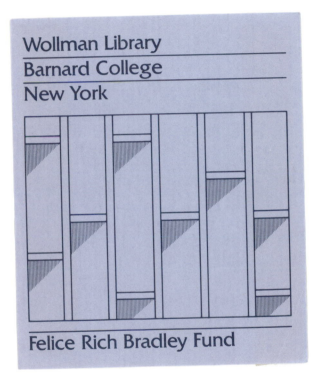

Society and Economy in Germany 1300–1600

TOM SCOTT

palgrave

First published 2002 by
PALGRAVE
Houndmills, Basingstoke, Hampshire RG21 6XS
and
175 Fifth Avenue, New York, N.Y. 10010
Companies and representatives throughout the world

PALGRAVE is the new global academic imprint of
St. Martin's Press LLC Scholarly and Reference Division and
Palgrave Publishers Ltd (formerly Macmillan Press Ltd).

ISBN 0–333–58531–3 hardback
ISBN 0–333–58532–1 paperback

This book is printed on paper suitable for recycling and
made from fully managed and sustained forest sources.

A catalogue record for this book is available
from the British Library.

Library of Congress Cataloging-in-Publication Data
Scott, Tom, 1947–
    Society and economy in Germany, 1300–1600 / Tom Scott.
        p. cm. – (European studies series)
    Includes bibliographical references and index.
    ISBN 0-333-58531–3 (cloth) – ISBN 0-333-58532-1 (pbk.)
        1. Germany–Economic conditions. 2. Germany–Social conditions. 3.
    Germany–Politics and government. 4. Germany–History. I. Title.
    II. Series

    HC283 .S27 2001
    943'.02–dc21   2001053167

10   9   8   7   6   5   4   3   2   1
11 10 09 08 07 06 05 04 03 02

Printed and bound in Great Britain by J. W. Arrowsmith Ltd., Bristol

In memoriam

R. W. Scribner
1941–1998

'men must have legends, else they will die of strangeness . . . '

Les Murray, *Noonday Axeman*

'Schließlich brauchen sie uns nicht mehr, die Frühentrückten . . . '

Rainer Maria Rilke, *Duineser Elegien* I

Contents

Maps

Tables

Notes on Usage

Place-names are spelt in accordance with modern political frontiers, though in eastern Europe the German names precede the Slav ones. All variants are cross-referenced in the index. In the German-speaking lands, only the commonest English usages have been retained in the case of cities (Munich, Cologne, Nuremberg), but many territories have well-established English names: the (Rhineland) Palatinate, Bavaria, Franconia, Saxony, Pomerania. I have preferred Hessen to Hesse (or even Hessia!), and render the lands east of the river Elbe collectively as 'east Elbia'. In the case of two Swiss lakes, however, the English name has been retained – Lake Constance and Lake Lucerne, even though their cities are given as Konstanz and Luzern, since the German names (Bodensee, Vierwaldstättersee) do not translate directly into English.

To avoid confusion, Estates (social corporations, political associations) are distinguished from estates (lands) by use of an initial capital for the former. Similarly, the religious Reformers and the Reformation of the sixteenth century are given initial capital letters in order to differentiate them from general movements of reform within the Holy Roman Empire in the fifteenth and sixteenth centuries.

Unless otherwise indicated, all measurements and distances are metric. One German mile equates to 4.6 statute miles (7.4 kilometres). The imperial coinage was denominated in guilders or florins (abbreviated fl.).

See also the Glossary.

Introduction

'Italy', as the Austrian chancellor Prince Metternich dismissively remarked, 'is a geographical expression.' That, at least, brings some advantage: an area clearly bounded on three sides by the sea and on the fourth by the mountain range of the Alps to the north. Historians of Germany are not so fortunate. Their task in describing Germany before the Napoleonic era is infinitely harder – both geographically and politically. Where were its boundaries to be drawn – or were they simply coterminous with that curious agglomeration, the 'Holy Roman Empire', of which Voltaire famously remarked that it was neither holy, Roman, nor an Empire? Since it was precisely in the period covered by this book that definitions of 'Germany' began to crystallize, it is worth reflecting at the outset on what contemporaries came to understand by German identity. Did they believe that 'German' institutions, culture, or social life were distinct from those of their neighbours – indeed, did their neighbours themselves think so? Or was the term 'Germany' so vague that it is no more than a convenient label to describe a variety of social and political formations at local or regional level within an area loosely defined as central Europe? Can a coherent social and economic history of Germany between 1300 and 1600 in fact be written?

At many stages in the gestation of this book I have been assailed by doubts. At a general level, social and economic developments in Germany seem to differ little in both character and chronology from other parts of western Europe. Several examples taken more or less at random may serve to make the point: the late medieval agrarian crisis, the growth of manufacturing and industry around 1500, the prevalence of the (west) European marriage pattern, the rise of a witchcraze in the late sixteenth century – all these are phenomena common to all or some of western Europe, whose predictable variations can easily embrace, rather than marginalize, the experience of

1

the German lands. But already the cancer of doubt sets in: why should the comparison be with *western* Europe? For one of the great fault-lines of European social and economic development is held to run through the heart of the German lands, that between the old-settled lands of the west, where landlordship (in the sense of manorialism) gave way to simple rent-extraction in the course of the later Middle Ages, and the new-settled 'colonial' lands east of the river Elbe, where in the same period a seigneurial regime which at the outset had weighed lightly on largely free peasants gave way to an intensified 'manorialism' as the precursor of large-scale commercialized agricultural domains using unfree and often landless labour. Even if recent scholarship has called into question the sharpness of this divide (only with hindsight does an air of inevitability seem to hang over it), other, though doubtless less clearly contoured, fault-lines can readily be discerned within Germany: the area of strong rural communes in the south, for instance, compared with the allegedly much weaker communes in the north; or the density of urban population in the south, contrasted with much sparser settlement in the north. This 'north–south divide' is echoed in the geopolitical map of Germany, with the northern lands remote from the influence (and the interests) of the monarchy, while in the southern lands, those 'nearest the crown' in the days of the Luxemburg and Habsburg dynasties, the presence or intervention of the monarch was a constant possibility.

The lack of an unequivocal or central focus to German history – no 'national' tradition of statehood, not even (more dialectically) a polarity of centre and periphery – not only makes its political history hard to write: its society and economy, too, threaten to crumble into a series of regional, or even local, histories which have little bearing upon each other. It would be possible to write such a kaleidoscopic history region by region, emphasizing significant diversity and interesting peculiarity; but even a book three times the length of the present one could not do full justice to that variety. In any case, it would not be desirable, for such accumulation of detail would only obliterate the broad outlines of development.

The chapters which follow are, therefore, deliberately selective in both scope and content. Broadly speaking, they take as their canvas Germany in the boundaries of 1914, that is to say, including Alsace and Lorraine in the west, and the districts of west Prussia, Poznań, and Lusatia in the east (all today in Poland). Nevertheless, reference is frequently made to northern Switzerland, whose social and economic history is largely of-a-piece with Upper (that is, southern) Germany in this period, though only occasionally to the Low Countries. Austria, on the other hand, presents perennial difficulties. Once the Habsburgs had established the Austro-Hungarian Empire (after 1526), its history is often taken as distinct from that of the Holy Roman Empire (of which the Habsburgs after 1438 were uninterrupted rulers until the mid-eighteenth century), and indeed it is often assigned to an 'east-European' model of development (or retardation). Whatever justification for such a view there may once have been, the new-found scepticism about the existence of a distinctively 'eastern' social and economic regime makes it hard to sustain nowadays. Yet to give a full account of developments in Bohemia and Hungary would be to stretch the narrative too far; the Austrian lands proper (including south Tirol, now in Italy) are discussed where appropriate.

The choice of topics has been even more selective. Those features of German society and economy which are commonplace in European historiography have been treated quite briefly in order to dwell at greater length on the regional differences within Germany, and in particular on certain themes which have been given less than their due in scholarship hitherto: the persistence of a highly feudal-aristocratic social and political structure, for instance, or the tensions between town and country consequent upon the commercialization of agriculture. At every stage, I have been at pains to show that social and economic history cannot satisfactorily be written without regard to politics and power-relationships. In Germany, a landscape without a centre, that implies not least an awareness of its political geography. For that reason, the analysis begins in Chapter 1 with the question 'What is Germany?' before dissecting its society and economy in a succession of chapters which seek to integrate structural and diachronic analysis.

Chapter 2 explores the character of a society of Estates to ask whether the three Orders of prelates, nobles, and commoners were as watertight as convention has implied. In particular, it investigates the status and mentality of the upper echelons of urban society – the so-called patriciate – to see if they were in any sense the harbingers of a bourgeois society and its values. Chapter 3 then outlines the broad sweep of population movement and social structure, drawing attention to the difficulties of accurate calculation in a pre-statistical age, and above all pouring cold water on the exaggerated claims made for the level, or at least the quality, of urbanization in several areas of Germany. It also sketches patterns of nuptuality and fertility, and considers the deteriorating role of women. In Chapters 4 and 5 the focus switches to the development of the rural and urban economies, including a discussion of commercial systems, transport links, and urban networks. It is suggested that the German lands can usefully be differentiated into three types of economic landscape, from the primarily agrarian to the largely industrialized, yet at the same time the emphasis is firmly on how far economic regions became ever more stamped by the interaction between town and country – or, indeed, by competition between them. This point is taken further in a survey of the development of civic rural territories in Germany, some of them coming close to city-states, whose main-springs were as much economic and commercial as political and jurisdictional. In this regard, Germany stands at the crossroads between the cultural splendour of the city-states of the Italian Renaissance and the commercial prowess of the metropolises of the Low Countries.

In Chapter 6 the spotlight is turned back upon the countryside, to the structures of lordship and subjection within a political-legal framework traditionally described as feudal. Three principal themes are pursued: whether there was a 'crisis of feudalism' which capsized relations between lords and peasants; whether the alleged late medieval economic slump can be held responsible for such a crisis; and why the eastern German lands should have experienced a re-intensification of seigneurial domination which seemingly did not occur in the west. From a comparison of the dispersion and deployment of serfdom in its various forms many of the traditional categories of explanation are called into question. Chapter 7 subjects the social and economic transformations within late medieval and early modern Germany both to the intellectual critique advanced by the proponents of reform within the Empire before and during the religious upheavals of the early sixteenth century, and to the palpable impact of popular rebellion in both town and country. Just as the preoccupations of the reformers were iterated over many decades, so the issues which impelled urban and rural dissent showed a remark-able consistency over several centuries, with the great revolt of 1525, the German Peasants' War, standing both within and without this continuum. Chapter 8, in conclusion, draws many of these strands together in a review of the cultural and mental shifts which emerged in the course of the sixteenth century, an age of confessional poli-tics, state intervention in matters of everyday life, and a search for order and discipline throughout society as a whole. These shifts, at once a reaction to prevailing conditions and an attempt to find solutions for contemporary concerns, over time culminated in a situation in which certain social groups were defined as deviant or marginal, whether by confession, occupation, or gender.

Underlying this approach is a belief that, all dislocations and fault-lines notwithstanding, society and economy in the German lands between 1300 and 1600 displayed as many continuities as caesuras. At the outset, therefore, it explicitly rejects the Rankean paradigm, which once saw 1500 (the consolidation of princely territories and the impact of the Protestant Reformation) as a watershed in German history, as quite irrelevant to much of its social and economic development. That is not to imply that our starting and finishing dates, 1300 and 1600, represent decisive turning-points in their own right. To begin at the onset of the fourteenth century allows an assessment of the late medieval economy and society which is not fixated upon the wave of pestilence that swept Europe in the middle of that century, the Black Death, whose repercussions have often been exaggerated. To end in 1600 is not to suggest that the Thirty Years War from 1618 to 1648 created *tabula rasa* in Germany; signs of crisis – fundamental dislocations in society and mentality – can already be observed in the closing decades of the sixteenth century. Nevertheless, the three centuries spanned by this volume have a coherence of their own: they witnessed the consolidation of a society of Estates within a fragmented constitutional polity. Both proved remarkably durable, surviving the undoubted cataclysm of the Thirty Years War, but each had come under exceptional strains during our period: the challenge to the hierarchy of Estates implied by the massive popular rebellion in the early sixteenth century; or the threat to the territorial balance within the Empire posed by the rise of confessional allegiances as the Reformation took root. The resilience of the Empire as a unique social and constitutional polity lends German history between the late medieval and early modern centuries its own fascination and should encourage us to look again at what Heinrich Heine, that most ambivalent lover of his father-land, sardonically called the 'mouldiest load of junk with all its trumpery'.*

---

* *Das alte heilige römische Reich/Stells wieder her, das ganze,/Gib uns den modrigsten Plunder zurück/Mit allem Firlifanze.* Heinrich Heine, *Deutschland. Ein Wintermärchen*, Caput XVII.

1   The Political Geography of Germany, 1300–1600

What was 'Germany'?

The term 'Germany' only became current usage in the sixteenth century. Before that, the sources spoke in the plural of 'German lands'. That linguistic shift points to a growing sense of German identity, but even after 1500 it would be unwise to equate that identity with clear geographical or political divisions. 'Germany' was never (until the late nineteenth century) a national or monarchical state, a supreme territorial jurisdiction, unlike France or England. Rather, it was a constituent of the Holy Roman Empire, whose sovereignty – at least in theory – extended well beyond the German lands, even if much of that sovereignty (for instance, in Italy) had by the fifteenth century dwindled from reality to mere assertion. By 1500 Empire and Germany were increasingly seen as coterminous, as the phrase 'the Holy Roman Empire of the German Nation', first officially recorded in 1492, suggests. But what did 'nation' or 'nationhood' in the German context imply? Certainly nothing that fits neatly into categories of geography, ethnicity, or language. The German lands west of the Rhine were a particular source of confusion. The river Rhine since the days of the Roman Empire had separated *Germania* from *Gallia*, and latterly the kingdoms of the East and West Franks. But a fourteenth-century chronicler of Strasbourg (well-positioned to speak with authority) could argue that the archbishopric of Trier, one of the seven electors to the Roman crown, the dignity of the rulers of Germany, whose lands stretched along the river Moselle, possessed political jurisdiction over that part of *Gallia* which lay 'on German soil' (*in tutschem lande*). And in the sixteenth century humanists in Alsace could engage in heated debate whether Alsace had been truly 'German' since the age of classical Rome. Sometimes, it is true, the lands west of the Rhine were called 'Alemannia', to distinguish them from 'Germania' proper, but the terms were also used quite interchangeably. The Rhine was no administrative frontier, though sometimes a legal one in terms of feudal law; several dioceses in the south-west – Strasbourg, Worms, Speyer, and Mainz – straddled it. And it was certainly not in any sense a national boundary: only after Alsace had been ceded to France in the aftermath of the Thirty Years War did the Rhine come to be regarded as France's natural eastern frontier, and even then the customs barrier remained the crest of the Vosges mountains until the Napoleonic era swept such distinctions away.

It is no easier to pin down a German identity in the north or east. Of course, the North Sea and Baltic coasts acted as a clear frontier, but between them lay the Danish peninsula, where Schleswig and Holstein were pulled by competing feudal and territorial claims of the Empire and the Danish crown. Along the North Sea littoral itself, the Frisians had settled on lands which were 'German', even though they themselves were ethnically distinct, while the northern provinces of the Netherlands, although populated by those of Germanic stock, were no longer regarded as part of the German lands by the sixteenth century. To the east, the waves of German colonization in areas which today lie within Poland and the Baltic republics brought within the German lands peoples who were Slavic.

From every angle, therefore, the notion of a German 'nation' or 'nationhood' seems to elude our grasp. The reason is simple: we are searching for an anachronistic definition of 'nation'. Those who spoke of a German *natio* in the fifteenth century had two distinct senses in mind. One was linguistic, as in the many plans for imperial reform, where it was used as the Latin equivalent of 'tongue', the linguistic community which set German-speakers apart from foreign (*welsch*) speakers. But even that community was not what it seemed, for the German lands were divided between areas of Low German (in the north) and High German (in the centre and south), not always mutually comprehensible. A standard German only evolved in the sixteenth century. The other usage was altogether technical, and has often been misunderstood, though it helps to explain the ideological connection between 'Germany' and 'Empire'. The split in the

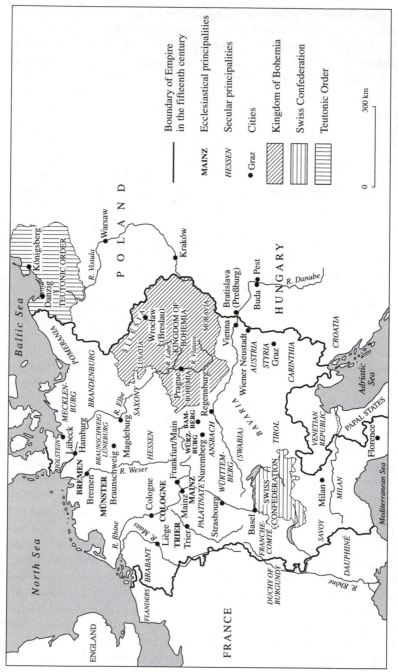

1.1 *The Holy Roman Empire, c.1500*

western Church at the end of the fourteenth century which followed upon the election of rival popes led to the convocation of a series of General Councils to heal the schism. Two of these, promoted by Emperor Sigismund, convened in the early fifteenth century on German soil, with those attending being identified by 'nations', a term originally used to categorize students at medieval universities. By mid-century the three ecclesiastical prince-electors in Germany (the archbishops of Mainz, Cologne, and Trier) could couch their demands for independence from Rome and a reduction in papal taxation as the 'grievances of the German nation'. High ecclesiastical politics had helped to bring the term 'nation' into wider public discourse. These developments underscored the spiritual task which had inhered in the sacred mission of the Germans to protect Christendom and to preserve Christian unity since the days of Charlemagne. And they were given a new urgency in the fifteenth century as it fell to the Germans first and foremost to combat the Hussite heresy in Bohemia and to bear the brunt of fending off Ottoman advances in the Balkans.

These events, which underscored the ideological resonance of the term 'German nation', had practical political consequences as well. The fiscal demands which arose from the Hussite wars led to the drawing up of a quota list of military contributions (1422) and the earliest attempt to impose a general poll-tax on all inhabitants of the Empire (1427). The debate among the imperial Estates which these proposals unleashed helped create a national public opinion with a sense of common fate and shared purpose so that, by the end of the century, 'nation' had come to apply to the political nation, the Estates of the Empire. When Emperor Maximilian invoked the 'German nation' at the great reforming diet of Worms in 1495, he was not calling up the spirit of some imaginary *Volk* but addressing his constitutional counterparts. By various channels, therefore, and with varying ideological overtones, we can say that by 1500 Germany meant the German nation, conceived of both as a people with a religious mission (under the Empire as a salvific ideal) and as a people with a political voice (under the Empire as a judicial-constitutional entity). By the later Middle Ages these two components, *imperium*, the Empire as ideal, and *regnum*, the Empire as a constitutional reality, began to pull apart, so that the latter, despite resting upon the dignity of the Roman crown, was identified essentially as Germany. Not surprisingly, this hybrid created its own anomalies.

In the west, certain 'German lands' such as Luxemburg, although it had been the homeland of the emperors of that dynasty from Charles IV to Sigismund, and Lorraine, in part Germanic, fell away from the Empire and passed under French influence. The western border of 'Germany', therefore, in effect ran northwards along the crest of the Vosges taking in Alsace but then bending westwards to embrace the Rhineland Palatinate along a line which still marks the frontier of France and Germany today. In the south-west, however, the Habsburgs, emperors from 1438 onwards, controlled the Free County of Burgundy west of the Belfort Gap and thus a French land: various schemes to administer it as part of their dynastic patrimony of Outer Austria (the Habsburg German lands on the Upper Rhine) were put forward after 1500, but in the end the Free County remained under the aegis of the Spanish Habsburg Netherlands.

The German lands in the south embraced the German-speaking members (canton is an anachronistic term) of the Swiss Confederation, but the inner communes around the Lake of Lucerne had been engaged in a protracted struggle from the late thirteenth century to assert their autonomy. This they did in (sometimes uneasy) alliance with their more powerful city neighbours, forging what later historiography often misconstrued as a common front against their feudal lords, among them the Habsburgs, whose own seat, the fortress of Habsburg perched above the river Aare near Baden, gave the dynasty its name before it was enfeoffed with substantial lands in the *Ostmark* (in effect, present-day Austria) and elevated to the dignity of dukes of Austria. The erosion of Habsburg power was by no means a foregone conclusion, but the defeat of a south German feudal array put into the field by the Habsburg Emperor Maximilian at the hands of the Swiss in 1499 not only dashed any lingering hopes of recuperating Habsburg power in Switzerland; it signalled the departure of the Swiss communes in fact, if not in law, from constitutional membership of the Empire. In social and economic terms, however, Switzerland north of the Alps continued to share the fortunes of its neighbours in southern Germany and is therefore included in the account which follows.

The eastern border of the German lands gives least occasion for confusion in our period. These embraced the Austrian duchies in the south-east, marched with the kingdom of Bohemia, took in the duchies of Lusatia and Silesia, and in the north-east encompassed the territories of Brandenburg and Pomerania. Yet, quite apart from the fact that the eastern lands contained a sizeable admixture of Slavs and other non-Germanic peoples, the discrepancy between

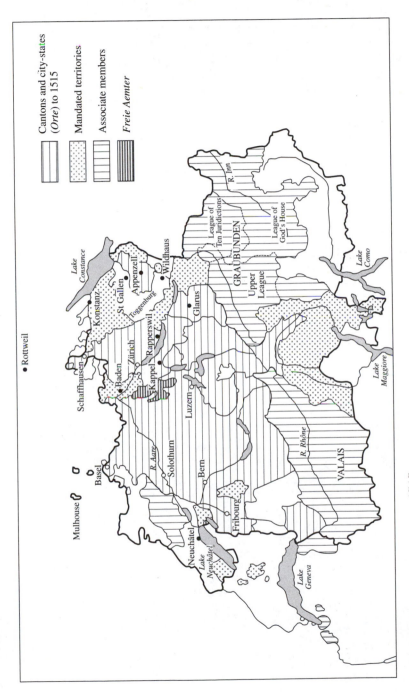

1.2 *The Swiss Confederation, c.1515*

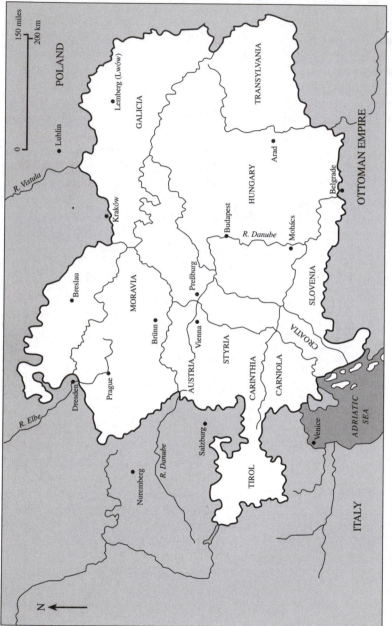

1.3   *The Austrian lands*

'Germany' and the Empire was here particularly obtrusive. On the one hand, the kingdom of Bohemia was part of the Empire: its king was one of the seven electors to the Roman crown. In the later fourteenth and early fifteenth centuries the crown was held (with interruptions caused by the religious revolt of the Hussites) by the Luxemburg emperors themselves, and subsequently after 1526 by the Habsburgs. On the other hand, the Teutonic Order, the military corporation of knights which had undertaken the mission of Christian conversion into the Slav lands – often with considerable brutality – had established a secular territory in east Prussia, which lay outside the Empire (although in the fourteenth century the Order had also acquired Livonia to the north, which was an imperial fief). Yet, both by recruitment and by religious mission the Teutonic Order was closely allied with the Empire as a universal Christian monarchy; if not of the *regnum* of 'Germany', it was certainly of the *imperium*. But debilitating wars in the fifteenth century saw the Order's land of Prussia succumb to Polish sovereignty and become in effect detached even from the *imperium*.

Even beyond the boundaries of Germany in the east, however, lay enclaves which were German both by origin and by function: the trading cities of the Baltic, which had been developed as merchant settlements by members of the Hanseatic League – Reval (Tallinn) in Estonia, or Danzig (Gdańsk) in Prussia, to mention two of the best-known. Aside from such thoroughly German outposts, there were German quarters in many eastern cities, notably in Prague, the Bohemian capital, where ethnic Germans dominated the civic administration and indeed the university, founded by Emperor Charles IV in 1346. These settlers and traders should not be ignored in any economic history of Germany.

Territorial Principalities

Because the imperial title never became attached to a national monarchy, the political geography of the German lands themselves remained highly disparate. Too often the history of the late medieval Empire has been written as a sorry tale of political decline and fragmentation, of centrifugal forces conspiring to rob the monarchy of its powers, so that Germany dissolved into a myriad of principalities, some large and relatively consolidated, but others diminutive, backward, and 'inefficient'. The fatal teleology of such a perspective need not detain us in a survey of social and economic developments. It is enough to point out that some of the most thriving polities in Germany – at least until 1500 – were its smallest, namely mercantile metropolises such as Nuremberg, Ulm, or Erfurt, all of which acquired rural territories and aspired to the condition of city-states. That was all the more true of the leading city communes of Switzerland. In the long run the German cities did find themselves at a disadvantage over against their princely neighbours with greater fiscal and military resources, but the Swiss city-states survived as an indispensable part of the constitution of checks and balances designed to reconcile rural and urban interests.

It is a truism that the princes dominated Germany. But this truism, as so often, tends to mislead. The most powerful prince of the Empire was the emperor himself, at least from the accession of the Habsburgs. Their problem in confronting the other princes was twofold: their dynastic lands lay largely remote from the heartlands of the Empire in the west (apart from their lordships in Swabia and on the Upper Rhine); yet in the east they were faced first with the challenge of 'national' monarchs such as Matthias Corvinus in Hungary, and then by the menace of the advancing Turks. Not only were the Habsburgs unable to devote sufficient attention to the affairs of the Empire proper; when they did seek to mobilize men and money for their campaigns in the Balkans (and latterly in Italy), it was not always clear to the Estates of the imperial diet whether they were being asked to contribute to the essential defence of the Empire or to the particular ambitions of the Habsburgs as dynasts. Once the crowns of Bohemia and Hungary fell to the Habsburgs in 1526, the latter's interest in the (western) Empire was further attenuated. In so far as the Habsburgs retained a stake in the west, it revolved after 1500 around their Burgundian and Spanish inheritance. This neglect of 'Germany' proper had decisive consequences at the onset of the movement of religious Reform initiated by Martin Luther and the emergence of a Protestant coalition of princes and cities in the early 1530s. As far as 'Germany' was concerned, Protestantism politically entrenched itself in those territories most remote from imperial influence, in the north and north-east, with numerous territories in the south (barring many imperial free cities) remaining loyal to the emperor and therewith to Catholicism.

The political map of Germany before and after 1500 may appear to be dominated by the larger principalities, but this gives a false impression in at least two respects. The lands of the great princes (with the exception of the one prince who was a sovereign in his own right, the king of Bohemia) were very far from being consolidated territories – states in miniature – a process which was not in full swing until well into the sixteenth century. The search for the origins of the German territorial state has at times led back to the thirteenth century, but it is a fool's errand. Princely lordship was not yet areal, that is, a territory marked out on a map with clear boundaries, wherein uniform subjection of its inhabitants to unitary jurisdiction prevailed. Princely dominion embraced a welter of claims and rights: cameral lordships (those administered directly by the prince's exchequer – if he had one), mortgages (lordships pledged to powerful vassals), fiefs (lands granted in feudal tenure), or lands held administratively or commissarially (the jointures brought into a princely marriage by his wife, for instance). But to lands were added regalian rights (mining and minting prerogatives, grants of market franchise), the stewardship of monastic foundations, and similar protective agreements, rights of access (to fortresses or towns in times of war), and various jurisdictional rights (the ban, the general right to command or prohibit; or lordship over serfs). Such rights could be and were exercised quite independently of any control over territory. Moreover, the steps along the path to a bureaucratic administration, functioning impersonally and independently of the prince, and staffed by trained lawyers, were at best halting until the mid-sixteenth century, even in relatively large and consolidated principalities such as Bavaria. It is true that laymen began to replace churchmen as princely chancellors before 1500, and German Latin as the language of administration, but the upper echelons of the prince's household remained firmly in the hands of the high aristocracy, even in a territory such as Württemberg where government by bureaucrats is supposed to have superseded personal rule by 1550. Württemberg is a cautionary example, in any case, for the administrative reforms of the 1540s and 1550s gave way to a return to cabinet government, with the ruler relying upon personal advisers, half a century later. The early modern territorial state in Germany, as it is often pictured, with its standing army, ostentatious princely residences, and elaborate court ceremonial, underpinned by universal taxation and an ideology of the public good (known in Germany as cameralism), is a feature of the seventeenth and eighteenth centuries rather than of the sixteenth, though a concern for 'good police', spurred in part by the teachings of the Protestant Reformers and the belated response of the Catholic Reform movement, had already begun to bring issues of public welfare and social disciplining onto the agenda in the decades after 1500.

This is not to argue that the princely territories of Germany were, in comparison with national monarchies elsewhere, 'backward', but only the seven electoral principalities were expressly forbidden to be partitioned under the terms of the Golden Bull of 1356, Charles IV's constitutional decree which remained the juridical cornerstone of the Empire until its dissolution. Partition left certain dynasties in a parlous position, notably the Welf house of Braunschweig, where only the senior line and imperial vassal, the dukes of Braunschweig-Lüneburg, retained any real political clout. Partitions remained commonplace, moreover, and primogeniture rarely prevailed until late in the sixteenth century. In itself, partition was not automatically a handicap, as the history of Bavaria shows, which in the fifteenth century was divided first into four, then three, and latterly into two lines, since its dukes, as rulers of agriculturally well-endowed lands, remained an important counterweight to the Habsburgs at least until 1504, or, to take another example, Saxony, where the division into electoral and ducal territories (with many fragmented and intersecting constituents) did not prejudice the functioning of the central and local administrations which had been set up after the civil wars of the mid-fifteenth century. What partition does underscore is how far the princes still regarded their lands as patrimonies. They thought dynastically, not territorially, and if they sought to augment their lands they chose to do so by enfeoffments, marriage or inheritance treaties, or mortgages, rarely by outright purchase or military conquest. The landgraviate of Hessen, a fragmented and second-rank territory before 1450, is a good example: by feudal grants and inheritance it had vastly extended its borders by the late fifteenth century and, even more importantly, its revenues, by acquiring control of strategic toll-stations on the river Rhine.

Partition, of course, posed no threat to Germany's ecclesiastical principalities – the archbishoprics, bishoprics, abbacies, and priories which constituted temporal territories under the Empire in their own right – for they knew no principle of dynastic succession. It would be logical to imagine that their unbroken territorial integrity must have guaranteed them an influence and resilience greater than that of many secular princes, but the truth is otherwise, for they were subject to external and internal pressures which threatened to destabilize them. Over time the ecclesiastical princes succumbed to *de facto* mediatization, whereby secular territorial rulers, in an extension of their own dynastic policies, installed their kin or leading councillors in neighbouring sees. A notorious instance was the Palatinate in the mid-fifteenth century, where Elector Frederick the Victorious secured the appointment of his younger brother as archbishop of Cologne, having already installed successive chancellors as bishops of Speyer and then Worms. The internal stability of the ecclesiastical principalities was jeopardized, moreover, by their elective character. Disputed elections and conflicts between bishops and their cathedral chapters easily capsized into wider political instability, as the numerous 'episcopal feuds' (*Stiftsfehden*) of the sixteenth century testify, for example the Bishops' War over the see of Strasbourg from 1586 to 1593, where rival candidates from the Guise house of Lorraine and the Hohenzollern dynasty of Brandenburg transformed a local squabble into an international incident. But the problems of the ecclesiastical principalities had begun much earlier, during the Avignon papacy in the fourteenth century, when the popes sought to reserve the right to nominate to vacant sees themselves by means of what were termed papal provisions. After 1400 several sees were so exhausted by legal and even military conflicts between episcopal nominees and renitent chapters that they teetered on the edge of bankruptcy, including the two archiepiscopal electorates of Mainz and Cologne. Cathedral chapters, whose canons were drawn exclusively from the ranks of the nobility, imposed upon episcopal candidates so-called 'electoral capitulations', that is, treaties which guaranteed the former's control of lucrative benefices and sinecures, and confirmed their stranglehold on the administration of the diocese. Although no ecclesiastical principality could (by definition) disappear, many led a shadowy existence from the fifteenth century onwards, for example, the electoral archbishopric of Trier sidelined under Burgundian influence, or the impoverished see of Eichstätt. Before the start of our period many residential capital cities had already succeeded in ejecting their bishops (though not their cathedral chapters), who were obliged to take up residence in lesser towns nearby (the archbishops of Cologne in Bonn, the bishops of Strasbourg in Saverne, or the bishops of Basel in Porrentruy, for instance). Those who remained were either lords of episcopal cities whose economic fortunes were on the wane (Bamberg, Passau, or Halberstadt), or else ecclesiastical magnates of the first rank, such as the wine-rich bishops of Würzburg or the salt-rich archbishops of Salzburg, whose impregnable fortresses perched menacingly above their cathedral cities.

More than the existence in itself of ecclesiastical principalities – a hallmark of the German lands almost without parallel elsewhere in Europe – their domination by the high aristocracy, and indeed by members of major ruling houses such as the Wittelsbachs in the Palatinate and Bavaria, coloured the fabric of German society until the end of the *ancien régime*.

Nobles, Knights, and Cities

Historians have focused, perhaps understandably, on the great spiritual and temporal princes, whose voice and vote dominated the political forum of the nation, the imperial diet. But they have sometimes overlooked the fact that at least a third of the German lands at the beginning of the fourteenth century was ruled by nobles of the second rank, margraves, counts, and barons. Many of these lineages died out, but certain regions of Germany – the Rhine-Main area, northern Hessen and Thuringia, or parts of Swabia – continued to be dominated by such families, who had originally risen in the service of the crown, and who colonized the upper reaches of the imperial Church. Leading comital families shored up their position by gaining entry to the ranks of the imperial princes – examples from the fourteenth century include the counts of Henneberg, Nassau, Mecklenburg, Berg, and Jülich, while the most spectacular elevation of the fifteenth was the raising of the counts of Württemberg to dukes in 1495. Historians obsessed with princes as rulers of 'states' have downplayed the role of these nobles who failed to consolidate their estates into a royal fief, contrasting their 'mere' family lands unfavourably with the princely territories, whose integrity was legally sanctioned under imperial law. But, apart from their smaller size, these dynastic territories (as Ernst Schubert calls them)[*] differed administratively barely one iota from the great principalities, at least until the need to provide for all members of the dynasty led to repeated partitions and in some cases to the enforced sale of the family lands to princes waiting in the wings.

But where such dynasties did survive they sought to differentiate themselves more clearly from the lesser nobility, the knights, with whom they had once combined in regional nobles' associations, by

---

[*] Ernst Schubert, *Fürstliche Herrschaft und Territorium im späten Mittelalter* (*Enzyklopädie Deutscher Geschichte*, vol. 35) (Munich, 1996), p. 16 f.

spurning intermarriage and by aligning themselves to the high nobility, the princes. In Westphalia and parts of Lower Germany (the broad plain stretching across the north) counties could match in size and organization some of the lesser principalities, the county of Oldenburg being a prime example (whose dynasty over the centuries was happy to supply monarchs to Denmark, Russia, and Sweden). Elsewhere, notably in Swabia and the Wetterau (north-west of Frankfurt) the comital dynasties closed ranks in regional unions in order to repel the danger of mediatization by the princes.

The threat of mediatization was felt most acutely by the imperial knights, whose ancestors had once been ministerials of the Empire, nobles bound by their person to serve the monarch. They were concentrated, as one might expect, in regions 'close to the king', especially in Franconia, Swabia, Alsace, and the Rhineland, all areas where Hohenstaufen dynastic power at the turn of the twelfth century had been at its strongest. Although the imperial knights were immediately dependent on the emperor, their position was more vulnerable than their superiors in the peerage, the barons and counts, for they were not princes of the Empire and did not constitute a separate Estate. Their best hope of self-protection was to band together in regional associations, the first of which received an imperial privilege from Emperor Sigismund in 1422. By 1500, however, the threat of being sucked into subjection to the territorial princes, on the one hand, and the pressure to submit to imperial taxation, such as the Common Penny of 1495, on the other, left the knights in a quandary. In the end, it was the issue of taxation to fight the Turks in the 1530s which drove the knights to establish a separate body of knighthood spanning the Empire, with the result that during mid-century the knights were able to withdraw from the territorial principalities and from memberships of their Estates. In Württemberg, for instance, the knights removed themselves *en bloc*, so that the Estates of the duchy thereafter formed a bicurial diet, comprising two benches, the first Estate of prelates and the third Estate of towns and administrative districts. Imperial protection and privileges undoubtedly helped to shore up a social group which is often held to have undergone a debilitating economic and social decline before 1500. Whatever the truth of such a verdict (to be examined in Chapter 6), it remains the case that on their family estates the imperial knights exercised 'princely' sovereignty in miniature, not merely as landlords (as any territorially dependent nobles might do), but as jurisdictional lords, usually with rights of capital jurisdiction, stewards of monastic houses, lords of serfs, and, where they embraced Protestantism, protectors of the Church. The only aspect of authority denied them as individuals was public taxation, for that was vested collectively in the local knightly associations (known as cantons). The very fact that the imperial knights were free to choose their confessional allegiance under the terms of the Religious Peace of Augsburg in 1555, despite their corporate identity resting on the sanction of a Catholic emperor, underscores the relative security and independence within the Empire which they had achieved by the mid-sixteenth century.

Within the political system of the Empire, dominated by the higher and lower aristocracy in church and state, the only counterweight consisted of the imperial free cities. Strictly speaking, imperial and free cities should be differentiated. The former, on old crown lands, derived their privileges from imperial charters; the latter had once been sees, which had gained their freedom by ousting their bishops. But by the later fifteenth century, when the cities began to make their presence felt in the imperial diets, the distinction had all but been elided. Although the registers of the imperial diet in 1521 recorded as many as 86 such cities, those who had managed to escape the clutches of the princes numbered in reality only around 68 in 1500. The most notable casualty was Erfurt, a commune of 18 000 inhabitants in the late fifteenth century, controlling the third-largest rural territory of any German city, which lost its independence *de facto* to the archbishops of Mainz. Erfurt is the exception which proves the rule, however, for the bulk of imperial cities lay clustered in the regions of southern Germany traditionally 'close to the king', along the Middle and Upper Rhine, in Swabia below Lake Constance, in northern Württemberg, and in Franconia. Here the cities had banded together from the late fourteenth century onwards in urban leagues to protect their collective political and commercial interests against princely encroachment. By that token, the few imperial cities scattered throughout the north were out on a limb: Mühlhausen, Goslar, Dortmund, Soest, and Aachen were the most prominent, but others, such as Brakel, Warburg, or Lemgo, were of little account. The imperial and free cities have enjoyed an unusually high profile in recent German historiography, not least on account of their pioneering role, first stressed by Bernd Moeller, in embracing and championing Reforming doctrines in the 1520s.* Certainly, the major mercantile cities of western and

---

* Bernd Moeller, *Imperial Cities and the Reformation: Three essays* (Philadelphia, 1972).

southern Germany – Cologne, Frankfurt am Main, Strasbourg, Ulm, Nuremberg, and Augsburg – with populations around or in excess of 20 000 present a glittering array of economic and social power. But they were not typical, even of the imperial cities themselves, some of which were little more than villages. The league of ten imperial cities in Alsace, known as the Decapolis, founded in 1354 (which did not include the free city of Strasbourg), was led by communes of the size of Colmar or Sélestat, with perhaps 5000 inhabitants each, but reached down to embrace diminutive settlements such as Kaysersberg, Turckheim, and Munster, sheltering no more than 1000 citizens, which were perhaps lucky even to have been granted a market franchise.

On the other hand, many imperial cities succeeded in establishing territorial control of their hinterlands; these urban territories, unlike the principalities, were indeed defined by clear areal boundaries, sometimes quite literally by ditches or hedges marking the extent of urban overlordship. And it was not always the largest or most powerful cities which acquired the most territory: Cologne and Augsburg had hardly any rural dependencies at all. Several cities of middling rank, such as Schwäbisch Hall, Rottweil, or Rothenburg ob der Tauber, built up quite sizeable territories, whose populations outstripped (sometimes quite dramatically) those of the cities themselves, and which constituted a far from negligible demographic, fiscal, and military reservoir (as we will explore further in Chapter 5).

It is tempting, at first glance, to compare these urban territories with the city-states of northern Italy, or with the leading Flemish cities of the Middle Ages, which carved up the countryside into separate spheres of influence (known as 'quarters') amounting in all but name to city-states. On closer inspection, the differences outweighed the similarities. Formally (that is, in strict juridical terms), the imperial and free cities were not sovereign but vassals of the emperor. In practice, many of them derived much of their commercial advantage and political influence from close co-operation with the emperor, who conferred upon them or their leading merchants trading privileges, concessions, and monopolies in return for raising loans on their capital markets. Moreover, apart from Nuremberg (and then only after 1504), their territories did not begin to match the 'quarters' of the Flemish cities or the *contadi* of the Italian city-states. If one wants to identify true city-states north of the Alps, then it is the Swiss urban communes which may lay proper claim to the title. Although also nominally under the Empire, they were in effect fully independent and indispensable components of the republican Helvetic constitution. They were also territorially ambitious, Bern being the most predatory, and the one city republic in the German lands which does indeed stand comparison with its Italian neighbours to the south. The city-states of northern Switzerland made up a solid urban belt stretching from the Burgundian frontier in the west to the Habsburg lands in the east. By contrast, the 'city-states' of southern Germany remained intruders in a landscape dominated by dynastic territories. The principles of communal liberty and civic humanism, the twin hallmarks of the Italian city-states of the Renaissance, found only a limited echo in Germany: the city patricians developed no civic or 'bourgeois' culture of their own; their ideals and values remained those of the feudal-aristocratic world in which they were embedded.

As members of the German political nation, the imperial cities were latecomers. They had no separate vote in the imperial diet until it was conceded in the peace settlement which followed the Thirty Years War in 1648. Their constitutional activity developed instead within the penumbra of the diets, in the form of separate urban diets, attested from 1471 onwards, which met before or during the full diets in order to co-ordinate policy. Yet the profusion of urban diets in the first two decades of their existence was a reflection of the weight of imperial taxation they were expected to bear, rather than the outflow of any collective solidarity or purpose. While the imperial knights achieved corporate status in the sixteenth century, the cities remained hamstrung by their unwillingness to grant plenipotentiary powers to their representatives at the diets; for all their attempts at concerted political action, the truth was that the cities remained fierce economic rivals amongst themselves, competitors constantly looking over their shoulders to those who might be stealing a march on them commercially. An older historiographical tradition believed that the imperial cities sought to present a united front against the princes, but even that is doubtful. The long-standing problem of lawlessness within the Empire, which reached a peak in the mid-fifteenth century, did indeed largely turn on the rivalry between princes and cities (in which the former were by no means always the aggressors). But when Bavarian expansion threatened to upset the balance of power in southern Germany, the solution, promoted by the Habsburg emperor (as an antagonist of the Wittelsbachs, to be sure) was to bring together the Estates of the region in 1488 in a defensive alliance, the Swabian League, in which

for the first time princes, prelates, knights, and cities stood, somewhat uneasily, on the same side of the fence. However tentative, the
consolidation of the Empire (or 'compression', to use Peter Moraw's
term) into a constitutional dualism of emperor and imperial Estates
had made great strides by 1500.[*] The emperor had found his counterpart in the political nation: together they constituted what we
know as 'Germany'.

Topography and Communications

Germany is a land which should be envisaged on an inverted
compass, that is, from south to north. From the crest of the Alps the
terrain becomes progressively less mountainous, with a series of
upland undulations in southern and central Germany, until it
broadens into the north German plain. With the exception of the
Alpine valleys, marked by an extreme climate and sparse population,
the lands of Upper Germany (so called precisely because of its altitude) were more populous, more urbanized, and economically more
vigorous than those to the north: in short, the physical gradient was
matched by a demographic and economic one. That may seem surprising given their remoteness from markets overseas in an age
before the revolution in transport (canals, and latterly with steam-
power the railway), when shipping goods by sea was always significantly quicker and cheaper than overland haulage. The explanation
lies in Germany's river system. With two exceptions, the rivers
Danube and Main (though they were vital east–west arteries),
Germany's principal rivers ran south to north: foremost among them
the Rhine in the west, the only continuous artery from Switzerland
to the sea; then the Neckar, as a tributary of the Rhine; and further
east the Lech and the Inn as tributaries of the Danube. Likewise,
beyond the hilly ranges of central Germany, the vast north German
plain was watered by the Ems, Weser, Aller, and Franconian Saale,
before the other great arteries of the German lands in the east, the
Elbe, and the Oder-Neiße, linked Bohemia to the North Sea, and
Silesia and Lusatia to the Baltic. Although the north German plain,
on account of its flatness, was criss-crossed by important highroads
running west to east – the best-known being the *Hellweg* which linked

---

[*] Peter Moraw, *Von offener Verfassung zu gestalteter Verdichtung: Das Reich im späten Mittelalter* (*Propyläen Geschichte Deutschlands*, vol. 3) (Berlin, 1985).

Cologne via Kassel, Erfurt, and Leipzig to Breslau (Wrocław) – land transport only came into its own for local trade, or else for the consignment of goods of high value but low bulk, such as spices, furs, or silks. By contrast, the grain which was exported in vast quantities to the far-flung markets of northwestern Europe by aristocratic agricultural entrepreneurs on their estates east of the Elbe from the sixteenth century onwards only made their fortunes because it was shipped down the river Vistula to Danzig, and then across the Baltic; if sent by land, its cost would have doubled after 375 kilometres (on the usual calculation), rendering any long-distance trade quite unprofitable.

The importance of the river system to Germany's economy, however, was not confined to trade. The river valleys of the south and west, often cutting through hilly terrain, caught and retained the heat of the sun and so became meso-climates appreciably warmer and drier than their surrounding uplands. Along the slopes of the Rhine, Neckar, Main, and Moselle viticulture flourished (much of it for export), sustaining a high level of population density, clustered in many small urban centres as relay- and distribution-points. The importance of fluvial meso-climates becomes even clearer in northern Germany, where viticulture of more than local significance was practised in Lusatia south of Frankfurt an der Oder, in Saxony around Meißen on the Elbe, and on the Unstrut from Naumburg to Freyburg, the core of present-day wine-growing in the territory of the former German Democratic Republic. But even the flatter riverlands to the east with higher rainfall could support a specialized agrarian regime: the linen industry of Swabia developed along the valleys of the Iller, Wertach, and Lech, where lush pasturelands supported dairy-farming whose milk was essential to the bleaching of linen-cloth. The same was true of parts of northern Germany, where Westphalian linen-manufacture prospered in the rolling countryside around Ravensberg, in effect the catchment area of the rivers Ems and Weser, or in southern Saxony along rivers flowing north from the mineral-rich Erzgebirge on the Bohemian border, the Gera, Ilm, and Saxon Saale.

Without access to an extensive river system, Upper Germany would have been hard put to achieve the commercial prosperity it experienced after 1300. But that prosperity was founded in turn upon its links across the Alps to the thriving mercantile communes of northern Italy. The cities of Upper Germany (both in Swabia and in Switzerland) were located on or near routes which linked river traffic to the alpine passes – Luzern, Zürich, Konstanz, Basel, and the cities north of Lake Constance, Ravensburg, Isny, Kempten. In our period it is impossible to quantify the trade which crosses the Alps (though we know what range of goods from the Mediterranean or further afield were sold at south German markets: cotton, ceramics, silks, and spices); it is scarcely any easier to assess how frequented some routes were. Historians have seized upon the opening up of the route over the Gotthard pass in the early thirteenth century as a crucial stimulus to commercial contacts between Upper Germany and Milan, but whether it was more travelled until the fifteenth century than the passes of Graubünden (such as the San Bernardino), or indeed the Brenner, linking north and south Tirol, which was traversible by carts and not merely pack-animals, has recently been cast into doubt.

To emphasize the greater economic vigour of Upper Germany threatens to ignore the great medieval trading association which bound together the cities of northern Germany, the Hanseatic League, with its 'factories' (commercial offices) in Bruges, London, Novgorod, and Bergen. As an organization it exerted an attraction so great that even the Grand Master of the Teutonic Order of Knights sought membership. As Philippe Dollinger, its most distinguished historian, has commented, although it 'had none of the traits characteristic of a state', it 'nevertheless wielded the power of a state'.[*] But that power manifested itself in the stranglehold which Hanseatic merchants exerted over commerce from Muscovy through Scandinavia to the North Sea, rather than in any political or economic dominance of the north German plain. For the Hansa was in essence an association of merchants (or latterly, with greater corporate cohesion, of merchant cities), engaged primarily in the carrying-trade through the Baltic, their chief ports – Lübeck, Danzig, or Reval – acting as entrepôts and staging-posts, rather than as outlets for the economy of their hinterlands. Not only did the Hansa not seek to usurp the political authority of the north German princes; its leading cities, unlike their counterparts in Upper Germany, rarely sought to extend judicial control of their hinterlands to the point of creating dependent territories. The bourgeois self-confidence and cultural identity of the Hanseatic merchant patricians which we encounter in the pages of Thomas Mann's *Buddenbrooks*, set in late nineteenth-century Lübeck, had no counterpart in the early modern period.

---

[*] Philippe Dollinger, The German Hansa (London/Basingstoke, 1970), p. 106.

Then, if merchants of the Hansa wanted to cut a figure, they bought up castles in the countryside.

To sum up, the social and economic condition of the German lands between 1300 and 1600 was deeply influenced both by political geography and by natural-topographical endowment, in the latter case river-systems in particular, vital arteries of commerce which princes were often keen to improve, as we shall consider in Chapter 5.

2 Society and Hierarchy

The Spiritual and Secular Aristocracy

Politically, by 1500, Germany was hamstrung by the constitutional dualism of 'king and Empire', the monarch and the imperial Estates. The Estates embodied a social as well as a constitutional principle. Medieval European society was divided into a hierarchy of three Estates, first, the prelates of the Church (archbishops, bishops, abbots, and latterly the Military Orders), then the secular aristocracy, and finally the third Estate of commoners, though usually only townsfolk, rarely peasants, had a political voice. This was the principle which underlay European society of the *ancien régime* up to the French Revolution; in Germany it was known as the *altständische Gesellschaft*, a society based on the ancient constitution of Estates. The hallmarks of this society were, first, a belief in the God-given legitimation of social inequality, in which the powerful few commanded the allegiance of the subordinate many, and, second, the configuration of the Estates as social corporations, that is, as bodies which marked themselves off by privileges, known as 'liberties' or 'immunities'; their status, in other words, was stamped by the exemption which they enjoyed from the rules and laws governing others – a classic instance being the exemption from civic jurisdiction enjoyed by the clergy resident within towns. However, this second feature requires some elaboration. On a general level, corporate privileges distinguished one Estate from another, but *within* each Estate subordinate corporate identities and interests vied with each other: regular *versus* secular clergy, counthood and baronage *versus* knighthood, or craft guilds *versus* merchant guilds, for instance. And corporative attitudes, of course, could run athwart individual or family interests.

In that sense, Germany was little different from other *ancien-régime* societies, except in one respect. The salvific character of the Empire had invested the Church in Germany with unusual eminence and independence: three of the prince-electors were prelates, while the archbishoprics, bishoprics, and abbacies were more than spiritual jurisdictions: they were temporal lordships in their own right. In English, diocese and bishopric are synonyms; in German *Diözese* and *Bistum* are differentiated from a third term, *Hochstift*, which describes the ecclesiastical principalities, whose boundaries, it should be added, by no means necessarily coincided with diocesan ones.

The immediate beneficiary of this German peculiarity was the aristocracy, for the highest offices in the imperial Church were reserved exclusively by the late Middle Ages to those of noble birth. Erasmus, the Christian humanist and biblical scholar, is famously reputed to have remarked that if Christ had sought admittance to the cathedral chapter of Strasbourg he would have been turned away on account of his lowly birth: all the canons had to show noble ancestry of at least two generations. To an unusual degree, therefore, the political system of the Empire and its social and cultural values were dominated by a privileged elite which made up no more than 1.5 per cent of the population, but which was undergirded by the symbiosis between the first and second Estates. The only change of significance after 1500 – indeed, up to the end of the *ancien régime* – was the impact of the Reformation, which loosened (but did not destroy) the close ties between aristocracy and Church in the Protestant territories while entrenching them in the imperial system as a whole, indissolubly linked as it was to the Catholicism of the Habsburg emperors.

Within the period 1300–1600, however, sections of the aristocracy are held to have undergone a profound transformation. The lower nobility, the knights in particular, have been seen as the victims of the late medieval agrarian crisis, which ruined their finances and led them into social degradation or exclusion. It is this 'crisis of the nobility' which is blamed for the increased lawlessness of the fifteenth century, manifested in the prevalence of feuding and the spread of 'robber baronage', and which allegedly provided the background to the Peasants' War of 1525. In a longer perspective, however, this 'crisis' all but disappears or else is revealed as propaganda by enemies of the nobility. Noble families were always 'rising' or 'falling', consolidating their social and economic position, or dying out. It is immanent in the nature of a personal or familial dignity that this should be so. The number of noble families whose lines died out can appear quite dramatic: from perhaps 1400 to 1500 families in Lower Saxony in the twelfth century to a mere 350 in the mid-sixteenth, for instance. But new families were waiting in the wings to take their place, particularly after 1500, when commoners entering princely service as bureaucrats were rewarded with titles of nobility. These 'nobles by patent' were often scorned by the ancient lineages 'of the blood', just as in other parts of Europe, but the unmistakable signs of social exclusivity, where proof of noble ancestry could be demanded back to three generations, or sixteen grandparents, belong (with the exception of some cathedral chapters) to the seventeenth century rather than before.* The mobility of the aristocracy – upwards as well as downwards – has been seen, therefore, as a continuous process of biological and social selection whose fluctuations evened themselves out over time. Those who failed to find suitable marriage partners, or who did not have the wherewithal to sustain a suitably noble lifestyle, might slip back into the ranks of commoners. The truth of this becomes all the clearer if one compares the contrasting fortunes of branches of the same family.

Recent research on the lower nobility of the Palatinate on estates flanking the Rhine, for instance, has identified three out of four branches of the von Zeiskam family prospering in the fifteenth century, while the fourth declined. Although the practice of dividing the patrimony could leave branches of a noble family in possession of estates insufficient to maintain their households, 'house treaties' (that is, testatory compacts between the various branches) usually ensured that lands reverted upon the extinction of one branch to the surviving branches, and that was the case with the von Zeiskam, where the one line remaining in the sixteenth century was securely established and held extensive property. A series of individual or family fates confront us, rather than a collective predicament specific to one or other tier of the aristocracy.

The 'substance' of the nobility also depended on new creations. But in our period new patents of nobility within the Empire (as opposed to elevations within the Habsburg crown lands) were

---

* Voltaire's mocking in *Candide* of the Westphalian aristocracy which insisted on 72 quarterings is a piece of satirical hyperbole.

relatively infrequent, as indeed were elevations of noble families into the ranks of the imperial princes, though that began to change at the end of the sixteenth century, when one princely house, the Bavarian Wittelsbachs, arrogated to itself (quite improperly under imperial feudal law) the right to confer noble titles. What does stand out, instead, is the relative indulgence shown by a succession of emperors towards the very knights who, down on their luck, are supposed to have been such notorious trouble-makers in the fifteenth century. That ranges from Sigismund's privilege of 1422 to Maximilian's patronage of such dubious figures as Götz von Berlichingen (subsequently implicated in the Peasants' War) and Franz von Sickingen (whose feud against the archbishopric of Trier in 1522–23 had limited support and does not merit the title 'Knights' Revolt'), and on to Charles V's recognition of the imperial knighthood as a corporation in the 1540s. An indication of the continuing social power and prestige of the imperial knighthood can be seen in their domination of the chapters of the major Rhenish and Main bishoprics throughout the early modern period – Mainz, Würzburg, Bamberg, Trier, Worms, and Speyer – where their families had always been prominent.

On account of their status, the imperial knights have received undue attention: the vast majority of the lower nobility were, and remained, territorial vassals of the princes, whether in possession of baronial or comital titles, or merely gentry entitled to the appellation 'von'. As a broad generalization it can be stated that these families flourished more in the larger principalities of northern Germany – achieving true political and social hegemony in many lands east of the Elbe – than in the smaller and more fragmented territories of the south. A partial exception is offered by the territorial nobility of the eastern Austrian lands in the sixteenth century, who banded together under the banner of Protestantism to resist the centralizing and rationalizing tendencies of the Habsburg administration. They were able to gain such leverage because they shouldered the burden of frontier defence against the Turks. Their Lutheranism, therefore, became a badge of political defiance, especially against Emperor Ferdinand in mid-century, though his successor, Maximilian II, who had Protestant sympathies, was more indulgent. A similar polarity can be observed in some of the south German bishoprics, in Würzburg, for instance, under the rule of its illustrious but unbending Counter-Reformation prelate, Julius Echter von Mespelbrunn, in the 1580s and 1590s. But such defiance was short-lived. When the reaction set in (as under Rudolf II in Austria), the nobles' political opposition in confessional clothing led in many instances to expropriation, exile, or imprisonment.

No such dangers faced the territorial nobility in northern Germany. Their economic fortunes were securely founded upon profitable agriculture, and they rarely found themselves at confessional odds with their princely superiors. The further east one goes, the more profitable that agriculture became after 1500, and the less powerful the princes, so that (to look for a moment beyond our German remit) the crown of Poland became a byword of constitutional paralysis, under the thumb of its magnates in what amounted to an aristocratic republic. The rise of Brandenburg-Prussia as the driving-force of early modern Germany, by contrast, may have had its origins in the sixteenth century, but it was only in the aftermath of the Thirty Years War and the Great Northern War of 1659–60 against Sweden that the path to monarchical absolutism was marked out by the margraves as electoral princes.

What can be said of the Empire as a whole is that the higher echelons of the nobility became increasingly keen to set a distance between themselves and their fellows of inferior rank. This was not simply achieved by negative means (such as by imposing ever more rigorous criteria of 'purity of the blood') but positively as well, by seizing the possibility of advancement in princely service or by espying new commercial opportunities, as with the large landowners east of the Elbe engaged in the grain trade. There the magnates often elbowed the lesser gentry out of the way. In Brandenburg, for example, a mere 14 families out of a total of 300 owned a third of all noble estates around 1500, and their holdings continued to grow at the expense of the less well-endowed. (Poland, again, provides an extreme example: a once-influential gentry in the sixteenth century was brushed aside by the great magnates, who held the crown to ransom.) Away from areas which favoured magnate entrepreneurs, however, the exclusive tendencies of the nobility could lead to their erosion. Bavaria is the prime example, where the counts and barons jealously guarded their eligibility to tourney against the knights and the urban patricians. From a total of 140 higher noble families in the late Middle Ages only 75 survived in 1503, and a mere 31 by 1652. Into their shoes stepped the lower nobility – perhaps numbering 250 families in 1500 – who achieved wealth and status in ducal service, though even then their charters of liberty distinguished between old and new families, the former enjoying greater rights of jurisdiction within their lordships.

Apart from the chase, the privilege which marked noble status above all others was the right to tourney. The fifteenth century witnessed a profusion of new jousting societies, access to which required proof of noble ancestry for all four grandparents. At the ball on the eve of an unusually well-documented tournament in Schaffhausen in 1436, for instance, no lady could be invited to take the floor unless her noble partner could demonstrate this pedigree. We should be cautious, however, in presuming always a conscious effort to maintain distance from commoners aspiring to noble rank, not least because the phenomenon was by no means confined to Germany. Tournaments, after all, were staged for the most part in urban settings – in the imperial cities, though by the later fifteenth century in the episcopal sees as well – where the jousting associations had their headquarters, as in Frankfurt am Main. At a tourney in Heidelberg, the seat of the electors Palatine, in 1489 it was decided to exclude any knights who had taken out burgher's rights in a town or who had marriage ties to patrician families; four years later, however, the decree was quietly dropped. Moreover, money talked: in Franconia, a noble who married a patrician's daughter was admitted to the tourney, provided that she brought a dowry of at least 4000 fl. with her, or 10 000 fl. if the noble in question had been eligible to tourney for no more than half a century! Intermarriage between local aristocrats and urban patricians was in fact much more frequent than the former chose to admit, certainly in southern Germany, where such ties between the elites of Augsburg, Ulm, Strasbourg, or Basel and their neighbouring noble families were commonplace by the fifteenth century – though still on occasion regarded as socially degrading. At the Schaffhausen tourney of 1436 already mentioned, Heinrich von Ramstein was denounced for having married beneath his rank, even if his bride was the daughter of a Basel patrician of gentle birth, Konrad von Eptingen. His fellow-noblemen shattered the helmet upon his head and would in all likelihood have killed him, had he not been wearing, as was customary, a smaller protective helmet underneath.

Nobles and Cities

Exclusiveness, in other words, was a natural reaction to the sense of social insecurity which such alliances occasioned. But in political and military terms the mutual self-interest of nobles and townsfolk led to

protective agreements and legal alliances which find little counterpart elsewhere in western Europe, apart from northern Italy and the
Low Countries. The most widespread practice was for nobles to
acquire rights of citizenship (without prejudice to their noble
status). Where seats were already reserved to them on the town
council, burgess rights were a *sine qua non* of holding political office.
None the less, many nobles chose not to reside in their adopted
towns – or did so only on special occasions or in times of emergency
– but continued to live on their rural estates. These noble outburghers, as we may call them (there is no agreed term in English),
were in most cases exempt from normal civic taxation; instead, they
paid an annual composition fee and were not subject to civic jurisdiction, except over property held within the town walls.
Outburghership was attractive to both parties. In general terms, the
towns secured military assistance from their nobles, and an indirect
lever of influence over the surrounding countryside. In certain
instances – Cologne is perhaps the best example – the contracts of
loyalty and service which the magistracy concluded with the nobility
of the Lower Rhine, including such powerful dynasts as Count
Wilhelm von Jülich, as well as many lesser noblemen, may be
regarded as the specific substitute for Cologne's failure to acquire a
rural territory (though that did not preclude its economic and commercial dominance of the surrounding plain, the *Kölner Bucht*). For
their part, the nobles, who in a land as fragmented as Germany
could as vassals scarcely count upon the protection of their liege
lords, saw economic and defensive reasons for having a foothold in
the towns, as well as enjoying the conviviality of nobles' clubs, to
which they could escape from their draughty, rat-infested castles in
the countryside. Traditionally, many had served on city councils;
indeed, their position as outburghers often reflected the fact that
they had their origins in the urban patriciate, only subsequently to
quit the towns and become absorbed in the local aristocracy. In the
course of the fifteenth century imperial cities, such as Worms and
Basel, as well as territorial towns found it increasingly hard to persuade noble outburghers to fulfil their civic responsibilities, though
in some instances, such as in Freiburg im Breisgau, the constitution
insisted that the burgomaster be nominated from their ranks. What
appears as a dereliction of duty did not spell the end of outburghership as an institution.

Of course, not all communes, whether free or dependent, welcomed nobles as outburghers, especially if they were seen to enjoy

an easement of the burdens which ordinary citizens had to shoulder. Ulm, a city economically powerful enough and with sufficient landed territory to be able to cock a snook at the Swabian nobility, accepted with reluctance five as outburghers in the later fifteenth century, on condition that they did not come near the town! Another, the council sardonically observed, would have brought 60 000 fl. worth of capital with him, if he had been admitted. On the other hand, Ulm did sign fixed-term military contracts with knights from the surrounding area, who captained the civic militia. Other south German communes – Ravensburg, Isny, Kempten – also kept the local nobility at arm's length, but the most prominent was beyond doubt Nuremberg (which also banned intermarriage), so helping to account for the notoriously strained relations between it and the Franconian nobility before and after 1500. The number of such cities is, however, far outweighed by others which for practical reasons were prepared to enter into alliances with the local nobility – Konstanz, Nördlingen, Augsburg, Memmingen, Lauingen, and Rottweil in Swabia, Strasbourg, Colmar, and Sélestat in Alsace, or Mühlhausen in Thuringia, to cite only a few examples. One particular advantage for the cities was the right of access to nobles' strongholds during any military emergency, though in the case of Frankfurt am Main this right of entry superseded noble outburghership in the fifteenth century, rather than being its usual concomitant.

Outburghership was also extended as a corporate privilege to many monastic foundations in the countryside, though here the benefits lay much more clearly with the convents than with their host communes. To immunity from civic jurisdiction, which as clerics they in any case enjoyed, was added exemption from tolls and market dues, so that convents were often able to undercut other sellers of agricultural produce and, by virtue of their tithebarns, to hoard grain until the best prices could be obtained. Noble outburghers, at least, rarely attracted the same degree of odium.

Citizens and Communal Values

However much aristocratic values were reflected in corporate privileges – the right to bear a coat of arms, access to the tournament, trial by one's peers – they were vested in individuals, or rather, in families, whose members were bound together by a code of honour.

Ancestry and chivalry informed their self-perception; exclusivity and rank marked their social standing. These features set them apart from commoners, who were born without privileges or inherited distinctions. In the feudal-aristocratic polity of the Empire the third Estate of burghers and countrydwellers may have had little constitutional voice of its own, yet within the individual principalities towns often took their place in the territorial diets, as did the rural commons on occasion. Was the political participation of the third Estate matched, therefore, by a distinctive set of corporate social values? If aristocratic self-perception was hierarchical and familial, based on lineage and rank, the mentality of the commoners, it is often argued, was horizontal and collective, expressed in communal associations and communal values. Much recent writing on the diffusion of Reforming doctrines in the 1520s and 1530s has sought to explain their appeal by pointing to the high degree of compatibility between the egalitarian and communal precepts implicit in the Gospel and the secular values of good neighbourliness and the commonweal already embraced by townsfolk (and by rural communes, too). In the case of the urban communities, however, it is conceded that the councils who deployed collective-corporative rhetoric chose to do so in order to buttress their own authority by implying an equality and mutuality of citizenship to which reality gave the lie.

Oaths of citizenship, it is true, were often premissed upon a sworn association of legal equals – that is the phraseology which can be found in many charters of urban liberty from the twelfth century onwards: in 1120 Freiburg im Breisgau's charter (to take a well-known and much imitated example) spoke of the *conjuratores fori*, the sworn confederates of the market, in a diploma designed to underpin Freiburg's foundation as a merchant settlement. But the growth and economic diversification of German towns ensured that by the late Middle Ages the citizenry had become both socially and legally heterogeneous. Because in the pre-industrial era urban populations did not replenish themselves naturally, they had to rely on a constant stream of immigrants from the countryside. Some who immigrated acquired citizen's rights, and many were able to slough off the bonds of serfdom, but the implication that towns became 'non-feudal islands in a feudal sea' is altogether misleading in the German context, where the urban elites, both collectively and individually, retained close ties to the feudal-aristocratic world of their agrarian hinterlands, even to the point of becoming feudal overlords themselves. To echo Perry Anderson's verdict on the Italian medieval communes, they did not so much subvert as usurp the authority of the landed aristocracy.* The reasons are not far to seek. While some urban communities were indeed dominated by those whose livelihood derived from commerce and manufacturing, many recruits to the urban elites were of ministerial origin, that is, they had been noble servants and officials of the monarchs, especially in Swabia and Franconia. Nuremberg's elite – the patricians who sat on the council – in the fourteenth century were largely ministerials who retained close ties to the surrounding nobility, while the von Auer family of Augsburg, which led a patrician *fronde* against the existing council between 1330 and 1334, were also ministerials by ancestry, who controlled castles in the countryside. In northern Germany, too, where the mercantile interests of the elites in the Hanseatic cities can easily blind us to their backgrounds, many of Lübeck's leading families, to take one example, were ministerials from Westphalia and Holstein, even if they had forsaken an aristocratic-chivalric milieu and devoted themselves purely to commerce.

A sense of social superiority, therefore, informed in part by noble ancestry, was intrinsic to the urban elites, who regarded their communities as hierarchies of authority and obedience. That is tellingly illustrated by the deliberations which preceded reforms to the civic administration and finances of even a modest territorial town, Freiburg im Breisgau, in 1476. The town council took as its ideological framework the anthropological topos of the commune as a body with head and members. The head represented the councillors themselves, who governed by virtue of their inborn reason as well as by divine and natural aptitude, using the urban officials as their eyes and ears, whose duty it was to protect and promote the arms and the hands (the handiworkers!), with the tillers of the soil and menials as the feet, who should honour their superiors out of love, not fear. A counterpart to this paternalism was the concern of the elites to maintain and reinforce their exclusivity. Modern historians have sometimes been accused of superimposing artificial divisions upon the urban population, derived from analyses of wealth contained in tax records, which do not reflect any historical distinctions. In truth, the urban elites of our period were no less keen to affirm and maintain such distinctions, the difference being that wealth alone was not a sufficient criterion of honourability. At the close of the fifteenth century, Conrad Celtis, the humanist and poet-laureate of the

---

* Cf. Perry Anderson, *Passages from Antiquity to Feudalism* (London, 1974), pp. 190 ff.

Empire, drew attention to the five categories of citizen which existed in Nuremberg, beginning with members of the small council, which exercised real power, followed by various groups within the large council, whose function was largely ceremonial. These gradations were no figment of his imagination; their main purpose, however, was not so much to assign the citizenry as a whole to its proper place in the social hierarchy as to mark subtle distinctions of rank and honour within the patriciate itself. Nuremberg's patricians may have been unduly sensitive in this regard; in other leading Upper German cities such as Augsburg and Ulm only three ranks of citizen status obtained. But there is no doubting that the general tendency was towards a greater refinement and precision of classification as the sixteenth century wore on, as the many sumptuary laws – those which regulated clothing, jewellery, and deportment – in the 1400s and 1500s testify. By 1628 the sumptuary code of Strasbourg elaborated six major classes of urban dwellers, with two further subdivisions. At the pinnacle stood, predictably, the councillors and urban nobles, followed by burgher families whose ancestors had been of council rank for at least a century; then the bigger merchants and various urban officials; next the guild aldermen; below them common artisans and day-labourers; and finally women in subordinate positions – domestic servants, seamstresses, laundrywomen.

To find women at the bottom of the pile comes as no surprise; the gendered nature of women's work and women's roles is a topic to which we will return in more detail in Chapter 3. What the Strasbourg legislation of 1628 does reveal, however, is the social ascent (albeit finely gradated) of the new professionals – lawyers and teachers – in the sixteenth century. The city's jurisconsults (legal advisers) claimed the top rank alongside the magistracy and urban nobles; high chancery officials and professors at Strasbourg's high school occupied the next rank down; graduate scholars without a doctorate came next, followed by lawyers without a higher degree, together with teachers at Strasbourg's grammar school (*Gymnasium*); and finally ordinary teachers, ranked on a par with the guild aldermen.

Urban Social Mobility

Such elaborate distinctions of status and prestige immediately prompt questions about social mobility. How rigid were these categories? Could they be transcended or ignored? Eligibility to sit on

town councils was always strictly controlled, as the example of
Nuremberg shows. The famous 'dance statute' of 1521 (which laid
down who was entitled to attend the council's balls) applied the twin
criteria of honour and ancestry to restrict access to twenty 'old' families, seven 'new', and a further fifteen parvenus who had acquired a
sufficient patina of respectability between 1440 and 1504. Graphic
though this example undoubtedly is, it can easily lead to false conclusions: ancestry and honour were attributes which could be
applied retrospectively (as in the case of the parvenu families they
indeed were); if these hallmarks of social acceptability had been
applied rigorously, sclerosis would quickly have set in. Between 1332,
at the beginning of our period, and the dance statute of 1521, half
the original thirty-five patrician dynasties of Nuremberg (all of ministerial origin) had died out, but they had been replaced by new-
comers, entrepreneurs to a man. In those towns and cities where a
specified number of seats on the council was reserved for patricians
or merchants, the ascendancy of the craft guilds from the mid-fourteenth century onwards led both to a dilution of the patriciate within
the towns and to the emigration of leading families, so that their
place had to be filled, by default, by common craftsmen. In this
regard, Nuremberg was something of an exception, being the one
imperial city in Germany which resolutely excluded craftsmen from
political power, an even-handed counterpart to keeping the local
nobility at a distance, as it were. But at the same time its patriciate
was much less ostentatious than Augsburg's, Cologne's, or Lübeck's.
These cities all boasted quasi-aristocratic convivial associations,
whereas the 'lords' drinking parlour' in the Franconian metropolis
was altogether less exclusive and its members were enjoined to avoid
any public display of wealth. Efforts to rein in public ostentation in
German towns were not attended by much success, as the repeated
promulgation of sumptuary laws attests. Yet the urban patricians and
nobles were able to demonstrate their status in more permanent
fashion by the mansions they occupied. Competition to build repre-
sentative residences can be observed as early as the twelfth century,
with the apeing of architectural styles prevalent in the north Italian
communes. The urban towers which today dominate the skyline of
Bologna in Emilia-Romagna or San Gimignano in Tuscany were
copied by the leading families of Cologne, Nuremberg, and
Regensburg. Few of these survive, except in Regensburg, where
twenty such towers out of a total of twice that number can still be
seen rising as many as seven or even nine storeys high above the

narrow streets. Imposing they may have been, but comfortable they were not. By 1500 the urban elites were building themselves palaces, grand town houses of lesser elevation, but with larger windows (glazed) and spacious public rooms, often with elaborate external decoration in the Gothic style, until once again Italian influences in the Renaissance encouraged a return to the simplicity and proportion of classical antiquity.

The urban elites remained anything but homogeneous, and the rise of the new professionals in the sixteenth century added further shades to the social picture. Nevertheless, in one respect they presented an increasingly closed front towards the rest of the urban population by 1500, in that they embraced new precepts of government, loosely derived from Roman law, which distinguished sharply between those fit to rule and those destined to be ruled. *Obrigkeit*, 'authority', not so much an impersonal term as a collective designation of those entitled to exercise authority, was counterposed to *Untertan*, no longer primarily the citizen, but the subject. Here, too, the prevailing view of the commune as a collectivity of equals (by legal status, if not by social standing) was being hollowed out – in so far as it had ever matched reality – and replaced by vertical notions of dominion and subordination. The dry legal categories of *Obrigkeit* and *Untertan* mark the first hesitant steps towards a system of universal public law with uniform dependence of the subject, which overlaid the older corporate categories but failed to destroy them, for the transition was accompanied by an often bitter struggle between council and commons. What historians blandly describe as oligarchic tendencies in the German towns manifested themselves to the citizenry at large as secrecy, corruption, and croneyism – and in general as a lack of accountability. The latter half of the fifteenth century and the early decades of the sixteenth were marked by frequent urban disturbances which at times escalated into full-scale revolts. This unrest had little or nothing in common with the so-called 'guild revolutions' of a century earlier, which had in many cases been straightforward attempts by the craft guilds to wrest a measure of power from the patriciate. Instead, it was a reaction to policies which threatened to marginalize or eliminate such participation in or scrutiny of public affairs as the ordinary townsfolk had already achieved. But we should be very wary of imputing to these movements of popular unrest any 'democratic' motive. Often they were led by malcontents on the fringes of power and social prestige, the 'outs' of civic politics who were resentful of the 'ins', and who did not shrink from stirring up support among the citizenry for their mostly partisan ends. One such was Ulrich Schwarz, who seized power as burgomaster of Augsburg in 1476. In an effort to reduce the civic debt and provide for more open accounting, Schwarz proposed that council membership be expanded to include representatives of all seventeen guilds, who should in turn report to a committee made up of three members of each guild. Although these commoners were regarded by the patrician families with complete disdain, the constitutional alteration was carried. But within two years Schwarz was toppled and the patrician regime restored. A harsher fate awaited Konrad Walzenmüller in Freiburg im Breisgau, whose faction had swept the board at the council elections of 1492, claiming to express the voice of a general guild committee which had been demanding to inspect the town's public accounts. Within weeks, Walzenmüller was killed under suspicious circumstances in a street brawl, whereupon the cry went up, 'The king of the Jews is dead!' When the restored council took statements from his followers, it emerged that even many humble citizens resented Walzenmüller's arrogance and distrusted his self-proclaimed role as champion of the people.

The Reformation afforded political *hasardeurs* further opportunities to make mischief. Foremost among them was Jürgen Wullenwever in Lübeck, originally an immigrant from Hamburg, who capitalized upon long-standing discontent over the city's debts and heavy burden of taxation to place himself at the head of the citizens' committee in 1530. In that capacity he encouraged the introduction of Lutheran doctrines, which had previously found only minority support, and for the next three years he ruled the city as a popular tribune, until he was officially elected burgomaster in 1533. Not content with domestic politics, however, Wullenwever sought to foment divisions within the Danish monarchy during a disputed succession (largely to protect Lübeck's control of Baltic trade from encroachment by Denmark), but his diplomatic intrigues backfired. Despite Lübeck's capture of Copenhagen in mid-1534, the city had failed to gain the support of most other Hanseatic League members and soon found itself up against a powerful coalition of neighbouring princes. Wullenwever was eventually captured and put on trial, before being executed in 1537. His fall brought the patrician council back to power, though by then Lübeck's allegiance to Lutheranism was firmly established.

Urban Social Inequality

One reason why political outsiders found it easy to harness communal opposition movements to their personal ambitions was that the structure of urban society was by no means as communal as it seemed (and as many modern historians have argued). The *Bürgerverband* – the association of citizens as a collectivity – was an ideological construct. Many towns and cities, it is true, had 'large councils', bodies of a hundred citizens or more, to whom the small council (which held actual executive power) was in theory accountable. But such assemblies met rarely, and when they were convened it was usually to rubber-stamp decisions already reached. In the turbulent years of the early Reformation, admittedly, citizens' assemblies could exert real power. In Mühlhausen in Thuringia, for instance, in early 1525 the radical evangelical Thomas Müntzer, together with the local Reformer Heinrich Pfeiffer, who had already come to prominence in communal agitation two years earlier, sought to oust the sitting council by summoning the citizenry at large to elect a new 'eternal council' which would govern by the Word of God alone. Since the voting took place in public, not in secret, with each citizen being asked his opinion in turn, it comes as no surprise that a majority of three to one in favour of the change was secured, but, as the author of the Mühlhausen chronicle sourly noted, this figure was swollen by intimidation and cajolery. In any case, less than half the eligible electors cast their vote.

Those were indeed stormy seas. In calmer waters, corporative sentiments were most directly articulated by specific interest-groups rather than by the community at large. It was the craft guilds, parishes and wards, rifle and archery clubs, or religious confraternities which affirmed a collective identity and upheld their rights and privileges as corporate associations against any encroachment by the council acting in the name of the commune as a whole. Amongst their members the maxims of peace, justice, and the commonweal – that familiar triad of communal values – may perhaps be taken at face value; from the lips of the urban elites, eager to underpin their hegemony, they should be taken with a hefty pinch of salt. But even within the interest-groups themselves an invocation of corporative-communal values should not be mistaken for a general commitment to fraternity, let alone egalitarianism.

This point emerges clearly if we look at the composition and policies of the craft guilds. Internally, most urban artisan guilds practised a form of apartheid: entry to the guild was restricted in many cases to the sons (or at least the relatives) of existing craftmasters. The apprentice system, with its culmination (often after several years) in the presentation of a 'masterpiece', was, of course, intended to maintain the proficiency of skills and quality of goods, but it also served as a convenient means of excluding outsiders, or of limiting the number of master craftsmen. In Wagner's comic opera, the mastersingers of Nuremberg used the rule-book to thwart the hopes of the impoverished nobleman Walther von Stolzing of winning the midsummer music competition, until its hero, the cobbler and mastersinger Hans Sachs, stepped in to the rescue. Similar ends could be attained by imposing higher entry-fines for guild membership or ceilings on production, as occurred in Basel after 1500, culminating in the craft constitution in 1526, which sealed the victory of the artisans over the four merchant guilds by forbidding any commerce in goods which could be produced within the city itself, and by granting its craftsmen a sales monopoly within the city and its territory. Such events might at first sight be taken to reflect the triumph of collective mentalities espoused by craft guilds over the individual interests of Basel's merchants and entrepreneurs, one of whom, Ulrich Meltinger, was notorious for subverting guild restrictions by employing rural weavers in Alsace through the putting-out system. But we should tread cautiously. How strictly the craft constitution was enforced is open to question; within a generation, in 1552, it had been revoked on the grounds that it had never been fully effective and had given rise to unrest among the guilds themselves. The reasons are not hard to discern. Those who argue that the craft guilds were by definition so imbued with the spirit of collectivism and egalitarianism that they shunned competition and disavowed production for accumulation, the capitalist profit-motive, can point with justice to the increasing efforts of the guilds to restrict masters to employing only a handful of apprentices and journeymen, in order that no great disparities of wealth and employment should arise. But that applied to the guilds only as producers, not as consumers. When Freiburg im Breisgau embraced a 'guild reformation' in 1495, which went a long way towards adopting protectionism as its guiding principle, the council was yielding to long-standing demands to banish all foreign merchants from the town who refused to join a guild or take up residence within the walls. In its justification, however, the council struck an apologetic note: it admitted that it was responding to pressure from the guild of haberdashers alone, which had begged it to ignore the inconvenient fact that the 'common man' – that is, the townsfolk at large – could buy his goods more cheaply from foreign retailers. Legislation which ostensibly favoured the craft guilds could not disguise the conflicts of interest which might arise between specific producers or distributors and the artisans generally. This analytic distinction has recently been deployed to account for the varying attitudes of Augsburg's guilds towards evangelical doctrines in the early years of the Reformation. The weavers' guild, fearful of competition from the countryside and of increasing social differentiation among its members in the face of capitalist manufacturing within the city, took refuge in the evangelical message of Christian brotherhood, which seemed to underpin its collective and corporate interests, whereas the butchers, dependent as individual cattle-dealers upon long-distance commercial contacts with regions which remained predominantly Catholic, showed understandably less enthusiasm for the new doctrines. It will not do, therefore, to treat the outlook of the craft guilds as all-of-a-piece, let alone as *pars pro toto* for the community as a whole, even if governed by a guild regime.

The Margins of Urban Society

Moreover, just as there were differences of background and status among members of the patriciate, so, too, was there a perceptible gradient of influence and prestige between the crafts themselves – quite apart from the traditional tensions between artisan and merchant guilds – which was not determined by economic clout alone. It is not always easy to pin down the social ranking of the various crafts, not least because in many communes quite disparate trades were lumped together in a single guild, or because guild affiliation depended upon residence, not occupation. The economy of the surrounding district might also have a bearing upon a craft's prestige: in areas of viticulture, for instance, coopers enjoyed a higher standing (and better income) than where there was less call for their skills. Butchers, too, are hard to classify: on the whole they ranked among the wealthier artisans, but their involvement in slaughtering at the shambles, and the sale of meat which included offal, brought them close to one of the so-called dishonourable professions, that of knacker. It is no accident that the butchers often obtruded as an unruly element in urban society.

As a rule of thumb, the greater the skill, the higher the social standing; those whose occupation was essentially rural – market-gardeners, wine-growers – were marked by inferior status and rights. Known as *Ackerbürger* (citizens who tilled the fields), these peasant burghers congregated in the suburbs, and were often denied full citizen's rights, being relegated to the category of *Hintersassen*, those with a right of abode but little else. The gulf between agricultural workers and handicraftsmen, even where both enjoyed citizen's rights and political enfranchisement, could be wide. Freiburg im Breisgau provides an instructive example during the Peasants' War. There the wine-growers' guild had on paper the same standing as the remaining eleven guilds, each electing two masters to sit on the council. But not only did the wine-growers never supply a master to high administrative or judicial office, they were the one guild in the town expressly forbidden to bear arms, an outflow of the council's deliberate policy of marginalization and surveillance. The guild was prevented from enforcing a closed shop or setting its own wage rates; instead, the council used it as a convenient dumping-ground for a variety of menial occupations and day-labourers. This policy almost fell victim to its own success in 1525, when the wine-growers became restive after a contentious guildmaster election, and might easily have provided a fifth column in the town for the rebellious peasants, had their agitation found any support from the other craft guilds.

Despite the fissures within and between guilds, mastercraftsmen and their families made up the majority of citizens in most German towns (unless they were predominantly agricultural communities fortunate enough to have been granted civic charters), but below them ranged a variety of urban denizens described by modern historians as the 'lower orders' (in German, *Unterschichten*). This is acknowledged to be an imprecise description, but broadly speaking it embraced two distinct groups in urban society, the poor, on the one hand, and the marginals (*Randgruppen*), on the other, though the categories could clearly overlap. Alas, 'poor' remains one of the hardest terms to pin down. In part, it was simply a technical term, used to identify those who fell below the lowest rung of taxable wealth. But this in itself can be a most misleading distinction. While many councils might classify those worth five florins or less as poor, some magistracies set the hurdle much higher, on occasion at as much as 100 florins, which in most circumstances would indicate a burgher of some substance. And on what basis was the assessment made? From the evidence accumulated by Freiburg's town clerk on his journey of enquiry in 1476, a huge diversity of practice in the south German cities emerges. It was common (if not universal) to assess capital, rather than income. But what capital? Were goods bought as stock for resale and the tools of trade (i.e. working capital) to be included? No, said Ravensburg and Ulm; yes, said Augsburg; yes, too, said Kempten, but at a reduced rate. Were moveable goods such as household items to be taxed, as well as real estate? Only the latter, said Landsberg, but on its annual yield, not its capital value; all goods except for armour, said Nördlingen. Often silverware, jewellery, and clothes were exempted (as in Augsburg and Ulm, though not in Rottweil), so that (in Kempten's words) 'citizens be inclined to jewels and wealth be increased through silver'. In an age which regarded bullion as a tangible measure of wealth, that view was not at all remarkable.

But even for those who by all ordinary criteria were undoubtedly poor the possession of pewter and silver objects, as a recent study of Nuremberg has suggested, had its own rationale. Such persons could not afford to buy an annuity to provide for them in their old age in the city hospital, nor could they afford to invest in civic bonds or buy shares in mining enterprises. Their only alternative was to put their meagre cash into household objects, intended for daily use but with some intrinsic value, so as to build up a deposit or reserve which could be passed on to heirs or used *inter vivos* as collateral for old-age provision. It was quite possible, therefore, to possess fair-sized inventories of household goods and yet remain 'poor'. Since direct taxation of income – unlike today – was extremely uncommon, the cash from sales and wages was fully disposable. The bulk of civic revenue derived instead from indirect taxes, especially tolls and excises on beer and wine. In that sense, these consumption taxes hit the wealthier and more extravagant households harder – a modest redressing of the balance in a tax system which in all other respects was highly regressive.

These complexities do not make the search for the urban poor any easier, but it is quite clear that for many townsfolk disposable incomes were almost entirely absorbed by the daily necessities of life. That was true, above all, of menial workers paid on hourly or daily rates, though once again a note of caution must be sounded. Wage-labourers, especially those in council employ, as the Nuremberg evidence shows, received many benefits in kind: not only food and drink, but lodging and clothes as well. In its cash equivalent, food could constitute as much as 40 to 50 per cent of a labourer's wage. The drawback for such public employees was the often seasonal nature of their work: builders, for instance, who were laid off during the winter months and who had to scratch around for other jobs on the open market. Even if they could find them, they were paid at freely negotiated rates, rather than according to a tariff fixed by the council. It became increasingly common in German towns (as elsewhere in Europe) in the sixteenth century to draw a distinction between the 'deserving poor' (who would take work if it was available, or, if incapacitated, were deemed deserving of charity) and the 'undesirable poor', who are too readily equated with the marginal groups. Beggars, vagrants, prostitutes, and criminals were by definition of dubious character, and subject to constant surveillance and supervision. In the case of prostitutes, the councils of many of Germany's leading cities decided by the fifteenth century that supervision was best achieved in civic brothels, as in Nuremberg, Munich, Memmingen, and Strasbourg; in Lübeck prostitutes were gathered into a separate guild. In a few cities – Frankfurt am Main and Mainz – the public brothels were in fact owned by the ecclesiastical authorities rather than the council. But attitudes towards prostitution were changing even before the Reformation; decrees restricting access to brothels, or banning street-walking, were issued from the 1470s onwards. Once the civic Reformers began to raise their voice against immorality, a string of brothels was closed down. To those of a cynical disposition, the panic caused by the wave of syphilis which swept Europe at the turn of the fifteenth century had as much to do with the growing hostility to brothels as any revival in Christian righteousness, yet all the cities which took such action in the first instance – Konstanz, Basel, Augsburg, Nördlingen, Ulm, Regensburg, or Frankfurt am Main – were without exception Protestant or Protestant-inclined. The Catholic authorities caught up later.

To the many prostitutes should be added on the fringes of civic society the necessary occupations of knacker and hangman, but such men commanded a good fee for their services. What set them apart was the 'dishonourable' nature of their trade. More difficult still to categorize were the Jews. Their faith – and their strong sense of separate identity – were bound to place them outside Christian society, but the attitude of German town councils towards their Israelite communities varied greatly. A tendency to banish their Jewish populations can be observed in numerous imperial cities from the fifteenth century onwards. Yet sizeable and economically prominent communities remained in Regensburg, Worms, and Frankfurt am Main. In Alsace, the Jews found shelter in several lesser towns, regardless of the latter's constitutional status, whether the small imperial city of Rosheim, or the territorial town of Bergheim ruled by the lords of Ribeaupierre. A descent into overt hatred may be observed in the latter half of the fifteenth century: a gruesome massacre of Jews in Endingen in the Breisgau in 1462 was the prelude to several others, and in 1519 the Jewish community in Regensburg, hitherto protected, was slaughtered, its synagogue razed, and a church dedicated to the Virgin as Queen of Heaven erected on the site. Nevertheless, pogroms and forcible expulsions had in fact been commoner in the period up to 1350, rather than afterwards.

The largest group of marginals in any German city, nevertheless, was the secular and regular clergy: parish priests, chantry-priests, and the inmates of convents, friaries, and collegiate foundations. Historians do not customarily include clerics among the marginals, but that is what they were, even if they had familial ties with sections of the urban classes. For however much their spiritual duties were seen as indispensable, the judicial and fiscal immunity which they enjoyed by virtue of their holy orders created a barrier of suspicion and resentment on the part of the laity. That applied especially to monastic foundations in the countryside who maintained town residences, extensive complexes of courtyards, stables, and granaries, as well as living quarters, where produce from their estates might be stored until the best market price beckoned. In point of fact, there were also antagonisms within the ranks of the clergy itself, with the parish priests accusing the friars of preaching to and hearing confessions from their own parishioners, as well as allowing burials in friary grounds rather than in parish graveyards. Although the nature and extent of anticlericalism in German towns has been hotly debated, the very fact that one of the earliest demands by those inclined towards Reforming doctrines was for the 'domestication of the clergy', that is, its integration into civic society and the suspension of its immunities, speaks for itself. Once they had acquired citizen's rights and submitted to civic taxation – in short, had been absorbed into the *Bürgerverband* – anticlerical feeling subsided (though it did not disappear).

No such steps were taken to dismantle the special corporate privileges of the universities in those German cities where they had been founded in growing numbers from the late fourteenth century onwards. Few foundations – Cologne is a notable exception –

derived from civic initiative; rather, they were established as vocational training colleges for doctors, lawyers, and theologians who would serve the Church or secular princes. Universities were granted immunities similar to those of the clergy (many masters had taken lesser orders, in any case), and rapidly became as propertied and economically influential as monastic institutions. The hostility of burghers towards students – the rivalry of 'town' and 'gown' – was pervasive: they were accused, often with some justice, of drunkenness, licentiousness, gambling, or running up debts, for which they could not be called to account in the civic courts.

Altogether, we are dealing with civic communities which might present a solid front to the world, and which upheld a vision of the commonweal as part of their necessary self-esteem, but where in reality corporate privileges and identities competed and conflicted with each other, and where precepts of status and honour served as much to exclude and to marginalize as they did to integrate and to foster an overriding sense of communal solidarity.

The Rural Commune

How far is that true of the majority of the population, who lived and worked on the land? There, as a welter of recent research has emphasized, corporative values reigned supreme. The undertow to this perspective is that the rural communes' corporate sense of identity was fundamentally collective and egalitarian. Yet, as with the towns, there were perceptible differences of status and power within villages and rural settlements, and the corporative principle could be as exclusive as in the towns. Indeed, in one south German territory noted for its 'openness' as a constitutional polity, namely Württemberg – described by Charles James Fox as the only state in Europe with a true constitution, aside from Britain – it is hard to put a knife between the social configuration of towns and villages, embraced as they were by a common constitutional framework, that of the district (*Amt*) as the building-block of political representation and administrative authority. In Württemberg, no one could participate in the life of the commune unless they possessed citizen's rights, either fully or as an accepted resident. Only that status conferred access to existential necessities: the use of communal resources, entitlement to poor relief, and, more generally, the right to marriage. These principles were first enshrined formally in the territorial constitution of 1621, but that merely ratified what had been long-standing custom, and they remained in force in Württemberg until the nineteenth century. A law of 1833 governing citizenship declared:

> No citizen of the state . . . can marry, take on public office, practice any occupation on his own account or with his own household, or even keep an independent dwelling, before he possesses citizenship or *Besitzrecht* [property rights] in a community.*

In practice, such rights – in Württemberg and elsewhere – were accorded to tenant farmers and their families, not to cottars, or landless labourers and hired hands. In some parts of eastern Swabia, cottars were admitted to the commune, even if they did not enjoy full equality, but the general rule was that peasant proprietors held the whiphand in village affairs.

Just how exclusive this sense of corporate identity could be is illustrated once again by the Württemberg evidence. Each village jealously guarded its own customs, which might differ perceptibly from those of its neighbours over such matters as weights and measures or calculating excise payments. These were set down in the village custumal (*Dorfbuch*). Property rights, in particular, were closely regulated. Neither land nor dwellings could be sold to those outside the community without the sanction of the village commune, and any property for sale had to be offered to members of the village first. This communal control of private property, in other words, went well beyond the familiar regulation of crop rotation, communal labour-services, and management of the common land (which included forest and water), which are regarded as the hallmark of village self-government based upon communal-collective values, and whose transgressions were punished at the annual disciplinary court composed of members of the commune.

It is widely argued that these values were communal in a double sense: they reinforced the rights and privileges of the village against outsiders; equally, however, they underpinned collectivist and egalitarian values within the village itself. It was not merely, for example,

---

* Cited in Sheilagh Ogilvie, 'The state in Germany: A non-Prussian view', in John Brewer and Eckhart Hellmuth (eds), *Rethinking Leviathan: The eighteenth-century state in Britain and Germany* (London/Oxford, 1999), p. 194.

that a villager could only drive beasts onto the common pasture by permission of the commune as a whole, but that the number of beasts should be limited to those which he required for his own household needs. This principle of 'household need' (*Hausnotdurft* in the German sources) applied in like fashion to the amount of wood which could be felled in the forest. But more important still was the extension of the principle to prohibit the sale of goods beyond the commune. 'Household need' allowed only for the satisfaction of immediate and family requirements; it excluded – indeed, it deliberately discountenanced – production for the market, and by that token individual or selfish pursuit of gain at the expense of the commonweal. This principle, as a case-study of Bavaria has suggested, initially determined the distribution of resources at local or communal level, but developed as the norm for *ancien-régime* society as a whole, though, as was only to be expected in a world of peasant proprietorship based in the main on secure and hereditary tenures (which Bavaria was), it was not inimical to individual property rights.

It is no criticism of the emphasis on 'household need' to point out that it was tailored to the situation of tenant farmers; its relevance to those villagers who had little or no land of their own, were not members of the commune, and in some cases lived principally from handicrafts rather than agriculture, was remote. Bavaria may have been in many respects the classic land of peasant agriculture on large and undivided farms, producing surpluses for export, but it was also at the end of our period a territory in which artisan activity was spreading to the countryside, albeit without the stimulus of the putting-out system. The principle of *Hausnotdurft*, it hardly needs to be stressed, could never be as compelling in those regions which were given over to commercialized agriculture (such as wine-growing), the cultivation of industrial crops, or which witnessed the spread of rural manufactures.

In one respect it was easier to maintain a sense of corporate solidarity at village level than in the towns, for the economic, charitable, and residential identities as discrete components of urban society fell together in the rural communes: the village as parish, commune, or agricultural entity could appear as a social unity, a world in miniature. But there were also corporate loyalties which cut across village solidarity. In those regions where the secondary economic sector – crafts and manufactures – had penetrated the village economy, artisans working in the countryside might be gathered into rural guilds.

It is often asserted, following the classic study of Pierre Goubert for the region of the Beauvaisis north of Paris,[*] that such occupations were never more than by-employments, supplementary sources of income intended to bolster the livelihood of those who lacked sufficient land to subsist from agriculture alone. In some cases this may be so, as the spread of spinning and weaving throughout the length and breadth of the Swabian countryside attests. But such craftsmen and -women, dependent outworkers of urban capitalists, for the most part, neither aspired to the status of craftmasters, nor were they organized in separate guilds. Elsewhere the picture was quite different. In parts of northern Switzerland and on the Upper Rhine rural artisanal guilds were commonplace. For Luzern it has been suggested that they represent a collective closing of the ranks to protect rural craftsmen against the economic downturn of the later sixteenth century. That is possible; but it does not dispose of the fact that regional guilds spanning town and countryside may well have existed much earlier. Where town and country were administered in districts (as in Upper Alsace and the duchy of Württemberg), artisan guilds embracing both can be encountered from the fifteenth century onwards; elsewhere, as in the county of Hohenlohe on the northern flank of Württemberg, sometimes only a century later.

In some principalities it became government policy to regulate crafts – and by extension the markets necessary to distribute artisan goods – for the territory as a whole, thereby deliberately ignoring or suspending the traditional liberties and franchises of the craft towns. That was a better strategy than unavailing attempts to suppress or restrict such rural crafts. In 1495, for instance, the margraves of Baden on the right bank of the Upper Rhine tried to concentrate artisan activity in the countryside in a mere four centres which were deemed to be markets, 'and similarly several other villages which we have allowed for their convenience and for reason of necessity',[†] but the ordinance soon became a dead letter.

One reason for trying to corral rural craftsmen into territorial guilds was precisely that they were not always casual or part-time occupations which might be assumed scarcely to have impinged upon the skills of trained urban masters. On the contrary, there is

[*] Pierre Goubert, *Beauvais et le Beauvaisis de 1600 à 1730*, 2 vols (Paris, 1960). See also Pierre Goubert, 'The French peasantry of the seventeenth century: A regional example', *Past and Present*, 10 (1956), pp. 55–77.

[†] Cited in Wolfgang Leiser, 'Zentralorte als Strukturprobleme der Markgrafschaft Baden', in Erich Maschke and Jürgen Sydow (eds), *Stadt und Umland* (Stuttgart, 1974), p. 8.

indirect evidence from the Upper Rhine, a region of economic diversification and close commercial links between town and country, that rural craftsmen had in some instances completed an apprenticeship to become masters in their own right; that training they can presumably have undergone only in the towns.

Rural Citizens and Communal Solidarity

The close links between town and country, evident in the diffusion of artisan trades to the countryside and the establishment of territorial guilds, are echoed, moreover, in legal and political relationships which historians have been prone to overlook. Just as the local nobility might acquire citizen's rights in neighbouring towns so, too, might ordinary villagers. The acceptance of rural commoners as burghers – usually described as paleburghers, rather than outburghers – had been expressly forbidden under the terms of Emperor Charles IV's Golden Bull of 1356, because it drove a wedge between the feudal lords and their peasant subjects. As a result, the number of paleburghers declined, but they certainly did not disappear. Not only were they to be found as citizens of several Swabian cities – Nördlingen, Memmingen, Lauingen, and Augsburg – (though Nuremberg, as always following its own line, observed the ban); they were common on the Upper Rhine, too, under imperial cities such as Konstanz and Strasbourg, and even under the jurisdiction of territorial towns such as the Outer Austrian communes of Freiburg im Breisgau and Breisach. They are encountered in the greatest numbers, however, as rural citizens of the Swiss cities. Indeed, there is now broad agreement that the consolidation of the Swiss Confederation in the fourteenth century was a direct result of the rural cantons' entering into a series of protective alliances with the leading cities of northern Switzerland, a development undergirded and impelled by the manumission of serfs on a grandiose scale, who acquired burgher's rights in Luzern, Bern, Zürich, and other smaller cities, sometimes in their thousands.

For the peasants, citizenship brought manifest political and legal advantages. They were legally answerable in the civic courts, not in the lord's village court; they paid civic taxes, not feudal renders (though, of course, they continued to owe rents to their landlords for their farms); and they were liable for call-up in the town's militia, rather than owing military service to their village lords. And, not

least, the disposal and inheritance of property fell under the provisions of urban law codes, not feudal custom. Outburghership, in
other words, conveyed a separate and privileged identity upon some
members of the village community. But it came at a price. If outburghership was the prelude to a general emancipation of the peasantry (as the case of Switzerland suggests), then it became an
aspiration which could be embraced by all; a vision of 'Swiss liberty'
encouraged many rural communes to the immediate north and east
– on the Upper Rhine, in Swabia, Vorarlberg, and Tirol – to seek to
'turn Swiss' at the close of the Middle Ages. But where outburghership served to discriminate between the fortunate few under the
aegis of urban jurisdiction and the less fortunate many who
remained at the beck and call of their village lords, then its impact
was bound to be divisive and to cause resentment. Moreover, in
those cases where noble outburghers controlled villages which also
contained peasant paleburghers of the same town, the likelihood of
conflict was great. That is exactly what happened with Freiburg im
Breisgau's peasant outburghers. Through chicanery and harassment
their rights were whittled away to the point where they were treated
no differently from the local lords' serfs; eventually the town council
sold off three of its largest outburgher communities after 1500 to
their village overlords, all of whom were noble outburghers of the
town!

So far, the discussion has focused on southern Germany and
Switzerland, regions where strong local communes were pervasive.
These were not confined to nucleated villages, but could embrace
landscapes of dispersed farmsteads, or take in entire alpine valleys;
by the same token, they were not peculiar to areas of diminutive or
fragmented lordships, but flourished in consolidated territories as
well; and, for good measure, they were not associated with regions of
partible inheritance alone (where the subdivision of farms might
pose a threat to the integrity of the commune), but were located in
areas of thoroughgoing impartibility as well, where large farms were
kept intact and the non-inheriting siblings paid off. There is no necessary correlation, therefore, between strong communes and particular agrarian regimes or landscapes (known in German as
Kulturlandschaften). Accordingly, historians in recent decades have
felt encouraged to search for strong communes in those regions of
Germany where they were traditionally supposed in the later Middle
Ages to have been either weak or absent: in much of the north
German plain, and the colonial lands east of the Elbe. Here the

picture is much patchier, but at least the prevalence of large dis-persed farmsteads in northern Germany is no longer taken as an unfailing indication that communes were deficient or redundant. Rather, peasants formed themselves into 'neighbourhoods', or collective associations simply termed 'peasantries'. Without nucleated villages as the focus of communal life, countrydwellers might come together in marcher associations (*Markgenossenschaften*) to regulate access to the common woods and pastures, or might take the parish as the framework of collective jurisdiction. Such was the pattern in much of Westphalia and Lower Saxony, towards the North Sea coast, though in the territory of Saxony itself communal organization was undoubtedly rudimentary. Even under the intensified seigneurial regime of eastern Germany, as it evolved from the fourteenth century onwards, rural communes were still able to make their voices heard, as will be explored in more detail in Chapter 6.

In exceptional circumstances, peasant communes could achieve real autonomy, whereby their corporate social status was elevated into political independence. That only happened, however, in areas remote from feudal lordship. There has been much debate, largely inconclusive, whether the alpine valleys of the Inner Swiss rural communes were ever fully penetrated by feudal domination, though it is now conceded that their early 'struggle for freedom', epitomized in the famous oath of confederation sworn by the men of Uri, Schwyz, and Nidwalden in 1291, was in fact directed against law-breakers and feuders within their own ranks, rather than against 'foreign' feudal overlords. But on the North Sea coast, the inhabitants of Frisia, bordering on the northern Low Countries, and of Dithmarschen, north of the Elbe estuary, established what were in effect free peasant republics by the later Middle Ages, the former in contempt of imperial authority, the latter in defiance of the titular authority of the archbishops of Bremen. Neither Frisia nor Dithmarschen, however, fully maintained their independence after 1500. Dithmarschen, indeed, was absorbed into the county of Holstein in 1559. A peasant republic such as Dithmarschen may strike us as the apotheosis of corporate identity, binding together in social and political solidarity a community of free and equal status. But even Dithmarschen had a hierarchy, based not on economic or social criteria but on membership of the parish assembly. Only those held worthy of partaking in the Lord's Supper were admitted to the assembly, which at its monthly meetings held in the churchyard acted as a consistory, supervising morals and manners, and dispensing charity to the deserving poor. Modern preconceptions of equality and democracy run the risk of misconstruing German society before and after 1500. However prevalent and powerful notions of the commonweal or the 'household good' might be, they were embedded in a fabric of social relations woven from corporate interests and liberties, which was grounded in privilege and oligarchy, exclusion and discrimination.

3 Population and Household

Population Decline and Recovery

A lack of reliable statistics before the eighteenth century makes the task of determining Germany's population between 1300 and 1600 no easy matter. But the difficulty is compounded by a lack of agreement over the appropriate geographical boundaries within which to calculate the population. The available figures may relate to Germany in its frontiers of 1914, in which case they include Alsace-Lorraine, the whole of west and east Prussia and province of Posen/Poznań or they may be based on the frontiers of 1937, by which time Germany had lost Alsace-Lorraine to France, and Poznań and part of west Prussia (the Danzig corridor) to Poland. Sometimes they comprehend the entire extent of German eastwards colonization and settlement, thereby taking in Austria. Rarely, however, do they include the German-speaking territories of Switzerland (though their omission is a historical nonsense), or, more justifiably, those parts of the Empire in the west which had become effectively detached in the course of the later Middle Ages (Luxembourg, the Low Countries) and were therefore not regarded as part of Germany. The rough totals are set out in Table 3.1. Were Austria and Switzerland to be included, the former might add 1.5 million to the 1550 total, and nearly 2 million to the 1600 figure; the latter around 0.6 million in 1500 and 0.9 million in 1600.

These are crude figures at best, showing orders of magnitude rather than precise totals. They derive from a variety of sources: tax records, rent-books, muster-rolls, citizenship registers, all of which list adult males, not women and children. Parish registers, which in

Table 3.1 Population of the German lands in the boundaries of 1914 (excluding Austria and Switzerland) in millions

1300	1400	1450	1500	1550	1600
14	9	8–9	9–10	13–14	16–17

Source: Christian Pfister, 'The population of late medieval and early modern Germany', in Bob Scribner (ed.), *Germany: A new social and economic history* (London/New York/Sydney/Auckland, 1996), pp. 38–43.

principle record all births, marriages, and deaths, except obviously of Jews, only survive in Germany in any number from the mid-seventeenth century. Unlike a modern census, therefore, it becomes necessary to find a multiplier to convert the number of adult males into a household total. Early demographers worked on a total of 5 or even 5.5 persons per household; this was the coefficient used by Fritz Koerner in his pioneering work on the population of Thuringia in the 1920s. Nowadays this figure is regarded as too high; a multiplier of 4 or 4.5 is preferred (which discounts those children who die in infancy, within a year of their birth). The element of uncertainty in calculating population totals is therefore considerable, but at least modern estimates err on the side of caution.

However the figures are calculated, what remains incontrovertible is the slump in Germany's population during the fourteenth century, with the estimated total of 14 million inhabitants in 1300 not to be reached again until the mid-sixteenth century. The most direct evidence of population decline comes from the abandonment of human settlements and cultivated land. It has been reckoned that as many as 40 000 settlements out of a total of 170 000 disappeared, either temporarily or permanently, that is, slightly less than one-quarter. As in other parts of Europe, the chief culprit was the Black Death, the wave of bubonic plague which swept over Europe after 1349, with further bouts of the disease afflicting the population at irregular intervals well into the sixteenth century.

The evidence of deserted settlements needs, however, to be interpreted with caution. Deserted lands as well as deserted villages – the German term *Wüstungen* is significantly much less restrictive than the common English usage 'deserted *villages*' – can be found before the onset of the Black Death, and should not automatically be taken as a sign of economic or demographic adversity. In east Prussia, it is true, the wars of the mid-thirteenth century may already have swept away numerous communities, but elsewhere the pull of burgeoning towns, the establishment of monastic latifundia given over to pastoralism (most commonly by the Cistercians), or the fusion of smaller settlements into larger ones could cause places – or, more tellingly, place-names – to disappear, as population was sucked or drawn off the land, or concentrated in fewer settlements. That is not to deny the impact of the plague when it came, but a loss of settlements or place-names cannot simply be equated with a loss of people. Marginal fields taken into cultivation when good land was becoming scarce as the population rose in the thirteenth century were subsequently abandoned when a demographic thinning of the ranks allowed survivors to migrate to areas where farms with better land had fallen vacant. Population loss, in other words, is complicated by migration and resettlement.

All that cannot take away from the fact that after 1350 the population in the German lands declined severely and, above all, rapidly, by on average one-third up to 1383, when another bout of plague struck. Given its highly contagious nature, the disease struck hardest in congested areas such as towns, rather than in the countryside. This helps to explain the otherwise paradoxical phenomenon that *Wüstungen* were commonest *both* in regions of existing population density (the heavily urbanized landscape of Silesia, for example), *and* where uplands or forests on the margins of agriculture had recently and too readily been cleared and colonized (as in the Harz mountains of central Germany).

After the 1380s stagnation set in for the best part of a century, until the first signs of demographic upturn appeared around 1470. During this century of stagnation, however, a subtle shift in the balance of population occurred. While rural population figures remained depressed, signs of urban recovery can be detected from 1430 onwards. In the western German lands, the total urban population, reckoned at 640 000 in 1350, slumped to 385 000 in 1430, but, it has been claimed, by 1450 had managed to regain the level attained just before the Black Death, at a time when the countryside was experiencing a further loss of approaching 200 000 souls. That represents a staggering two-thirds increase in twenty years, which seems hardly credible. As a percentage of the population as a whole, however, the urban share in this period seems to have gone up on one estimate by as much as 6 per cent, from 10 per cent to 16 per cent, or, on a more conservative estimate, from 10 per cent to 13 per cent or 13.5 per cent . Either way, this suggests a recovery both rapid and remarkable.

Urban Population Ratios

Yet the most recent compilation of urban population statistics for Europe as a whole lends little credibility to the figures. Out of fifty towns in the German-speaking lands (including Alsace and Switzerland) for which we have any kind of reliable and *consecutive* information between 1300 and 1600, no more than twenty managed to increase their population by 1500, and in most cases it was a slow and protracted recuperation after the losses of the later fourteenth century, rather than a dramatic spurt in the mid-fifteenth. After 1500, a handful of towns and cities did begin to display significant growth up to 1600. For these, as in the case of communes which were flourishing before 1500, their demographic health was attributable to specific economic circumstances and opportunities: it was not the outflow of a general recovery in urban populations. The Saxon mining boom of the late fifteenth century spurred the growth of Eisleben (with reserves of copper), and the silver towns of Freiberg, and Annaberg on the Bohemian border. The rise of the north German brewing industry, as hopped ale began to displace wine as the everyday drink, accounted for the development of Einbeck, Braunschweig, and Goslar. Some cities were able to grow because they could feed their populations on grain imported from the Baltic (the ports of Bremen, Hamburg, Rostock, and Stralsund); others prospered as the capitals or main residences of the emerging princely territories (Munich, Dresden, Heidelberg). Only a few very prominent cities, however, can be said to have expanded because of the underlying vigour of their manufacturing and commercial enterprises. They include Augsburg, Nuremberg, Aachen (as an aspiring rival to Cologne), Görlitz (as the entrepôt between woad production in Thuringia and the textile centres of Lusatia and Silesia); or Leipzig, which displaced Erfurt as the principal staging-post on commercial routes into eastern Europe.

The majority of towns and cities in Germany, by contrast, were hard pressed to achieve demographic stability in the course of the fifteenth and sixteenth centuries. Not only were some smaller and middling craft towns exposed to competition from rural crafts and country markets (the towns of the Austrian Breisgau on the right

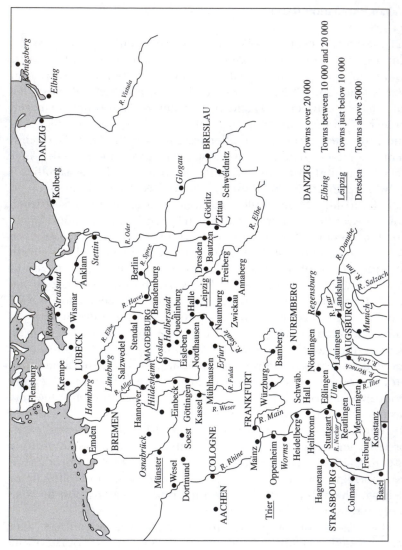

3.1 Population of German towns in the sixteenth century

bank of the Upper Rhine being a well-documented example); their economic vitality might be sapped by the overwhelming power of metropolises bent upon dominating their hinterlands, as the difficulties of Swabian manufacturing centres such as Nördlingen and Memmingen in the face of Augsburg's predatory commercial policies in the sixteenth century attest.

At the same time, no German city in this period encountered the problem which had confronted the leading Flemish cities in the fourteenth century and which was to beset the gateway cities of monarchies with overseas empires, such as Naples and Seville, in the sixteenth and seventeenth centuries, that is, hypertrophic populations of immigrants desperate for work – or beggars content to scrounge – who acted as an economic drag upon their host communities.

Only by the mid-sixteenth century did Germany's population regain the level of the early fourteenth century, and it continued to rise until the onset of the Thirty Years War. Around 1550 the chroniclers speak once more of land hunger, rising land prices, and the taking-in of marginal lands. As the chronicle of the counts of Zimmern in Swabia put it, there was 'scarcely a patch, even in the bleakest forest and on the highest hills, which remained uncleared and uncultivated'.* The proliferation of territorial forest ordinances after 1500, from Tirol through Württemberg and northwards to Hessen and Braunschweig-Wolfenbüttel, designed to prevent indiscriminate felling and burning, offers further indirect evidence of land hunger on the part of a swelling population. Subsistence crises reappeared, especially during a string of harvest failures in the early 1570s, so that Germany's population was already knocking against its sustainable limits well before the demographic catastrophe of the Thirty Years War.

That can already be seen from the startling tilt in the balance between urban and rural populations after 1500. If Germany's overall population went up from around 10 million in 1500 to around 17 million at the beginning of the seventeenth century, only three-quarters of a million at best was added to the urban total, a differential of 20 per cent. Very little of that increase, moreover, is attributable to the larger cities. The inhabitants of communities over 5000 may have numbered 0.7 million in 1500, but only 0.78 million

---

* *Zimmersche Chronik*, ed. Karl August Barack, 4 vols (Bibliothek des Litterarischen Vereins in Stuttgart, 89–93) (Tübingen, 1867–69), vol. 4, p. 304.

in 1600 (as a percentage of the entire population a fall from 7 per cent to a mere 4.6 per cent). The urban component as a whole declined from around 15 per cent to 13 per cent, and even the metropolitan centres over 10 000 inhabitants, which are often regarded as having held their own, fell proportionately from 4.5 per cent to 3.1 per cent. It should immediately be added, however, that these figures are at variance with the calculations of the leading demographic expert, Christian Pfister, who sets the urban percentages appreciably higher. On the other hand, they are still far greater than those compiled by three leading French scholars for European towns as a whole, who give Germany's population as rising from 10.5 million in 1500 to no more than 12.5 million in 1600, with the degree of urbanization never exceeding 8.5 per cent of the total (see the Bibliography of Works in English, pp. 271–82). That would give an urban population of just over one million in 1600. From the database compiled by Bob Scribner of towns in present-day Germany (a highly restrictive criterion, since it excludes Alsace-Lorraine, Switzerland, Austria, and the former German territories now in Poland) this figure is so low as to be quite implausible. Scribner's figures will be discussed in more detail below, but for the moment all that can be said is that there is no consensus among historians either on the absolute population figures for Germany in this period, or on their method of calculation, though there is broad agreement on the peaks and troughs and the population trend in general, which largely mirror those elsewhere in western Europe.

Perhaps in the end the absolute figures do not matter very much; what is truly significant is the vast regional variation in population density. Too often a simple contrast has been drawn between western Germany and the lands east of the Elbe. After the Black Death the former may have had between 15 and 18 persons per square kilometre, the latter no more than 12 to 15 persons. Even for the west these figures are appreciably lower than those for France or England in the later Middle Ages. Yet all this is to paint with a very broad brush, for the fluctuations over quite small areas could be remarkable. Around 1500 the number of houses (not individuals) per square kilometre in thinly settled Mecklenburg (2) and Pomerania (1) east of the river Oder stands in marked contrast to Württemberg (8) and the western Black Forest (10). If we apply a conservative multiplier of four, that gives a population density in parts of south-west Germany of anything between 32 and 40 persons per square kilometre, figures altogether comparable with the Paris basin, Lombardy, or even Sicily. But even these figures do not tell the whole story. Within south-west Germany population density on the uplands of the Swabian Alp or in the Black Forest never reached the levels of the principal river valleys of the Rhine, Main, or Neckar. A commercialized economy geared to exports, the prevalence of partible inheritance, and good communications along arterial waterways encouraged a settlement density as great as anywhere in Europe, and which certainly far exceeded most of central and northern Germany, except for the areas bordering on the Low Countries.

These valleys, moreover, were highly urbanized, but the point often missed is that, with the obvious exception of the metropolises and larger regional centres – Basel, Strasbourg, Speyer, Worms, Würzburg, Frankfurt, Eßlingen, Heilbronn, or Heidelberg – the vast majority of south-west German towns were 'farm towns' or 'peasant burgher towns', many engaged in viticulture or market-gardening, whose populations might not top 500, and certainly only rarely exceeded 2000. In social structure and economic function, therefore, they barely differed from neighbouring villages which never received an urban franchise. Along the Neckar and its tributaries, to take a particularly striking example, there were at least 15 such dwarf towns dotted between Eßlingen and Heilbronn, a distance of no more than 35 kilometres; yet taken together, they never approached the clustering of urban centres which Jan de Vries has posited as the launching-pad of European modernization.[*] Their 'urban quality', in other words, was absent or deficient, so that the much trumpeted distinction between urban and rural populations, with their different trajectories of growth, may be fundamentally unenlightening or even positively misleading.

A tabulation of urban populations in sixteenth-century Germany makes sobering reading. There were probably no more than 2200 towns in the German-speaking lands as a whole (including 88 in Switzerland, 150 in Austria, and around 70 in Alsace-Lorraine), far less than the figure of 4000 encountered in the older literature. Taking a cohort of 1865 towns that lay within the boundaries of present-day Germany, we find that over 50 per cent had populations of 2000 or less, and that figure is likely to be considerably inflated by the one-third of towns about which we have no information at all. The distribution would hardly vary, were figures for Switzerland, Austria, and Alsace-Lorraine to be included.

---

[*] Jan de Vries, *European Urbanization 1500–1800* (Cambridge, MA, 1984).

Table 3.2.   Population of German towns in the sixteenth century

Category	Population	Number	Percentage of total
1. Metropolises	20 000+	10	0.54
2. Sub-regional metropolises	10 000–20 000	18	0.97
3. Regional centres	5000–10 000	57	3.05
4. Sub-regional centres	2000–5000	186	9.97
5. Local centres	1000–2000	298	15.98
6. Dwarf towns	up to 1000	668	35.82
7. No information		628	33.67

Source: Regrouped from Tom Scott and Bob Scribner, 'Urban networks', in Bob Scribner (ed.), *Germany: A new social and economic history* (London/New York/Sydney/Auckland, 1996), p. 116.

Everywhere in the German-speaking lands the tide of urban foundations, which had flowed so strongly in the later Middle Ages, was ebbing by 1500. In Saxony, seventeen new towns had been founded from the beginning of the fourteenth century, almost all of them in the Erzgebirge, the mineral-rich mountain range bordering Bohemia, with its deposits of silver and tin; their growth could be spectacular. The principal mining communities of Annaberg, Schneeberg, and Marienberg had all been granted urban charters by 1500, and they boasted populations of 5000 or more (in Annaberg's case perhaps even 12 000, which far outstripped Leipzig!), though none of them came close to Schwaz, the centre of the Tirolean mining industry, with a population of 20 000 (and no urban charter, as it happened!). But these were Klondykes, whose decline, as seams were exhausted, might be as swift as their rise. Annaberg, strikingly, only had 3400 residents in 1600. The leading silver-mining town in the Vosges in the early sixteenth century, for instance, was Ste-Marie-aux-Mines – a settlement of squalid houses and rapidly run-up shacks, in effect a squatter camp – which may have given shelter to more than 5000 persons at its peak, but which by the latter part of the century was all but a ghost town. While urban populations might thus fluctuate dramatically, the actual number of new foundations in the three centuries after 1500 amounted to no more than 200. This figure includes several towns specifically created as refugee settlements, designed to harness the skills of those fleeing religious persecution, examples being the worsted weavers of Frankenthal in the Palatinate, the hosiers of Hanau in Hessen, or the cabinet-makers of Neuwied in the county of Wied on the Rhine.

But while new town foundations might be a rarity, the number of villages which received market franchises – a key indicator of urban quality – increased dramatically. In Switzerland alone, with not a single urban foundation between 1400 and 1800, the total of village markets in the same period went up from 30 to 300. That reminds us of the need for caution in distinguishing 'town' and 'country' when analyzing not only comparative population figures but the scope of commercial and economic activity as well.

The Jewish population of the German lands was concentrated at the beginning of our period largely in the towns, with some strikingly sizeable communities, perhaps numbering 1000 each, in both Nuremberg and Erfurt, amounting to between 5 and 10 per cent of those cities' inhabitants. But elsewhere the population was much lower, less than 1 per cent of the population. A total figure of 100 000 Jews has been conjectured for the period around 1300; a century later that total had fallen to 40 000 at best, in line with the general slump in population. Whether the number of Jews recovered significantly after 1500 is hard to determine, given their gradual dispersion into smaller towns and villages, for which usable statistics are essentially lacking.

Mortality

Periodic snapshots of Germany's population between 1300 and 1500 will always be tainted by the quantitative imprecision inherent in a pre-statistical age, but at least they give us a general impression of demographic growth and recession. What they do not do is explain those fluctuations. Over the last few decades historians have shown considerable ingenuity in uncovering the underlying rhythms of population development – the respective roles of mortality, fertility, and migration. Investigations into family structure and reproductive behaviour were long taboo in German historiography because of the shadow cast by the Nazis' misuse of demographic data to compile registers of local family lineages (*Ortssippenbücher*) designed to document racial purity. Until recently, it has largely been left to Austrian and Swiss historians to make up lost ground. On two points, a consensus seems to have been achieved. Early modern European society until the agrarian and industrial revolutions was the prisoner of a 'system of zero growth' in agricultural production; that is to say, peasant agriculture was incapable of raising output to the level necessary to break free from periodic subsistence crises, for against a background of marginal returns and climatic variations any increase in agrarian production simply encouraged population to grow to a point where it knocked up against available resources and toppled over into decline as the result of plague, famine, or warfare. Yet at the same time, populations could also recover remarkably quickly from periodic adversities and restore what has been called the homeostatic or self-regulating balance. If on the one hand they were the victims of mortality crises, so on the other could they adapt by controlling patterns of fertility. Just how the limits of the demographic regime – its 'carrying capacity' – were achieved, in particular how population growth and economic development interacted, remains controversial, but it is now recognized that social constraints must be set alongside ecological constraints, so that the structural limits to population growth determined by the influence of topography and climate upon agrarian output can only properly be interpreted within the framework of unequal distribution of that output. The German lands are no exception to this general western European pattern, but that does not preclude variations at local or regional level. The difficulties of analysis begin with the mortality rates. Epidemics, whether caused by bubonic plague, smallpox, or dysentery became less common, less widespread, and less virulent after 1500, though severe social disruptions caused by warfare continued to trigger local crises, especially during the Thirty Years War. The reasons are not well understood. It is true that territorial and urban authorities became much more alert to the importance of environmental hygiene in the later sixteenth century, issuing quarantine edicts and concerning themselves with the purity of the public water supply. But these measures remained halting and sporadic for many years to come, and in any case the decline in epidemics was already observable much earlier. Moreover, it is only a mild exaggeration to say that epidemic crises were replaced by subsistence crises during the sixteenth century. Not only did years of bad harvests with subsequent deaths and famine often not come singly, but in clusters – 1527–30, the mid-1550s, 1569–74, 1586–89, 1593–97 – the clusters themselves became more frequent after mid-century. This has been attributed to a downturn in the climate lasting from the mid-1560s to the end of the 1630s. Much of the evidence for this deterioration is (almost by definition) impressionistic; meteorological records were unknown. And yet the sources lament with striking unanimity hard winters with excessive snow and late frosts, or wet springs and summers with too much rain and too little sun. Crops failed to bud, or turned rotten on their stalks, thereby leading both to small harvests and to the risk of fungal diseases such as ergot. Here the social dimension of mortality immediately obtrudes, for those who were able to store grain from times of good harvest in tithebarns and ventilated granaries held the whiphand. Convents could regrate stocks of grain at market at inflated prices which the poor could not afford; town magistracies, caught between a concern for the commonweal and a fear of bread riots, could dole out grain or flour to needy citizens. Those beyond the reach of such benevolence might well starve. During the particularly severe subsistence crisis of the early 1570s, scores of villages on the right bank of the Rhine up into the Black Forest sent appeals to Strasbourg for doles of corn from the city's famous granary. The magistrates did their best to meet the requests (though they scaled them down *pro rata*), and the communes in this instance seem to have been able to pay for the emergency supplies without running up large debts. But not all villages were lucky enough to have a Strasbourg on their doorstep.

Mortality caused by disease or famine is by its nature unpredictable. But perinatal mortality, always much higher than in modern societies, showed unmistakable regional variations throughout the German lands which require explanation. Areas where breastfeeding was customary show much lower rates (between 9 per cent and 25 per cent in much of northern Germany) than those where infants were fed off the breast (southern Germany, with rates up to 33 per cent). Where infants were weaned on floury gruel and unsweetened juices, as in eastern Switzerland, perinatal mortality could top 40 per cent. Yet the discrepancy was much more evident in the case of three- to four-year-old children than with infants in their first two years of life. A comparative case-study of two communities, the Lutheran parish of Hesel in east Frisia and the Catholic village of Gabelbach in Bavarian Swabia – admittedly from the seventeenth century – has sought to shed light on manifest differences between low infant mortality in the former (around 13 per cent) and high in the latter (around 34 per cent). These differences, however, only emerged after the first twelve months. In Gabelbach, infants were weaned shortly after birth, with the result that their mothers quickly became pregnant again, whereas in Hesel children were kept on the breast precisely in order to prevent or delay further pregnancies. However, prolonged breastfeeding at the same time helped to reduce the mothers' mortality rate, which was 25 per cent higher in Gabelbach than in Hesel. The question remains whether confessional differences compounded the cultural difference between north and south in breastfeeding practices. Arthur E. Imhof, the author of this case-study, cautiously supports this thesis.[*] He points on the one hand to the trauma inflicted on Gabelbach by the ravages of the Thirty Years War, which may have led to a resigned acceptance of high infant mortality, whereas Hesel in remote east Frisia was spared. But on the other he suggests that Catholic beliefs may have made it easier for parents in Gabelbach to accept high mortality rates, quite apart from the shorter span of breastfeeding. Evidence from the late eighteenth century in the small wine-growing town of Oppenheim on the left bank of the Rhine does highlight lower perinatal mortality rates among the town's Protestant population than among its Catholic citizens – but in the first half of the century no such distinction was apparent! The search for definitive answers for earlier periods is likely to remain fruitless.

Fertility and Nuptuality

The pattern of fertility and nuptuality, by contrast, is much clearer. The seasonal weighting of conceptions and births remained constant over the centuries, with pregnancies commonest in the early summer, leading to parturition in quieter winter months, when mothers could devote more attention to their infants. The link to the rhythms of the agricultural cycle is obvious: conceptions were less frequent at harvest time. Exhaustion during the busiest months of the calendar may well have accounted in part for a drop in fertility, but there is no doubt that couples practised various forms of deliberate birth control as well, quite apart from simply refraining

---

[*] Arthur E. Imhof, *Lost Worlds: How our European ancestors coped with everyday life, and why life is so hard today* (Charlottesville, VA/London, 1998).

from sex. Prolonged breastfeeding was one; temporary separation of partners through seasonal migration of labour was another. But the commonest (by presumption, though not attested everywhere) was coitus interruptus, especially after the birth and survival beyond the immediate perinatal years of the first children. The ability of the population rapidly to make good losses sustained by epidemics before levelling off once more underscores the use of rudimentary controls upon fertility, though it has been pointed out that perhaps as many as one-third of conceptions in the wake of epidemics resulted in spontaneous abortion. The major check on fertility, however, was the age of marriage. In this respect the German lands corresponded by and large to what has been termed the (west) European marriage pattern, whereby marriage was dependent upon the spouses leaving home to set up their own household. Within the rural population – but to some extent in urban ones as well – marriage was indissolubly bound up with inheritance entitlements, property rights, and the availability of labour. Parents would not assent to their offspring marrying unless and until rights of succession and provision for their old age had been established. By the same token, the choice of marriage partners was restricted. In Upper Bavaria, for instance, in the country areas, marriage was possible only where the male had the prospect of inheriting a farm and the woman could provide a suitable dowry. These constraints were underpinned by the territorial administrations, especially in areas of impartible inheritance, which were concerned to preserve the viability of family farms. But restrictions could be imposed by the local communities themselves: in the upland commune of Törbel in the German-speaking part of the Valais, couples could not marry unless they had sufficient land to farm, along with access to the communal pastures and forests, an entitlement granted to natives of Törbel alone, not even to men who had married women from the commune.

Two corollaries immediately and predictably followed: the age of marriage was high (perhaps as much as 30 for men and the mid-20s for women), which reduced the span of annual fertility for women by around one-third; and the opportunity for cottagers, landless labourers, domestic servants, or apprentices to marry was seriously curtailed, at least until their status improved, as when apprentices became mastercraftsmen. It might be supposed that late marriages were accompanied by high illegitimacy rates, but this was not necessarily the case. Quite apart from the sanctions imposed on extramarital sexual relations by Church and state, the pressure exerted by family or community – specifically, exclusion from inheritance or banishment from the commune – had its effect, though that effect was naturally weaker on those without prospect of inheritance or on the margins of the community. Another reason was the later age of sexual maturity. A generally poor diet, deficient in proteins, and the labour which children were expected to perform combined to retard sexual development. Quite unlike today, when sexual maturity often precedes legal majority by several years, children were treated as adults at a surprisingly early age: Heide Wunder instances apprentices hired from the age of eleven; fourteen as the age of legal responsibility, or twelve the age for bearing arms (in the city of Konstanz).[*] But the lowest age for marriage was set at eighteen for men and sixteen for women. At the same time, though, she emphasizes that these age limits varied over time and from territory to territory; they are an indication of social and legal mores, not a hard-and-fast guide.

Employment and Gender

Given the undeniable steady rise of the population during the sixteenth century, with an annual growth rate of 1.4 per cent in certain parts of Germany, it is legitimate to wonder just how far the European marriage pattern was the norm in our period. In the lands of the south-west, with partible inheritance and commercialized agriculture, the sanctions on early marriage were less severe, especially if some of the rural population derived its livelihood in part from crafts and manufactures. The strongest growth rates are visible here: in the territories of Zürich and Bern, in Swabia generally (including in the north the county of Hohenlohe, with an annual increase in mid-century of 3 per cent!), in Hessen (where the population doubled in a century), and even in Thuringia, on the borders of partible and impartible inheritance, but with a thriving and diversified rural economy. These examples suggest that marriage cannot have been quite as restricted as once thought. Attempts to break these figures down between town and country, or between different social strata, have been bedevilled by a lack of statistical sources, and even when such sources exist they do not speak an unequivocal lan-

---

[*] Heide Wunder, *He is the Sun, she is the Moon: Women in early modern Germany* (Cambridge, MA, 1998).

guage. The one exception appears to be life expectancy, where differences between town and country – based on a case-study of northern Hessen in the early seventeenth century – stand out, male peasants living longer on average (to 62) than members of urban elites (to 48), with an even greater divergence amongst women. The reasons, however, remain obscure, though the clergy lived longest, perhaps because of a more nutritious diet.

As far as we can tell, women as a rule somewhat outnumbered men. After outbreaks of famine or disease the pressure on widows to remarry and bear second families became considerable. Despite that socio-biological imperative, and notwithstanding the authorities' widespread suspicion of 'masterless women', the number of women as heads of their own households was surprisingly large, at least in the towns. Figures compiled for cities in Upper Germany for the late fourteenth and the fifteenth century reveal that as many as one-quarter of all households (according to the tax registers) had women at their heads – in Frankfurt, Trier, Basel, and Friedberg, with slightly lower totals in Schwäbish Hall and Bern. In many cases, these women were the widows of mastercraftsmen who were carrying on their husbands' trade, having not (yet) remarried. It was rare, though not unknown, for women to pursue careers as independent breadwinners, but opportunities for women became increasingly restricted after 1500 as new patterns of the division of labour reduced many urban males to the status of wage-workers. As a consequence, the search for gainful employment which defined male gender roles made men hostile towards female competition in the workplace. This is particularly evident amongst journeymen, anxious about their chances of becoming masters, whose sense of honour and status inclined them to draw a sharp distinction between their labour and what was properly women's work. In the countryside, where the peasant family as a group constituted the productive unit, these tensions were less marked. In viticulture, for instance, the seasonal tasks in vineyard and cellar were divided amongst men and women, though as landlords began to replace labour-services with wage-work at the close of the Middle Ages women were paid up to a third or even a half less than men for their labour. Yet, as Heide Wunder has concluded, the gendered nature of relations between men and women lacked the universal structural force which it was to acquire in the bourgeois society of the nineteenth century, for age, civil status, and social class still bore crucially upon gender roles in a society dominated by the corporate principles of Estate and hierarchy.

4   Economic Landscapes

The Determinants of an Economic Landscape

The German lands from the fourteenth to the early seventeenth century remained a predominantly agrarian society, with anything up to 80 per cent of the population living and working on the land. Nevertheless, during this period significant shifts in the economy took place. Some of these occurred within the primary sector itself – the switch to pastoralism in the late Middle Ages before a retreat to tillage in the later sixteenth century, or the concentration upon specialized crops, in certain areas of western Germany, and the rise of an intensified cereal agriculture on large commercial estates east of the Elbe. Others marked the dissolution of a purely agrarian regime through the spread of industrial crops and rural manufactures. A few areas, moreover, began to develop as fully industrialized regions based upon mining and metallurgy. Taken together, these developments encouraged the emergence of distinctive economic landscapes throughout Germany.

Such landscapes clearly depended both upon endogenous conditions – soil, climate, altitude, natural resources – and upon exogenous circumstances – location, transport, the organization of production, and consumer demand. But these factors are insufficient in themselves to explain the rise of specifically *economic* landscapes beyond the level of basic description. What was decisive was the interplay, often highly complex, of endogenous and exogenous factors, above all the interdependence of complementary economic regions. It is worth pursuing this point in some detail before giving a more general account of the various types of economic landscape. In the case of agriculture, many parts of Germany remained wedded to mixed agriculture (tillage and pastoralism side-by-side) and the traditional pattern of open fields, parcelled out into strips, which had been the common pattern throughout most of western Europe from the high Middle Ages. But by the late fourteenth century, a concentration upon either tillage or stock-rearing and dairying can be observed. Yet even in such instances, arable and pastoral husbandry could not exist in isolation from each other. Tillage was impossible without draught animals for ploughing and carting; their dung was needed to manure the soil; and their meat and milk provided an essential source of protein and energy. Without large-scale cattle-grazing on the marshes of Frisia and Emsland along the North Sea coast, or in low-lying parts of Mecklenburg between the Elbe and Oder, intensive cereal agriculture in adjacent areas could not have flourished, because the latter depended on the annual ploughing over of the topsoil humus admixed with stable dung. As a result, an agrarian region of perpetual rye cultivation developed, by means of a one-field system which was able to dispense with traditional crop rotation and fallowing.

In regions of rural manufactures alongside agriculture the interconnectedness of the primary (agricultural) and secondary (manufacturing) economic sectors is readily apparent. A classic example is that of the Upper German linen industry in Swabia between the Allgäu in the east at the foothills of the Alps and the northern littoral of Lake Constance in the west. Here the cultivation of flax and its manufacture into linen can be traced back at least to the thirteenth century. The low-lying tracts of marshland flanking the rivers Iller and Lech flowing northwards to the Danube provided suitable conditions for flax-growing, but once it had been spun and woven into linen, the cloth still had to be bleached. The various stages all used milk, either for bucking (that is steeping in an alkaline dye) or for soaking in vats of buttermilk, before the cloths were finally crofted (spread out and kept moist on bleaching-grounds for several months). None of that would have been possible without the existence of widespread dairying, which benefited from the lush pastures of a well-watered landscape with high rainfall, at least in the east. A particular pastoral regime, therefore, functionally conditioned the growth of the linen industry. When linen-weaving spread in the sixteenth century to parts of Westphalia and Flanders with strong dairying traditions the rapid growth of the industry created a huge demand for milk which led to periodic shortages of supply for bleaching.

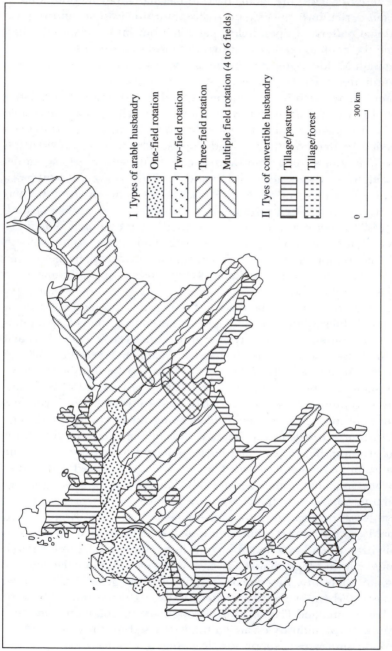

I Types of arable husbandry

  One-field rotation

  Two-field rotation

  Three-field rotation

  Multiple field rotation (4 to 6 fields)

II Tyes of convertible husbandry

  Tillage/pasture

  Tillage/forest

0   300 km

4.1 *Agricultural systems (after W. Abel)*

The example of the Swabian linen industry, however, alerts us to other interdependences which lay beyond the sphere of production and supply. For topography, climate, and agrarian regime were not uniform throughout Swabia. The Allgäu was – and still is – a region of dairying, with a cool climate and high rainfall, but the western fringes of Swabia, shading into the Alemannic lands of the Upper Rhine, were warmer, drier, and with less emphasis on dairy cattle. On the other hand, their location in terms of communications and transport was more favourable. Yet even an explanation grounded in advantage of distribution and marketing, as opposed to production, does not work too well, since the linen industry around Lake Constance was well established long before the rise of the great Swiss or Swabian merchant houses of the fourteenth century and after. We need instead to look to extraneous stimuli such as the relatively dense urbanization of the area below Lake Constance, which created consumer demand, and population growth in the countryside, which led to pressure within the primary sector for rural by-employment in textiles, whose output the towns could absorb.

Where regions were given over to mining and metallurgy, the links between available resources, the choice of location, and the nature of production were the most complex of all. Without the natural resources offered by the belt of forest stretching across central Germany, much of the extractive and metal-working industry of Franconia and Hessen would initially have been unable to develop. But the forests themselves were ultimately less important than the by-products derived from them, especially charcoal as the principal fossil fuel. Many upland areas of the Sauerland, at the headwaters of the river Ruhr, were given over to charcoal-burning, with entire villages dedicated to supplying the local iron-foundries, to the point where the organization of production began to display rudimentary forms of vertical integration, as miners, charcoalers, ironsmiths, and iron-founders – that is, wage-labourers, independent artisans, and forgemasters – combined in a single craft guild. Within much the same area, however, the availability of timber helped stimulate a quite different branch of industry, which did not rely on wood for fuel, but as a constituent of the manufacturing process itself. In the oak forests of the Siegerland, abutting the Sauerland to the south, the practice of coppicing, that is, cutting over young trees before they became timber-trees, commonly in order to make wooden spokes, handles, or hoops, served here to provide tanbark (by stripping and drying the bark of young trees) which was used in the preparation of leather. By the same token, the extensive glass industry which grew up in eastern Westphalia and northern Hessen depended upon timber resources, in this instance the supply of potash made by leaching woodash which was then evaporated in pots. In their organization and technology, therefore, the iron-, leather-, and glass-manufacturing of much of northern central Germany all depended in various ways on the availability of timber.

The most intricate equation between natural resources and the location of industry occurred in the mining and refining of those base and precious metals which required heavy capital investment. All forms of extraction and smelting required limitless supplies of wood and water, but these were not always to be found in the vicinity of the ores themselves. In the case of the Thuringian copper-mining industry, which flourished from the fifteenth century, the ore was found and mined in northern Thuringia, around Mansfeld, Eisleben, and Sangerhausen, but the smelteries were, with one exception, situated much further south beyond Erfurt and Weimar, where the countryside was thickly forested and watered by the rivers Gera, Ilm, and Saxon Saale. But these natural features cannot of themselves explain the location of smelteries. The industry came to rely on the new and expensive technology of liquation, which required extensive plant, with as many as six to eight furnaces in a row covering a considerable area. Because of the capital costs involved, liquation works had to be located with good access to per-ceived markets, a prime example being the Augsburg merchant house of Fugger's smeltery at Hohenkirchen in the Thuringian Forest, which was conveniently sited where trade routes to and from Nuremberg, Frankfurt, and Leipzig intersected. Indeed, the tech-nology on occasion outstripped the capital investment. Several new technical processes, such as the invention of the wet stamping-mill, and the switch from bloomery to blast-furnace, quite apart from liquation, had already been perfected in the early fifteenth century, but lay idle until much later, when entrepreneurs could at last see a return on their considerable financial outlay.

Agricultural Landscapes and Inheritance Customs

These preliminary reflections need to be borne in mind when we turn to examine the three basic types of economic landscape in greater detail. Within the predominantly agricultural sector farming practices may have been influenced by inheritance customs, field systems and crop rotation, patterns of tenure and landlordship, or any combination of these, but it remains notoriously difficult to disentangle cause from effect. A particularly thorny issue is inheritance practices, for through the German lands, uniquely in western Europe, ran a fault-line dividing what have commonly been seen as Mediterranean from Nordic customs. In most of Germany, as in Scandinavia, impartible inheritance was the rule, that is to say, the farm, its buildings, livestock, implements, and stores were passed on intact to a single heir, often but by no means always the eldest son (primogeniture). Sometimes the youngest son might take over the farm (ultimogeniture), as in east Frisia (or even, in the territory around Osnabrück, by default the youngest daughter), but elsewhere the choice of heir was left to the parents (as in Bavaria and Braunschweig-Wolfenbüttel). Where impartibility was the rule, as the population began to recover quite rapidly in the late fifteenth century, a well-established class of tenant farmers with good proprietary rights faced a growing band of cottars or landless labourers – often their own siblings – who, without hope of taking over a farm, were obliged to move to other districts or to the towns, or else had to subsist through by-employment as craftsmen or hired labourers. The economic viability of the peasant holding was preserved at the expense of social dislocation and marginalization.

In south-west Germany, the Middle Rhine, much of Hessen, and pockets of Silesia, by contrast, partible inheritance prevailed, whereby all the heirs (or the male heirs, at least) were entitled to equal shares of the moveable and immoveable farm inventory. In theory, such a custom would have led to the irretrievable fragmentation of holdings into unsustainable parcels; in practice, the heirs came to arrangements amongst themselves how the shares could be bought out, or the parcels of land recombined into viable farmsteads. An easy, but misleading, view would be to imagine that partible inheritance was widespread where the natural endowment and good communications made a more intensive and diversified agrarian regime both possible and profitable. Although it is true that partible inheritance first spread along the fruitful river valley and basin landscapes in the warmer latitudes of the south-west, any inference that soil, topography, or climate were its chief determinants is quickly refuted by its establishment in the less fertile upland areas to the west and east of the Rhine, the Hunsrück and Eifel ranges, the Westerwald, and the Bergisches Land.

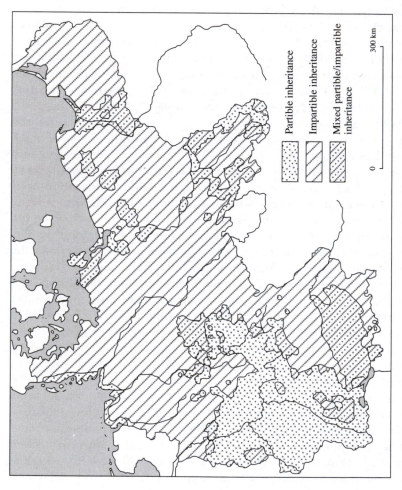

4.2 *Inheritance customs (modified after B. Huppertz)*

The geographical peculiarity of impartibility in the German lands, wedged between partible areas in the Latin west and the Slavic east, has long been a puzzle to historians, who once were tempted to search for an explanation in ethnic or racial differences. The integrity of the Germanic kinship group, it was argued, demanded the indivisibility of landholdings, a practice which the migrant tribes carried southwards and westwards into territories colonized by the Romans. If that were so, the partible inheritance of the south-west must have represented a subsequent retreat from the advance of Germanic custom. When that might have occurred is altogether unclear. What is clear, at any rate, is that the era of internal colonization in the twelfth and thirteenth centuries witnessed the spread of impartibility to the newly settled upland areas in Swabia, Franconia, and the Black Forest, where partibility in many instances continued on the lower ground. In general, however, what stands out is the remarkable continuity in inheritance patterns throughout Germany from the ninth to the twentieth century; that should discourage us from seeking too close a causal connection between specific inheritance practices and certain forms of agriculture. It is true that areas of partible inheritance, especially in the Rhineland, displayed an abundance of specialized and industrial crops, together with rural crafts and cottage industries. They also happened to be the areas of greatest urban density in late medieval and early modern Germany. But landscapes with these features were by no means confined to the south-west. They arose in areas of predominant impartibility as well, such as eastern Swabia and Westphalia. Partible inheritance, therefore, may have provided a favourable milieu for economic diversification and specialization, leading to the growth of genuine proto-industries in the seventeenth century and beyond, but there was certainly no straightforward causal link.

In our period, especially with renewed pressure on land after 1500, both landlords and existing tenants in areas of partibility were keen to prevent the further subdivision of holdings and to make impartibility legally binding. In southern Germany, they had some success in the Black Forest and Upper Swabia but less in the wine-growing valleys of central Württemberg. In Thuringia, by contrast, where the river Saale (*not* the Elbe, it should be noted) marked the frontier between the two inheritance practices, the impartibility of holdings east of the Saale was in fact undermined, though not destroyed, in the course of the sixteenth century by the spread of partibility to the margraviate of Meißen and the ore-rich mountains of the Erzgebirge (possibly because of the new opportunities which mining offered the rural population).

In any case, impartibility was not always the absolute principle it appeared. Land, or farmsteads, might be passed on undivided, but wealth and moveable goods shared out. And even with land, as a recent study of the county of Hohenlohe in northern Württemberg has shown, the prevailing impartibility of the Hohenlohe plain kept family farms intact, with those outside the kinship group held firmly at arm's length, but did not prevent the rise of a lively market in smaller parcels of land and vineyards. This underscores the wider point that inheritance practices – and the social reproduction that they embodied – were not set in tablets of stone, but were influenced by the play of political and economic circumstances and subject to contesting and conflicting interests.

As prevalent as, and largely coterminous with, impartible inheritance was the traditional system of open fields, parcelled out among the tenants into strips. On them winter cereals (wheat and rye, or in parts of the south-west, principally Württemberg, spelt) were followed by summer grains (oats and barley) and then fallow in a regulated rotation. These principal grains were those which the peasants brought to market, and in which their feudal rents in kind were denominated. But within their own households many peasants subsisted on lesser grains such as buckwheat and millet, or oats, eaten as gruel, whose importance in the diet of the common man has been obscured because they were rarely seen as market crops. Together with the three-field pattern of tillage, beasts were grazed on the common land or forest, though often the fallow year itself was used for pasturing, rather than repeated ploughing to aerate and improve the soil. In some areas with sufficient access to manure, this classic system of mixed agriculture could be intensified to enable a one-field system with continuous cultivation of rye to develop, as we have already indicated for stretches of the north German plain.

The three-field system was also widespread in areas of partible inheritance, but here, especially in the Rhineland and its fringes, it co-existed with a two-field alternation whose origins are much harder to pin down than other variants of the three-field rotation. It was certainly the ancient and primitive method of cultivation which had typified Roman agriculture beyond the Mediterranean up to the ninth century, and survived on what had once been the eastern border of Gaul, particularly in the upland regions of the Palatinate. Here the prevalence of loess soils, liable to erosion, hindered the continuous cultivation of meadow, pasture, and forest, so that the fallow had to be extended over time and space in order to provide enough manure. In such instances, a three-year rotation was practised on an infield, while on the outfield fallow succeeded oats on a two-year cycle in what is known as alternate husbandry.

This ecological constraint did not apply, however, to the lower-lying riverine lands along the Moselle and the Middle Rhine, downstream of Koblenz, which were also tilled in a two-year rotation, with even the infield being given over to a simple alternation of rye and fallow. The prevalence of a two-field system in the valleys of the Rhine and its tributaries has prompted some writers to assert that, far from being the remnant of a primitive agriculture, it reflected the growth of specialized and commercialized crops throughout the Rhineland, and some support for this view is afforded by the spread of a peculiar form of alternate husbandry, known in German as *Lohheckenwirtschaft*, whereby tillage was succeeded by coppicing in order to provide both tanbark and vine-props. By the beginning of the sixteenth century the two-field system had apparently penetrated Alsace, in response to intensified cereal cultivation, a thriving viticulture, and the planting of industrial crops such as hemp or madder (and in the seventeenth century tobacco).

Correlations of this kind clearly existed, but they must not be pressed too far: not all areas of loess soils had two-field systems; and the changes in land-management observable in Alsace did not occur in other areas of commercial crops such as Swabia. Moreover, the link between a two-field rotation and viticulture is not straightforward. Structural requirements in wine-growing – for copious labour and plentiful manure – may have been more important than the functional stimulus of the export market in encouraging the two-field system because they restricted the scope for traditional mixed agriculture. Necessity, not opportunity, may have encouraged its spread. It is also questionable whether the two-field system was indeed a newcomer in Alsace. Patches of it can be found centuries earlier on both banks of the Upper Rhine, sometimes interchangeably with an open-field system without a regulated crop rotation.

Intensified Tillage and Pastoralism

In certain parts of Germany mixed agriculture was giving way at the end of the Middle Ages either to multi-course rotation, or else to a concentration on stock-rearing and dairying. In the rich pasture-lands of Schleswig-Holstein and along the Frisian coast to the Dutch border a form of regulated convertible (or 'up-and-down') hus-bandry developed, in which a series of corn years could be followed by anything from three to six years' grazing. This rotation could even dispense with a fallow year, provided that fodder crops (such as nitrogenous legumes and vetches) were planted as catch-crops in the intervening period. This pattern foreshadows the 'improved' agricul-ture of the eighteenth century. Cattle-pastures were created by intakes from both forest and waste, and from the existing common, but these usually involved only hurdling or folding (temporary fencing), rather than permanent enclosures, and a limit was set on the stint of beasts allowed to graze the cattle-gates. In the moun-tainous regions of Switzerland, by contrast, where good pasture was at a premium, much more common land was bought up by nobles and peasants to be turned into private hay-meadows for summer grazing, in order to release low-lying fields for winter fodder. In general, cattle-rearing in northern Germany tended to serve the market for both meat and dairy produce, whereas in the Alps there was a greater emphasis on dairying. Indeed, the sharply increased demand for meat from the urban centres of southern and western Germany could no longer be covered by purely regional supplies. Instead, the cities came to rely upon livestock imports driven on the hoof, often over immense distances, from Burgundy, Hungary, Poland, and Scania. The belt of pastureland in east-central Europe affords an illuminating contrast to the grain-producing latifundia further to the north and west, for it indicates how regional inter-dependence could be writ on a much larger canvas; in southern Germany, however, the one comparable instance – namely the symbiosis of two agriculturally specialized regions, cereal Swabia and pastoral northern Switzerland – only developed after the Thirty Years War.

Although much less significant than cattle-raising throughout Germany as a whole, sheep-rearing made serious inroads in the six-teenth century in parts of upland Franconia, as well as Saxony and Thuringia, in response to a growing demand for wool. It has been reckoned that a million sheep were kept by Saxon landlords in this period. But here, too, there was no widespread enclosure movement along the lines of England. Conflicts – and they were numerous, especially during and after the Peasants' War – revolved around pro-tecting the common from encroachment and regulating the right to drive sheep to pasture across fields and tracks, rather than over any obligation to allow grazing on the peasants' own lands. Despite the lords' best efforts, peasants themselves even took to rearing flocks of sheep, though their numbers never approached those of cattle held. Although pastoral agriculture was bound to encroach on the land available for cereal cultivation, the greater amount of manure available to be spread on the fields helped to raise crop yields, especially when, as in Saxony, sheep were folded overnight for their dung: it has been reckoned that 400 sheep could produce the equivalent of 40 quintals[*] of byre dung from cattle every night. As with the lesser grains, the importance of pig-rearing has often been overlooked in discussions of the rural economy. Strictly speaking, pigs were not part of the pastoral economy, since they rooted rather than grazed; as relatively sedentary animals, there was no question of an international pig-trade developing, or of pigs driving men off the land through the spread of enclosures. Nevertheless, the largest cities in Germany created a demand which encouraged a regional market in pigs: Augsburg bought pigs on the trotter from its Bavarian hinterland, while Cologne was dependent on supplies from Westphalia (the Münsterland), the Saar, and Lorraine. These, however, were exceptional instances. More broadly, what the rearing of pigs illustrates is the symbiosis between animal husbandry and forestry, for pigs fed not only on kitchen scraps or bran from milling (hence the close connection between bakers and pig-farming), but above all were fattened in autumn on acorns and beechmast in deciduous woodlands. As domestic animals, pigs – and for that matter chickens – were vital components of the immediate local economy and household diet, even if they had little significance in the wider commercial economy. For Saxony, indeed, it has recently been suggested that the increase in pastoralism, particularly commercial cattle-rearing, occurred specifically at the expense of pig-farming.

The great contrast to the spread of pastoralism in the west – or the simple continuity of mixed agriculture – is the rise of cereal production as a monoculture, geared to overseas markets, in the lands east of the Elbe. Because labour-intensive grain cultivation on large commercial estates – latifundia – in the hands of the nobility is held to have been made possible by the intensification of seigneurial lordship able to command the necessary labour-services, the nature of the agrarian economy, even the actual extent of grain-growing itself,

---

[*] A quintal is 100 kg.

has often been obscured by arguments over the character of east-Elbian domanial lordship, its exploitation of the peasantry, and the emergence of a 'second serfdom'. These issues will be discussed in Chapter 6, as will the reasons for the spread of cereal monoculture itself. In terms of economic landscapes, however, the essential point to grasp is that large tracts of east Elbia remained untouched by commercial cereal husbandry, even if they still fell victim to intensified seigneurial lordship. Brandenburg provides an excellent illustration. There local feudal lords by the end of the Middle Ages were heavily involved in direct exploitation of their estates, some on *Vorwerke*, arable domain farms, unhelpfully and misleadingly described in English as manors, but others on *Meiereien*, which might be either beef- or dairy-cattle farms, and still others on *Schäfereien*, sheep-farms, all serving different markets and involving different patterns of land-use and labour-recruitment. Given the topography of Brandenburg, that is no more than might be expected. The sandy soils of the Uckermark, north of Berlin, were principally arable, but on the alluvial flatlands in the Altmark on the east bank of the Elbe in the Prignitz, stock-rearing predominated. The principal landscapes of cereal monoculture were strung out along the Baltic coast, from Mecklenburg through Pomerania, the Polish crown lands, east Prussia, and Lithuania. But within that area there were considerable variations. In west Mecklenburg, for instance, the demand for rye and wheat seems to have outstripped barley and oats, so that the production of grain, initially at least, may have been destined for the domestic market – the thriving Wendish port cities of the Hanseatic League – or else near-neighbours, such as Hamburg and Holstein. Poland's exports, by contrast, which expanded dramatically in the sixteenth century (over twentyfold), went almost entirely overseas to the Low Countries, not least because the lower urban density of Great Poland and Masovia meant that domestic demand was much weaker.

Where monocultures, or intensified forms of mixed agriculture such as 'up-and-down' husbandry, developed, crop yields could increase substantially: figures of 1:8.6 for wheat or 1:6.5 for rye are recorded for parts of the Rhineland on commercial leasehold farms from the fifteenth century. But these were very much the exception. It has been calculated that in normal circumstances 1.6–2 quintals of seed per hectare would give a harvest of between 4.5 and 5.5 quintals. After deducting the seed to be retained for next year's sowing, the farmer was left with a net return of two-and-a-half to three times the seed sown per hectare. Anything less would bring the farmer to the point of ruin and starvation, unless he had been able to build up a stock of seed from earlier years. Apart from sharp annual harvest fluctuations, what made it so hard to raise productivity on peasant farms was their relatively small size. Domain estates east of the Elbe might exceed 100 hectares (though even then their surpluses were achieved by intensified labour-input in the form of *corvées*, rather than by any agronomic advances), and some large peasants – often sneeringly described as kulaks – in parts of northern Germany (Lower Saxony, Schleswig-Holstein, and some of Westphalia) might farm holdings only slightly smaller, but the further south one goes, the smaller the farms become, with many in the area of partibility in the south-west less than ten hectares, and sometimes no more than five. Only in Bavaria and parts of Swabia (usually with secure inheritance rights) were the farms more substantial, though the other side of the coin, of course, was the profusion of cottagers' smallholdings, insufficient on their own to support a family group, of as little as 1.5 hectares.

A rough correlation can be also observed between the size of holdings and the quality of peasant proprietary rights. In much of western Germany landlords had divested themselves of their demesne land by the beginning of our period, and leased it out to the peasantry. That was true even of the Cistercians, who had pioneered the direct exploitation of their estates on a commercial basis – granges, as they were called – in the twelfth and thirteenth century. Hereditary tenure against the payment of an annual rent, usually in cash, became commonplace on the large farms of Bavaria (with heritable leases), or northwestern Germany, when a form of copyhold (*Meierrecht*) developed. Revocable leases for fixed terms were only common where agriculture had become strongly commercialized or even proto-capitalist, that is, on the Middle and Lower Rhine stretching into the Low Countries, and on the coastal strip of Frisia and western Holstein. Here the tenurial dependence of the peasantry was superseded by a purely contractual obligation, although feudal landlordship survived as the framework for the socio-legal subjection of the peasantry. Short-term leases, by the same token, were characteristic of areas of partible inheritance, where a land market was beginning to emerge. But even then the general tendency by the sixteenth century was for fixed-term leases to be transformed, in fact if not in law, into hereditary ones. Here the contrast with the new seigneurialism in the eastern lands is particularly stark.

Viticulture and Commercial Crops

Although mixed agriculture remained the principal source of livelihood for the vast majority of the German population throughout
our period, we should not overlook the widespread cultivation of
non-industrial specialized crops, in particular vines, hops, and
legumes. Apart from the northernmost latitudes and the alpine
valleys, there was scarcely a region of Germany which had no viticulture at the end of the Middle Ages, yet by 1600 the area under vines
had begun to contract dramatically. To explain such a rapid reversal,
two points need to be borne in mind. In the first place, in the main
growing regions viticulture became restricted to the most favoured
sites, whose vines could command a premium beyond the immediate
locality, as land was taken back into cereal cultivation to feed a
swelling population after 1500. In the second, the high price of wine,
determined above all by the labour-intensiveness of viticulture, made
it vulnerable to competition from other beverages, principally beer.

Vineyards – at least seasonally, and on the steeper sites – could
require up to eight times the manpower of cereal agriculture, as well
as regular provision of manure, vine-props, barrels, and staves. It is
no surprise, therefore, that they should chiefly have flourished
where population and consumer demand were greatest, that is, the
urbanized regions of the south and west. But by the same token,
vineyards might be planted wherever there was a hunger for land,
subdivision of holdings, and the chance of ready sale at market, that
is to say, not always in places where quality was best assured.

Towards the end of the sixteenth century as many as 350 000
hectares were under vines, on average perhaps five times the extent
of viticulture today. But in some areas the discrepancy is altogether
startling: Franconia, an important wine land then as now, once had
between 40 000 and 45 000 hectares of vineyards, fifteen times
greater than the 3000 hectares today. On the fringes of the main
growing areas, vines crept into the narrower, shadier valleys and up
the cooler slopes: up into the Eifel, the valleys of the Upper Ahr and
Lahn, on to the higher reaches of the Haardt plateau in the
Palatinate, across into Lorraine, onto the foothills of the Swabian
Alp, Lower Bavaria, and the Danube valley. Vines were even planted
on the Lower Rhine, and on the north German plain, stretching as
far eastwards as Mecklenburg, Brandenburg, and east Prussia. These
marginal areas were naturally the first to contract in the course of
the fifteenth century, but there were other growing regions of signif-

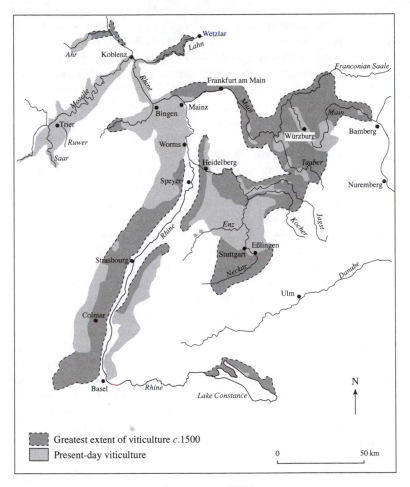

4.3   Viticulture in western Germany, c.1500

icance which have now completely vanished, such as Lusatia. It is
often forgotten that viticulture of more than local importance flourished in Thuringia and parts of Saxony, the remnants of which on
the Elbe around Meißen, and the Saale and Unstrut from Naumburg
to Freyburg, still survive. The main reason for the insupportable
expansion of viticulture was that it provided a cash crop which gave
employment to a sizeable labour-force at a time of population
recovery and renewed pressure on land. Only that can explain the
otherwise bizarre phenomenon of an increase in viticulture in the
county of Hohenlohe in northern Württemberg in the sixteenth

century on the poorest land at a time when prices were falling. Moreover, the loamy soil of the plain was easier to till than the slopes of the river valleys (Kocher and Jagst), which were liable to flooding or soil erosion, even though quality was only to be achieved in these steep and warmth-retaining meso-climates.

The main areas of good-quality wines, in marked contrast, have remained remarkably unchanged from the Middle Ages to the present day – Alsace and Baden, the Neckar valley and Württemberg, the Lower Main in Franconia around Würzburg, the Moselle and its tributaries, and the Rhine from Speyer down to Koblenz. The importance of the Rhine as a vital artery of transport which enabled the better German wines to be sold outside their region of origin cannot be overstated. That was true, above all, of Alsace, whose wines had the furthest to travel to reach northern Germany or overseas to England, and therefore incurred the highest transaction costs, though they were sold throughout the German south-west and Switzerland as well. The reputation of Alsatian and Rhenish wines lay essentially in the white grape varieties, but it is hard to say with any confidence which varieties were grown and in what proportions before 1700. In Alsace, the best wines in our period were probably made from muscat and traminer grapes, with riesling the only varietal of true quality on the Rhine and Moselle. But these grapes are unlikely to have constituted more than a fraction of production, the bulk of the harvest being made up of lesser varieties such as sylvaner and elbling. Surprisingly, perhaps, red-wine grapes were widely planted in Alsace and Baden (principally pinot noir), and much of the harvest in Württemberg, then as now, may well have been of light red wine.

Württemberg is in fact the one region in the sixteenth century not to have experienced a decline in the extent of land under vines. As many as 13 500 hectares were newly planted between 1514 and 1568, while after mid-century its ruler, Duke Christoph, even planned to make the upper reaches of the Neckar navigable in order to promote exports. Elsewhere, the decline was gradual, and some peripheral sites only disappeared after the Thirty Years War. It is worth noting in this regard that in 1600 there were still 432 identifiable wine-producing villages in Thuringia.

Only in the sixteenth century did beer begin its triumphant march into the front rank of German beverages. Up to that point, beer made from malted barley had usually been flavoured with herbs such as bog-myrtle or rosemary. This brew – small beer, or grout, as it was known – was cheap and not designed for long-keeping. With the extended cultivation of hops, however, beer – now properly called ale – acquired a fuller (usually more bitter) flavour, and improved with a certain length of keeping. Not only did that make the beer more palatable, it could now be shipped over some distance as an export commodity. In north Germany, where wine had always been less readily available and comparatively expensive, several of the Hanseatic cities emerged as major brewing centres – the ports of Hamburg, Lübeck, Wismar, Rostock, and Danzig along the Baltic coast, and the inland cities of Hannover, Einbeck, Goslar, and Braunschweig in Lower Saxony. But there also developed a famous brewing industry in eastern Franconia (Kulmbach, Bamberg, and Nuremberg), with hops sourced from the nearby growing area south of Regensburg in Bavaria. Only in the late seventeenth century, however, did Bavarian beer come to be highly prized; before then parts of the duchy had been better known for their wine-growing. Hop-cultivation was labour-intensive (almost as much so as viticulture), so that it could mop up surplus labour in localities which in general were stamped by impartible inheritance. Moreover, the profits from ale could encourage cereal specialization around the brewing centres. That was true of not only cities such as Braunschweig, which as a major buyer of barley from the plains around Magdeburg encouraged a switch by local lords from rental management of their estates to direct exploitation, but it could apply to much smaller towns as well. As a recent study of the eastern Saxon administrative district of Grimma, for instance, has shown, barley production was intensified in the course of the sixteenth century to supply the local breweries. Although not a district famed for its ale, the small towns of eastern Saxony – Colditz, Leisnig, Wurzen, Freiberg, and Torgau – were producing over 7 million litres annually, mostly consumed locally, though Torgau's output of 3 million litres clearly served, at least in part, an export trade. This suggests that ale-brewing could give a direct stimulus to the local economy, even in areas which were not renowned as brewing centres.

Vines and hops were the most visible signs of agricultural landscapes with specialized crops grown on a commercial basis. But they must not be allowed to obscure the importance of catch-crops (that is, crops grown alongside the main cereal crop in order to regenerate the soil and improve yields), and horticulture or market-gardening. The favoured catch-crop was vetches, which helped restore nitrogen to the soil; these were sown on the fallow in the Rhineland from at least the early thirteenth century. Their popularity was enhanced by their use as horse fodder. Other fodder crops, notably clover, had of course been widely planted in earlier centuries, but new varieties such as purple medick or lucerne (in the United States: alfalfa) became popular in the later Middle Ages, and they were joined by a variety of root-crops, such as brassicas and beets. The six-teenth-century Rhenish agronomist, Konrad Heresbach, advocated a new rotation of rye, followed by beets or buckwheat, followed by rape (*brassica napus*), which would allow farmers to dispense with regular fallowing. But he also pinned his faith in more obscure catch-crops, such as corn spurry. Since an intensified agrarian regime held one of the keys to the decisive transformation of the Dutch economy in the seventeenth century, one must ask why the German Rhineland, only a little way up river, with a similar natural endowment, failed to follow suit. One reason is undoubtedly that the open-field system and rotation by course, collectively supervised by village communities, placed a brake upon the deployment of inten-sive cultures dependent upon individual initiative and investment, for which enclosures were a precondition. Another is the absence (or disappearance) of seigneurial lordship in many parts of the northern Low Countries by the end of the Middle Ages, which removed legal and social restraints upon peasants who saw opportu-nities in commercialized agriculture: a free peasant on free land is his own master, and can engage in the market at will.

But alongside catch-crops, the spread of market-gardening is a salient feature of the late medieval German agricultural landscape, particularly along the course of the Rhine. In Alsace, both Strasbourg and Colmar were major growers of onions, whose seeds were shipped down river for sale in Cologne; although the quantity fluctuated wildly, an average of around 900 kg per annum was by no means unusual. Fresh produce too – lettuces, radishes, cabbages, beets – could be sent to market over surprising distances: fast skiffs supplied Cologne from as far away as 60 kilometres. Without the Rhine as the vital conduit, these regional commercial contacts would have been palpably attenuated.

Landscapes with Rural Industries

Diversification and specialization within the primary sector could reach the stage where we may identify a new type of economic land-scape, in which manufacturing was based upon the cultivation of

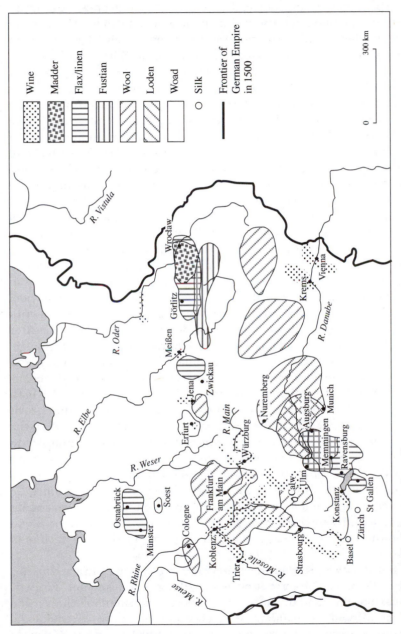

4.4 *Specialized crops and textiles*

Legend:

- Wine
- Madder
- Flax/linen
- Fustian
- Wool
- Loden
- Woad
- ○ Silk
- ▬ Frontier of German Empire in 1500

0   300 km

Map labels:

R. Vistula, R. Oder, R. Elbe, R. Weser, R. Rhine, R. Meuse, R. Moselle, R. Main, R. Danube

Wrocław, Görlitz, Meißen, Jena, Zwickau, Erfurt, Würzburg, Krems, Vienna, Nuremberg, Augsburg, Munich, Memmingen, Ravensburg, Ulm, Calw, Konstanz, St Gallen, Zürich, Basel, Strasbourg, Trier, Koblenz, Frankfurt am Main, Cologne, Münster, Soest, Osnabrück

industrial crops to make cloths or dyestuffs. There could be no
sharp boundary, of course, between such landscapes and purely
agricultural ones, because by far the most extensive textile sector in
late medieval and early modern Germany remained wool, whose
production did not involve an industrial crop. The areas of manufacture ranged from northern Swabia, Franconia, and Bavaria,
through central Württemberg, much of Lower Alsace and the
Middle Rhine, to the district west of Cologne (the *Kölner Bucht*), and
on eastwards through Hessen into Thuringia, and, indeed, Bohemia
and Moravia beyond the German-speaking lands though within the
Empire. Because flocks could be driven to market (or the place of
shearing) and because fleeces in any case were not as heavy to transport as ore or metal, the symbiosis between areas of oviculture and
centres of the woollen industry remained loose: woollen manufacturing never set its stamp on an economic landscape in the way that
linen and fustian production did. By the same token, woollen textiles were somewhat less exposed to the characteristic early capitalist
organization of production through the putting-out system.
Production was largely concentrated in towns, with only spinning as
a part-time, and above all female, occupation in the countryside.
The rapid expansion of woollen manufacturing in the sixteenth
century, however, coupled with the development of lighter, softer
cloths, known collectively as the 'new draperies' brought a change.
In some areas, notably northern Swabia, woollen cloths began to displace other textiles: Nördlingen, for example, which had been a
centre of linen- and then fustian-weaving in the late Middle Ages,
progressed to the specialized manufacture of loden, the heavy,
felted, short-pile cloth used for blankets and coats. By the end of the
sixteenth century loden production had spread north-eastwards into
many Bavarian towns as far as Munich. In this regard, Cologne's production represents an anomaly. It, uniquely in Germany, had specialized up to the fifteenth century in linsey-woolsey (*Tirtey*), a
mixed cloth with a linen warp and a wool weft. But the demand for
lighter cloths encouraged a switch to a fustian (linen-cotton) blend
known as sarrock, whose rise exactly corresponded to the decline in
Tirtey.

But it is the so-called 'new draperies' which have attracted particular attention. The term itself is something of a misnomer. Properly
speaking, the new draperies were short-staple woollen cloths, first
manufactured in Flanders as a cheaper alternative to traditional
luxury woollens, whereas the new cloths widely made in Germany

(and in England, too) were either worsted (that is, long-staple cloths), or else blends with a worsted warp and a woollen (short-staple) weft. These light, unsheared cloths – known as sayes and serges – were already being promoted by the territorial authorities in Baden and Württemberg around 1500, and by mid-century the leading textile cities of southern Germany – Strasbourg, Ulm, and Augsburg – were likewise making sayes under a variety of names such as barracans and grosgrams. These innovations achieved a new organizational identity only after the Thirty Years War, however, with the establishment in 1650 of the Calw Worsted Company (*Calwer Zeughandlungscompagnie*), which traded its cloths extensively throughout Europe, as well as setting up its own bank. In the Calw merchant company lay the germ of true proto-industrialization, in which an entire landscape, spanning town and country, was vertically integrated into a system of factory production. Before 1600, putting-out remained confined to the towns: in southern Thuringia, for instance, urban weavers were obliged to accept piecework contracts from merchant drapers. And Cologne, as a major metropolis of both production and distribution, used outwork to extend the manufacturing area of cloth entitled to bear its seal of quality as far afield as Aachen. But these were exceptional instances, not the rule. Neither Strasbourg, which stood at the head of a group of five urban woollen towns clustered in Lower Alsace, nor Braunschweig, the most export-oriented of the Hanseatic cities, resorted to any degree of putting-out. In the case of Strasbourg, the reason may lie in the fact that its workshops were geared to the production of cheaper cloths, such as ticking used in linings, rather than new quality draperies; in Braunschweig, the clothmakers' guild, which controlled all stages of production, did not display the common early-capitalist division between merchant drapers on the one hand, and independent masters in their workshops or piece-working wage-labourers on the other.

If it is wrong to see the organization of production in woollen manufacturing as necessarily dependent upon putting-out, that applies even more to the spread of linen-weaving in south-west Germany. We have already pointed to the natural endowment of the Upper Swabian and northern Swiss landscape which favoured the growing of flax, whose processing into linen-cloth can be traced to the thirteenth century, well before the rise of the major trading companies. Initially, town and country existed in simple symbiosis, with production concentrated in the larger towns and cities – Konstanz, St Gallen, Lindau, and Kempten – which drew unprocessed flax from the surrounding countryside. But in the course of the fifteenth century production began to move out to the smaller towns and villages, where weavers made and marketed their own types of cloth, imposed their own quality control, and shunned the cloth-exchanges of the larger centres. It would be unwise to ascribe this shift to the rise of putting-out alone. For one thing, linen-manufacturing by virtue of the multiple stages involved in turning flax into linen offered a ready means of by-employment for a gradually recovering population. For another, the spread of putting-out was highly uneven. In the western districts below Lake Constance and in northern Switzerland it was seldom encountered, but in eastern Swabia it had been deployed from the outset. In the case of Memmingen, the urban weavers were so alarmed at the threat of rural competition that they banded together to enter into collective guild contracts with merchants to supply cloth at an agreed price. Another, more formal, way of bringing rural weavers under urban supervision was to subject them to civic jurisdiction by extending citizen's rights to them. Although the link between out-burghership and rural manufacturing can only be inferred, rather than demonstrated directly, it is surely suggestive that in the 1470s in Kempten, the centre of the Allgäu linen industry, 400 urban weavers with 300 apprentices were matched by 600 outburghers in the surrounding villages which were largely given over to linen-weaving. Nearby Isny, too, with 250 weavers and 200 apprentices in the town, is recorded as having an unspecified number of out-burghers in its hinterland.

By the sixteenth century other areas of linen-production were emerging as competitors to the linen landscape of Upper Swabia. The principal one was Westphalia, where woollen manufacturing was in decline. In its place linen-weaving began to flourish, particularly in the rolling countryside between Osnabrück, Ravensberg, and Minden, and on the plains between Diepholz and Hoya, in effect the catchment area of the rivers Ems and Weser. Flax was also grown around Münster, and further south in the Bergisches Land east of Cologne. In eastern Germany, flax was widely cultivated between the Erzgebirge in southeastern Saxony and Upper Lusatia. Chemnitz was the focal point of Saxon production, while in Lusatia, a group of cities bunched together – Görlitz, Bautzen, Löbau, and Kamenz – not only manufactured linen but acted as entrepôts for the trade in woollen cloth and woad from Thuringia to the west. Flax was also grown further east across the Neiße in Silesia, around Reichenberg

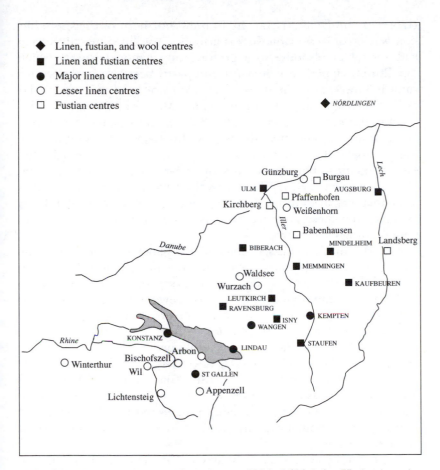

◆ Linen, fustian, and wool centres
■ Linen and fustian centres
● Major linen centres
○ Lesser linen centres
□ Fustian centres

4.5 The Upper Swabian textile industry, 1300–1600 (after H. Ammann)

(Liberec) and Neiße (Nysa). In all these northern districts, production was organized by outwork, partly because linen-manufacturing had spread in response to a growing international market which rapidly outstripped local demand, and partly because of the need for rural by-employment in areas which (with the exception of Silesia) were governed by impartible inheritance. Moreover, a relatively weak guild tradition in the towns left the field open to capitalist entrepreneurs, some of whom held thousands of cottage weavers under contract. Initially these merchants were local, from commercial cities such as Leipzig, but over time south German entrepreneurs from Nuremberg and Augsburg, perhaps thwarted in their opportunities in Swabia, began to invest in Saxony and Silesia. By the 1560s linen exports from these areas were penetrating southern Germany and undercutting local cloths.

With the much increased demand for paper (as opposed to the more expensive parchment) after the invention of moveable type in the mid-fifteenth century, flax, as the fibre for linen manufacture, took on a new importance since it also provided the raw material for the making of rag-paper, which was already flourishing in several south-west German and Swiss cities before the advent of printing. There were concentrations of paper-mills around Ravensburg, Basel, Fribourg (Freiburg im Üchtland), as well as Épinal in the Vosges, all of which were already centres, or within landscapes, of linen (and subsequently fustian or cotton) manufacturing. The technique of paper-making, however, was quickly transferred to other centres of printing throughout Germany which had no necessary history of linen-production.

The natural conditions which favoured the cultivation of flax also applied to hemp, from whose fibres rough canvas and ropes were made, as well as a coarse cloth known confusingly in German as hempen linen. Although there were some similarities in the working of hemp and flax – the need for retting and hackling – hemp never dominated the production of any one region so as to stamp it as an economic landscape in its own right: demand was smaller, and the production process simpler and cheaper. The only exception was in northern Germany, where districts such as the Münsterland around Tecklenburg or the coastline of Frisia were heavily engaged in manufacturing canvas for the shipping industry of the Hanseatic ports.

Textiles and the Putting-Out System

It was with the rise of fustian manufacturing from the late fourteenth century onwards that early capitalism in the form of outwork came to dominate the heartlands of the textile industry in Upper Germany. Because fustian was a mixed cloth, woven from a linen warp and a cotton weft, its manufacture depended upon the import of raw cotton, which grew only in the warmer climate of the Mediterranean. In other words, it had to be transported by long-distance merchants who then supplied the local spinners and weavers. At first, putting-out was confined to the larger towns where the merchants maintained their headquarters – Nördlingen is a prime example – but then spread quickly to the countryside, as entrepreneurs sought a cheaper and less regulated source of labour. In striking contrast, where fustian did not supplant linen as the principal textile – St Gallen is the most obvious instance – putting-out was hardly deployed before the sixteenth century. Competition between country weavers who supplied their capitalist employers by piecework directly, and the craft weavers of the Swabian cities, at once protected and restricted by their guild regulations, intensified during the fifteenth century. The latter tried to ban all outwork in textiles within a radius of 10, or later 20 or more, kilometres, but such edicts availed little against powerful merchant companies such as the Fuggers (whose founder, Hans Fugger, had himself been a peasant and part-time weaver who emigrated to Augsburg in 1367 from the village of Graben in the Lech valley to seek his fortune). The Fuggers simply grouped their rural weavers round smaller, rival centres of production and marketing – Weißenhorn and Pfaffenhofen, for instance, ranged against the metropolis of Ulm in western Swabia. The latter tried to hit back by enforcing more stringent quality controls and by imposing higher inspection fees, but that only elicited protests from neighbouring competitors bound to the Ulm production standard. Similarly, Biberach saw its trade slip away to rural weavers in the pay of the Haug merchant company of Augsburg, and the Zangmeisters of Memmingen. Even the merchants of middle-ranking textile centres, however, found the pull of the great metropolises hard to resist. The Zangmeisters remained as leading patricians in Memmingen, but their rivals, the Vöhlins, at the beginning of the sixteenth century threw in the towel, upped sticks, and relocated to Augsburg.

Another bone of contention arose in the early 1400s as rural spinners began to warp linen-yarn ready for the loom by winding it onto beams – themselves known as warps – which could be sold on as half-finished goods, thereby encroaching on the more advanced stages of production. The cities vacillated in their response: some, in the Allgäu, strove to confine putting-out to the countryside, so that their own citizens, at least, were not depressed into the condition of dependent pieceworkers; but others, in the breadth of Swabia, were ready to tolerate production both within their walls and in the countryside, provided that its organization through putting-out could be altogether suppressed. In general, the division of labour which marked fustian production could bring certain advantages to urban weavers, provided that they were given the opportunity to concentrate on the more complex finishing processes with greater added value and hence greater rewards. The switch from linen to fustian, which was such a salient feature of the textile industry of the later Middle Ages, and which had such a profound impact on the relations between town and country, was not confined to Upper Germany. Saxony, too, underwent a similar transition, though usually with an appreciable timelag: only in the 1530s did Chemnitz, the Saxon textile capital, turn to fustian, again characteristically organized by collective guild contracts with a single putting-out distributor, and also to dyeing, but even then much of rural Saxony continued to produce simple linenware.

Woollens, linens, and fustians were all produced for a mass market both domestic and foreign; only some of the 'new draperies' can be classified as luxury cloths. But side-by-side with the latter, a few centres began to specialize in higher-priced textiles, notably cotton, silk, and satin (silk woven with the weft uppermost), all of which relied entirely upon the import of raw materials. Basel had already developed a cotton industry, based on putting out work to weavers in Alsace and the Breisgau in the fifteenth century, and south-west Germany also saw the rise of satin manufacture, especially in the countryside. Silk-weaving was a speciality of Cologne, the only important centre of production in the fifteenth century outside the south-west. In the 1490s Cologne was processing more than 100 000 florins' worth of raw silk annually, which placed silk manufacture as the most valuable branch of the city's textile industry. By the middle of the sixteenth century, however, Cologne's pre-eminence was being challenged as refugees from Tridentine Italy began to bring their expertise in silk-weaving over the Alps to Zürich and other Protestant cities.

Textiles sold undyed were known as greycloths, but from earliest times a variety of dyestuffs was employed, often simply berries or crushed leaves. Black dye was obtained – at least in Upper Germany – from the leaves of the bear-berry, an alpine shrub of the heath family (*Erica*) common from the Allgäu over the Alps and into south Tirol, whose sale throughout the region was handled as a monopoly by peasants of the Upper Lech valley in the sixteenth century. Other dyeplants, already known, became more commonly grown after 1300. Yellow was derived from weld (dyer's weed), a plant poisonous to animals and emitting a vile stench, doubtless accounting for its restricted cultivation, principally to the west of Bonn into the uplands of the Eifel. Red could be obtained both from madder, grown on the Middle Rhine around Speyer and Worms, by the six-teenth century extensively in Silesia, as well as around Breslau (Wrocław), in Lower Alsace north of Strasbourg, or else from saf-flower, again common along the course of the Rhine. But these dyestuffs paled into insignificance compared with the cultivation of the principal blue dye, woad, which did contribute to the shaping of distinctive economic landscapes. Although widely grown, with pockets of cultivation on the Westphalian plain, it set its stamp on two distinct regions of Germany: Thuringia around Erfurt (whose fortunes were made by woad-dealing), and the area between the Lower Rhine west of Cologne and the river Maas (Meuse), stretching into the district of Hesbaye (Haspengau) in present-day Belgium. The woad plant was easy enough to grow, though it preferred a warm climate, and rich, well-fertilized soil. Where those conditions pre-vailed, it could grow as profusely as a weed, giving two crops a year. But the skill – and the expense – lay in its processing. Once picked, the leaves had to be chopped and compressed into balls; that in itself was a cumbersome business, requiring animal- or water-powered mills to grind the leaves. Next the balls were delivered to urban centres for further processing, which involved moistening and hanging for several months to allow mould to set in and the dye juice to emerge by fermentation. Only then were barrels packed with pulpy dye ready for the market. The necessary investment, and the timelag in receiving the profits from sale, ensured that woad fin-ishing and marketing lay in the hands of merchants who, in the case of Thuringia, banded together to form an urban cartel comprising Erfurt, Gotha, Arnstadt, Langensalza, and Tennstedt. Other towns tried to get round the monopoly by purchasing direct from the peasant growers, but Erfurt, which controlled the most extensive rural territory in northern Germany, was able to keep outsiders largely at bay through the enforcement of civic jurisdiction and monopsony (the exercise of a purchasing stranglehold) collectively and the landholdings of its burghers and merchants individually. For that reason, Erfurt's woad industry had no need to rely upon putting-out or share-cropping; instead, by the fifteenth century much of the harvesting was done by seasonal migrant labour. Likewise, much of the processing within the towns was carried out by wage-labour.

In the Lower Rhenish woad-producing area, the elements of capital concentration and monopolism were much less pronounced. Several reasons for the contrast with Thuringia come to mind. Much of the woad grown between Rhine and Maas was used in the local textile industry, rather than being exported: Erfurt's symbiotic relationship with the Lusatian woad entrepôts as staging-posts to the east, and its extensive annual shipments to Nuremberg, find no parallel in Cologne. Despite its size and economic clout, moreover, Cologne controlled no rural territory whatsoever; it relied instead on the pull of its market and the extension of its quality control to dominate the economy of its hinterland, rather than on jurisdictional and political weapons. It is also the case that its economy – and that of its nearest rival, Aachen – was much more diversified than Erfurt's, so that it was less inclined – or had less need – to resort to restrictive practices in order to control a single source of economic strength.

Woad cultivation, in any case, was a mixed blessing. On the one hand, it could be integrated into the existing three-field system by being planted on the fallow; its leaves were too sharp to be eaten by sheep, but the stalks which remained after harvesting provided fodder for cattle. On the other hand, the permanent cultivation of woad impoverished the soil (as Martin Luther, who accused the Thuringian peasants of abandoning tillage in favour of woad cultivation for the sake of filthy lucre, bitterly complained), so that it was essential periodically to revitalize the soil with fertilizers such as marl or woodash, which again increased the costs of cultivation. When alternative sources of blue dye became available in the sixteenth century, woad cultivation declined, though even in 1600 around 300 villages in Thuringia still grew woad, despite the availability of indigo. It is a sign of what Immanuel Wallerstein has called the beginnings of the modern world-economy under merchant capitalism[*] that it became cheaper and more convenient to use dyestuffs

---

[*] Immanuel Wallerstein, *The Modern World-System*, vol. 1: *Capitalist Agriculture and the Origins of the European World-Economy in the Sixteenth Century* (New York/London/Toronto/Sydney/San Francisco, 1974).

from overseas – not only indigo which gradually ousted woad, but the dark red of brazilwood and the scarlet of cochineal. The other essential component of dyeing was alum, a mordant used to fix the colour in the dyeing process. This crystalline solution was derived from alum rock, found mostly in Italy, but the potash with which it was commonly admixed was widely available in the heavily afforested German lands.

Mining and Metallurgy

The third type of economic landscape, that of the mining and metal-working industries, has sometimes been seen as the pacemaker in a decisive transition towards a fully industrial economy based on capitalism. Yet quite apart from the restricted geographical dispersion of such areas up to the end of the sixteenth century, it should be remembered that the twin hallmarks of industrial production – the factory system and the replacement of manual labour by machines – only existed in rudimentary form; 'proto-factories', as the example of Nuremberg's metallurgy shows, could survive for centuries without giving rise to any widespread industrialization. In one particular branch of the extractive industry, moreover, salt-mining, the nature of production in fact inhibited the development of a factory system. Where salt was extracted by evaporation from brine, as in the salt-springs of Frankenhausen in Thuringia, Allendorf-Sooden in the Harz mountains of Hessen, or Halle on the river Saale, the capital of Anhalt, the work was neither capital-intensive nor technologically complex. In Thuringia individual salt-mines were engaged in extended commodity production rather than in early capitalist entrepreneurialism, though the Allendorf salt-springs were run as a state monopoly on a capitalist footing by the landgraves. By contrast, where salt had to be hewn from saliferous rock, as with the alpine salt deposits in Bavaria and Austria, the techniques of extraction were more costly. Winches and pulleys were needed to bring the salt to the surface, while the salt-pans installed in Hall in Tirol, for instance, were on an industrial scale. The principal salt-mines in the German lands were strung out from west to east on the northern slopes of the Alps from Hall in Tirol through Reichenhall in Bavaria to the salt-rich deposits of the Salzkammergut around Hallein, and onwards to further Habsburg salt-mines in Aussee and Hallstadt.

Because salt, as other minerals, was a regalian right, it was firmly

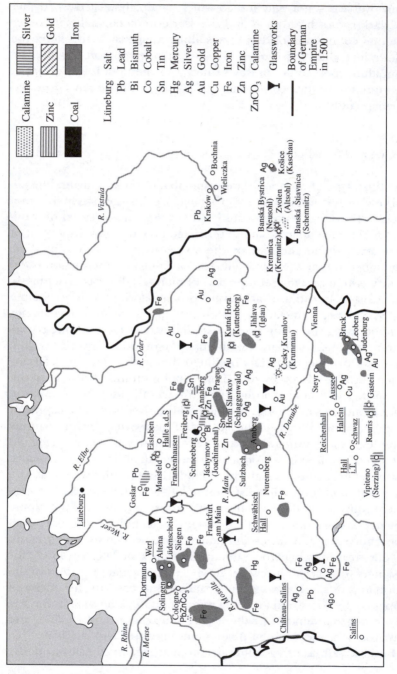

4.6 *Minerals and mining, c.1500*

under princely control from the thirteenth century onwards, providing a major source of revenue – it underpinned the magnificence of the prince-archbishops of Salzburg who controlled the Salzkammergut. Salt was essentially a commercial commodity, shipped and sold well beyond its immediate area of production. Alpine salt was traded westwards into Swabia, Württemberg, and the Upper Rhine (although the latter had convenient access to the salt of the Burgundian and Lorraine frontiers), and northwards into Franconia and Bohemia. To the south, however, it faced competition from sea-salt from the Venetian lagoon; up to 1500 considerable sums were invested by the princes to improve roads over the Alps in order to make their salt more attractive in north Italian markets. Other centres of production in Germany, all of them based in brine-pits rather than salt-mines, were of only regional importance, and could extricate themselves on occasion from princely control. The fortunes of the imperial free city of Schwäbisch Hall were built on salt: it dominated the market in northern Württemberg and on the Middle Rhine. A string of small salt-towns, Werl the most prominent, ran along the northern fringes of the Sauerland, east of Dortmund. But the leading salt city of northern Germany was undoubtedly Lüneburg on the river Ilmenau south of Lübeck. It succeeded in casting off the authority of the dukes of Braunschweig-Lüneburg in the fourteenth century and, as a member of the Hanseatic League, sought outlets for its copious salt-deposits both inland and overseas. After the construction of the Stecknitz canal in 1396 – financed in large measure by Lübeck merchants – Lüneburg acquired direct access to the Baltic via Lübeck. By the mid-sixteenth century half Lüneburg's salt trade was being shipped by canal, and even when it was threatened by competition from sea-salt (as were the Alpine mines by Venice), it was able to compensate by building up exports overland through northern Germany and the lands east of the Elbe.

The other extractive industry which did not necessarily involve new techniques of production was glass-making. Glassworks, as the case of Hessen mentioned earlier suggests, were less dependent on the location of raw materials – lime and silicates – than on the availability of the derivatives used in the manufacturing process itself. Both quartz sand and clay (for the firing ovens) were plentiful enough in the forests of northern and southern Hessen, the Reinhard, Kaufungen, and Spessart districts. But glassworks also flourished in areas where timber (and hence potash) abounded but the soils were not especially siliceous, notably in the Black Forest, where quartz sand was hauled up from the Rhine valley. Glass foundries might be grouped into a federation of producers, as in Hessen, but it was just as common for glassmakers to remain journeymen who staked out a plot of forest which they felled until exhausted, before moving on to a fresh site. For that reason, along with the relatively straightforward technology, glass-making remained an industry without any significant capitalist penetration of production and distribution, and one which, by the same token, rarely dominated a particular region for long enough to constitute an economic landscape. Even in Hessen, the extensive glass industry, which had already moved northwards in the course of the sixteenth century, was in decline by 1600, as woodland resources were exhausted. A similar fate was later to befall the Thuringian Forest glass industry, despite a bounteous natural endowment and state promotion of glassworks.

Technological Innovations

The extraction and processing of precious and base minerals, by contrast, could in general expand only with sufficient capital backing and the stimulus of new technology. Open-cast mining provides a partial exception, but it was largely confined to tin-mining. Brown coal (lignite), of which there were sizeable deposits in several parts of Germany, was also obtained by open-cast mining, but it was not mined to any extent until the sixteenth century. Instead, the first seams of mineral coal (pit-coal) were being worked as early as the fifteenth century. Bituminous coal was found in regions which were already heavily engaged in mining and metallurgy, such as the Ruhr, the Aachen basin, and southern Saxony, but in our period it made only a marginal contribution to the fuel requirements of those industries, which continued to rely principally on timber and charcoal.

Where copper, silver, lead, and iron were plentiful – in southern Westphalia, Saxony, Bohemia, the Upper Palatinate (east of Nuremberg), Tirol, and Styria – the first genuinely industrial landscapes of late medieval and early modern Germany emerged. In many of these districts, moreover, subsidiary deposits of other minerals were discovered: gold in parts of Bohemia and Lusatia; bismuth and cobalt, rare metals but indispensable as alloys, or tin (used to coat iron to prevent rusting, in the form of tinplate, all in southern

Saxony. Other areas rose to prominence through the prevalence of a single metal ore: calamine (zinc carbonate; in the USA smithsonite) was discovered west of Cologne, and was alloyed with copper to produce brass; the Rhineland Palatinate held resources of mercury (quicksilver), whose fluidity over a broad temperature band allowed it to dissolve other metals into amalgams.

Perhaps the most remarkable transformation occurred in the processing of silver. From the high Middle Ages silver had been mined wherever argentiferous lead ores were discovered – in the Carpathian mountains of Slovakia, in the Erzgebirge straddling southern Saxony and northwestern Bohemia, throughout the Austrian Alps from Tirol to Carinthia, in the Harz mountains around Goslar, and in parts of the Black Forest and the Vosges mountains on the Upper Rhine. The silver was separated from the lead ore by means of cupellation (a technique known to antiquity), whereby the lead was melted in a marl-lined hearth and then oxidized, so that the silver was left as a metal 'bun' on the hearth. In the fifteenth century this process was overtaken by the invention of liquation, whereby silver could now be extracted from argentiferous raw copper through the admixture of lead. In liquation, the lead was entirely burnt up, producing white lead (lead oxide), which could then be retrieved as metal by reduction through charcoal (though the wastage of lead remained high). The discovery of liquation transformed the mining industry of central Germany, the Bohemian crown lands, and subsequently the Alps, where new argentiferous copper deposits were discovered near the existing lead ores. Henceforth, in these areas copper, lead, and silver production went hand-in-hand, creating major industrial landscapes which relegated smaller and less abundant areas of silver ore without copper deposits to relative insignificance. Liquation allowed the volume of silver to be gained from argentiferous rock to increase dramatically, but it was a costly and time-consuming process, in which the ore was smelted in a chain of blast-furnaces which might cover several hectares. Above all, the process required copious supplies of lead. In the copper-shale district of Thuringia, on whose southern fringes the greatest concentration of liquation works was to be found, lead, despite its weight, had to be imported from the Harz mountains, the Eifel (with Cologne as an important entrepôt), Silesia, Poland, and even overseas from England. One reason was the Fuggers' decision to make their smelting at Hohenkirchen, to whose convenient commercial location we have already referred, the centre of its operations for ore brought in from far-flung mines. Around 1500 the Hohenkirchen plant was refining 11 000 quintals of copper ore per annum sent from the Fugger mines at Neusohl (Banská Bystrica) in Slovakia, alongside the output of the Mansfeld mines in Thuringia. The expense and organization involved in shipping the ore in convoys of 220 waggons over 600 kilometres, taking up to eighty days there and back, beggars belief – but at the same time indicates the enormous profits which could accrue from silver-mining, with net margins of up to 40 per cent.

Up to the late fifteenth century it is reckoned that central Europe produced around 20 tonnes of refined silver annually, alongside 4000 tonnes of raw copper, mostly from Saxony, Bohemia, and Slovakia. But after 1470 the picture changed markedly as the alpine mines began to yield a substantial output. In the following half-century silver production increased to around 65 tonnes per annum, split almost evenly between Saxony on the one hand, and Bohemia, Slovakia, and Tirol on the other. The claim that around 1500 Schwaz in Tirol was alone producing 80 per cent of the silver and 40 per cent of the copper of central Europe does, however, appear fanciful. The production figures, in any case, make up only a fraction of the silver mined throughout Europe as a whole. Despite the opening-up of new mines in the period (Kitzbühel in Tirol, Ste-Marie-aux-Mines in the Val de Lièpvre in the Vosges), silver-mining remained a precarious business, caught between boom and bust. One simple reason was the exhaustion of the ore-seams. As noted in Chapter 3, Schneeberg's resources of ore, which had made it one of the leading south Saxon mining towns by 1500, were worked out by 1540, while Ste-Marie-aux-Mines, which by 1525 was home to 3000 miners, many of them squatters, was all but a ghost town a generation later. But there were other causes at work. The cost of pumping water out of the deeper shafts – despite the use of hydraulic pumps – and the difficulties in hauling up ore from remote galleries – despite the advent of improved winding-gear such as the whim, a vertical rope drum turned by horse-power – rendered the lesser minefields too risky: that was why the silver reserves of the Black Forest (a source of great wealth up to the fourteenth century) were gradually abandoned in favour of new and shallower deposits across the Rhine in the Vosges. Another blow was struck by the flow of silver imports from the Americas. If the tonnage amounted to no more than 10 tonnes per annum before 1540, over the next two decades it had shot up to 80 tonnes per annum, then to 120 tonnes, and finally, in the last two decades of the sixteenth century, to 270 tonnes. Even though these figures remain somewhat conjectural, they suggest an order of magnitude which by mid-century was clearly outstripping production in central Europe with a corresponding depression in the price of silver.

Nevertheless, the advantage of the technological breakthrough of liquation was that it allowed a new phase of metallurgical enterprise to flourish through a switch in emphasis to copper production. By mid-century, for instance, the bulk of Thuringian mining output was copper rather than silver. Even though there appears to have been a gradual decline in the demand for copper for household goods after 1550, raw copper was still exported from Thuringia (and Slovakia) to the burgeoning metallurgical centres of Aachen and Stolberg, where it was processed with the local deposits of zinc and calamine to make brass, which supplied the growing armaments industry of the sixteenth century. The lucrative potential of zinc was recognized by the formation of joint-stock companies to invest in its mining and alloying; these comprised both investors from the locality itself (such as the Altenberg company), and outside speculators, including entrepreneurs from Nuremberg who pioneered the use of embossing hammers, which could turn ten times as much sheet-metal into semi-finished or finished wares in a day as hand-beating (much to the annoyance of the local guildsmen, who saw their craft livelihood put at risk).

Mining regions, in other words, that were not dependent upon a single mineral were able to sustain their industries in a changing market. This is aptly demonstrated by southern Saxony, whose copper, lead, and silver output may have declined in the course of the sixteenth century, but where tin-mining expanded rapidly. From an annual yield of not more than ten tonnes before 1470 (less than the amount of silver produced!), the output in centres such as Altenberg, Oelsnitz, Lauterbach, and Schönbrunn had shot up to around 200 tonnes per annum in 1600. Notwithstanding open-cast mining, expansion on this scale could not have been accomplished without outside investment by putters-out, at first from mercantile cities in Saxony itself such as Leipzig, but latterly from south Germany as well.

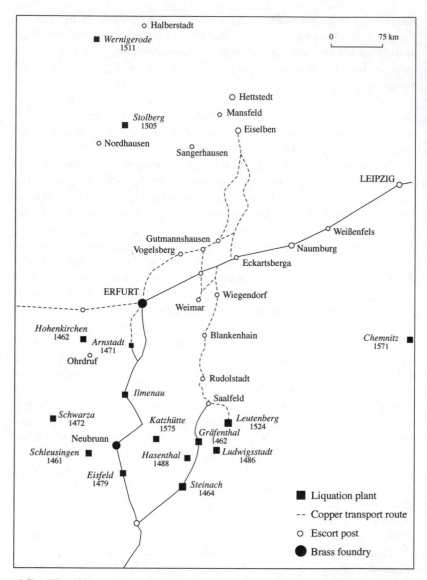

4.7   *The Thuringian copper industry, c.1500 (after E. Westermann/W. von Stromer).*

Industrialized Landscapes

It is easy to be lured by the glitter of silver and other precious metals into imagining that Saxony and Thuringia or the Alps were the most important and dynamic industrial regions of late medieval and early modern Germany. While there is no doubt that silver-, copper-, and lead-mining in Saxony gave a direct stimulus to the economy of the region as a whole, their impact was chiefly observable in the primary sector, in the expansion of wool, woad, and flax production. In areas of iron production, by contrast, the entire secondary sector might be invigorated by the manufacture of high-value metalwares – precision tools, clocks, and scientific instruments – provided that sufficient capital and technology were available. Iron-ore deposits had been found in many parts of the Empire in the Middle Ages – the Saar valley and the Eifel and Hunsrück ranges in the west, the Siegerland and Sauerland east of the Rhine, the Harz mountains, parts of the Black Forest and northern Swabia, the Upper Palatinate, eastern Saxony around Pirna, much of Bohemia into Moravia and Lusatia, and in the Austrian duchies of Styria and Carinthia, to name only the major areas. Indeed, in terms of output, iron left copper and silver in the shade, with perhaps 30 000 tonnes of iron being produced over against 4500 tonnes at best of copper and silver. Only two areas, however, made the successful transition from isolated forges employing primitive technology and supplying local needs to fully industrialized landscapes with specialized factory production by the sixteenth century. One was the Süderland, the county of Mark in the western Sauerland; the other was the Upper Palatinate in Franconia. It is no accident that these two districts lay near major international trading cities – Cologne and Nuremberg – and enjoyed good communications and a strategic market position. In the Süderland, the towns of Solingen, Altena, Iserlohn, and Lüdenscheid were already famous in the fifteenth century for the manufacture of wire (by drawing, not smithying), as well as tools, and household metal goods such as cutlery which required the use of moulds and presses as well as forges and furnaces. So advanced was production that the Süderland came to concentrate on finished articles, and was content to import pig-iron from further south in the Siegerland. But even there the pace of technological change had not slowed. By 1500 blast-furnaces had replaced bloomery (the first firing of the ore), and the working of the malleable ore by chafery (the second furnace) was aided by hydraulic power to drive the hammers which shaped the metal. Yet although the Siegerland iron industry was organized by putting-out, it never attained the status of a fully industrialized region, unlike the Süderland, largely because of its remoteness and the lack of entrepreneurial initiative: iron-working remained under the control of local lords or the landgraves of Hessen, who were more concerned to promote domestic manufactures than engage in export markets.

The most advanced industrial region in Germany was undoubtedly the district round Nuremberg, which drew on iron supplies from the Upper Palatinate with its twin metallurgical centres of Sulzbach and Amberg. By the early fourteenth century the technique of tin-plating iron had been pioneered, which for long remained confined to Nuremberg and Wunsiedel in the Fichtelgebirge. Likewise, the technology of wire-drawing was in use from the early fifteenth century, though it was not to be fully automated until the late sixteenth. Wire-mills were established all around the city on the rivers Rednitz and Pegnitz – one of which was depicted in a famous water-colour by Albrecht Dürer, the greatest German artist of our period. Just as in the Süderland, Nuremberg as the region's economic powerhouse sought less to control all stages of the metallurgical process than to secure supplies of semi-finished ironware through recourse to putting-out, which it could then manufacture into specialized finished goods. A list of crafts organized by putting-out in the city in 1535 records hook-, blade-, compass-, knife-, needle-, and wire-making, as well as armourers and tinsmiths (not to mention certain clothing trades, such as fustian-weaving and glovemaking, and printing). The city and its entrepreneurs used the putting-out system less to organize the surrounding countryside into an industrial zone of mass production – unlike the Upper Swabian cities with their rural linen and fustian industries – than to reserve the latter stages of production to urban craftsmen in their employ, and to export their wares to foreign markets. The concept of the 'economic unit' embracing town and country, which Hektor Ammann advanced on the basis of his study of Nuremberg's industry,* implied not so much dominance by the city of its hinterland as the fulfilment of mutual needs: the smaller surrounding towns were as eager to grab a share of Nuremberg's industrial prosperity as the city's merchants were to control local production. A measure of the region's industrialization

---

* Hektor Ammann, *Die wirtschaftliche Stellung der Reichsstadt Nürnberg im Spätmittelalter* (Nuremberg, 1970).

can be seen from the fact that perhaps one-quarter of the population of the Upper Palatinate was engaged in some stage of iron-mining and smelting, with the area accounting for one-third of Germany's entire output of iron in 1600.

The hallmark of the emergence of economic landscapes in late medieval Germany was the intensification of town–country relations, most evident in the spread of the putting-out system from towns to the countryside. In it, the artisan was divorced from the product of his labour, which is why the system has traditionally been regarded as the forerunner of capitalist production. This judgement, however, needs to be treated with circumspection. It is true that labour was treated as a commodity, but the wage-working artisan, whether urban or rural, still retained some independence: a weaver might own his own loom, even if he was dependent on the putter-out for the supply of raw materials (yarn) and was obliged to sell his cloth to the putter-out, who distributed it in local and international markets. But putting-out, unlike the factory system of industrial capitalism, was decentralized, with goods in many cases being shipped from their primary place of production as semi-finished wares to be finished and marketed in centres of higher rank. The early capitalist element, particularly in mining and metallurgical enterprises, resided in the division of labour and capital, rather than in volume of output or capital accumulation. That is why it can be misleading to focus on the great banking and trading companies of early modern Germany – the Fuggers, Welsers, Höchstetters, Paumgartners, and the like – with their overseas investments and 'factories', as if they were typical of its economy as a whole. Not only was the putting-out system, as we have argued, already well established, particularly in parts of Upper Germany, long before the sixteenth century; the economic landscapes in which they operated were not dependent on the meteoric rise and fall of these shooting-stars. Between 1556 and 1584, to take a striking instance, seventy firms in Augsburg went bankrupt, but others quickly stepped in to take their place, and the zenith of Augsburg's industry and commerce was not reached until the following century. Indeed, one reason for the resilience of the German iron industry in our period lay precisely in the fact that it was not dominated by a handful of oligopolists, but benefited from a proliferation of medium-sized firms in a variety of urban centres bound together in mutually stimulating competition – as the Süderland or the Upper Palatinate demonstrate.

That, in turn, leads on to a final reflection. Economic landscapes could only emerge where town and country constituted an economic unit. Where cities earned their livelihood as entrepôts and their merchants as middlemen and carriers, there was no reason why such activity should impinge on their hinterlands at all. That is most noticeably the case in the coastal cities of the Hanseatic League, whose trade derived much less from importing to and exporting from northern Germany than from long-distance cargo-carrying between Russia, the Baltic, and western Europe. In cities such as Lübeck and Hamburg the urban economy of small commodity producers remained largely intact; the division of labour, capital-intensive production, and the putting-out system were underdeveloped before the sixteenth century; and there was little attempt to extend commercial influence to the countryside. Only in the course of the sixteenth century did cities such as Lübeck, the Hanseatic capital, begin to employ put-out rural workers in the copper industry and in cooperage. These differing problems of town–country relations will be explored more fully in the next chapter.

5 Commercial Networks and Urban Systems

Markets and Urban Regional Systems

The period from the mid-fourteenth century until the end of the Thirty Years War, it is commonly agreed, witnessed the greatest efflorescence of the urban economy in the German-speaking lands. In broad terms this verdict is accurate, but it needs to be qualified in several particulars. It stands in stark and conscious contrast to the alleged crisis of the late medieval feudal-agrarian economy, even though the intensification of town–country relations in this period led to growing interdependences of production and distribution which must render any polarity suspect. The flowering of the urban economy, moreover, has too often been identified with the fortunes of individual families and family enterprises, particularly the galaxy of merchants and financiers with a European network of branch-offices and business partnerships, rather than with the collective economic performance of particular cities. Indeed, in terms of gross domestic product (if we could begin to measure it in a pre-statistical age) it is highly unlikely that international and overseas trade had more than a marginal impact on the development of the German economy.

Of much greater significance is the growth of local and regional markets and commercial networks to the point where we can speak of urban regional systems. In some parts of Germany, especially the south-west, these systems were admixed with and enhanced by wider ambitions to control hinterlands by political and judicial means, to the point where certain cities could claim (as in Switzerland) to be fully fledged city-states or (as in Upper Germany) to aspire to that condition. As a concomitant of the spate of late medieval urban foundations came the proliferation of market privileges in the form of weekly markets and annual fairs. Emperors and princes allowed themselves to be remunerated handsomely for the confirmation and extension of these privileges – Emperor Maximilian, notoriously strapped for cash, showed himself altogether amenable to such petitions in the 1490s and beyond. The immediate benefit of market privileges is self-evident: to establish a place of exchange which could attract suppliers from the town's hinterland, and to cream off cash into civic coffers through tolls and stallage-charges. But the wider advantage lay in the franchises which charters of market rights conferred upon the recipients. One was the creation of a precinct around the town, usually of one to two German miles (4.6 or 9.2 statute miles; or 7.4 or 14.8 km), within which no other markets might be held, and whose inhabitants were often required to sell only at the civic market (the right of monopsony). An unmistakable feature of the fifteenth and sixteenth centuries in Germany, as we shall discuss in detail later, was the effort by towns large and small to extend their precincts – or to vary them according to the products for sale – as a means of underpinning economic influence over their hinterlands. These attempts could easily shade over into legislation to prevent not merely village markets but rural crafts as well (unless they were under the control of urban putters-out), or to outlaw informal marketing on feast-days and at church-ales. In particular, urban councils repeatedly passed decrees banning the sale of produce direct to itinerant dealers and merchants, a practice known as forestalling, which could lead to artificial shortages and price inflation. One of the commonest complaints of the age concerned the activities of pedlars, often described in the sources as Savoyards or Scots, though in reality they could come from anywhere abroad or even from an adjacent territory. In 1543, for instance, the magistrates of Nördlingen were exercised over whether to allow foreign traders to frequent the city's market, but decided on balance that a ban was inadvisable since otherwise the latter might simply resort to hawking their wares in the countryside and drag the city's handicrafts along in their wake, as was already happening. In other words, however oppressive market legislation might appear from the perspective of those in the city's environs, much of it was driven by the need to respond to overt competition from the countryside, which prompted an unending stream of lamentation from urban magistrates and guildsfolk.

Attempts to combat market competition and forestalling were notoriously ineffective – not surprising in a country as territorially and judicially fragmented as Germany. Just as the earlier urban leagues of the thirteenth and fourteenth centuries in Swabia and the Rhineland had expressed collective solidarity in the face of threats to their liberty from monarchs and princes, so too in the late fifteenth and early sixteenth centuries urban communes banded together for economic reasons to prevent forestalling on a regional level: in 1491 Kempten and Memmingen launched an initiative which was then supported by other Swabian communes – Isny, Leutkirch, Kaufbeuren, Mindelheim, and Biberach; or again in 1530/31 further west, when Ravensburg agreed with Lindau, Überlingen, and Radolfzell to enforce the exclusive sale of corn at urban markets. These, of course, were temporary measures in the face of dearth, which were suspended when plenty returned. And they did not always meet universal acclaim: it is significant that the communes which acted in concert were middle-ranking cities with a modest economic sphere of influence, rather than the larger metropolises such as Ulm or Augsburg whose commercial clout allowed them to stand aside. Nevertheless, in the course of the sixteenth century, the imperial free cities of Upper Swabia extended co-operation from reactive measures against forestalling to the active pursuit of intelligence about the workings of the regional grain market. This underscores the point that the primary theatre of the urban economy in our period was regional rather than international, and that within the region relations between town and country were stamped as much by conflict and competition as by the mutually reinforcing division of functions implied by the putting-out system and the concept of an 'economic unit' with a town and its hinterland subsisting in mutual dependence.

Commerce: Opportunities and Obstacles

Markets, however, were not simply the focal points for the exchange of goods between a central place and its immediate hinterland. As the location of fairs and as entrepôts or places of transshipment, towns could also play a commercial role which extended well beyond the region. Here the problem of language obtrudes. In German, the annual civic fairs – *Jahrmärkte* – are readily contrasted with the *Messen*, the international trade fairs, usually held twice a year, which survive up to our own day in Frankfurt am Main and in Leipzig, but for which there is no straightforward translation. Glittering occasions they were, but these latter international fairs are a poor guide to the economic standing of the cities in which they were held. Both Frankfurt am Main and Leipzig were populous and powerful cities in their own right, but they were the exception. Other international fairs were held in cities of middling rank such as Frankfurt an der Oder, Nördlingen, or Zürich, but one major fair was held in the small Swiss town of Zurzach, on the Rhine above Basel, with a population never greater than 3000, which reverted to economic slumber once its fair-fortnight had passed. That was even truer of those fair-towns specializing in one commodity, usually cattle: however advantageous their location at the point of intersection between adjacent regions, it cannot reasonably be claimed that the international cattle-market at gateways to the German lands in Cernay (Sennheim) in Alsace, Buttstädt in Saxony, Brieg (Brzeg) in Poland, or Raab (Györ) in Hungary imparted to these communes a dynamic of economic development which they would otherwise have lacked: within their own regions they remained minor players. As a rule of thumb, the most prominent manufacturing and trading cities of Germany – Cologne, Nuremberg, Strasbourg, Augsburg, or Basel – were not also the sites of international *Messen*, largely because their merchants and manufacturers were keen to keep their economic prosperity to themselves, rather than let foreigners partake of it.

On the other hand, even leading commercial metropolises might try to organize interregional trade to their advantage where they functioned as entrepôts in an arterial commercial network, rather than as outlets for their hinterlands. Cities exploited their location by imposing staple rights, that is to say, the obligation to discharge loads, offer part or all of the cargo for sale at the local market, sometimes at below the going-rate, before allowing reloading and onward passage. These rights could be augmented by the compulsion on merchants to use only designated routes and to pass prescribed toll-posts on water or on land. That was the case with Cologne for shipping on the Rhine before the fourteenth century, and for Vienna for trade on the Danube. As long as overseas demand flourished and staple rights were not too onerous, these measures could bring clear financial advantage to the cities concerned. But it is not hard to see how, during a commercial downturn, they could aggravate a deterio-

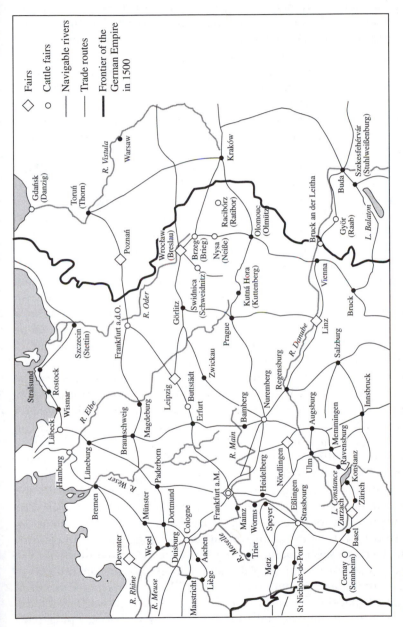

5.1 *Trade routes, fairs, and navigable rivers*

rating situation. In the much altered circumstances of the late six-teenth century Strasbourg decided to introduce a wine-staple for the first time, with foreign merchants initially obliged to offer fewer barrels for sale than native ones, though the differential was later abolished. This took place at a time when Alsace wine was already suffering from shrinking markets in northern Germany in the face of rising beer consumption, and from viticultural competition in Switzerland. Not surprisingly, the merchants claimed that the magis-tracy was simply compounding the problem. Similar complaints were voiced when Hamburg began to enforce a staple on the river Elbe in the same period.

By the same token, it has frequently been argued that the prolifer-ation of tolls and toll-stations in itself acted as a barrier to inter regional and overseas trade. Whether levied as turnpike tolls or as customs dues, these charges were bound to increase transaction costs. The example invariably cited is the succession of toll-posts on the Rhine, where 31 survived from the Middle Ages to the Napoleonic era, mostly concentrated between Mainz and Cologne. In our period, however, these tolls were essentially transit dues rather than protectionist imposts; by extension, a toll levied for purely fiscal purposes at a rate so high that it blocks the flow of goods must lead logically *ad absurdum*. Goods shipped on the Rhine in any case often paid a flat-rate considerably lower than the sum of individual tolls, while the weights and measures used to calculate toll-charges were frequently much less than those applied to the goods themselves. The truth of this argument is reflected in the pop-ularity of Alsace wines in overseas markets until the mid-sixteenth century: the most sought-after German wines were those which had to pass the greatest number of toll-stages.

Quite a different impediment to trade before the sixteenth century was supposedly presented by a shortage of bullion. Bullion crises occurred around 1420 and again at the end of the 1450s, when cities in northern Germany complained of a lack of struck coin. The bottleneck was only relieved, it is suggested, when the new mines of Saxony and Tirol came on stream towards the end of the century. The German silver boom, of course, quickly collapsed in the face of cheaper imports from the Americas. It is extraordinarily difficult to assess the impact of bullion shortages. That they occurred is not in dispute; that they seriously disrupted trade is quite another matter. Although Germany lagged well behind Italy in bookkeeping tech-niques, merchants trading overseas were already quite familiar with bills of exchange and sureties by the fifteenth century, which obviated the need for ready cash until the agreed settlement date, when balances had to be cleared. Credit arrangements in the form of moneyless transactions were commonplace between Cologne and the Upper Rhine, for instance, before the fifteenth century. It can be argued that shortage of coin created difficulties within the local economy – an escalating silver price had repercussions for wage-workers if it meant that there was insufficient coin to pay their wages – but in their daily life as consumers even artisans and labourers often ran a slate, which was wiped weekly or monthly, rather than handing over small amounts of precious coin for each transaction.

On the other hand, it has been argued that bullion shortages stifled technological innovation in the mining industry, for expensive hydraulic drainage techniques had been known at least 120 years before they were finally deployed. That investment was so dependent upon available bullion is not altogether self-evident: social relations of production (as Karl Marx emphasized) bore directly upon the willingness of investors to harness new technology, for as long as labour was plentiful and cheap, the incentive to switch to machines was diminished. By the fifteenth century that was not the case, so that a bullion shortage in the early 1400s can perhaps best be seen as a delaying factor rather than as an absolute deterrent. On the other hand, the signs were once again reversed with the population recovery after 1470. The abundance of labour in the mines of Schwaz in Tirol is evident from the wages totalling 15 000 florins which were paid to the 600 mineworkers who formed a continuous human chain, working in four-hour shifts round the clock, to drain water by bucket off the mine shafts. Only twenty years later was a horse-powered pump-wheel deployed, even though it had been invented at least a century earlier.

The principal obstacle to trade remained the sheer cost of transport, though shipment on water was always appreciably cheaper than overland. Nevertheless, necessity – in the case of the supply of essential foodstuffs, for instance – could override considerations of cost. The largest cities were obliged to import grain from a radius of at least 30 kilometres. In the case of Cologne that might rise to 50 kilometres over land from the bishopric of Cologne and the duchy of Jülich, but as much as 130 km on water downriver from the Rheingau. Nuremberg, too, regularly drew supplies from as far afield as 100 km, and these distances could escalate markedly during famines and harvest failures. The same was true of the booming mining areas. The mining communities of the Erzgebirge in southern Saxony, with a collective population of 70 000 by 1500, relied upon grain imports from 60 to 80 kilometres away from the plains south of Leipzig; only one-third of annual consumption could be sourced locally. The Saxon mining industry reminds us, too, that opportunity – the prospect of profit – could outweigh cost, as we have already seen in the case of the furnaces strategically located at Hohenkirchen on the edge of the Thuringian Forest, where convoys of copper ore arrived from Neusohl (Banská Bystrica) in Slovakia, over 600 km away. High-value commodities, traded internationally, could in such circumstances appear to defy the laws of transaction costs, and the same applied to bulk shipments of grain across the Baltic to supply the towns and cities of the Low Countries. But the German lands, bound by political constraints, never witnessed the concerted efforts to improve the infrastructure of commerce which characterized the Dutch economy in the early modern period: the digging of canals (or the rectification of river courses) and the construction of paved roads. The Stecknitz canal linking Lübeck to the salt-town of Lüneburg to the south, built at enormous cost at the end of the fourteenth century, is remarkable precisely because it is exceptional. The river Rhine, the main artery of commerce between north and south Germany, meandered in its upper stretches through shoals and sandbanks; not until the nineteenth century was its channel straightened and deepened by the so-called 'Rhine regulation'. The importance of the river network to Germany's commercial prosperity was, nevertheless, fundamental, and on a local level the authorities began to invest in improvements by the fifteenth century, especially to the tributary rivers which enabled traffic on the major arteries to penetrate into more remote areas.

One example is the river system fanning out from the Weser, which flowed from the Hessian uplands through the north German plain to the sea beyond Bremen. Navigation on its tributaries the Aller (linking Braunschweig to the Weser via the Oker) and the Leine (up to Hannover), as well as on the Weser itself, was improved to allow grain to reach the northern ports, and stone and lime from the Harz mountains to be exported. These princely initiatives were complemented in the sixteenth century by the dukes of Braunschweig-Wolfenbüttel who took in hand the dredging of the Oker, which provided an outlet for Harz ores and timber. A parallel can be found in Württemberg, where Duke Christoph after 1550 planned to make the upper reaches of the Neckar navigable in order to boost wine exports – one reason why (as we have argued in the previous chapter) the duchy was the only viticultural region of Germany not to have experienced a slump in the later sixteenth century.

But improvements in transport and the lowering of transaction costs also had their price. Just as the leading Flemish cities of Bruges and Ghent had clashed violently in the mid-fourteenth century over the construction of a canal, the New Leie between Bruges and Deinze, which threatened to divert trade from Ghent's grain staple, so the cities of the north German plain watched jealously over their toll and staple privileges, wary of intruders such as Braunschweig taking advantage of improvements to the Oker, and keen always to force traffic to use their quays, warehouses, and exchanges at the expense of others'. That is why so many attempts by cities to establish leagues of commercial co-operation were short-lived: however much they needed to stand shoulder-to-shoulder in the face of princely aggression or the vagaries of the harvest, their individual interests might ultimately conflict.

The Hanseatic League

The one shining exception to this rule was the survival of the league of north German merchant cities known as the Hansa, which dominated the trade of the Baltic and the north Atlantic from the thirteenth to the sixteenth century. But the success of the Hansa was attributable directly to its character as an association of individual merchants, or latterly cities collectively, engaged in the carrying-trade overseas, rather than in competition with each other as market outlets for their hinterlands. Another reason lay in the fluidity – or imprecision – of the Hansa as a legal entity. Because it had no proper institutional identity (at least until the establishment of the Hanseatic diet in the 1350s) – no army, no fleet, no officials, and no seal – it should perhaps not be called a league at all, but rather an association or community of merchants or cities banding together in defence of common external interests which betokened no other solidarity or obligation. Originally those interests were not even primarily commercial, or at least directed towards the overseas carrying trade. For the three regional alliances of cities which coalesced into the Hansa – in Westphalia, Saxony, and of the Wendish cities of the Baltic coast – were concerned as much to protect their own domestic economies from princely encroachment or the incursions of Flemish

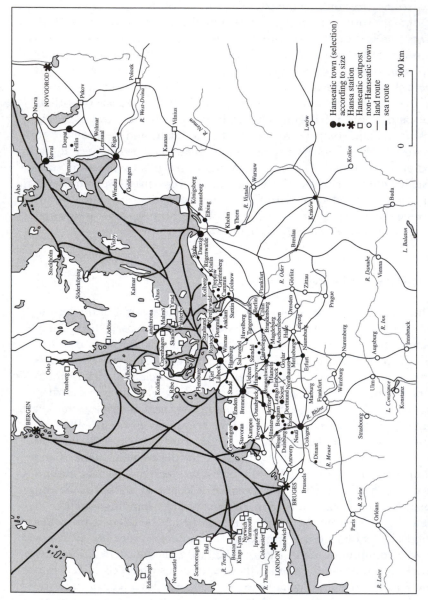

5.2 *The Hanseatic League (after J. Schildhauer)*

merchants as to act in concert on overseas ventures. Yet at no stage were Hanseatic merchants accorded preferential treatment in other Hanseatic cities as a general rule.

The defining period of the Hansa came in the second half of the fourteenth century. Against the background of economic conflict with the Flemish cities and war with the Danish crown, what had been a community of merchants yielded to an association of cities numbering over eighty at its peak. But the city councils remained suspicious of the independent 'factories' – the headquarters which the Hansa merchants collectively maintained in their most important overseas trading-stations, Bergen, Novgorod, Bruges, and London (where the Hanseatic factory was known as the Steelyard). More broadly, regional tensions bedevilled Hanseatic history. Its members found themselves pulled either towards its capital city, Lübeck, and therewith to commercial engagement in the Baltic, or else towards its rival Cologne, which dominated the trade of the west German interior down the river Rhine. Cologne and Lübeck were at opposite poles in another respect, too: the latter saw itself principally as an entrepôt for the carrying-trade; the former, although a key staging-post along the major commercial artery of Germany, was also an important centre of manufacturing, controlling the output of its hinterland.

These rivalries, writ large in the diverging interests of the Hansa's inland Westphalian and Saxon members, on the one hand, and the Wendish coastal cities of the Baltic, on the other, made greater institutional cohesion unlikely. The only step towards more formal and regular consultation was the development of the Hanseatic diet, first convened in 1356 to deliberate on measures against Flanders. Yet only rarely could the Hansa agree on a common foreign policy. Its overseas expeditions (sometimes in alliance with foreign princes) were *ad hoc* affairs, wars of piracy or deterrent raids on commercial rivals. The Hansa never sought to control foreign territory, apart from several short-lived invasions onto Danish and Norwegian soil.

By the close of the Middle Ages it is often reckoned that the Hansa as a commercial force was on the wane. This judgement rests on several questionable assumptions. The lack of strong institutions is often cited, and it is perfectly true that the advantages of flexibility which loose organization afforded might become a Trojan horse in the face of concerted opposition. But the Hanseatic cities' response to the attrition of the north German princes, themselves eager to lay hands on the profits of commerce, was to form regional defensive alliances, known as *tohopesaten*, which could be quite effective. Again, north Germany was not absolved from the effects of the late medieval economic crisis; declining populations meant a downturn in demand. Nevertheless, the pattern of migration eastwards, observable since the days of east-Elbian colonization in the thirteenth century, continued, as Westphalian towns offered shelter to Rhinelanders, and Bremen welcomed new burghers from the Low Countries and Frisia. In the cities of the Baltic, immigrants might outnumber natives in the ranks of the merchants – in the late fourteenth century one-quarter of Danzig's population hailed from west of the Elbe. Although each Hansa member guarded its own interests, a remarkable feature is the ease with which incomers could make a career in their new cities – the tribune of Lübeck in the 1530s, Jürgen Wullenwever, was in fact a native of Hamburg. Of greater account may be the rudimentary character of the financing of overseas ventures and Hanseatic business practices in general. The voyages of commercial fleets were funded by shareholders who initially took quarter-shares in each ship, but these stakes were subsequently split into much smaller holdings, which diluted individual risk-taking and made accounting difficult.

Certainly, the Hanseatic cities never witnessed the rise on any scale of the large merchant companies – amalgams of industrial enterprises, finance houses and speculative cartels – which came to dominate the south German urban economy. This argument remains truer, however, of the Baltic cities of the Hansa than of its Rhenish members. For by the fifteenth century the centre of gravity within the Hansa was switching from Lübeck towards Cologne, a city endowed with strategic-geographical advantages and stamped by the dynamism of its merchant elite. What on the upper stretches of the Rhine was a hindrance to passage proved at its estuary to be a positive boon: it debouched in numerous channels prone to shifting and silting, which hampered the rise of a great gateway port as a competitor to the Rhenish metropolis upriver. Tiel, Dordrecht, and Kampen in the course of the Middle Ages all failed to establish themselves as serious competitors – Rotterdam's importance dates from the nineteenth century after the canalization of the estuary in the New Waterway. By contrast, Cologne developed its commercial links with Antwerp – no direct rival at the mouth of the Scheldt – with many merchants taking up residence there: over half the foreigners in Antwerp at the turn of the fifteenth century were German, mostly from the Rhineland and Cologne. These contacts intensified in the sixteenth century, as Cologne's loyalty to Catholicism gave it privileged access to the fulcrum of the Habsburgs' overseas commercial empire.

About financial techniques it is difficult to be precise. Double-entry bookkeeping (which was widespread in south German merchant houses by the mid-fifteenth century) seems to have become prevalent among Hansa members only in the sixteenth. But bills of exchange and futures contracts were commonplace. What was lacking were city- or state-backed financial institutions to facilitate and underwrite credit transactions. The first fully fledged deposit and clearing bank within the Hanseatic area was not established until 1619, with the foundation of the Hamburg Bank, though it was largely a response to the monetary chaos and accelerating inflation of the period of debasement known as the *Kipper- und Wipperzeit*.

In the end, what weakened the Hansa collectively was commercial competition on its own doorstep. It failed to counteract the activity of its rivals in the Low Countries, because its members in the eastern Baltic – the German settlements of Reval (Tallinn), Riga, and Memel (Klaipeda), as well as its one aristocratic corporate member, the Teutonic Order – who were already the beneficiaries of a burgeoning grain trade with the Low Countries refused to play ball by helping to blockade Flanders. At the same time, as the fifteenth century wore on, south German merchants began to penetrate northwards, carrying goods of domestic and Italian manufacture. The traditional commercial artery via the Baltic ports was challenged by the ascendancy of new routes which ran eastwards from Frankfurt into Poland, and, above all, via the stepping-stones of Frankfurt and Cologne to Antwerp.

The most obvious sign of commercial reorientation came with the closure of the Hansa's factory in Bruges and its transfer to Antwerp in the early sixteenth century. But the Germans who continued to trade there did so less and less as Hanseatic members than as individuals in partnership with native Antwerpers or the many Iberians who flocked there. To draw up a balance-sheet is by no means easy. Some Hanseatic cities prospered throughout the sixteenth century: by 1600 Lübeck's tonnage had increased twofold from the beginning of the century. More broadly, the rise of the Baltic grain trade conferred a particular advantage on Lübeck, Hamburg, and not least Danzig. To what extent this helped to compensate for the decline in fishing – by the mid-fifteenth century the staple of the Baltic fishing industry, the herring, had disappeared from its spawning grounds off Scania, either through overfishing or migration of shoals to the North Sea – is uncertain. The Hanseatic cities got fresh wind in their sails, moreover, in the wake of the political crisis in the Spanish Netherlands: the closure of the Antwerp market in 1569, and the sack of the city two years later.

A verdict on the Hansa, therefore, must set any collectively declining fortunes against the vitality of some of its leading cities, and recognize that such vigour was the result both of accident (including political and diplomatic hazards) and design. What remains unresolved is the balance between domestic and international trade. Although the Hanseatic cities were known as cargo-carriers, the value of Lübeck's inland trade with Cologne, Frankfurt, and Nuremberg, as Philippe Dollinger has pointed out, probably equalled, if it did not exceed, that of its maritime trade, at least in the fifteenth century.

South German Merchant Companies

This point needs to be borne in mind as we explore the differences between the Hansa and the merchant companies of Upper Germany. Too much can be made of the contrast between the loose and constitutionally fluid character of the Hansa and the tighter structure of south German enterprises operating as firms with a hierarchy of responsibilities and modern methods of accounting. If, as Wolfgang von Stromer has suggested, the Hansa was effectively a cartel to gain and maintain economic pre-eminence by political means,[*] then the judicial and seigneurial privileges which the array of market franchise monopolies, and the control of territory afforded to south German cities and their merchant dynasties, particularly in underpinning the putting-out system, achieved similar ends by different means. What distinguished the commerce of Upper Germany – and ultimately gave it the edge over the Hansa – was not so much its organization as its output. The merchants of the Hansa traded predominantly in raw materials – fish, grain, timber, furs – dependent on the primary sector, which were inexpensive to produce, beer being the obvious example. The only advanced industrial sector was shipbuilding itself. But Upper German firms mar-

---

[*] Wolfgang von Stromer, 'Verflechtungen oberdeutscher Wirtschaftszentren am Beginn der Neuzeit', in Wilhelm Rausch (ed.), *Die Stadt an der Schwelle zur Neuzeit* (Linz, 1980), p. 21.

keted not only a variety of textiles – including by the sixteenth century the more refined 'new draperies' – but a range of metallurgical goods on the back of the mining and smelting industries, switching from objects of everyday use – pots, pans, needles, pins – to sophisticated and complex wares – armour, artillery, clocks, scientific instruments. And to that end, large stretches of the countryside were harnessed to their production (in its early stages) through the putting-out system. That is not to deny the genuine differences in business organization and methods between the Hansa and its south and west German counterparts.

In the twelfth and thirteenth century a series of urban leagues had arisen – the Middle Rhine town league (before 1226), the league of cloth-producing towns in the Hesbaye (Haspengau), in the east of present-day Belgium, centred upon Liège and Maastricht, concluded in 1230, or the Swabian Town League of 1376, led by Ulm (not to be confused with the peace-keeping Swabian League of towns and princes a century later) – whose origins and motives bore some resemblance to the Hansa. But these leagues were of short duration, often responses to military or diplomatic emergency; they did not provide the basis of long-lasting commercial associations. Instead, south Germany witnessed the rise of large trading companies, and latterly family firms. Both might open branch offices in other cities, and overseas, working in partnership with local merchants, or else maintain factories owned by the company itself (unlike the Hansa) and run by agents. The best-known of the companies, established in 1380, was the Great Ravensburg Trading Company. It was founded by three merchant families, only one of which came from Ravensburg itself (the others were from Konstanz and Buchhorn), to exploit the burgeoning linen industry of western Swabia by gaining a monopoly on the marketing of its cloths at home and overseas. At the height of its prosperity around 1500 it embraced well over one hundred shareholders from two dozen Swabian cities, disposed of working capital amounting to 130 000 fl. and had offices in Spain, the Low Countries, Italy, and Switzerland. Its strength – and ultimately its weakness – was that it remained deliberately a purely trading company, handling and distributing goods, exports of linen in return for metal goods and spices. It did not seek to interfere in the production of linen-cloth (by putting-out), and it did not diversify into credit and banking. Having missed the opportunity to engage from Lisbon in the East Indies spice trade, the company was wound up in 1530. In its organization, it remained a halfway house

on the road to the family firm: an association of partners for specified terms, whose contracts were reviewed every six years; its
accounting procedures remained correspondingly cumbersome.

Another company whose fortunes were made on the back of the
eastern Swiss linen industry was the Diesbach-Watt Company of St
Gallen. From its origins in the early 1400s it opened branches in St
Gallen, Nuremberg, and Bern to handle linen-cloth, brass, and ironware, which it exported to Poland and Silesia in return for peltry and
wax, and to Catalonia and Aragon in return for the highly prized
commodity of saffron, used as a spice and as a dyestuff. Although it
did deploy putting-out in the linen industry of eastern Switzerland, it
shied away – just as the Ravensburg Trading Company – from investment in industry, mining, or finance. By the late 1450s the Diesbach-
Watt Company was in serious difficulties, caused not so much by
imprudent investment or diminishing entrepreneurship, but by the
political upheavals in northern Switzerland at the time of the Old
Zürich War. By 1460 it appears to have been wound up. Though
never matching its Ravensburg rival in size or in capital, the
Diesbach-Watt company was particularly successful in Spain, helped
by the resettlement of one of the Ravensburg Company's major
family investors, the Mötteli, to St Gallen in the 1450s.

By the end of the fifteenth century the age of the trading companies with multiple shareholders was passing. Into their shoes there
had begun to step aggressive and single-minded family firms,
accountable only to their immediate kin, and often run patriarchally
like families themselves. In any account of these firms, the rise of the
Fuggers from the peasant and part-time weaver in the Lech valley,
Hans Fugger, who emigrated to Augsburg in the mid-fourteenth
century, to Jakob Fugger two centuries later, already dubbed 'the
Rich' by his contemporaries, the greatest tycoon of his day, claims
pride of place. It is not to quibble with this verdict to point out that
the Fuggers – indeed the Augsburg commercial dynasties in general
– were relative latecomers, having been foreshadowed in the scope
of their operations and in innovative business practices by
Nuremberg merchant houses up to a century earlier. At the turn of
the fourteenth century the Kreß and Mendel in Nuremberg were
keeping their books *alla Venezia*, in the Venetian manner, that is to
say, using counterposed columns of debtors and creditors with trial
balances, while fully fledged double-entry bookkeeping was being
deployed by the Praun and Tucher by the 1480s. These accounting
practices, which permitted much greater supervision and control of

cash flow and capital reserves, were adopted in 1498 by the Welsers in Augsburg, and by other houses shortly thereafter. What made the Fuggers exceptional was both their deliberate engagement in banking – the Fugger Bank was founded in 1486 – whose capital was underwritten by their extensive investment in precious and base-metal mining ventures in eastern Europe and latterly Tirol, and their recognition that the success of their business depended upon polit-ical capital as well. The close alliance with the Habsburgs brought them monopolies and, above all, allowed them to acquire trading privileges and regalian rights in the mining industry (not least Tirol). By the mid-sixteenth century the Fuggers as a merchant house and as a bank had factories and branches spanning the globe. This commercial empire was secured upon a rigorous business struc-ture which allowed only direct male relatives into the firm's partner-ship and which conferred its managing directorship on a single man. Other family firms, such as the Welsers, admitted into partnership those who were related by marriage or even had no family connec-tions at all.

One measure of how far the Fuggers outstripped the Ravensburg Trading Company is to compare their working capital. The latter's capital of 130 000 fl. around 1500 had already been approached by the Fuggers in the 1460s. By 1527 the latter had amassed 2.8 million fl., and twenty years later, at the firm's peak, a staggering 7 million fl. This meteoric rise was abetted, however, by astute joint enterprises sealed through marriage alliances. Just as the Völhins left Memmingen for Augsburg, where they intermarried with the Welsers, and these in turn married into the Rem and Gossembrot dynasties, so the Fuggers' mining investment in eastern Europe was underpinned by marital links with the Thurzo family of Carpathian Germans, already involved in the industry. By the same token, thanks to its business structure, it was possible for branches of the family to fail without bringing down the entire concern, as happened when the Fugger vom Reh, based in Breslau (Wrocław), became extinct in 1586.

Partnerships, whether based on marriage alliances or not, were in fact much more common than the focus on single commercial dynasties suggests, whether it was the Gruber-Podmer-Stromer in fifteenth-century Nuremberg or the Haug-Langnauer-Linck in Augsburg in the sixteenth. That prompts in turn a wider question how far the fortunes and interests of individual firms can be equated with the economic performance of the cities as a whole in which they resided. The merchant houses in terms of their commercial clout and financial investments together comprised what Wolfgang von Stromer has termed a concentration of 'Upper German high finance',[*] but the collapse of that system in the second half of the sixteenth century did not necessarily spell the economic decline of individual cities such as Augsburg, whose true economic zenith may only have been achieved in the following century. Again, the role played by the Fuggers was somewhat unusual. Although Jakob Fugger and his brothers were notable benefactors of the city – they founded and endowed a vast complex of almshouses in the suburb of St Jakob known as the Fuggerei, which despite severe damage sustained in the Second World War still exists today – politically they remained at arm's length, at least until Emperor Charles V suspended the guild constitution in 1548. Unlike other leading merchant families such as the Welser, Rehlinger, Langenmantel, or Herwart they eschewed public office, placing the interests of family and firm before those of the commonweal. Their detachment was, of course, abetted by their resolute (and politically coloured) adherence to Catholicism as the city trod gingerly towards Protestantism up to mid-century. The investigation of economic mentalities – the search for the spirit of capitalism – has with some justice been discredited in recent years, but the Fuggers do offer an intriguing case-study precisely because their exceptional individualism and familism, combined with a ruthless pursuit of accumulation, have often been regarded as expressing a Protestant spirit, but, in their case, were in fact allied to staunch Catholicism.

After mid-century, as we have earlier remarked, many of the Augsburg merchant houses went bankrupt. Chief culprit was undoubtedly the injudicious (though politically essential) loans to ruling princes. When the Habsburg Philip II of Spain suspended interest-payments on his debts after 1550 (or, more accurately, defaulted), the knock-on-effects, and not only in Germany, were considerable. Similarly, the collapse of the French consortium of lenders to the crown, the Grand Parti, in which merchants of Strasbourg were involved, had dire repercussions for the city's trading firms. Most deeply implicated were the Ingolds, who became effectively insolvent by 1571; a string of bankruptcies in other houses followed over the next few years – the Mesingers, Minckels, Brauns, Engelmanns, and Marstallers – putting an end to Strasbourg's role

---

[*] Wolfgang von Stromer, *Oberdeutsche Hochfinanz 1350–1450*, 3 vols (Wiesbaden, 1970).

as a European centre of finance. Even the one merchant family who escaped, the Prechters (who had never lent to the French crown), were weakened by family deaths.

In Augsburg a change of generations at the head of many family firms around this time has also been observed, with less capable sons laying their hands on the tiller. Yet it was only those who had flown too close to the sun who plummeted, Icarus-like, to earth. The fortunes of middling entrepreneurs who had resisted the lure of high finance continued to flourish. That confirms the suspicion which we have already voiced, namely that the links between the fortunes of the leading commercial dynasties and the wider economic performance of the urban economy of Upper Germany were attenuated – the collapse of the former precipitated no conjunctural or structural changes in the latter. And, in passing, it might be added that the reverse could also apply. The hostilities with Burgundy, when Charles the Bold laid siege to Neuß in 1475, ruined Cologne's civic finances – Neuß was on its doorstep – but left its merchants and craftsmen relatively unscathed. For the cities of southern Germany as a whole we are confronted with the familiar image of the relay-race: as some centres declined, the baton passed to others which continued to prosper: in the west Ravensburg faltering as Ulm maintained its pre-eminence; or in the east, the supremacy of Regensburg in the fourteenth yielding to Nuremberg in the fifteenth, and that in turn to Augsburg in the course of the sixteenth century.

The reasons lay as much in the shifting pattern of trade routes – Regensburg's strategic position on the Danube could not halt the drift of commerce westwards to Franconia – or in political upheavals – Konstanz found its hinterland cut off when the Swiss took control of the Thurgau in 1460 – as in flagging enterprise on the part of their merchants. That, of course, applied generally throughout Germany: Erfurt, the centre of the Thuringian woad-trade, found itself sidelined by the rise of Leipzig in the course of the sixteenth century, as the Saxon dukes, backed by imperial privileges, promoted it as the preferred entrepôt – complete with international fairs – on the routes northwards from Franconia to Saxony, both regions of advanced mining, metallurgy, and manufacturing.

An assessment of German cities' commercial vitality is in any case further complicated by the growing involvement of princes in mercantile activities. The Fuggers' capital in their Slovakian and Carinthian mines had been raised in part from Hungarian prelates as well as from the prince-bishop of Bressanone/Brixen, Cardinal

Melchior von Meckau, who advanced a staggering total of 300 000 fl. But those were passive stakes; active partnerships could be forged as well. This can be seen in Thuringia, where Nuremberg and Augsburg merchants were heavily engaged in copper- and silver-mining and smelting. In 1524 a partnership was agreed between the counts of Mansfeld and Jakob Welser, for which they stumped up a total of 70 000 fl. By the 1540s, however, the counts were left as majority shareholders in the Mansfeld mines, as urban investors found themselves overstretched. Direct princely investment in mining was also undertaken by the dukes of Saxony, who took a stake in a tin-producing company in 1491, along with other share-holders drawn from the ranks of their officials, and who invested heavily in silver-mining in the Annaberg district on the Bohemian border, holding as many as 700 mining shares scattered over more than forty workings in 1535. Such partnerships or stake-holding might come as a welcome reinforcement for urban risk-capital, but princely initiatives could also be intended as competition for urban merchants. In the late sixteenth century, the dukes of Württemberg set out to challenge Ulm's ascendancy in the linen industry of western Swabia by reorganizing and extending existing production in the districts east of Stuttgart, and nominating Urach as the central place for bleaching and pressing linen-cloths, as well as for spinning silk yarn. This scheme, launched in 1598, was financed by the dukes using putting-out. Alas, the local weavers did not welcome this bureaucratic intervention, and the venture collapsed ten years later. The future of textile manufacturing in Württemberg was to remain in the hands of urban entrepreneurs and partnerships such as the Calw worsted manufacturing company, which we have already encountered.

Central Places and Town–Country Relations

The spread of commercial networks throughout the German lands in the centuries after 1300, linking the economies of regions to wider markets domestically and overseas in an ever-tighter mesh, went hand-in-hand with the intensification of urban systems, mani-fest in cities' attempts to control their hinterlands by economic and commercial as well as legal and political means. How we may best understand the cities' economic relations with their hinterlands has been suggested by the Swiss historical geographer, Hektor Ammann, whose researches were deeply indebted to the pioneers of central-place theory in Germany, above all Walter Christaller. Around any city, Ammann argued, three zones of centrality may be discerned. At first there was the immediate marketing area – the smallest unit of an urban economy – constituted by those who regularly visited the town's weekly market to exchange their produce and goods for urban supplies and manufactures. A second, wider marketing space extended beyond this zone, comprising a sphere of economic influence in which the town's manufactures were sold and from which outside artisans and merchants were periodically attracted to the town. Depending on the goods offered for sale, this broader market area could be quite extensive, even encompassing the narrower market areas of smaller towns. This area was roughly equivalent to the catchment area of the town's annual market. The third area of economic influence was determined by the intensity of long-distance trade, and corresponded by-and-large to the recruitment of a town's larger regional annual market or, in some instances, international fair. In practice, the radii of these three circles might range from 10 to 30 kilometres for the immediate market area (known in German as *Umland*); the wider market area (or *Hinterland*) might stretch up to 50 or 60 kilometres, but rarely further; while the outer sphere of influence (*Einflußbereich*), from which visitors to the annual fair might be drawn or migrants attracted to the city's labour market, could extend to 100 kilometres, or, in the case of true metropolises, even further.[*]

As we shall see, this pattern is extraordinarily suggestive in high-lighting changes in the extent of cities' domination of their sur-rounding countrysides, but it suffers from two immediate drawbacks, one theoretical, the other practical. It quickly comes up against inconvenient anomalies, with some areas of Germany woefully underprovided with towns of any kind, while others had clusters of towns jostling for centrality, giving rise to overlapping and appar-ently competing hinterlands. One obvious example is Württemberg, where the five largest towns in the area – Heilbronn, Schwäbisch Hall, Stuttgart, Eßlingen, and Reutlingen – all competed fiercely for space. Elsewhere, as in Saxony, the relationship between centres of similar rank-size seems not to correspond to concentric circles (or, as Walter Christaller systematized it, into a series of interlocking hexagons), but to comets' tails or chain-links, the prime instance

---

[*] Ammann, *Wirtschaftliche Stellung*, pp. 194 ff.

being the concentration of economic activity around Erfurt as the centre of Thuringian woad-production, at one pole, and Görlitz dominating the textile industry of the Silesian-Lusatian borderlands, on the other. These two cities appear as barbells at either end of a rod, linked by reciprocal supply and demand along a commercial axis with Naumburg, Leipzig, Freiberg, and Dresden as staging-posts along its route. In other words, centrality can be axial as well as radial, with towns being linked as nodes, junctions, outposts, or relays in a trading network. In a country whose communications were so heavily dependent on its river system, that point hardly needs to be laboured: the wine-exporting communes of Alsace, for instance, were located along the river Ill until it joined the Rhine at Strasbourg at regular intervals like 'pearls on a string' (again, Christaller's phrase),[*] with their market areas no longer circular but squeezed into ellipses, whose short axis was formed by the river, so that they resembled the sails of a schooner mirrored in the water, with the ellipses projecting both skywards and downwards. Again, topography and natural endowment might render centrality dendritic, that is, shaped like the trunk of a tree with branches emanating from it, so that the metropolis appears as the gateway of an elongated hinterland. That was the case with many ports, which channelled goods from a delta-like hinterland through a narrower outlet, or else of towns located where mountain valleys debouched into the plain. Many of the coastal Hanseatic cities functioned in this way, which helps to explain why, despite appearances, ports such as Lübeck, Wismar, Rostock, and Stralsund, huddled together on the Baltic littoral, did not, in fact, compete for space.

These varieties of centrality, moreover, were neither mutually exclusive nor immutable. Erfurt's centrality, for instance, rested upon a tripod: its position as the economic capital and chief market of Thuringia (radial); its location as a node of trade routes which intersected north–south and east–west (axial); and its umbilical relationship to Görlitz (a variant of portal centrality). In the course of the sixteenth century, Erfurt's radial centrality dwindled in parallel with the downturn in woad-production – as a result of competition as a dyestuff from indigo; its axial centrality was challenged (as we have noted) by the rise of Leipzig as a major entrepôt. Or take Nördlingen in northern Swabia, which had lost much of its significance as a long-distance trading city, boasting an international fair,

---

[*] Walter Christaller, *Central Places in Southern Germany* (Englewood Cliffs, NJ, 1966), p. 58.

by the middle of the sixteenth century. The city was gradually reduced to no more than a market centre for its hinterland, as its council turned cautiously to strengthening control over its immediate market area. Often, however, control of a city's *Umland* was only the launching-pad for a much more ambitious policy of regional economic hegemony, where commercial privileges buttressed the influence which was already being exerted through the putting-out system.

It is at this point that the practical drawback to any perfect-mesh system of centrality becomes evident, for the efforts by German cities to control the economy of their hinterlands were matched by vigorous competition from rural craftsmen and village markets. We shall pursue these points in turn. In principle, within a town's market precinct (*Bannmeile*) any attempts to evade or pre-empt the urban market by forestalling or hawking were forbidden, and foreign lords prohibited from levying tolls or turnpike charges. In the period 1350 to 1600 cities strove to expand their precincts from the usually restricted radius of one or two German miles, though not necessarily on all commodities. To take evidence from Swabia, which has been exhaustively investigated by Rolf Kießling,[*] a small town such as Lauingen doubled its general franchise in the mid-sixteenth century from one to two miles in a deliberate move to fend off commercial encroachment from Augsburg, but at the same time imposed a four-mile franchise for loden cloth subject to its quality control, since the town could not obtain sufficient supplies of wool in the locality. Larger metropolises were noticeably more aggressive in extending their precincts. Augsburg had begun in the fifteenth century with a modest one-mile franchise, but by 1500 this had risen to three miles, and thereafter was extended to six or even ten miles (74 km) on occasion. The goal which prompted these measures was nothing less than the attempted subordination of the textile production of eastern Swabia to the city's quality control, so that Augsburg could dominate its marketing and distribution. By contrast, a small Swabian territorial town such as Mindelheim had no need to impose a market franchise or insist on monopsony at all, since its lords, the Frundsbergs, while stripping the community of any political autonomy, ensured that it functioned as the principal central place for their territory as a whole, so that its geographical boundaries at

---

[*] Rolf Kießling, *Die Stadt und ihr Land. Umlandpolitik, Bürgerbesitz und Wirtschaftsgefüge in Ostschwaben vom 14. bis ins 16. Jahrhundert* (Cologne/Vienna, 1989).

the same time constituted Mindelheim's market precinct. By the six-teenth century the franchise area for most medium-sized towns in Swabia had reached two to three miles, for the larger cities six to eight miles.

How effective these measures were is another matter. One of the contradictions of the cities' policies was that they simultaneously sought to encourage manufacturing in their hinterlands, provided that they could organize it to their own advantage through the putting-out system, while lamenting the competition which they faced from rural crafts and village markets. All the legislation to extend franchises and enforce monopsony seems to have had little effect. In Swabia, Nördlingen, Memmingen, and Kempten all com-plained at the challenge to their chartered markets posed by rival foundations (or informal marketing) in their hinterlands. Even the territorial town of Mindelheim, just cited, despite being insulated from any immediate threat by the *cordon sanitaire* of Frundsberg terri-torial lordship, found itself confronted with market competition from beyond its (admittedly not very extensive) borders.

The proliferation of country crafts and village markets was by no means confined to Swabia. Within Germany there is scarcely a region, from Mecklenburg or Saxony in the north, to Bavaria, Swabia, and Switzerland in the south, where the threat of rural com-petition did not exercise urban magistrates or territorial rulers. It is generally agreed, however, that the greatest concentration was in south-west Germany and Switzerland, areas of relatively dense popu-lation and of partible inheritance, to be sure, but ones with few obvious signs (until the closing decades of the sixteenth century) of rural immiseration, such as the rise of a cottar class. On the Upper Rhine the middling territorial towns seem to have been hit harder than the larger independent imperial cities, which might indicate that the construction of a rural territory offered some protection against economic competition from the countryside. That has cer-tainly been argued for the imperial cities of Swabia and, switching focus, for Westphalia, where the city of Soest – a powerful inland member of the Hanseatic League – used its territorial sovereignty to suppress artisan activity and to enforce monopsony in the sur-rounding area, known as the Börde, under its rule. As a general statement, however, this explanation does not hold water, for it ignores, above all, the experience of the powerful Swiss city-states, whose metropolises without exception were exposed to burgeoning crafts and informal marketing in their cantonal hinterlands.

After 1500, moreover, country craftsmen frequently banded together in rural guilds outside civic control. The evidence for Switzerland (which is plentiful, unlike the rest of the German-speaking lands) shows just how intractable the problem was. Some cities (and not necessarily those which controlled the most territory) were able to suppress the guilds as formal associations – Zürich, Basel, and Schaffhausen succeeded, though Luzern's efforts partly failed. But that did not make the underlying problem go away. In the wake of the so-called Waldmann affair in 1489 (a political upheaval engineered by a demagogic mayor) Zürich had been forced to make sweeping concessions to craftsmen, petty traders, and middlemen in its hinterland; elsewhere, Bern and Luzern acquiesced in a policy of partial toleration. The most interesting case, though, is that of Fribourg (Freiburg im Üchtland), where the council pursued a differential strategy according to the craft in question. Weavers of quality woollen-cloth were required to move to the town and submit to civic inspection; the linen-weavers and other lesser textile workers were allowed to stay put, while the tanners – a significant trade in an area of commercial cattle-rearing – were permitted for occupational reasons to remain in the countryside, but had to submit to integration into and regulation by the urban tanners' guild. Whether any of these attempts to restrict rural crafts were crowned with much success is open to question. In the long run, the issue was resolved for the territorial towns by their princely rulers 'territorializing' crafts and manufacturing, that is to say, integrating rural crafts into a common structure embracing town and country, Bavaria being the classic example. But that solution was only achieved at the price of eroding or destroying the traditional liberties and ancient market privileges of the territorial towns. For their part, the imperial and free cities had to shift as best they could.

Stages of Urban Expansion

In many cases their survival was buttressed by the construction of a dependent rural territory, a hallmark of the belt of small but often economically vibrant urban polities in Europe stretching from northern Italy over the Alps to the German lands and the Low Countries, which at their most consolidated and powerful deserve the name of city-states. Within the spectrum of territorial expansion the cities of Germany stand halfway between the experience of the leading cities of Flanders and the achievement of the germanophone city-states of the Swiss Confederation. In the case of the former – Ghent, Bruges, and Ypres, powerful manufacturing and commercial metropolises exercising economic sway over their hinterlands, known as 'quarters' – attempts to carve out truly independent city-states were thwarted by the authority of the counts of Flanders and, at one remove, the French crown; for the latter – Bern, Luzern, Zürich, and Basel – the establishment of rural dependencies meant in the first instance the political and judicial subordination of their surrounding areas, though the cities were certainly not blind to the economic and fiscal opportunities which their territories afforded. The German cities were strung out at intermediate points between these two poles. Some, such as Nuremberg, sought to acquire land which would directly serve their commercial interests as a source of labour and raw materials; others, such as Augsburg and Cologne, came to dominate the economies of their hinterlands without ever amassing (or being able to amass) a landed territory of any size. Nuremberg was a city-state in all but name; Augsburg and Cologne echoed the regional economic sway exercised by the Flemish cities.

Urban territorial expansion in Germany has traditionally been seen as unfolding through three distinct stages: first, the acquisition by individual citizens of property rights and revenues in the countryside; then, the development of personal or corporate ties between countrydwellers and cities in the form of outburghership, or else of protective agreements which afforded cities access to strategic strongholds in times of military emergency or more continuous supervision of turnpikes, toll-stages, and bridges in peacetime; finally, the acquisition of lands and subjects by the city as a corporation, either as a mortgage which might later be redeemed, or as the launching-pad for consolidation into a dependent territory, over which the magistracy possessed exclusive jurisdiction. These stages are not always clearly distinguishable, let alone chronologically successive. In some instances measures to control a city's immediate market area (*Umlandpolitik*) might go much further towards securing domination of the countryside than the formal construction of a rural territory. Some historians have shied away from the term 'territorial policy', advocating instead a more neutral description such as the 'acquisition of rural estates', precisely because a deliberate territorial policy with anti-feudal and anti-princely overtones so rarely informed the motives of the ruling elites of German cities.

By examining these stages in turn, the mixture of motives – including reversals and contradictions – underlying territorial expansion will emerge. For a string of south German imperial cities in Swabia the acquisition of rural property by individual burghers was the necessary – though not always the sufficient – prerequisite of any subsequent territorial consolidation. The range of such acquisitions corresponded closely to the size, or the economic pull, of the city itself. For Augsburg, the regional metropolis, the radius of bourgeois property extended as far as 40 or even 60 kilometres; for sub-regional centres such as Memmingen, Nördlingen, or Kaufbeuren it was no more than 20 kilometres; but for local market towns such as Kempten, Donauwörth, or Lauingen a mere 10 to 15 kilometres. In the case of Augsburg (which was too hemmed in by its bishopric and the duchy of Bavaria to convert these extensive individual rights into a fully fledged territory) citizens might invest in land for a variety of reasons: status and privilege – to assemble over time a congeries of estates as the nucleus of a dynastic lordship upon which a patent of nobility might be conferred; financial insurance – to use estates as a security or cash reserve to offset risks incurred in long-distance trade; or commercial exploitation – to use land as the vehicle for agricultural improvement. One instance is the Fuggers (who might well qualify under each of the preceding headings) in their lordship of Mickhausen, south-west of the city, where they ruthlessly enclosed land, evicted sitting tenants and established cottars in their place, in order to reap the profits from intensive sheep-farming. This pattern is repeated in the Wendish cities of the Hanseatic League along the Baltic coast. Here, too, burghers bought up estates as a capital reserve or substitute bank, and the turnover of such estates could, not surprisingly, be rapid. But this essentially conservative motive contrasts with the aggressive intervention of certain Stralsund merchants in the grain and wool production of the island of Rügen in the early fifteenth century, where they established a purchasing monopoly and made substantial profits. The rate of return on landed property was modest; around 3 to 5 per cent (as figures for Nuremberg suggest) seems to have been usual. The much higher rate posited for the Wendish cities, of around 8 to 9 per cent, strikes one as implausibly high.

What was essentially a defensive investment contrasts with agricultural improvements elsewhere. In Thuringia, where land was being bought up for sheep-pastures, burghers of Erfurt were acquiring land to cultivate woad, to the city's benefit as processing and distribution were channelled through Erfurt's guilds and market. A similar development can be traced in Cologne's hinterland around Düren and Jülich, where citizens were sowing vetches and clover as catch-crops to improve the nitrogen content of the soil on their rural estates as early as the fourteenth century. In the same period in the environs of Nuremberg pine trees were being planted on sandy soil ill-suited to tillage, until two centuries later council and citizens combined to turn the dry land into lush meadows by improved irrigation through the use of bucket-wheels.

Where not only individuals but urban ecclesiastical and charitable foundations acquired rural property, magistracies gained an added political opportunity, for they frequently held the stewardships of such corporations. As a bulwark against the designs of the surrounding nobility, the smaller and less powerful cities of Swabia showed themselves particularly adept at extending control of their hinterlands by stealthily appropriating their hospitals' rural holdings. That could occur in the larger cities as well. Memmingen's Lower Hospital, effectively under civic control by the fifteenth century, played a crucial role in the city's construction of a rural territory, while even Augsburg initially acquired indirect domination over its hinterland through holding the stewardship of the city's hospitals, parish funds, and friaries. In this manner, not only their lands and subjects but the jurisdictional authority over them passed into civic hands.

Such a conflation of landlordship and jurisdictional lordship encouraged cities to extend rights of citizenship to their allies and dependents in the countryside in the form of outburghership. The granting of citizen's rights to countrydwellers was a pervasive institution in the German-speaking lands, though its significance has been downplayed by historians content to emphasize the cities' areal expansion. Only in Switzerland and in the Low Countries has outburghership been accorded its due weight, but a comparison between them underscores the very contrasting purposes that it served. What determined the growth of the Swiss Confederation in the fourteenth century was the network of protective alliances which the inner valleys and communes concluded with leading cities to the north. Undergirding this development was the large-scale manumission of serfs, who thereupon acquired burgher's rights – in some cases in their thousands – in cities such as Luzern, Bern, and Zürich. Outburghership could be as much in the cities' as in the peasants' interests: indeed, it was the principal means whereby Bern contrived to undermine the power of the local nobility and to construct a vast rural territory which became the largest city-state north of the Alps.

In the southern Low Countries, by contrast, outburghership was not used as an instrument of state-building. While the three leading cities of Flanders – Bruges, Ghent, and Ypres – all held outburghers (including members of the local nobility), it was the lesser towns which most assiduously granted citizen's rights to the rural population, not least as a demographic and economic insurance policy against being overwhelmed or swallowed up by the three metropolises. Indeed, there are some indications that the counts of Flanders themselves encouraged the lesser towns to acquire outburghers as a political counterweight to their arch-rivals, the *drie steden,* as they were called. Whereas Bruges, Ghent, and Ypres regulated outburghership strictly, for instance by attempting to enforce a requirement to reside for part of the year within their walls, the lesser towns often found themselves faced with the problem of double citizenship, as their outburghers took out citizenship in other small towns or in the larger cities. This underlines the essentially commercial benefits which outburghership was seen as offering those whose livelihood depended on access to urban markets; politically, it worked to thwart, not to abet, any territorial consolidation in the form of city-states.

Within Germany proper the function of outburghership fell unevenly between the two poles of Switzerland and Flanders. Up to the mid-fourteenth century many free and imperial cities, particularly in southern Germany, had acquired outburghers under several headings: individual noblemen, convents as corporate citizens, or even peasants (who were usually called paleburghers). Once Emperor Charles IV's Golden Bull of 1356 had outlawed the acceptance of paleburghers, the number of peasant outburghers generally declined, though they rarely disappeared altogether. Only Nuremberg, with its strong imperial connections, seems to have observed the ban on paleburghers rigorously, requiring any such countrydwellers to immigrate to the city within a given time limit. In the case of Frankfurt am Main, another city with close imperial ties, the institution of paleburghership was superseded by the assertion of judicial sovereignty over all its rural dependents (which amounted to much the same thing), while noble outburghership was replaced in the later fifteenth century by a series of bilateral service and protective alliances, which included access to the nobles' castles. Nevertheless, a string of Swabian cities – Nördlingen, Memmingen, Lauingen, as well as Augsburg – managed to retain both noble and peasant outburghers, while in Alsace the number of Strasbourg's peasant outburghers may even have increased. Most surprising of all, some territorial towns, whose subordination to princely overlordship should have rendered outburghership well-nigh impossible to sustain, also acquired and retained rural citizens. Outburghership, indeed, might serve as the specific substitute for a city's failure to construct a rural territory. For Cologne, caught between powerful ecclesiastical and secular princes (just as Augsburg), the treaties of alliance with the local nobility in the form of outburghership helped compensate for its inability to pursue territorial expansion. Elsewhere, binding wealthy rural convents to civic interests by obliging them to acquire corporate citizenship, as practised by Augsburg, was a useful means of harnessing and channelling their economic clout as substantial landowners.

In general, outburghership was embraced for essentially defensive purposes – to secure a demographic and fiscal reservoir which would buttress the oppidan population and finances, and to reinforce the civic militia in times of war. How much a lifeline it afforded can be seen in the case of Freiburg im Breisgau, which, despite being a territorial town within Habsburg Outer Austria, clung grimly to its rural peasant citizens throughout decades of economic and demographic crisis in the fifteenth century, even though it was assailed on all sides by the margraves of Baden and its own noble outburghers. Freiburg's rural subjects may have added another 10 per cent to the urban population; only in the first two decades of the sixteenth century did the council throw in the towel and sell the three largest of its outburgher communities to their village lords (themselves noble outburghers of the town!), but by then Freiburg had turned the corner economically. The evidence for Swabia which we glanced at in Chapter 4, however, provides a hint that on occasion outburghership may have operated in tandem with cities' attempts to control the manufacturing output of their hinterlands, as the examples of linen-weavers alongside outburghers in Kempten and Isny seem to suggest, in an echo of the experience of the lesser Flemish cities.

The Construction of Landed Territories

The most visible manifestation of cities' growing control of their countrysides from the fourteenth to the sixteenth centuries remained, none the less, the construction of landed territories. Here an immediate difference between north and south Germany obtrudes. While many south German imperial cities, including quite small ones, and even some territorial towns, were able to convert a miscellany of estates, jurisdictions, privileges, and protective agreements into consolidated dependencies, in the north only a handful of larger cities succeeded, and even then mainly by means of mortgages rather than outright purchases (Erfurt being the prominent exception). That was especially true of the leading Hanseatic cities: Braunschweig and Lüneburg as inland members relied almost exclusively, and the major ports of Bremen, Hamburg, and Lübeck to a large degree, upon acquisitions by mortgage. Despite the political constraints which stood in the way of a concerted territorial policy in northern Germany, the recourse to mortgages was determined in the end by commercial considerations. For the members of the Hansa, the protection of trade routes and the maintenance of commercial privileges were much more important than the acquisition of rural territories for their own sake. Mortgages were a convenient means of reaching an accommodation with neighbouring princes who might otherwise prey upon the cities' merchants.

This can readily be illustrated by the decision of the Lübeck magistracy in 1392 to hand back a string of mortgaged lordships to the dukes of Braunschweig in return for the proclamation of a regional public peace. Commercial interests also hold the key to the location of mortgaged territories. Rather than being grouped around the cities, as would have been the case if they had been the hinterlands of cities acting as central places in a market network, the mortgages were distributed axially, rather than radially, along strategic trade routes, overland or by sea. That is clearly visible in the case of the Hanseatic capital Lübeck, which acquired the town and bailiwick of Mölln, 25 kilometres due south, from the dukes of Saxony-Lauenburg in 1359, and held them in mortgage for over three centuries until 1683. Mölln was a vantage-point southwards on the river Stecknitz, a vital artery to the lucrative brine-pits of Lüneburg which the city had canalized at the end of the fourteenth century. Over the next two hundred years similar motives prompted Lübeck to purchase as mortgages the island of Fehmarn (1437–91), overseeing shipping routes in the western Baltic, from the dukes of Schleswig, and then the island of Bornholm (1525–76) off the southern coast of Sweden after its capture by the Hanseatic League from the Danish crown. Any financial benefit from these mortgages was an entirely secondary consideration. Lübeck's expenditure on Mölln at one point greatly exceeded its income, yet up to the seventeenth century the city never increased taxes or renders from the town or bailiwick. Fehmarn, for its part, had cost Lübeck 18000 marks in 1437, but in the 53 years of the mortgage the city made a net profit of no more than 24000 marks, the equivalent of an annual rate of return of a mere 2.5 per cent.

Mortgages were a shifting sand upon which to construct any lasting territorial policy, for they could so easily be redeemed. Lübeck – whose control of Mölln for over three hundred years was quite exceptional – made but one attempt to erect a territorial buffer (as opposed to a commercial vantage-point) when it took on the mortgage of the sizeable bailiwick of Segeberg from the counts of Holstein in the mid-fourteenth century, but that experiment lasted no longer than a generation. All told, many Hanseatic and north German cities lost territory over time from their heyday in the fourteenth century – Lübeck (despite its later mortgages), Braunschweig, Lüneburg, Soest, and Goslar. And that also applied to the one imperial city in central Germany which had resorted to a mortgage policy, namely Frankfurt am Main. Of its 19 acquisitions by mortgage between 1300 and 1500, mostly concentrated along commercial arteries to the north and north-west of the city, only 13 remained at the beginning of the sixteenth century: the rest had been redeemed.

Yet some Hanseatic cities did build up modest territories in the fifteenth century. Of the Wendish ports, that was true of Rostock, Greifswald, and Stralsund; only Wismar had almost none. There territories were sometimes physically demarcated by a so-called *Landwehr*, a rampart-and-ditch, surmounted by a thorn hedge, with the roads passing it being guarded by gates and watchtowers. Lübeck (which owned a good deal of land close to the city, aside from its mortgages further afield), Hamburg, and Braunschweig all had *Landwehren* marking off their jurisdictions, though the best-known examples of such fortified boundary-lines were those of Rothenburg ob der Tauber and Schwäbisch Hall in the south. The few imperial cities in northern Germany – Dortmund, Soest, Goslar, and Mühlhausen – all managed to acquire dependent territories, but the most remarkable instance – a fish out of water – remained Erfurt. Despite being effectively shorn of its imperial status by the archbishops of Mainz in the later fifteenth century, Erfurt could boast in 1500 a territory of at least 610 square km., comprising over 60 villages and the small town of Sömmerda. This achievement is not solely intelligible against the background of Erfurt's considerable investment in Thuringian woad-production; it also stemmed from its axial centrality at the intersection of major trade routes, and its reciprocal commercial ties with the textile manufacturing towns of Lusatia and Silesia – the tripod of centrality which has been described above.

It remains true, none the less, that the greatest concentration of civic territories was to be found among the ranks of the south German imperial cities (see Table 5.1). Leading the way, and twice as large as its nearest rival, was Nuremberg, once it had acquired the *Neue Landschaft* from the Palatinate in 1504, whose territory comprised six towns, seven chartered markets and more than 70 villages. Next came Ulm, which began buying up lordships in western Swabia from its surrounding secular and ecclesiastical nobility in the late fourteenth century; by the sixteenth, its territory encompassed three towns, 55 villages and 22 other dependencies. After Erfurt, in third place, came the Franconian city of Rothenburg (whose territory derived largely from the estates of one bourgeois proprietor amassed around 1400), Schwäbisch Hall in northern Württemberg, Rottweil on the eastern fringes of the Black Forest, and Strasbourg, the metropolis of Alsace. Apart from their status as imperial or free cities, these cities had no common denominator. They were, however, only

Table 5.1 Territories of German and Swiss cities in the early sixteenth century (in square kilometres)

	German cities	Size		Swiss cantons	Size
1	Nuremberg*	1200	1	Bern**	9000
2	Ulm	830	2	Zürich	1700
3	Erfurt***	610	3	Luzern	1485
4	Rothenburg ob der Tauber	400	4	Solothurn	780
5	Schwäbisch Hall	330	5	Basel	460
6=	Strasbourg	220	6	Schaffhausen	295
	Rottweil		7	Zug	240

*   Includes the *Neue Landschaft* (1504). Some authorities give 1600 sq. km., but this is incorrect.
**   Includes the Vaud (acquired 1536).
***   Other estimates put the figure at 900 sq. km., but this figure is much too high.

the tip of the iceberg. In Upper Swabia alone, apart from Ulm, and Biberach's very scattered possessions, two further groups of cities can be distinguished: those with medium-sized territories of some influence, among them Memmingen and Lindau, and others whose territory barely extended beyond the immediate urban precinct, such as Kempten (confined by its powerful abbey), and Isny.

The economic and demographic significance of these rural territories for the cities of Germany, however, cannot be measured by size alone. For the largest city territories, those of Nuremberg and Ulm, the rural population may have added another 40 per cent and 60 per cent respectively to the urban total; in Rothenburg and Schwäbisch Hall, by contrast, each with a population of 5000 or just over, their territories added as much as 150 per cent and 220 per cent respectively to the oppidan figure. Beyond Swabia, the population of Strasbourg's directly controlled territory came to 10 000, that is, just under half the number living within the city walls, but if the lands indirectly under civic control (bourgeois estates and the properties of convents and charitable foundations) are taken into account, they add another 13 000 (and 500 sq. km.!) to the previous total. And even Frankfurt's territory, though diminutive (a mere 100 sq. km.), was densely populated, with 5000 subjects at the end of the *ancien régime.*

However impressive these figures may be, the fact remains that German city territories rarely rivalled their Swiss counterparts. Even a relatively insignificant canton such as Solothurn was larger than any German city-state except Nuremberg and Ulm. And indeed, the comparison shows how poorly size correlates with economic clout. In the course of the sixteenth century, Basel became the financial nerve centre of the Confederation, with almost 59 per cent of finance for public loans being raised on the city's capital market, yet its territory, hemmed in by topography (the Jura alps to the south) and by political geography (the block of Outer Austrian lands in Upper Alsace) remained relatively modest in size. In terms of manufacturing and commerce, moreover, it is arguable that Zürich was much more important than the essentially agricultural Bern, a huge territory more than five times its extent. Much the same applies to Germany, where only the first three cities had territories commensurate with (and contributing to) their economic ranking. Rothenburg, Schwäbisch Hall, and Rottweil, by contrast, had an economic pull decidedly inferior to, say, Nördlingen, Konstanz, or Memmingen. And spanning the emergent political frontier on the Upper Rhine in the sixteenth century, Basel (Swiss from 1501), despite the constraints already mentioned, still controlled a territory twice the size of the regional metropolis, Strasbourg, a linch-pin of Germany's international commerce.

Such discrepancies should counsel us against assuming too uniform or consistent a purpose in the territorial policies of the German cities. As often as not, territorial expansion was opportunist and piecemeal, beset by hesitations and reversals. Even singlemindedness and success might exact their price – as Nuremberg discovered after its conquest of the *Neue Landschaft* unleashed a string of suits before the imperial court of chancery which continued unabated up to 1806! On occasion both Nuremberg and Ulm spurned the chance of acquiring yet more territory, reckoning that on balance it would bring more trouble than it was worth. Yet the fact that so many cities chose to pursue a territorial policy at all (however haltingly) suggests some underlying common strands.

Defensive considerations were paramount. The cities' need to secure their own subsistence meant that protecting supplies of essential foodstuffs, above all grain, was a constant preoccupation. Beyond that, rural dependencies provided a useful source of income, at least for the south German cities, if less so for Hanseatic communes. A broadly typical rate of return was 5 per cent, as Rothenburg ob der Tauber, for instance, achieved from its territory. But in some cases the figure could be much higher: around 10 per cent of Frankfurt's civic taxes came from just 10 of its villages, while in years of good harvest a startling 22 per cent of Ulm's income derived from its extensive rural territory.

The cities undoubtedly saw their territories as a demographic reservoir, compensating for the notorious inability of pre-industrial towns to reproduce their populations without immigration. But that betokened no willingness to accord their rural subjects any preferential status, let alone citizenship. Almost without exception the latter were, and remained, serfs, though – to take the case of Ulm – the inhabitants of its three dependent towns (Geislingen, Albeck, and Leipheim) lived under a lighter form of residential serfdom than its villagers, who were bound by a more onerous personal or bodily serfdom. By contrast, where towns had already acquired peasant outburghers (paleburghers) on some scale, the experience of Freiburg im Breisgau towards 1500 shows that in the constant friction with local lords their status was in practice being eroded to that of serfs, on a par with the feudal lords' dependants.

But defensive interests did not preclude more aggressive motives, which might be as much political as commercial. The leading Swiss city-states offer a useful comparison. The city fathers of Bern, aristocrats in all but name with extensive feudal estates, were primarily concerned to buttress their rural power, rather than to invest in trade, with the result that the pursuit of territorial aggrandizement, culminating in the conquest of the Vaud from the house of Savoy in 1536, became the city's *raison d'être*. Bern was extraordinarily successful, but the economy of its hinterland was left largely untouched. Its rival Zürich, on the other hand, whose magistracy most certainly included feudal magnates and pensionaries profiting from the trade in mercenaries, was also a city of textile manufacturers and merchants, who likewise had seats on the council. Zürich's territorial policy, therefore, was driven not only by the need to protect its patricians' landed interests but also by commercial imperatives, above all control of the rivers which bore Zürich's trade northwards to the Rhine and southwards over the alpine passes to Italy.

Patterns of Integration and Subordination

The protection and promotion of commercial interests, however, need not depend upon the control of a rural territory, nor was the size of the latter any sure indicator of the cities' ability to absorb or ward off economic competition from their hinterlands. Cologne and Augsburg, after all, had no rural territory worth speaking of. To make sense of these anomalies we may, in conclusion, usefully set the experience of Germany's three leading commercial metropolises – Nuremberg, Augsburg, and Cologne – against each other to see what underlying patterns may be discerned. Nuremberg, with the largest territory of any German city, brought neighbouring towns and cities beyond its immediate market area into the orbit of its cloth- and metal-working industries. This was more than an act of economic imperialism: the communities themselves were eager to grab a share of Nuremberg's industrial prosperity and marketing power, though on occasion they drew the short straw: Wöhrd's textile industry on Nuremberg's doorstep was stripped of its independence by the beginning of the sixteenth century, with quality control brought firmly under the supervision of the drapers' hall in the city. Beyond this hinterland lay an arc of cloth-producing towns to the south-west and another of metallurgical centres to the east, both possessing sufficient economic centrality to set bounds upon Nuremberg's radius of influence. Within these arcs – in effect a circle – lay Nuremberg's economic unit (to use Hektor Ammann's term), in which metropolis and subaltern central places combined in a mutually reinforcing integrated regional economic system. Beyond that lay, of course, a wider sphere of influence, but once the levers of economic power were no longer direct but indirect, with the city reliant upon middlemen and agents, then this outer third circle was clearly no longer part of the city's 'economic unit'.

In the case of Cologne, a city without a landed territory, the 'economic unit' was not only somewhat larger than Nuremberg's, with a maximum radius of around 70 kilometres as opposed to the latter's 50 kilometres, it was less thoroughly integrated, too. If we plot Cologne's 'economic unit' cartographically, what stands out is the highly fluctuating size of its trade-specific areas of supply and putting-out. These range from a tightly drawn ellipse for hops, through a somewhat larger oval for cloth, to a circle of steel suppliers lying entirely eccentric of the city east of the Rhine, with a yet larger and irregular circle of copper and iron suppliers concentric around the city, to the largest circle of all, that of suppliers of peltry. It would be hazardous simply to equate Cologne's 'economic unit' with the largest circle *tout court*, not least because peltry was of much less importance to the city's economy than metal goods or cloth. Rather, we should conceive of the city's 'economic unit' in terms of variable geometry, with different configurations and levels of intensity, provided that we avoid the twin errors of supposing that Cologne as the metropolis must necessarily always lie at the centre of its component hinterlands, or that the immediate market area closest to the city must constitute its essential regional core. Instead, Cologne's centrality is clearly comprised of radial, axial, and portal elements (rather like Erfurt's).

With Augsburg, by contrast, Cologne's direct counterpart as an overseas manufacturing and trading city without a dependent territory, an entirely different situation confronts us. Its 'economic unit', it is true, had a radius of around 60 to 70 kilometres; by 1550 its active textile hinterland, in terms of weavers under civic control or of migrants to the city, may even have amounted to no more than 40 kilometres, with the small and medium-sized towns situated therein fulfilling the role of sub-central collection points or intermediate markets in a smoothly integrated system. But on the fringes of its economic unit, where its influence should have been weakest,

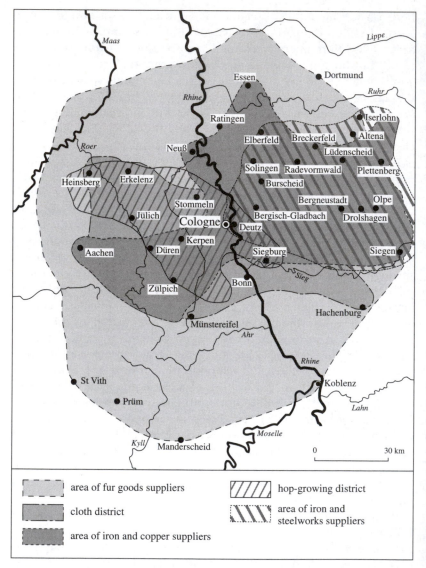

5.3   Cologne's economic hinterland, c.1500 (after F. Irsigler)

Augsburg began to act as a predator with overt monopolistic tendencies. The city's fustian merchants and putters-out began to throttle
the textile industry of towns at the fringes of its economic unit –
Lauingen just within the 70-kilometre radius, Nördlingen and

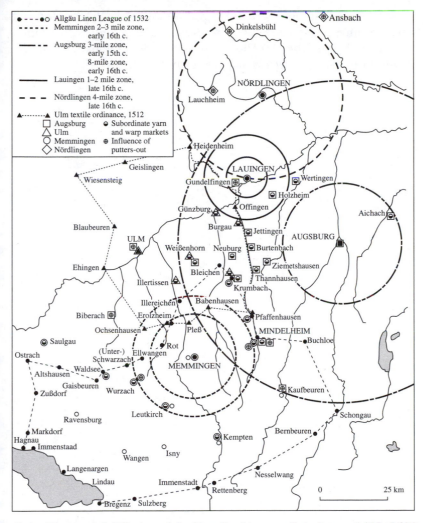

5.4   The spatial diffusion of the East Swabian textile industry, 1400–1600 (after R. Kießling)

Memmingen just outside – and even threatened the western Swabian metropolis of Ulm. This in large measure accounts for Nördlingen's switch from fustian to loden production, and Lauingen's turn towards wool or the coarse linen-cloth known as *Golschen*. In the long run, the middling cities of eastern Swabia found their economic vitality stunted in the shade of Augsburg's commercial upas-tree – a contradictory result of market integration and the intensification of town–country relations which in the German context remained exceptional, but which seems to reflect a general pattern in the economy of early modern Europe as a whole.

6 *Lordship and Dependence*

The Late Medieval Agrarian Crisis

Rural society in the German-speaking lands throughout our period rested, as elsewhere in Europe, on the twin pillars of seigneurial domination and the village commune. By 1300 the old manorial system of the high Middle Ages was in the last stages of dissolution. Landlords were abandoning the direct exploitation of their estates by labour services in favour of leasing out their lands to tenants who paid rents in kind or in cash. In parallel, the old instruments of seigneurial control through the manorial court, which bound peasants to the lords' exclusive jurisdiction, were yielding to a rural polity comprised of communes – in villages, valleys, or coastal regions – with considerable powers of local autonomy and self-policing. Membership of the commune became the hallmark of peasant status, rather than subjection to a manorial constitution.

For the centuries after 1300, therefore, the existential issue for rural society was the ability of lords to maintain their social and economic position through the extraction of rent, and the repercussions upon the village commune if their income should decline. By the end of our period, in 1600, the remarkable fact is that in western Germany the basic fabric of rural society had barely altered: a landowning aristocracy living in large measure from rental income side-by-side with a peasantry enjoying good security of tenure (often hereditary), with a recognized place (albeit lowly) in the social and legal order, and sometimes with a measure of political representation at territorial level. All this despite the agrarian crisis of the late Middle Ages, sharp fluctuations in population, prices, and wages, and despite an undercurrent of peasant resistance to seigneurial demands which burst forth in numerous agrarian uprisings, most notably in the so-called German Peasants' War of 1524–26, which engulfed much of southern and central Germany, as well as tracts of the Habsburg dynastic lands in Austria and south Tirol. In the lands east of the Elbe, in marked contrast, lord–peasant relations underwent a profound transformation, whereby landlords recurred to direct exploitation of their domains, using servile labour, and progressively eroding not only the peasants' legal status but their social and economic position as producers who possessed the land they tilled and who determined its use and productivity as well. Here the peasantry was degraded and expropriated in the name of a new form of domanial economy, driven not by manorial self-sufficiency (as in the high Middle Ages) but by commercial cereal agriculture serving overseas export markets in western Europe.

That, at least, is the traditional picture, which, in its broad outlines, may indeed be accurate. But it is an account which raises more questions than it answers, and which evades fundamental issues of definition and causation. To take only the two most obvious: how can the late medieval agrarian crisis (assuming that there was one) explain such divergent development between eastern and western Germany? And wherein did the origins of that crisis lie: in a slump in population following plague and epidemic, leading to tumbling grain prices, higher wages, and a collapse of seigneurial revenues; or in the mode of production itself, the social relations between landowners who creamed off the peasants' surplus, and the peasants themselves as producers, as lords sought to extract more surplus by extra-economic coercion (their judicial and political power as feudal overlords)?

A furious historiographical debate surrounding these questions for Europe as a whole was unleashed by Robert Brenner in 1976, whose participants felt compelled to align their responses according to their willingness to accept Brenner's neo-Marxist categories of analysis, in short, whether they spoke of an agrarian crisis or of a crisis of feudalism.[*] Because that debate largely ignored the German-speaking lands (aside from a brief account of developments in east Elbia) it might be thought to be of no concern here. Yet in the case of Germany we cannot ignore the historiography for

---

[*] T. H. Aston and C. H. E. Philpin (eds), *The Brenner Debate: Agrarian class structure and economic development in pre-industrial Europe* (Cambridge, 1985).

two compelling reasons: first, the point of reference for adherents of the 'agrarian crisis' theory remains the classic study by the German economic historian, Wilhelm Abel, first published in 1935, and translated into English as late as 1980 from its third edition (1978), as *Agricultural Fluctuations in Europe from the Thirteenth to the Twentieth Centuries*, to which there has been until very recently no serious challenge amongst non-Marxist historians; second, because during the forty years of its existence, historians in the German Democratic Republic were committed to elaborating a Marxist analysis of feudal society, emphasizing the social relations of production rather than the movement of prices and wages in response to supply and demand in the market, a task which acquired an especial piquancy because their state occupied some of the east-Elbian territory where there was indeed a 'feudal reaction' in the late Middle Ages leading to what Frederick Engels called the 'second serfdom'. In a reunited Germany these differences, it might be supposed, could usefully be laid to rest, but in point of fact the belief among scholars in an iron curtain of differential social and economic development dividing German rural society – in the west simple rental landlordship, in the east commercial domains using coerced labour – dies hard.

The empirical divergence between east and west has been matched by a historiographical divide, with little attempt to investigate the nuances and anomalies of both practice and theory. This gulf is all the more regrettable since recent German scholarship, exemplified by Peter Kriedte, has argued convincingly for a reconciliation and integration of the two approaches, following Guy Bois's pioneering attempt to redefine relations between lords and peasants in eastern Normandy between 1300 and 1550.[*] In his book, misleadingly entitled *The Crisis of Feudalism*, Bois alters the terms of the debate by redefining concepts of feudalism and feudal appropriation to include levies by the state, especially during the Hundred Years War. The evidence from France, with its national monarchy and centralized administration, cannot be easily applied to a polity as fragmented as Germany, but Bois's conceptual categories offer some hope of overcoming a historiographical stalemate.

---

[*] Peter Kriedte, 'Spätmittelalterliche Agrarkrise oder Krise des Feudalismus?', *Geschichte und Gesellschaft*, 7 (1981), pp. 42–68; Guy Bois, *The Crisis of Feudalism: Economy and society in eastern Normandy, c. 1300–1550* (Cambridge/Paris, 1984).

In trying to make sense of the extraordinary vicissitudes to which German rural society in east and west was exposed in the three centuries after 1300, four preliminary observations must be made. In the first place, it is quite unnecessary to pursue the bogey of 'feudalism' through the historiographical thickets. Leaving aside the deliberately ideological deployment of feudalism in Marxist discourse, what is at stake is perfectly clear: how lords, within a landed society, brought their array of power to bear upon a dependent peasantry in order to extract its surplus. Whether one calls that a feudal regime, or a seigneurial one, or a patrimonial one is of little account. Forget notions of mutuality implicit in the oath of fealty between liege lord and vassal which characterized the high politics of the central Middle Ages: the relationship between lord and peasant did imply the duty of protection in return for service, rendered as physical labour, but this reciprocity was a cloak for a hegemonic relationship whose main constituent was appropriation or exploitation. Secondly, this relationship, by the late Middle Ages, was being profoundly affected by the rise of the state or, in its German context, by the consolidation of the territorial principality. If it had ever been proper to regard relations between lord and peasant as purely bilateral, by the fifteenth century it was certainly no longer so. The intervention of princes in what became a triangular relationship could often work to the advantage of the peasant against the landlord. Bavaria was the classic example, but other instances from east of the Elbe, such as Brandenburg, should caution us against seeing rural society in eastern Germany as a story of unrelieved oppression. To put it another way, the growth of principalities afforded the territorial nobility opportunities to prosper in the service of the prince, which may have compensated for a shortfall in direct feudal levies upon their peasants and hence may have broken the vicious circle of ever-increasing feudal demands leading to ever-greater economic under-performance by the peasantry, which Bois attests for Normandy. Thirdly, as previous chapters have argued, the social structure and economic life of the German countryside – especially in Upper Germany – were being transformed in the late medieval centuries by the spread of rural crafts and village markets, and by the penetration of urban capital in the form of the putting-out system, which could not help but have a profound effect upon the exercise of lordship at local level as well as the more obvious impact upon the fabric of the village community. And lastly, it should be self-evident (though alas to many social historians it is not) that any analysis of the fortunes of the rural population in Germany must begin, not with the majority, the peasantry, but with the minority, the nobility, both secular and ecclesiastical lords, for it is their social and economic situation which bore directly upon the fate of the peasants and their communes, even if the peasants as a possessing class had some freedom of manoeuvre both economically and politically.

The Economic Situation of the West German Nobility

At the close of the Middle Ages, we are informed in all but the most recent accounts, the lesser nobility of Germany, both territorially dependent nobles and imperial knights, was in crisis. The stock figure of robber barons, so beloved of the romantic literature of the nineteenth century, still stalks the pages of otherwise reputable works of history, preying upon hapless peasants or ill-protected merchants from their fortified lairs in draughty, rat-infested castles. Such men were caught in a spiral of social and economic decline, forced to resort to brigandage to keep themselves and their families afloat, or else they hid behind threadbare notions of honour to launch feuds against other nobles, or more often towns, to rectify alleged slights and injustices, but in reality to hold them to ransom. Perhaps the most notorious was the Franconian knight with an iron hook in place of the right hand which he had lost in battle, Götz von Berlichingen, who had been placed under the ban of the Empire for declaring a feud upon the city of Nuremberg in 1513, and who subsequently became involved in the Peasants' War as a captain of the Odenwald-Neckar valley band which stormed the fortress of the bishop of Würzburg. Others hired themselves out as mercenary captains to princes, lured by booty and ransom, but had to finance their operations out of their own pocket.

Some contemporaries agreed that the nobility had fallen upon hard times. One was the Carthusian monk Werner Rolevinck, writing from a Westphalian vantage-point around 1500. He praised the noble lineage and fine physique of the knights he knew, but they had been drawn into evil ways by the poverty which had befallen them. Their fields would have been left waste as not worth cultivating, had they any choice but to till them. 'You could not contemplate without tears', he went on, 'how these fine knights have to struggle for their daily bread and clothing, running the risk of the gallows or the rack [on account of raids and feuding] simply to avert misery and hunger'.[*] But others took a different view. The German moralist and advocate of the new religious doctrines of the early sixteenth century, Sebastian Franck, placed the nobility squarely among the backsliders.

> They know no other trade than hunting, carousing, and gambling; they wallow in luxury and excess from rents, interest-payments and annuities. Their time is all spent in duelling and jousting, bragging of their ancestry and coats-of-arms; they commit acts of war and raids, rule arbitrarily, live indolently and arrogantly . . . they maintain palatial residences and give themselves such lordly airs.[†]

That much of this is rhetoric is obvious – part of the commonplace critique of the members of a society of Estates which can be found a generation earlier in the Strasbourg preacher Geiler von Kaysersberg's lambasting of the moral failings of both clergy and citizenry. In this so-called *Ständekritik* no one was exempt – not even the peasantry – but what marks it in this context is precisely its ambivalence. Were the nobles depraved by virtue of their birth and upbringing, which afforded them the money and the leisure to behave licentiously (as Franck saw it), or was their lineage indeed an honourable one, which desperation and necessity had driven them to traduce (as Rolevinck saw it)?

Only within the last generation have German historians tried to come to grips with the reality of the nobility's situation by careful local case-studies. Their results have swept away the old clichés and replaced them by a more subtle understanding of the nobility's predicament. The traditional interpretation – deriving essentially from Wilhelm Abel – can be summed up as follows: an overstretched rural economy (too many families chasing too few resources) was peculiarly susceptible to sharp reversals precipitated by periodic harvest failures and subsequent famines up to the mid-fourteenth century. This labile balance toppled into systemic crisis after the inroads of epidemic pestilence from 1348 onwards. The decline in seigneurial incomes which was the consequence of the slump in cereal prices in the wake of falling population and demand could

---

[*] Cited by Rudolf Endres, *Adlige Lebensformen in Franken zur Zeit des Bauernkrieges* (Würzburg, 1974), pp. 6–7.
[†] Ibid., p. 8.

not be compensated within the agrarian economy, so that lords were faced with a stark choice: they were either obliged to sue for offices and perquisites in the princes' household and administration, or else were consigned to feuding and brigandage.

At every stage, this concatenation of cause and effect breaks down. The objections can be summarized under two headings: first, the link between cereal prices and general economic cycles is far weaker than once thought; second, nobles' incomes were much less dependent on the profits of landlordship than usually assumed. It is not even certain that nobles who did rely upon landed incomes had generally switched to receiving rents in cash (with the risk of debasement) rather than in kind. In the southern Palatinate rents in kind outweighed rents in cash: the latter derived almost exclusively from estates which nobles had specifically leased out for cash payment. In Franconia the situation was similar. By extension, it was perfectly possible for landlords to revert to, or intensify, direct exploitation of their demesne to compensate for falling rents, that is to say, to act as agrarian entrepreneurs supervising their tenants, rather than deploying servile labour. That has been demonstrated for Franconia in the case of the Schenk von Schenkenstein (who derived around one-quarter of their income from managing their own estates in the mid-fifteenth century), while the Frankenberg line of the von Hutten dynasty was obtaining around one-third of its annual crop of grain from its own demesne in the 1530s. What advantage, it might be objected, did that bring if faced with a slump in cereal prices? The answer is simple: lords – and not merely ecclesiastical institutions – had tithebarns or granaries in which to store their grain, so enabling them to take advantage of the wide seasonal fluctuation in grain prices to sell their surplus on the open market at the most opportune moment.

The activity of nobles as grain speculators was matched, moreover, by a willingness to diversify out of purely arable husbandry. That could include setting down new saplings in areas of viticulture, or greater reliance on market-gardening (fruit, vegetables, and, as we have remarked earlier, on the Upper Rhine onion-seeds). But above all it could entail a switch to pastoral agriculture. Along the North Sea coast and in the Alpine valleys, lords had always been active as cattle-ranchers, but by the later fifteenth century in Thuringia and parts of Franconia nobles began to invest heavily in sheep-farming. The maintenance of sheep-runs and the enclosure of fields for pasture encroached upon the peasants' own grazing rights on the common land. But that is only half the story. The very notion that nobles' incomes were dependent upon the yield from agricultural production is in itself quite misleading. Landlords still possessed extensive rights of seigneurial (or feudal) jurisdiction – banalities, as they are technically called – such as brewing, milling, or distilling, as well as arrogating to themselves regalian rights (those pertaining to the crown), such as mining and minting. These rights were often underpinned by further privileges which reserved distribution of produce to the lords alone, for instance, monopsony, whereby peasants under a particular lordship were forced to sell their produce exclusively to their seigneur, or else offer it for sale only at markets under his jurisdiction. Lords also had the opportunity to turn their seigneurial powers to good advantage in other ways, by erecting toll-bars on roads traversing their estates, or levying customs dues on river-borne trade, or escort-fines on merchants' convoys – or by imposing a protection fee on Jewish communities, as in the case of the Palatine family von Weingarten, who also controlled the turnpike toll at Rheinzabern. Where the balance in nobles' incomes between production and distribution (or commerce) should be struck is, in a pre-statistical age, well-nigh impossible to judge, but, as the grievance lists in the Peasants' War made plain, lords were often as concerned to exploit the financial potential of their jurisdictional authority as they were to maximize their returns from landlordship. In sum, landlords were of course affected by trends in agrarian prices, but the nobility in general as an Estate derived its income from highly diverse sources, the most significant of which by the dawn of the fifteenth century have not yet been discussed: the opportunities for profit afforded by mortgages and loans.

Nobles, Feuding, and Territorial State-Building

When we speak of mortgages, we are referring both to grants by princes to their noble vassals, and to transactions within the nobility itself. Such pledges were by no means confined to land: they might include regalian and banal rights – markets, mines, public taxes – as well as stewardships, fortresses, or even entire towns; they might indeed be conferred by the emperor himself. To take one striking example of the latter: during the reign of Emperor Sigismund in the early fifteenth century three noble families resident at the western end of Lake Constance – the von Bodmann, von Homburg, and von

Klingenberg – had acquired by mortgage the imperial taxes in twelve Swabian cities. Before 1400 such mortgages were rare. It is true that Sigismund's successor, Emperor Frederick III, tried in principle to redeem these mortgages (a policy known as 'revindication'), but while he granted no new ones, he did confirm several existing ones. For the territorial princes mortgages served a double purpose: they were the most direct means of raising money to finance their burgeoning administration; and they offered a convenient way of binding the territorial nobility to princely service as a powerful clientele with a financial vested interest in the well-being of the principality.

The relationship between prince and noble mortgagees was, therefore, mutually beneficial – though at the same time inherently precarious. In Hillay Zmora's words, for princes 'noblemen were the most suitable pledgeholders: only they were sufficiently wealthy to hold a pledge without at the same time being sufficiently powerful to usurp it. No prince was willing . . . to pledge property to other princes or to imperial cities.'[*] Yet at the same time, their interests were not identical: by its own logic, the process of territorial consolidation was ultimately inimical to the nobles' private jurisdictions and social independence. As a result, princely efforts to territorialize the nobility – that is, politically to subordinate them and integrate them into the framework of the territorial Estates – were constrained by the fact that the nobles themselves had become, through mortgages and office-holding, an indispensable component of territorial administration. The princes, in other words, were riding a tiger, though in the end they rode it successfully. The political ambivalence of this relationship stands out, as we shall see, when it comes to the motives behind noble feuding.

For the moment, however, one conclusion is blindingly obvious: nobles would have been useless as agents of princely state-building if they had been impoverished: they could not have afforded to acquire the mortgages in the first place. These mortgages fell into two types: originally, their holders had enjoyed plenipotentiary authority over the pledged lands, rights, or revenues; but by the fifteenth century it was commoner not only for the grantor (such as a prince) to retain full proprietary rights over the mortgage, but to confer the pledge upon a noble who in return served simultaneously as the governor of an administrative district (*Amt*). These districts

---

[*] Hillay Zmora, *State and Nobility in Early Modern Germany: The knightly feud in Franconia, 1440–1567* (Cambridge, 1997), p. 46.

(in the plural *Ämter*) were the cornerstone of late medieval and early modern princely states in Germany. Where nobles were invested with such *Ämter*, they stood to gain hugely in financial terms, for they could use their public office to determine the marketing of produce throughout their district in the towns under their ostensible protection. This, at least, is what has been suggested for Franconian territories such as the bishopric of Würzburg and the margraviate of Brandenburg-Ansbach. Although scholars concede that the evidence here is patchy, indeed impressionistic, it does seem that, in the case of commercial sheep-farming, the nobles involved were drawn mostly from the ranks of district governors, pledge-holders and other princely officials.

What is altogether beyond doubt is that nobles made up the vast majority of princes' creditors. The debts which princes ran up in the course of their territorial state-building were colossal: in the first half of the sixteenth century nearly 1 million florins in Hessen; 750 000 fl. in Bavaria by 1514; 500 000 in the Palatinate in 1476; a staggering jump from just under 250 000 fl. to over 700 000 fl. in the space of less than thirty years between 1515 and 1542 in Brandenburg-Ansbach-Kulmbach. Wherever one looks, these debts were essentially secured on loans from the nobility: over 80 per cent in Württemberg, a figure of 24 per cent in the Palatinate, but in reality much greater; over 50 per cent in electoral Brandenburg but in terms of value much higher. In turn, these loans were extended against the receipt of pledges. In Würzburg most of the bishops' towns and castles had been mortgaged to nobles by 1450; in the archbishopric of Cologne a few years later all the district governorships and jurisdictions had been mortgaged for a total of 600 000 fl. In Brandenburg-Ansbach most of the margrave's creditors were noblemen, and while only 16 per cent were at the same time district governors the value of their loans amounted to 26 per cent of all credit. Moreover, within the ranks of the nobility itself the largest creditors were fellow-nobles. When the von Klingenberg, despite holding imperial taxes in many Swabian cities in pledge, were forced to sell two of their residences, Hohenklingen in 1457 and Blumenfeld in 1462, to make provision for an excess of sons and daughters (the Achilles heel of so many noble families), it transpired that over half their creditors came from the ranks of the nobility in the Lake Constance area, the von Schönau, von Landenberg, and von Bubenhofen in particular. It is also worth adding – not least because it contradicts the stereotype of noble brigands, down on their luck, preying upon innocent townsfolk – that nobles lent to urban communes as well: to Lüneburg, for instance, in the late fourteenth century, when by rights they should have been at their lowest ebb.

Yet the awkward fact remains that reforming tracts of the fifteenth century excoriated knights and nobles for their propensity to feud – to pursue private vendettas at the expense of public peace and order. By the time of the great reform diet of 1495 in Worms, which declared a general public peace throughout the German lands and outlawed all who feuded, feuding had become identified with brigandage as such, that is, as a criminal breach of the peace. That nobles feuded – and profited thereby from ransom and booty – is incontrovertible; but which nobles feuded and for what reasons is quite another question, which recent research has begun to answer in altogether unsuspected ways.

We may pass over swiftly the legitimacy of the feud itself, which so exercised an earlier generation of historians. Suffice it to say that the views, once so influential, of Otto Brunner, the Austrian historian whose work *Land and Lordship* first published in 1939, argued that medieval concepts of law, justice, and rulership were entirely alien to a modern understanding of the state, public authority, and government, no longer carry the day.[*] His insistence on the lawfulness of the feud within the context of an aristocratic perception of right, seen as the maintenance of peace within the land by those enjoined by their lineage and dignity to uphold it, has given way to the recognition that the distinction between (internal) feud and (external) war is completely bogus. The rationale of the feud, as Werner Rösener suggested two decades ago, was merely an attempt to justify what was otherwise illegitimate violence.[†] But that violence was often perpetrated on behalf of third parties – the territorial princes themselves! When Konrad Schott declared his defiance of the city of Nuremberg in 1498, it provoked an outcry throughout Germany; the feud culminated in Schott's cutting off the right hand of a city councillor, Wilhelm Derrer, the following year. Though there is no direct evidence that the feud was initiated by Margrave Friedrich of Brandenburg-Ansbach (it arose over a disputed inheritance), he

---

[*] Otto Brunner, *Land and Lordship: Structures of governance in medieval Austria* (Philadelphia, 1992).

[†] Werner Rösener, 'Zur Problematik des spätmittelalterlichen Raubrittertums', in Helmut Maurer and Hans Patze (eds), *Festschrift für Berent Schwineköper zu seinem siebzigsten Geburtstag* (Sigmaringen, 1982), pp. 469–88.

seems to have fomented it, for both Schott and his accomplice, Christoph von Giech, were already, or shortly to be, margravial officials. Similarly, when Peter von Mörsberg, from an Upper Alsatian dynasty which made its fortunes in Habsburg service, launched a feud against Basel between 1445 and 1450, the hand of Duke Albrecht of Austria was pulling the strings behind the scenes: he received over half the share of booty from what proved an unusually profitable campaign by von Mörsberg, even though in the end the latter sustained losses because of reprisals against his own lordships, including the burning of forty villages. Likewise, Margrave Friedrich of Brandenburg-Ansbach, in engaging the brothers Hans and Wilhelm von Rechberg as partisans in his campaign against Cologne and Liège in 1436, laid down in advance equal division of the expected spoils. What was at stake in feuds against cities was not simply the commercial clout of their mercantile elite, but the cities' policy of seigneurial expansion as well – both Nuremberg and Ulm posed a threat to the integrity of Brandenburg-Ansbach's territory. It is not surprising, therefore, that those who feuded were drawn, not from the ranks of nobles of lesser standing and wealth – the supposedly impoverished – but overwhelmingly from those of high status, usually with close connections to the princely court and administration. For Franconia it has been calculated that around three-quarters of all those prosecuting feuds against fellow-aristocrats or against cities were rich and powerful nobles from prominent families. Feuding, after all, was a risky business. It could only be undertaken by those who possessed the necessary resources to equip their troops, and the danger of reprisals against one's own estates and subjects was ever present, as not only Peter von Mörsberg, but other leading dynasties of the south-west, the von Rechberg, von Thüngen, and von Berlichingen, discovered. Against this background, booty was the means, rather than the end, of feuding.

What emerges from this analysis is a much more complex and less clear-cut image of the German nobility in the wake of the late medieval demographic and agrarian crisis. As Regina Görner concluded from her study of the Westphalian nobility, there was no general impoverishment or loss of political function.[*] Nobles remained effective partners for the territorial princes, both financially (as lenders), politically (as proxy wagers of war), and adminis-

---

[*] Regina Görner, *Raubritter: Untersuchungen zur Lage des spätmittelalterlichen Niederadels, besonders im südlichen Westfalen* (Münster, 1987).

tratively (as district officials, often holding their offices in pledge). Princely service, therefore, was not so much an indication of economic frailty or political submission as an opportunity for advancement. Nobles were certainly under no economic compulsion to feud; and the feud cannot be seen as a despairing attempt to shore up the nobles' position in the face of territorial consolidation by princes. As Roger Sablonier has shown for eastern Switzerland,[*] the nobility had begun to adjust to territorialization even before the late fourteenth-century crisis, and the same applied to Westphalia.

None of this is to deny that nobles were confronted with additional economic burdens at the close of the Middle Ages. The cost of ever more formal tournaments grew; the apeing of rich urban patricians involved new expenditure on buildings, clothing, and servants. Segments of the nobility were indeed plunged into financial extremity: the landed incomes of the knights of the Ortenau on the Upper Rhine were halved by 1400 as the result of coinage devaluation and the slump in cereal prices, and among the lesser nobility of Swabia only one-third could boast of an annual income in excess of 200 florins. Yet the evidence suggests that there was no general pattern. The nobility became more stratified; and the fortunes of various branches of one family could differ widely, as has been shown clearly for the southern Palatinate. In areas of diversified agriculture, nobles had more opportunity to switch production; elsewhere, nobles could hitch their star to the emerging territorial principalities. Those who chose to stand aside – the imperial knights – benefited from the protection extended to them collectively by Emperor Maximilian and latterly his grandson Charles V, even though their numbers included such genuinely dubious figures as Franz von Sickingen and Götz von Berlichingen, who do at first sight appear to fit seamlessly the role of robber barons.

But von Sickingen was the exception that proves the rule. He was only able to launch upon a career of feuding because his father and grandfather had grown rich in princely service with the elector Palatine. Fresh from a feud against Worms in 1515, von Sickingen became a military commander under Emperor Maximilian. He was anything other than a backwoodsman: open to the intellectual currents of his day, he embraced Reforming doctrines, and stood forth, alongside his friend Ulrich von Hutten, as a champion of Martin

---

[*] Roger Sablonier, *Adel im Wandel: Eine Untersuchung zur sozialen Situation des ostschweizerischen Adels um 1300* (Göttingen, 1979).

Luther. Not content with his public fame, however, von Sickingen launched a feud against the archbishopric of Trier, allegedly in the name of the Gospel, in 1523. Although he had many Franconian knights on his side, von Sickingen's campaign was not a 'Knights' Revolt' (as it used to be called), but the carefully calculated attempt of a nobleman without title to acquire with one bound a territorial principality and high dignity. The attempt failed because it was, in Hillay Zmora's words, 'unprecedented and intolerable' within the established hierarchy of Estates.[*] Overvaulting ambition, not indigent desperation, was von Sickingen's downfall. In that sense, his was a unique case. Götz von Berlichingen was altogether more typical of the Franconian knighthood, a man who despised learning and took to a life of feuding against cities and merchants, principally Nuremberg, supported by other Franconian freebooting gentry. Yet their days were numbered. At a general assembly of the Franconian knighthood in Schweinfurt in 1523, attended by 400 nobles, collective resistance against princes who unlawfully attacked any knight was agreed, and only feuds without just cause were condemned. But the Swabian League put an end to this truculence by sending an army into Franconia which destroyed 23 nobles' castles in a month, a foretaste of the much harsher retribution which the rebellious peasants were to inflict two years later. The Schweinfurt union offered no help to the afflicted, and the princes stood idly by. Feuding had outlived its usefulness, leaving Götz von Berlichingen to find alternative employment in the peasants' army in 1525.

Ecclesiastical Lordships in Western Germany

So far the discussion has concentrated on the fate of the secular nobility below the rank of territorial princes. We must now consider how ecclesiastical lordships – abbeys, priories, convents, commanderies, chapters – fared in the wake of the late medieval agrarian crisis. In principle, religious foundations had one salient economic advantage over secular lordships: as institutions, they were spared the partitions of inheritance which afflicted noble dynasties, and the need to make provision for widows and daughters through jointures and dowries. It has additionally been suggested that clerical literacy enabled such institutions to manage their estate accounts more com-

---

[*] Zmora, *State and Nobility*, p. 120.

petently and efficiently. It is certainly true that the sources are much more plentiful for ecclesiastical institutions than for small noble dynasties, but the current state of research leaves much to be desired. While there are numerous studies of individual religious houses, little attempt has been made to compare their fortunes, with the exception of the bailiwicks (*Balleien*) of the Teutonic Order, and the many convents in Swabia and on the Upper Rhine. Visitors who inspected the twelve bailiwicks in the western lands from which the Teutonic knights were recruited found a dismal state of affairs in 1361. Debts of 80 000 fl. had accrued, and several *Balleien* had been forced to dispose of estates and rents. Almost a century later, the debt had risen to 106 000 fl., a figure which would have been much higher if the Teutonic Master from his headquarters in east Prussia had not advanced a loan of 60 000 fl. in 1394, which was subsequently written off. When the tables were turned early in the fifteenth century, as the Order in the east plunged into debt, all appeals for help from the west were met with empty hands. This was not a ploy: between 1351 and 1450 the total income of the bailiwicks fell from 23 370 fl. to 19 649 fl., a drop of 16 per cent. Moreover, as the German Master (responsible for the western bailiwicks) lamented a few years later, in 1456, attempts to sell or mortgage the Order's castles, houses and lands had elicited no interest from the princes, nobility, and towns. The income of the cathedral chapter of Schleswig, to take an instance from northern Germany, calculated in terms of tonnes of hard grains, in this case barley, sank from 7609 tonnes in 1352 to a mere 2421 tonnes in 1434, a drop of 68 per cent, for which the fall of population and deserted farmsteads were mainly responsible. These two examples are the principal evidence cited by Wilhelm Abel in support of his thesis of a late medieval agrarian crisis. While the figures may be reliable, their interpretation is open to the same objections as have been put forward in the case of the secular nobility. Recently it has been suggested that the situation of the western bailiwicks of the Teutonic Order was not as bleak as Abel suggested. Levels of indebtedness varied considerably (the virtual bankruptcy of the Thuringian bailiwick in the fifteenth century stands alone), and in any case the figures for 1450 are distorted by the loss of the bailiwick of Alsace-Burgundy, whose liabilities were redistributed among the other bailiwicks. The main slump in landed incomes now seems to have occurred before 1400; thereafter the bailiwicks recuperated by abandoning demesne farming and reducing the number of knightly brothers. Some individual commanders spied

new economic opportunities in pastoral agriculture: the comman-
dery of Kapfenburg in the bailiwick of Franconia went over to sheep-
farming and cattle-ranching on a large scale, supplying the market in
Nördlingen with fleeces for its growing wool-weaving industry, and
bought up new estates on the profits. Sometimes the reason for the
economic predicament of bailiwicks lay not in any structural crisis,
but in the costs of warding off attempts to integrate them into the territorial principalities – in the long run a forlorn hope.

In the south-west, research into the Cluniac priory of St Alban in
Basel has revealed a depressing picture of collapsing landlordly revenues by the end of the fourteenth century, and that applies to other
convents in the city as well. But elsewhere what we find is a
sloughing-off of outlying and unprofitable lands in favour of managing the core estates more efficiently, as both the Dominican
nunnery of Adelhausen in Freiburg im Breisgau, and the Cistercian
abbey of Ebrach in the Steigerwald in Franconia achieved in the
course of the fifteenth century. Ebrach also began to diversify out of
tillage into forestry and pasture on the uplands and into viticulture
on the slopes of the Main. Yet southwestern Germany offers evidence
of a quite different kind – not connected to prices and wages, or
rental incomes – that an agrarian crisis after the Black Death confronted monastic houses with a compelling need to retrench, and to
reassert their seigneurial authority. The weapon to which they had
recourse was the revival of serfdom. In the high Middle Ages
monastic subjects had been bound to their ecclesiastical lords by a
general status of serfdom, known as *Eigenschaft*, which knew no distinction between servile lands and servile persons (or, to put it in its
technical English form, between villeinage and neifty). To recoup
their losses and to retain control of their subjects, convents from the
late fourteenth century onwards began to impose a new form of
serfdom attaching to the person, or to the subject by virtue of his or
her residence under monastic jurisdiction, known as *Leibeigenschaft*
(corporeal or bodily serfdom). The link between the agrarian crisis
and a revived serfdom has been explicitly demonstrated for Swabia
and the Black Forest by the acknowledged master of south-west
German agrarian history, Peter Blickle, in his comparison of the
abbeys of Schussenried in Upper Swabia, and St Blasien in the Black
Forest.[*] St Blasien's tighter restrictions on the freedom of its subjects

---

[*] Peter Blickle, 'Agrarkrise und Leibeigenschaft im spätmittelalterlichen deutschen Südwesten', in
Hermann Kellenbenz (ed.), *Agrarisches Nebengewerbe und Formen der Reagrarisierung im Spätmittelalter
und 19./20. Jahrhundert* (Stuttgart, 1975), pp. 39–55.

can be traced to the immediate aftermath of the Black Death, certainly before 1370. Up to that point the abbey's serfs had enjoyed freedom of movement and inheritance. But in the wake of unrest amongst its subjects resident in the Austrian cameral lordship of Hauenstein, it emerged that the abbey had apparently been seeking to extend its tenurial jurisdiction by declaring immovable property liable to the heriot (the fine which equates to death duty). In response, St Blasien's subjects were deserting their holdings in droves to seek refuge in the towns. A provisional compromise was brokered by the Austrian governor, whereby the abbey only had the right to seize moveable goods, while serfs' lands went to their next-of-kin. In 1383 a longer-term agreement was reached, which allowed subjects to move to those towns which upheld St Blasien's right to claim a heriot on death, but those serfs who simply abandoned the abbey's jurisdiction forfeited both moveable and immoveable property. Then, in 1467, a new bargain was struck, whereby any freedom of movement was suspended in return for a reduction of the heriot to the best head of cattle. Serfdom, in other words, was initially intended both to counter the landflight of subjects when epidemics had thinned the ranks of tenants, and to appropriate more of the peasants' inventory. What prevented the abbey from extending serfdom to all its tenants and ultimately from insisting upon a sweeping right of heriot was both the opposition of St Blasien's Austrian stewards, wary of its creeping designs upon the Hauenstein subjects, and persistent resistance by the peasants themselves (a tradition which lasted in the southern Black Forest for the best part of four hundred years).

In the case of Schussenried, the abbey's recourse to serfdom began in the 1380s, but intensified appreciably in the 1430s, when groups of subjects collectively had to swear a servile oath which recognized the abbey's right to pursue and reclaim those who had fled its jurisdiction. Schussenried was by then laying claim to half of both moveable and immoveable property as a heriot, but the abbey's measures provoked a sharp reaction, when its peasants rose in 1439. The upshot was a new compact which reduced the heriot to the common requirement of the best head of cattle (for men) and best dress (for women). In return, freedom of movement was cancelled, and those who married outside the abbey's jurisdiction were punished on death – quite apart from the heriot – by the confiscation of two-thirds (male) or one-third (female) of their estate. Other renders, however, were to remain fixed. Somewhat later, by contrast, – from the middle of the fifteenth century onwards – when the worst effects of the agrarian crisis were surely behind it, the abbey of Kempten began to impose servile status and renders upon its hitherto free tenants, in a series of ordinances which increased heriots from their nominal level as recognition-fees to half the property. By then, the purpose of serfdom had clearly begun to shift.

The Revival of Serfdom

The chronological discrepancy in the initial recourse to an intensified serfdom can be explained, Blickle believes, by the early decline of the Upper Rhenish and Swiss towns, whereas the Swabian cities were still in full flower up to 1450, so that landflight remained a real possibility for the subjects of Swabian lordships much later than further west, with a corresponding need for countermeasures. The difficulty with this line of argument is that the consequences of the agrarian crisis to a certain degree cancelled each other out: if landflight into the flourishing Swabian cities continued until the 1450s, then by the same token their populations must have sustained a brisk demand for grain, which would have staunched any slump in cereal prices. The example of Kempten and other lordships from the mid-fifteenth century should alert us instead to the wider political and territorial ambitions that serfdom could serve. That these buttressed the convents' economic foundations at the same time, regardless of the agrarian crisis, need hardly be stressed.

Yet there were also convents in Swabia, according to Blickle, which hardly resorted to serfdom at all in the fifteenth century, Ottobeuren being an instructive example. The convent's jurisdictional authority and revenues were under threat throughout the fifteenth century from the territorial aggrandizement of its neighbour, the imperial city of Memmingen. Although Ottobeuren therefore had good cause to deploy serfdom to bind its subjects politically and economically more closely to its overlordship, it only seems to have done so much later. The explanation may lie in its ability to increase its revenues from landlordship, since the latter was exercised over a relatively compact congeries of estates, given over to tillage and settled with nucleated villages, and that by extension allowed more or less exclusive jurisdiction over the peasants under its control. In regions of pastoralism, scattered settlements, and isolated farmsteads, by contrast, landlordship could not be mobilized in so effective a manner, which is chiefly why the abbey of Kempten, further east in the Allgäu, in an area of stock-rearing and dairying, did resort to serfdom. More recent research, however, has questioned whether Ottobeuren's subjects were free. The precondition of taking over a farm was acceptance of serfdom under the abbey's jurisdiction, so that by the sixteenth century most of Ottobeuren's subjects were serfs, either of the abbey itself or of other lords. Nevertheless, the status of its own serfs as property-holders had clearly been enhanced, so that they were on the whole better-off than the serfs of other lords, or the freemen.

In any case, we should recall that many Swabian religious houses were situated in a countryside already penetrated by rural industries and the putting-out system. There is no reason in principle why convents should not have recast their estate management to profit from the opportunities presented by the rise of linen- and fustian-manu-facturing. Here the evidence is sparse indeed, but one small clue points in this direction. In 1410 the abbot of Ottobeuren entered into a contract with an Augsburg merchant to deliver 32 cloths to the Memmingen exchange the following spring. The abbot was clearly acting as a middleman for the linen-production of his subjects; he was, in other words, stepping into the shoes of urban putters-out.

The obstacles to using serfdom as a straightforward measure of ecclesiastical lordships' response to the agrarian crisis, however, are twofold. In the first place, it was not intensified by some convents until after the mid-fifteenth century, by which time any direct link to the economic dislocations after 1350 was clearly attenuated. In the second, serfdom was a weapon used by territorial princes and imperial cities as well, whose motives presumably had little to do with a crisis of seigneurial agrarian incomes. These points require elaboration. It is again Peter Blickle who has alerted us to the use of serfdom as an instrument of territorial consolidation in south-west Germany.* The abbey of Kempten provides an instructive case-study. Lying in the Allgäu, its authority was circumscribed by the so-called 'Allgäu custom', whereby jurisdictional and fiscal powers over subjects lay with the lord who possessed rights of servile lordship over

---

* Peter Blickle, 'Leibherrschaft als Instrument der Territorialpolitik im Allgäu: Grundlagen der Landeshoheit der Klöster Kempten und Ottobeuren', in Heinz Haushofer and Willi A. Boelcke (eds), *Wege und Forschungen der Agrargeschichte: Festschrift zum 65. Geburtstag von Günther Franz* (Frankfurt am Main, 1967), pp. 51–66.

them; he could thereby pursue them wherever they resided since they enjoyed freedom of movement. In the course of the fifteenth century serfs of convents became scattered over a wide area, which hampered the exercise of seigneurial powers, and specifically any attempts to concentrate such powers in a consolidated areal lordship – a territorial principality in miniature, as it were. By 1500, therefore, lords with servile authority were busy exchanging serfs amongst themselves (sometimes in their thousands) to create exclusive jurisdictions without foreign allegiances. This was only possible, however, by treating all subjects on the same footing, namely as serfs, so as to create a uniform legal dependence. The consequence, in the case of Kempten, was that the abbey began to treat its free tenants, whose only obligation was the payment of an annual rent and recognition of the abbey's landlordship, as serfs by introducing the custom of the 'poorer hand', whereby children took the status of the legally inferior parent, rather than, as previously, the status of the mother, as well as forbidding marriage outside its jurisdiction. Within generations the abbey hoped thereby to reduce all its free peasants to serfs. Not surprisingly, the abbey's legal chicanery provoked serious unrest among its subjects which burst forth in 1491, and again in the Peasants' War. Kempten's harsh imposition of serfdom in the name of territorial exclusivity was a particularly crass instance, but other ecclesiastical lordships were bent upon the same end. St Blasien in the Black Forest, having ridden out its earlier economic misfortunes by means of serfdom, turned after 1500 to deploying it as a political tool. Although the abbey never exchanged serfs on the scale of Swabian convents such as Kempten, and was unlikely to achieve the same territorial success because of Austrian misgivings already mentioned, it began to offer the male subjects of foreign lords married to St Blasien female serfs lifetime leases only, so that their successors, thanks to the principle of the 'poorer hand', were only able to enter upon their inheritance as the abbey's serfs. Serfdom in the German south-west, in other words, although it is regarded essentially as a jurisdictional and territorial device, could underpin rights of landlordship. St Blasien as a member of the Outer Austrian territorial Estates was in no position to carve out a sovereign lordship for itself, unlike the imperial abbeys of Swabia, who used serfdom to buttress their territorial independence and integrity.

It lay in the logic of serfdom as an instrument of territorial consolidation that once it had achieved its purpose, its sting was drawn. For all the hatred which it drew upon itself, the abbey of Kempten's exchange of serfs with surrounding lordships, monastic and secular – the counts of Montfort, the bishopric of Augsburg, the abbeys of Isny and Ottobeuren, the city of Kempten, the lords of Werdenberg, or the Truchseß of Waldburg – meant that by 1560 it had largely removed foreign subjects from its territory, and the corollary was that the 'Allgäu custom' could then be abolished: it had run its course. What remained were purely nominal annual recognition-fees and oaths of homage. Tendentially, therefore, territorial serfdom was less oppressive than serfdom as an instrument of economic appropriation. That can be observed where princes and cities treated their rural subjects as serfs. By the sixteenth century in Württemberg, for instance, the dukes held most of the land and exercised high jurisdiction throughout their duchy; this sovereignty was expressed in a territory-wide servile dependence defined by residence, whose obligations included an annual Shrovetide fowl (or eggs) as a recognition-fee, and payment of a heriot (the best head of cattle or best dress, or a small proportion of the inventory). By extension, there was no automatic freedom of movement. The same applied to the margraviate of Baden, where serfs could not freely marry those of other jurisdictions. As territorialization was completed, serfdom became little more than a residential restriction; at the same time, margravial subjects were represented in the principality's Estates! There is scarcely an imperial free city in south-west Germany, moreover, which did not treat the inhabitants of its rural territory as serfs: in Ulm and Heilbronn all were serfs; in Schwäbisch Hall and Rothenburg ob der Tauber most; while Memmingen and Basel abolished serfdom in the wake of the Peasants' War. Yet Basel illustrates how serfdom as a legal disability was merely the prelude to a general territorial dependence. The city had allowed its serfs freedom of movement but not of marriage, so that abolition in 1525 brought with it the cancellation of merchets (marriage-fines) as well as heriots – or rather, it did not, for these fines were simply imposed on the rural population as a whole! Seven years later restrictions on *formariage*, marriage outwith the city's jurisdictional overlordships, were reintroduced, largely as a means of delimiting its territorial authority over against its neighbour to the south, the canton of Solothurn. For its part, Memmingen later reintroduced serfdom as a general condition of territorial dependence, and that continued well beyond the sixteenth century. Yet both before and after 1525 the economic burdens of serfdom were trivial. That holds generally good for serfdom in the south-west in the period after 1500. In essence, serfdom afforded a legal basis for the levying of dues which constituted a recognition of territorial authority; labour-services, the hallmark of serfdom in the high Middle Ages, were of little account. That it persisted in many parts of the south-west up to the age of the French Revolution was less a sign of strength than of etiolation. It survived only because it had outlived its purpose: by 1600, the end of our period, it had become a vestige of seigneurial dominion without any degrading connotations (though the subjects of the Austrian county of Hauenstein in the early eighteenth century sang a some-what different tune).

For that reason, serfdom in the west German lands has customarily been seen as a peripheral curiosity, confined to the urbanized and territorially fragmented south-west, where it fulfilled a transitional role in the shaping of the territorial state; it had little or nothing in common with the hereditary subordination and expropriation of the peasantry which developed east of the Elbe. Elsewhere in the west, it is argued, peasants were personally free and occupied tenurially unencumbered farmsteads. This view is misleading. Even in Upper Germany serfdom was more widespread than commonly supposed, and cannot always be pressed into the categories of explanation – a response to the agrarian crisis, or an instrument of territorialization – which have been adduced for the Upper Rhine and Swabia. That applies to serfdom in the Rhineland Palatinate, which was certainly no more onerous than elsewhere, but where it did not comprise a legally fixed category. Rather, Palatine subjects who resided under foreign lords were treated as serfs, but should they return to Palatine territory their servile status was discharged and they became subjects with full rights. In the Palatinate, moreover, serfdom never served as the basis of a general legal subordination, manifest in impediments to marriage or freedom of movement. Where neighbouring lord-ships did impose such restrictions (as did the bishopric of Speyer in 1470), the gradual process of territorialization led to the conclusion of bilateral compacts guaranteeing freedom of movement for serfs between their respective jurisdictions. Here serfdom served if any-thing as a hindrance, not a help, to territorial consolidation. In the county of Hohenlohe to the east, serfdom was deployed as a weapon of state-building, but it went hand-in-hand with a policy of agrarian improvement (in a region of poor soils) on the part of Count Kraft VI in the late fifteenth century, who remitted or eased servile dues for those prepared to clear and settle new land, in order to encourage agricultural production for the market.

Further afield, but still in Upper Germany, serfdom survived in the ecclesiastical (though not the secular) principalities of Franconia, notably the bishopric of Würzburg and the abbacy of Fulda. There servile dues had largely been tenurialized, that is to say, attached to the land held from the lord, rather than to the person. And this is the pattern which obtained in areas of north-west Germany, in particular Westphalia, where what Werner Rösener has called 'remains of the old form of personal dependence' (from the age of classical manorialism, that is) were still to be found.[*] While personally free, peasants in many ecclesiastical and secular territories – the bishoprics of Osnabrück and Münster, the counties of Ravensberg, Lippe, and Hoya-Diepholz – could only take on the lease of a farm if they accepted the status of villein (as it would have been called in the days of English manoralism), but with a difference. The peasant was not bound to the landlord's exclusive jurisdiction (as had been the case on the manor), but he enjoyed no absolute right of possession, merely the hereditary usufruct of the farm, which was only conceded after rendering a substantial heriot, originally half the moveable property, though this was later reduced to a more modest payment in cash.

Moreover, it is not the case that this particular form of villeinage (known in German as *Eigenbehörigkeit*) had simply superseded all forms of personal or bodily subjection. In the county of Lippe both forms of servile dependence continued side-by-side, the difference being that the villeins had to pay an entry-fine on taking over a holding, whereas the serfs in addition paid a heriot. Furthermore, the villeins could not be sold without their farms, whereas the serfs could. That these were not merely residual powers is demonstrated by landlords' attempts after the Thirty Years War (in a reprise of the situation after the Black Death three centuries earlier) to compensate for deserted tenancies by drawing the reins of villeinage more tightly. Elsewhere in Westphalia, as in the bishopric of Hildesheim, servile tenants also had to pay a merchet. Despite the fact that *Eigenbehörigkeit* entailed tying peasants to the soil, servile dues, and residual labour-services, Walter Achilles has no hesitation in classifying it as a variant of west German landlordship, essentially based on rental income.[†] By implication, this type of lordship was in

---

[*] Werner Rösener, *Agrarwirtschaft, Agrarverfassung und ländliche Gesellschaft im Mittelalter* (*Enzyklopädie Deutscher Geschichte*, vol. 13) (Munich, 1992), p. 38.

[†] Walter Achilles, *Landwirtschaft in der frühen Neuzeit* (*Enzyklopädie Deutscher Geschichte*, vol. 10) (Munich, 1991), p. 30.

principle not oppressive, especially since a third of the land in north-western Germany was farmed by free peasants, yet the simultaneous survival of both *Eigenbehörigkeit* and *Leibeigenschaft* in some places suggests that this judgement may be too sweeping.

Because serfdom in Westphalia was a means to underpin rental landlordship, it is therefore sometimes known by the altogether confusing name *Realleibeigenschaft*, (bodily, i.e. personal) serfdom applied really (that is, to property, tenurially: compare the American usage 'real estate'). However unfortunate this term, it points us in useful directions – away from the ghetto of the south-west, and towards an understanding of serfdom which is not obsessed with personal status and disability. For such forms of tenurial serfdom can also be found in Bavarian landlordships and further east as well. Acceptance of a tenancy implied recognition of the landlord's right to levy labour-services, and fines on the exchange of tenancies which could be quite substantial, though this servile status was cancelled on emigration or vacation. On lands under the direct administration of the dukes, by contrast, services and dues were of less account; serfdom was simply the mark of princely subjection. Yet the Bavarian territorial code of 1616 still distinguished between *servitus personalis* (personal serfdom) and *servitus realis* (tenurial serfdom), a distinction which was far more than the casuistry of hairsplitting lawyers. For it is quite easy to identify areas in the south of Bavaria (where monastic lordships predominated), in which *Realleibeigenschaft* was indeed used as a reinforcement of landlordship, and other districts in the west along the river Lech (where the dukes were judicial overlords), in which *Realleibeigenschaft* was cast as residential serfdom in order to underpin territorial jurisdictional authority. The persistence of forms of serfdom, especially of tenurial obligations, beyond south-west Germany has implications for the analysis of intensified seigneurialism east of the Elbe, as we shall see in due course.

Divisions within Village Communes in the West

The transformation of seigneurialism in the west, it emerges, should not be ascribed to any one overriding cause. The impact of the late medieval agrarian crisis cannot always readily be distinguished from the wider political imperatives which confronted feudal lords, especially those with smaller dominions in areas of territorial fragmentation and overlapping jurisdictions. By the same token, the consequences for the peasant commune were equally diverse. Resistance to the encroachments of feudal superiors, which led communes to present a united front to the outside world as a collectivity, was accompanied by increasing social and economic differentiation within the village itself. Whether that stratification was in any sense the outflow of changes in the seigneurial regime, however, is debatable. Historians have understandably enough paid more attention to the former than to the latter. Yet growth of a class of cottars, peasants with holdings too small to sustain a family by agriculture alone and who therefore had to rely on by-employment, was an unmistakable feature of German rural society from the fourteenth century. In areas of rural crafts and manufacturing its rise has been inextricably linked to the spread of linen- and fustian-weaving. That has been demonstrated beyond all doubt for eastern Swabia from the fifteenth century onwards, and for Saxony in the course of the sixteenth. The customary view is that these villagers were noticeably poorer than their counterparts, the tenant farmers on full holdings, and that they were excluded from participation in decisions of the village commune. This view, however, requires modification in several respects. In eastern Swabia, a region where partible was giving way to impartible inheritance, a third category of villagers, as Hermann Grees has shown, can be identified from at least the early fourteenth century, that of the lodgers (*Hausgenossen*), those who lived under the roof of the tenant or cottar as landless labourers.[*] In comparison with these, the cottars had a real stake in the village: they were members of the commune and did have access (albeit limited) to the common pastures and woodland. With renewed population pressure towards 1600, tenants and cottars could be found closing ranks against the lodgers, though in some villages, regarded as 'open', access to the common was not denied them. For western Swabia earlier in the century, David Sabean has identified a struggle over resources within the villages under the lordship of the abbey of Ochsenhausen, where those with too little land were encouraged by the commune to seize and enclose the common in order to establish new farmsteads, in the teeth of opposition from existing tenants, who saw their pasture being alienated.[†] The Ochsenhausen evidence, however, on closer inspection reveals that it was the abbey itself that was taking in land in order to create new sheep-pastures.

---

[*] Hermann Grees, *Ländliche Unterschichten und ländliche Siedlung in Ostschwaben* (Tübingen, 1975).

[†] David W. Sabean, *Landbesitz und Gesellschaft am Vorabend des Bauernkriegs* (Stuttgart, 1972).

Nevertheless, in Saxony and Thuringia the expansion of seigneurial sheep-farming did coincide with the appearance of a cottar class, some of whom were settled on the common land. For western Swabia Sabean also points to the abbey of Weingarten's attempts to shorten the span of leases, turning hereditary tenures into two- or three-life tenancies, in order to take advantage of the pressure on resources and the rise in land prices which overpopulation had begun to cause from the late fifteenth century onwards. In this instance, the convent's exercise of lordship may well have exacerbated existing divisions within its villages, pitting those with inferior tenures against peasants with secure rights. Whether such triangular tensions, evident in the 1530s and 1540s, can be identified elsewhere and at other times is a moot point: Sabean's findings remain controversial. Certainly there were complaints at the growing number of cottars, but their impact on village life is not easy to gauge.

Where partible inheritance was the rule, and especially in those districts of specialized and intensive agriculture alongside rural crafts, the extent of social differentiation within the village is much harder to assess. It is not altogether helpful to take Swabia, with its wage-working rural proletariat under the control of urban putters-out, as a template. The area of the German-speaking lands which showed the greatest incidence of rural crafts at the close of the Middle Ages was the Upper Rhine (including northern Switzerland), where the putting-out system in textiles or metallurgy was conspicuous by its rarity. Instead, the sources speak of coopers, cartwrights, butchers, cobblers, carpenters, tailors, bakers, furriers, tilers, potters, pewterers, saddlers, and fullers, few if any of whom worked as put-out labourers, and many of whom were mastercraftsmen. To regard such villagers as economically indigent, socially inferior, and politically marginalized is hazardous. The signs of immiseration which are usually taken to accompany the proliferation of rural craftsmen and labourers were entirely absent on the Upper Rhine until the later sixteenth century. One possible reason is the extent of viticulture, which was labour-intensive, requiring up to eight times the manpower of cereal agriculture, thereby enabling it to mop up surplus labour. The attitude of local lords in this area to the profusion of rural craftsmen is hard to judge, though we have earlier seen what city councils thought of it.

Divisions (let alone tensions) within the village – whether of occupation, social standing, or legal status – were deliberately suppressed in any conflict with feudal superiors. It was the commune which opposed, negotiated, or rebelled, even though not all villagers were members of the commune. The collective principle is best seen at work in the numerous 'treaties of lordship' which were hammered out between ecclesiastical lords in Upper Swabia and their subjects as a whole during the fifteenth century. The former's attempts to whittle away the peasants' rights, not least by the intensification of serfdom, provoked collective resistance, as we have briefly discussed in the case of Schussenried and St Blasien above. The outcome was invariably concessions on the part of the monastic lords, set down in public deeds, of which both parties received a copy. These treaties went well beyond the many medieval village custumals in scope and legal standing. In 1502, for instance, the abbey of Ochsenhausen was obliged to recast the entire array of its landlordly powers: by converting life-leases into hereditary tenures, by limiting entry-fines to 5 per cent (on entry) and 10 per cent (on departure) of the value of the farm, by reducing heriots to the best head of cattle, by allowing serfs to inherit freely, by permitting them freedom of movement, and by safeguarding the peasants' usufruct of the common. A simple tabulation reveals 14 such treaties in Upper Germany and Switzerland concluded by monastic lordships and their peasantries collectively, eight before 1460 and six thereafter, with two further treaties signed by secular lords (the Truchseß of Waldburg-Zeil and the count of Montfort). The treaties offered no copper-bottomed guarantee against further chicanery on the part of seigneurs: all subjects of the Swabian ecclesiastical lordships joined the Peasants' War in 1525. But the treaties demonstrated that the rural polity could not function without the active participation of the peasant communes. Why ecclesiastical lordships were much more prey to collective resistance then secular ones (if the number of treaties has any statistical significance), and why such treaties of lordship are seemingly unknown outside Upper Germany is to ask questions which can only elicit conjectures. It may well be that the institutional and impersonal character of monastic lordship made it easier to conclude treaties which were intended to have legal force in perpetuity (and in several instances were indeed still being cited by peasants in the imperial courts in the eighteenth century), rather than with secular lordships, under personal rule and liable to partition or extinction. Peter Blickle's view that the monastic lordships of Upper Germany were peculiarly exposed to demographic erosion through landflight to the many imperial cities cannot entirely convince, for this argument would presumably apply in equal measure to the secular lordships of the region. What can be said is that there is no evidence that ecclesiastical lordships were worse hit by a demographic and economic downturn than secular lordships, or that the former reacted more harshly than the latter. The balance of probability if anything tilts the other way, as the administration of mortgaged lordships by the secular nobility illustrates.

In the two decades before the Peasants' War Habsburg subjects in the Outer Austrian lands in the Black Forest and Alsace complained repeatedly at the abuses perpetrated by nobles who held Austrian lordships in pledge. In the county of Ferrette (Pfirt) in southern Alsace between 1511 and 1513 peasant unrest was vented against its two mortgagees, the brothers Marx and Jakob Reich von Reichenstein. Their crime, the peasants alleged, was to have abandoned their subjects without defence in the face of the repeated military emergencies on the Upper Rhine from the mid-fifteenth century onwards – the incursions of footloose mercenaries, known as Armagnacs, in the aftermath of the civil war in France in the 1440s, followed by the Burgundian occupation of the left bank of the Rhine between 1469 and 1474. 'We and our forebears have spilt blood for the sake of our lord and master', they lamented, 'but we have never heard of a bailiff of Ferrette being killed.'[*] In 1523 there were complaints at the Outer Austrian diet that the pledge-lords of Rheinfelden, Wehr, Reinach, and Rotberg in the southern Black Forest should be required to attend the assemblies so that they, alongside the other Austrian towns and administrative districts, should bear their reasonable share of territorial taxation. The third Estate of Outer Austria, the selfsame towns and districts, went on to issue a general plea that Archduke Ferdinand, the Austrian ruler, should allow no further mortgaging of castles, villages, and jurisdictions unless they first be offered to the prince or his territorial subjects.

These instances were only the tip of the iceberg, however, as a far more protracted and serious conflict within Austrian territory at the western end of Lake Constance reveals, an affair all the more telling because it led straight into the first stirrings of the Peasants' War. The counts of Lupfen, a dynasty that had long served the Habsburgs as administrators, held several lordships at the western end of Lake Constance, including the county of Stühlingen in the southern Black Forest whose subjects rebelled at midsummer 1524 against Count Sigismund von Lupfen, and submitted a list of 62 grievances the fol-

---

[*] Günther Franz (ed.), *Der Deutsche Bauernkrieg: Aktenband*, 2nd edn (Darmstadt, 1968), p. 40.

lowing spring in a lawsuit to be brought before the imperial court of chancery. This dispute was the climax of a hundred years of attrition between the counts and their subjects. Sigismund's forebear, Count Hans, the Austrian bailiff of the Aargau, Thurgau, and Swabia had also acquired the lordship of Hewen, comprising the town of Engen and 13 villages in the Hegau, a little further east, as a mortgage in 1404 from the Habsburgs (who had themselves acquired it from the lords of Hewen), but in 1419 Duke Frederick IV of Austria was expressing alarm at Count Hans's attempts to impose a general levy on his subjects. Although the mortgage of Hewen brought an annual income of 823 florins, von Lupfen also sought to jack up income from tolls, rents, and tithes, very possibly as compensation for arrears of salary as bailiff. Between 1440 and 1445 the counts of Lupfen became embroiled in a dispute with the town of Engen over rights of inheritance, the free sale of salt, iron, and steel, and excessive labour-services. All these grievances recurred in the so-called Hegau Bundschuh of 1460 (which was in fact an uprising confined to the lordship of Hewen itself) and they resurfaced undiminished in the Peasants' War itself.

What was at stake in this running conflict was not simply arbitrary rule by the counts, but the fact that they were treating their mortgaged lordship and its inhabitants as a commodity, which could be traded at will. The counts of Lupfen were not an isolated instance; similar examples of the ruthless exploitation of subjects by mortgagee lords can be found under Wilhelm von Grünberg in Rheinfelden in 1448 (a situation which, as we have seen, was still giving rise to complaint in 1523), or under Peter von Torberg in his lordship of Wollhausen in inner Switzerland in 1376, held in pledge from Austria. In 1525 subjects of the bishop of Basel in Porrentruy (Pruntrut) affirmed in their articles of grievance that 'all burdens which the mortgagee lord lays upon us shall not be tolerated. . . . We demand to remain with the burdens formerly imposed before the territory was mortgaged'.[*] The commodification of landholding by pledge-holders has also been identified as a major source of grievance on the part of subjects in Franconia. In sum, the evolution of lordship in the west German lands and its repercussions on the peasantry in our period cannot be reduced to a simple aetiology predicated upon the late medieval agrarian crisis. Responses to that crisis were far from uniform, spatially and chronologically, and

---

[*] Günther Franz (ed.), *Quellen zur Geschichte des Bauernkrieges* (Darmstadt, 1963), p. 264.

determined as much by the varying pattern of seigneurialism as by economic exigency pure and simple. Moreover, the intensity of reaction to the lords' attempts to retrench was shaped as much by the existing rights and self-perception of the peasant commune as by the level of exactions themselves.

In Upper Germany both the spread of rural crafts and the prevalence of mortgaged lordships introduced into the seigneurial equation elements of commercialization and commodification which buckle the framework of a purely agrarian crisis. The recourse to serfdom, moreover, was plainly more than a response to economic difficulties. The concentration on Upper Germany is justified by the structural changes which were taking place in the countryside, as well as by the incidence of agrarian unrest before 1525, a phenomenon confined exclusively to districts south of the river Main, where the peasant commune was most developed. Yet we still know too little about northern Germany (with the exception of Saxony and Thuringia) to understand why relations between lords and peasants seem to have been less fraught, all the more so once the widespread assumption that all forms of servile dependence had been swept away in the face of purely rental landlordship has been shown to be false. Indeed, the existence of tenurial restrictions upon peasants in parts of Westphalia suggests parallels with the development of seigneurialism in the lands east of the Elbe, to which we must finally turn.

Intensified Seigneurialism in East Elbia

The classical view of the harsh regime of landlords east of the Elbe, known as junkers, was most trenchantly expressed, originally over fifty years ago, by the emigré German scholar Hans Rosenberg. The junkers rose to power at the cost of 'the legal and social degradation, political emasculation, moral crippling, and destruction of the chances of self-determination of the subject peasantry'.* Rosenberg was writing of Brandenburg-Prussia from the fifteenth century onwards, but his scathing judgement is held to have applied equally to other territories in northeastern Europe beyond the Elbe.

---

* Hans Rosenberg, 'Die Ausprägung der Junkerherrschaft in Brandenburg-Preußen, 1410–1618', in idem, *Machteliten und Wirtschaftskonjunkturen: Studien zur neueren deutschen Sozial- und Wirtschaftsgeschichte* (Göttingen, 1978), p. 82.

Research in the last three decades, however, by historians in east and west, for all their ideological differences, has qualified this verdict in three essential respects. First, the development of intensified seigneurialism, which brought together in the hands of one noble family landlordship, jurisdictional powers, and (latterly) servile authority (and on occasion rights of clerical patronage too) preceded, sometimes by as much as three centuries, the rise of intensified commercial agriculture by means of direct exploitation of the lords' own demesne. Second, the spread of seigneurialism was not uniform (and in any case never exclusive) east of the Elbe. Its pattern varied considerably not only between 'west' and 'east', that is to say from Brandenburg, Mecklenburg, and Pomerania, on the one hand, through to Poland-Lithuania and east Prussia (the lands of the Teutonic Order, transformed into a secular principality after 1525), on the other – quite apart from the distinctive and much later development of serfdom in Russia – it also extended into regions which were neither primarily agricultural (tillage) nor dominated by a landholding aristocracy, but rather areas of rural crafts and a profusion of towns, such as Silesia and Lusatia, and spilled over west of the Elbe to the Altmark of Brandenburg, parts of Holstein, as well as Saxony and Thuringia. Third, the expansion of seigneurialism rested economically upon the taking-in of waste or deserted land, and politically upon the arrogation of jurisdictional powers long before there was any resort to servile lordship, the imposition of labour-services, let alone the expropriation of peasant farms (*Bauernlegen*), or the compulsion of peasants' children to work for fixed terms as servants on the demesne (*Gesindezwangdienst*), which together have been taken as the hallmark of junker rule; in reality, they were both late and partial. The peasant with a family farm, the three-field system with rotation by course, or the village commune with its management and allocation of pasture, wood, and forest were not crushed east of the Elbe – and neither was peasant resistance.

The late medieval agrarian crisis struck at the economic foundations of lordship in the east no less severely than in the west, and it elicited similar countermeasures – in attempts to halt the flight of peasants to towns, as tenancies were left vacant and cereal prices shrank; until the late fifteenth century rents from farm leases tended to fall. In Brandenburg, for instance, rents in 1480 were 17 per cent lower than a century earlier. This is no more than what one would expect. That the outcome in the longer term was to be a regime of intensified demesne agriculture followed no intrinsic economic

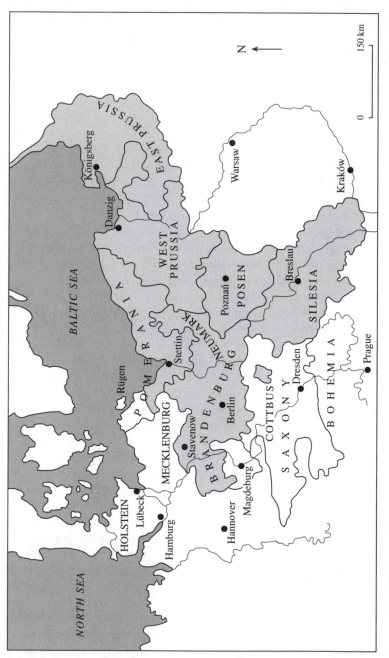

6.1 *East Elbia and the rise of Prussia*

logic: its mainsprings lay in a different configuration of the nobles' social and legal powers, combined with patterns of demography and settlement which allowed them – perhaps even obliged them – to find other ways of recouping their fortunes.

Because the lands east of the Elbe had been colonized in the twelfth and thirteenth centuries under the supervision of noble administrators known as *locatores*, the rights of landlords were already more extensive over against their territorial superiors, the princes, and more compact over against their dependants living in planned village settlements (even if the latter, as colonists encouraged to migrate eastwards, originally enjoyed freedom of personal status). During the fourteenth and fifteenth centuries noble landlords, who already exercised lesser jurisdiction over their subjects, acquired rights of high or capital jurisdiction which had previously been reserved to the princes. Their ability to do so derived both from the relative economic weakness of the princes, who were themselves too dependent on revenues from cereal agriculture, unlike their counterparts in western Germany, who buttressed their income through regalian mining rights (as in Saxony) or customs dues (as in the Rhineland Palatinate), and from the extraordinary political disruptions which afflicted the territorial powers in northeastern Europe at that time: civil war among the Brandenburg nobility in the 1330s and 1340s, conflict between Brandenburg and Mecklenburg for control of the Prignitz at the turn of the century, and most notably the debilitating wars of the Teutonic Order against the crown of Poland-Lithuania in the early 1400s, which all but led to the former's demise. In the long run, only those princes survived and prospered who could raise public or state taxes, in addition to feudal renders. In Mecklenburg, where capital jurisdiction had largely been alienated to leading vassals by 1450, the dukes became the virtual prisoners of their nobles' Estate, which was notorious for exercising the harshest rule over its peasants anywhere east of the Elbe: there legal rights were already being eroded in the fourteenth century. In Brandenburg, by contrast, they were also dependent on feudal-agrarian revenues, with only limited opportunity to defy their nobles by playing them off against the towns, but after the Thirty Years War the electors were at last able to impose a territorial excise, confine nobles' political and legal powers to their own estates, and even extend the peasantry a modicum of state protection. This bundling of seigneurial powers in one hand not only enabled lords in many cases to round off and consolidate their estates to the threshold of territoriality, but also created the preconditions for whittling away at peasants' titles to their farms and bringing large tracts of land under their direct management.

But preconditions are not accomplished facts; the lords were afforded opportunities east of the Elbe which barely existed elsewhere. The sparsity of population in comparison with western Germany left many farmsteads in the wake of the Black Death not only deserted but with no prospect of new tenants, quite apart from the prevalence of feuding and wars which wiped out many noble families themselves. These deserted holdings, known as 'wastes' (a term which does not imply poor or uncultivatable land) were incorporated by the surviving lords into their own demesnes. This was a gradual business – there was no obvious economic incentive to expand the demesne – in which the lords acted, as it were, by default. Even in 1500, around 30 per cent of the land in Brandenburg as a whole was still described as 'waste'; in the Uckermark (northern Brandenburg) the figure reached 40 per cent. In the course of the sixteenth century the general figure fell to 17 per cent, but villagers still held half the land in 1620, the lords only 32 per cent.

That is not to say that no great seigneuries were established before the sixteenth century; rather, these seigneuries – known in German as *Gutsherrschaften* – were carved chiefly out of waste land – just under half in the Middle Mark, but three-quarters in the Uckermark – and were seldom the result of expropriating peasant farmsteads. Only when all remaining waste had been reclaimed did the assault upon peasants' smallholdings begin, but that was a rarity before the mid-sixteenth century. Of course, given the imbalance between land and population, lords tried to restrict their peasants' freedom of movement by invoking their jurisdictional powers, as happened in Mecklenburg, Pomerania, and Brandenburg even before 1500, but the prohibition on landflight – or its enforcement – depended on territorial decrees, which were rarely enacted until the sixteenth century; the earliest appears to have been in east Prussia in 1496. What was at stake can be seen from the legislation in Brandenburg. The nobility had unsuccessfully demanded that the elector ban freedom of movement from 1484 onwards; when he at last agreed to a partial restriction in 1518 (a full prohibition only followed in 1536), it permitted movement within the entire territory (Brandenburg was not small!), provided that tenants left their farms fully equipped and stocked with beasts; those without farms had to offer their labour to their own lord first. In other words, the primary concern was to maintain the integrity of a lord's tenant farms, not to impose personal serfdom; indeed, as the German term *Schollenge-bundenheit* indicates, peasants were being bound to the sod (*Scholle*), that is, subject to tenurial restrictions. There were few signs at the time of any demand for increased labour-services, too often seen as the hidden agenda behind *Schollengebundenheit*. One exception was the estates of the von Arnim family in the Uckermark on their lord-ship of Boitzenburg near Prenzlau. At the beginning of the sixteenth century labour-services (and renders in kind, not cash) were a signif-icant component of the estate's economy, which was already engaged in exporting cereals from waste taken in under tillage, and that increased after the family had acquired the lands of the Cistercian nunnery of Boitzenburg as well after its secularization in 1539. Nevertheless, as the century wore on, the amount of land under direct demesne cultivation (using labour-services) declined; instead the number of cottars on smallholdings shot up, until the Thirty Years War swept them away.

By 1470 the population in the east, just as in western Germany, was beginning to recover, and therewith demand in local markets for cereals began to pick up. The nobility, given its seigneurial powers and extensive estates, was in a better position to take advantage of the recovery in grain prices than the peasantry, though there were coun-tervailing forces which had no wish to see the nobility corner the market. One was the Hanseatic League, which as a commercial associ-ation dominating trade in the Baltic had good reason to integrate peasants into the circulation of goods and encourage their own pro-duction for market, in order not to be confronted with an aristocratic cartel. Another was the princes themselves. In Mecklenburg, Duke Magnus VI (1477–1503), in a deliberate attempt to restore the terri-tory's finances, excluded the nobles from the markets of Wismar and Rostock, and took over the distribution of grain in mercantilist fashion as a state enterprise, selling Mecklenburg rye into Hamburg and other Baltic ports. He even planned to boost state exports by con-structing a canal to link the river Elbe through Lake Schwerin to Wismar on the Baltic coast. The nobles of Mecklenburg only appeared as large-scale grain exporters after his death, from the 1510s to the 1540s. In Brandenburg, Elector Joachim had already sought to ban cereal exports from the von Arnim estates in 1491, though he did not try to set up a state enterprise. The electors were concerned, however, to ensure the financial viability of their peasantry; hence in

1536 it was decreed that the peasants could sell their corn freely throughout the territory, and four years later the nobility was expressly forbidden to market any grain other than from their own estates. Both monopsony and monopoly were to be prevented.

Intensified Commercial Agriculture in East Elbia

All this suggests that the opportunity to make vast profits from the sale of grain existed. But this explains neither why cereal agriculture should have been so lucrative in the east (at a time when in the west the agrarian economy was marked by increasing pastoralism, the cultivation of industrial crops, and the spread of rural manufacturing), nor why grain-growing should have been organized by direct demesne production, rather than by encouraging greater peasant production for market and creaming off the surplus through higher rents. Until recently, historians allowed themselves to be mesmerized by overseas demand from the Low Countries, whose merchants, along with the Hansards, descended in droves upon the Baltic to sweep the granaries of Danzig and other ports clean of stocks of grain. That demand existed, but it is doubtful whether it amounted to much before 1500, despite a trickle of exports from the Vistula estuary from the end of the thirteenth century. Moreover, it affected the eastern parts of east Elbia (Poland and east Prussia) much more than the western (Brandenburg and Pomerania, though Mecklenburg became a large exporter).

The higher degree of urbanization in Brandenburg (leaving aside Berlin, which in 1500 was only just beginning its rise to a metropolis) created local demand in the first instance, with the gentry keen to protect their peasants' right to sell, rather than to impede it, if only to counteract the efforts by urban merchants to corner the market. The seigneurial economy, moreover, was by no means confined to tillage; we have noted earlier the spread of cattle-ranching and sheep-rearing, which created much less demand for labour-services, but which impacted on the peasant economy and village commune in other ways. On Brandenburg's western border, local demand similarly spurred the intensification of tillage, supplying cities such as Magdeburg, with a population of well over 20 000, with food grains, and brewing centres such as Braunschweig with barley.

The contrast with Poland and east Prussia is striking. These were areas of very sparse population indeed, where modest local demand meant that seigneurs had an incentive to export much more of their cereal production overseas. The overwhelming proportion of Poland's grain – from Great Poland and Masovia, nearest the coast – went through the German city of Danzig, whose exports shot up from 11 000 tonnes in 1491 to 240 000 tonnes on the eve of the Thirty Years War in 1618, more than a twentyfold increase. Yet Danzig's grain exports were unusually high, even by eastern standards: 80 per cent of its export volume was grain, compared with the Livonian ports of Reval (Tallinn), 50 per cent of whose exports were of rye and oats, and Riga, two-thirds of whose exports were not cereals at all, but flax and hemp. These export figures, moreover, are much higher than for the Wendish ports of the western Baltic. We should be cautious, therefore, of equating large-scale overseas grain exports straightforwardly with the rise of intensified commercial agriculture on seigneurial demesnes (the system known as *Gutswirtschaft*, or domanial economy), for *Gutswirtschaft* was much more prevalent than the areas of intensive cereal husbandry. At the same time, this system of domanial economy (sometimes referred to in the English literature as a manorial economy, though this arouses all sorts of false associations with the manorialism of the high Middle Ages) varied greatly in intensity throughout northeastern Germany and the Baltic. Even where *Gutswirtschaft* was widespread – as in Mecklenburg, Pomerania, and the Uckermark, as well as east Holstein, and Upper Silesia (by some accounts) – only between 40 and 50 per cent of farm land was subjected to a domanial regime; elsewhere – in western and southern Brandenburg, and in the Neumark (the new march of Brandenburg lying east of the Oder river, in modern-day Poland), as well as Middle and Lower Silesia – only 30 per cent of the land was under direct seigneurial exploitation.

Nevertheless, the evidence for a boom in cereal prices and an expansion of the domanial economy using labour-services in the sixteenth century, whether stimulated by local or overseas demand, remains incontrovertible. But that alone cannot explain the concentration on cereal agriculture. Two other factors need to be considered: natural endowment, and opportunity costs. It is clear, on the one hand, that the lighter sandy soils of the Baltic littoral were uniquely suited to grain-growing; on the other, it is unclear what alternative forms of profitable investment could have been available. The sheer size of seigneurial estates, and the availability of wasteland, made tillage an attractive proposition without the need for huge investment or an increase in crop yields, provided the demand existed in the first place. That lords were willing to invest and to diversify into other crops where the land did not favour grain cultivation can be seen from other parts of east Elbia, such as Lusatia. But we are still left with the puzzle of why lords resorted to direct demesne exploitation, instead of rack-renting. The answer seems to be that where the quota of grain destined for the market reached as much as 70 or 80 per cent of the entire crop, direct labour not only became the most efficient way to organize production, but also far more lucrative than revenues from rents and feudal renders, many of which were in any case fixed by custom.

The parallels with the use of indentured labour on the plantation economies of the Caribbean and Latin America are not far to seek. And, indeed, the large estates of eastern Europe are sometimes, with some justice, known as latifundia, a term which is often used to describe colonial planters' estates. It is also likely, given the sparsity of settlement, that it would not have been easy for nobles to find tenants willing or indeed able to pay rents at a level commensurate with the profits of direct marketing. The evidence from the Stavenow estate in the Prignitz in northwestern Brandenburg, which has been extensively studied by William Hagen, shows that in the course of the sixteenth century the value of the estate soared five-fold, with the income from grain and livestock sales in the demesne amounting to 32.3 per cent of its capitalized value in 1607, but fixed labour rents only 12.6 per cent, and rents in grain and cash a mere 3 per cent and 1.3 per cent respectively! The astonishingly low figure for rents in kind and cash has a simple explanation: the Stavenow peasants accepted an increase of labour-services only in return for the freezing or lowering of ground-rents.* Labour-services were already on the increase in the second half of the fifteenth century (as the von Arnim estate in Boitzenburg shows), but it was only after 1500 that a spectacular growth occurred. The Brandenburg evidence shows *corvées* in 1500 amounting to no more than a few days' labour a year on the lords' demesne, but by 1600 that had shot up to several days a week – a fiftyfold increase! It is important to remember that the compulsion to perform labour-services was grounded in the elision of seigneurial rights of landlordship and jurisdictional authority (that is to say, *Gutsherrschaft*); it was only 'manorial' in character inasmuch as it was vested in the peasants' *Schollengebundenheit*,

---

* W. W. Hagen, 'How mighty the junkers? Peasant rents and seigneurial profits in sixteenth-century Brandenburg', *Past and Present*, 108 (1985), pp. 80–116.

their tenurial subjugation. It was not, at the outset, derived from any personal (that is, corporeal) dependence: labour-services and *Leibeigenschaft* east of the Elbe must, at least in the sixteenth century, be kept separate. That applies not only to Brandenburg but to Poland and Lithuania as well, though here labour-services were already higher in the early fourteenth century; in Masovia (the region north of Warsaw) one day a week was expected from 1421. The decades after 1500 were, let us not forget, a period of population recovery and rising cereal prices, in which the question of personal serfdom, with the restrictions on movement and marriage which it entailed, was not acute. That situation changed dramatically after the Thirty Years War, whose devastation and depopulation were reminiscent of the conditions in the wake of the Black Death three centuries earlier. The issues of labour shortage and landflight once again became pressing, and it is in the seventeenth century, beyond the period with which we are primarily concerned, that the true enserfment of the east-Elbian peasantry occurred. This can readily be seen in the welter of legislation – at territorial level – consigning peasants to perpetual personal bondage and to forced labour – 1616 in Pomerania; 1620 the forced-labour ordinance in Brandenburg; 1646 a similar statute in Mecklenburg; 1645 the extension of the 1616 legislation to encompass *Vorpommern* (Pomerania west of the river Oder). And it is essentially in the seventeenth century and beyond that the phenomenon of the expropriation of peasant holdings (*Bauernlegen*) manifests itself. Much of the sorry tale of peasant degradation lay, no doubt, in the logic of a domanial economy (*Gutswirtschaft*) superimposed upon, and indeed only operable on the basis of, intensified seigneuralism (*Gutsherrschaft*), but whether the system would have acquired its most oppressive characteristics without the social and economic dislocations of the Thirty Years War (and the Northern War of 1655–1660 between Sweden and Poland, which finally detached east Prussia from the Polish crown and joined it to Brandenburg) is a moot point.

Yet there were areas east of the Elbe where intensified seigneuralism was *not* the precursor of a domanial economy. The prime examples are Silesia and Upper Lusatia. There as much as 80 per cent of the land was held by peasants with good title and hereditary tenure, who were personally free. Many of their holdings, however, were very small, 10 hectares or less, and partible inheritance was widespread. Rural by-employment and specialized crops were common. In Silesia linen-production was widespread, and madder was cultivated in the district round Breslau (Wrocław); while Upper Lusatia was known for its wool-production, organized in part by putting-out from a cluster of trading centres, such as Görlitz, Bautzen, Kamenz, and Löbau. Western Silesia, too, had become an urbanized landscape by 1500, as a string of towns was founded along the mountain ranges on the left bank of the Oder, largely on the back of a mining boom in iron, gold, and silver. Against this background a domanial economy as previously described was most unlikely to develop, though after 1550 there is some evidence of lords taking in waste to enlarge their existing estates. Nevertheless, *Gutsherrschaft* – intensified seigneurial jurisdiction – was on the advance in the second half of the sixteenth century, but the nobles used their concerted rights of lordship to batten onto existing economic activity by promoting crafts and textile production. Instead of expropriating tenants, they released demesne and common land for new settlement by cottagers, and lured linen-manufacturing away from the towns to their own estates, where it was integrated into the system of feudal rents. Rather than seeking to control production, these lords used their seigneurial power of extra-economic coercion to enforce monopsony or to capitalize upon their banal rights, such as the monopoly on brewing.

A high proportion of the peasantry escaped the clutches of hereditary serfdom, so that Silesia and Lusatia remained regions with a highly variegated structure of social and economic relationships. Across the border in Bohemia, however, hereditary serfdom did become widespread in the sixteenth century, as in the lordship of Friedland (Frýdlant), though, as Sheilagh Ogilvie has pointed out, its legal disabilities do not seem to have prevented the peasantry engaging in the market or pursuing new economic opportunities as they arose.[*]

A different configuration of *Gutswirtschaft* can also be observed in the districts spanning the Elbe. In the swathe of territories stretching from eastern Lower Saxony and Anhalt through Thuringia, Mansfeld, and the duchies of Saxony (as well as in parts of Bavaria and Upper Austria), we encounter an interval type of landlordship, using both wage-labour from free peasants and the labour-services of serfs to manage large demesnes, which Alfred Hoffmann has termed

---

[*] Sheilagh Ogilvie, 'The economic world of the Bohemian serf: Economic concepts, preferences and constraints on the estate of Friedland, 1583–1692', *Economic History Review*, 2nd series, 54 (2001), pp. 430–53.

'economic lordship' (*Wirtschaftsherrschaft*).[*] In the fertile district around Magdeburg, for instance, commercial leases on the larger peasant farms co-existed with a landless workforce within a single estate, and even then the proportion of free wage-labour far outweighed servile *corvées*. Because the chief means of production, namely land, remained in peasant hands, this type of domain should be regarded as a special form of western landlordship (*Grundherrschaft*), rather than as a watered-down variant of *Gutswirtschaft*. That applies also to Bavaria, where the dukes owned 20 per cent of the land, and the church 50 per cent, so that most of the land was simply not available for conversion into large-scale seigneurial enterprises; their nearest equivalent, the Bavarian *Hofmarken*, were much smaller and did not rely upon the labour of personal serfs. In Schleswig-Holstein, by contrast, the large estates of eastern Holstein were run as domanial economies, heavily dependent upon serf labour, but central Holstein remained a classic landscape of large peasant farms, hereditary and free, as in much of northern Germany.

It is striking, moreover, that the rise of *Gutsherrschaft* is intimately bound up with the rise of the junkers, the secular nobility and gentry. The evidence from monastic estates – little of which survives in the form of cadastres or rent-rolls – points in a different direction. The land registers of the Cistercian abbey of Zinna, south-east of Berlin, reveal a convent which had long since abandoned the typically Cistercian agrarian regime of direct farming on so-called 'granges' in favour of rental landlordship pure and simple. By 1471 only 12 hides of demesne were left on its Brandenburg estates; the convent's peasants were personally free, occupied hereditary tenements, and were even able to take over additional land from retrieved waste to bolster their livelihoods. At no stage did Zinna show any inclination to revert to demesne farming by apeing the *Gutswirtschaften* of its secular neighbours.

The Burdens on the East-Elbian Peasantry

The picture of east-Elbian seigneurialism painted by historians in recent years permits no easy conclusions about the burdens placed upon the peasantry. In the broadest of terms it may be possible to

---

[*] Alfred Hoffmann, 'Die Grundherrschaft als Unternehmen', *Zeitschrift für Agrargeschichte und Agrarsoziologie*, 6 (1958), pp. 123–31.

discern a gradient of subjugation growing steeper the further east one travels, but that cannot apply to the lands of the Teutonic Order in east Prussia, where communal rights were being consolidated well into the fifteenth century in the face of resistance by the Estates, formalized in the Prussian Union of 1440, to the Order's fiscal rapacity and arbitrary government. What determined peasants' ability to resist seigneurial demands was in any case often not so much their legal status, or the powers of the village commune, as their access to the territorial courts. Here the contrast between relatively good peasant rights in Brandenburg-Prussia (from the seventeenth century), where the electors were – for their own financial and military reasons – committed to a policy of (limited) protection, and the dire situation of the peasantry in Mecklenburg, which was run by aristocratic gangsters out of princely control, obtrudes: yet both were 'western' lands within the compass of the Baltic.

Just how burdensome labour-services were is also hard to determine. The evidence from the Stavenow estate shows that the value of new labour obligations considerably outstripped the older feudal ones. But at what cost to the peasants themselves? – or rather, to which peasants? – for tenants, cottars, and landless labourers were not in the same boat. The full peasants, Hagen suggests, did not resent the lost manpower so much as the abuse of their beasts as horsepower.[*] It was in any case commonplace for tenant farms to hire landless labourers to perform the *corvées* they owed. Perhaps the question is in fact wrongly put, given that a possessing peasantry still held most of the land. In the early seventeenth century in the Middle Mark of Brandenburg peasants farmed 77 per cent of the land, the church held 5 per cent, and the junkers the remaining 18 per cent: although demesne land had, since the late medieval agrarian crisis, increased by 71 per cent, the peasants still held almost four-fifths of the available farmland.

However much peasants east of the Elbe, as individuals or as households, may have enjoyed greater security and freedom than once supposed, it is still frequently assumed that their ability collectively to resist seigneurialism was undermined by the weakness of the village commune, at least in comparison with Upper Germany. But now even this verdict has been called into question. Both Lieselott Enders and Heide Wunder, acknowledged authorities on rural social structure east of the Elbe, argue that lords could not simply ignore

---

[*] Hagen, 'How mighty the junkers?', p. 107.

or overrule the commune; they had to enter into negotiation – however fraught – with the village bailiff, who was by no means a tool of the seigneur. Enders and Wunder speak, therefore, of lordship 'with' peasants, rather than lordship 'over' peasants.[*] When peasants had access to the courts (as in Brandenburg), increases in labour-services were not taken lying down: they were accompanied by much local resistance (though rarely open revolt), in which legal redress was the preferred option. Enders indeed suggests that Brandenburg peasants had scope for collective action similar to that enjoyed by their counterparts in Bavaria and Saxony – though, not, we must add, to Swabia or the Upper Rhine, the classic areas of strong communes: east Elbia never witnessed the treaties of lordship, hammered out after collective peasant resistance, of south-west Germany.

The Elbe, in other words, marks no clear divide in the evolution of lordship and dependence in the German-speaking lands – geographically or categorically. Patterns of western *Grundherrschaft* (in itself far from homogeneous) shaded off into a seigneurial regime in the east, which began as intensified seigneurialism (*Gutsherrschaft*) and developed in certain areas (but not in others) into a domanial economy (*Gutswirtschaft*), with interval or mixed forms such as 'economic lordship' (*Wirtschaftsherrschaft*) straddling the two. Equally, *Gutsherrschaft* could provide the legal foundation for an intensified economic regime, as in Silesia and Lusatia, which was not identical with *Gutswirtschaft*. Broadly speaking, there is now a consensus on this issue. More controversial remains the insight that patterns of subjugation and dependence form a gradient from west to east. Once we have overcome an unhealthy fascination with south-west German *Leibeigenschaft* and have recognized that *Eigenbehörigkeit* in Westphalia entailed tenurial restrictions, and once we have further acknowledged that serfdom east of the Elbe was originally vested in tenurial, not corporeal, subjugation, the way is open towards truer understanding of the fate of the peasantry in the east. No one has put this better than Lieselott Enders herself in her studies of Brandenburg. She argues for a threefold typology of servility: simple subjection as a concomitant of taking over a farmstead and accepting the landlordly and jurisdictional obligations to the seigneur which that entailed

---

[*] Lieselott Enders, 'Die Landgemeinde in Brandenburg: Grundzüge ihrer Funktion und Wirkungsweise vom 13. bis zum 18. Jahrhundert', *Blätter für deutsche Landesgeschichte*, 129 (1993), pp. 195–256, here at p. 205; Heide Wunder, *Die bäuerliche Gemeinde in Deutschland* (Göttingen, 1986).

(*Eigenbehörigkeit*); hereditary subjection (*Erbuntertänigkeit*), whereby the previous terms of tenancy fell automatically upon the heirs (though they could buy themselves free); and bodily serfdom (*Leibeigenschaft* in the narrow sense), which involved inferior rights of tenancy and the obligation to perform unlimited labour-services.[*] Enders admits that all three forms of servility could exist side-by-side, but insists that it is simple subjection (grounded in tenurial dependence) which was prevalent up to the end of the sixteenth century. Only later, particularly after the dislocations of the Thirty Years War, did the harsher forms of servility, extending to personal bondage, become commonplace – in 1653 the electors of Brandenburg enshrined *Leibeigenschaft* in territorial law in response to pressure from the nobility. A similar deterioration in the terms of tenancy from hereditary leases to leases for fixed terms with onerous obligations attached can also be observed in Mecklenburg. The spectrum of subjugation stretched, therefore, from *Eigenbehörigkeit* through *Schollengebundenheit* to the true stigma of personal hereditary serfdom (*Leibeigenschaft*), but, in its origins as *tenurial* dependence, servility existed both west and east of the Elbe.

Why those north German areas which already had forms of tenurial dependence did not then go the way of the east is, however, a question to which no satisfactory answer has ever been given. Those who point to the countervailing power of the monarch, or the cities, or even the sheer profusion of lordships in competition with each other, and with small hope of augmenting their domains by taking in vacant land, may appear to have a point – until we recall that it was precisely in the densely settled, urbanized south-west, an area where the royal writ still ran (or at least where royal influence could make itself felt), that personal serfdom (*Leibeigenschaft*) was most intensively imposed, not least by cities which had rural territories themselves. If relations between lord and peasant in Germany from 1300 to 1600 varied so widely, it is fruitless to search for the source of the variations solely in a late medieval agrarian crisis, undoubted though its demographic and economic consequences were. Equally, a 'crisis of feudalism' is far too broad-meshed a concept to capture the variety of forms and applications of seigneurial dependence or the deployment of extra-economic coer-

---

[*] Lieselott Enders, 'Entwicklungsetappen der Gutsherrschaft vom Ende des 15. bis zum Beginn des 17. Jahrhunderts, untersucht am Beispiel der Uckermark', *Jahrbuch für Geschichte des Feudalismus*, 12 (1988), pp. 119–66.

cion, though there is no doubting that Marxist categories of analysis come closer to comprehending the rationale of intensified seigneurialism in the east than neo-classical economic theory. What neither model accords sufficient weight to is the play of high politics – the impact of territorialization, both the mobilization of landed estates in the service of the prince through mortgages, and the uneasy balance between the separate, though reciprocal, interests of the state and the interests of the aristocracy.

7 Reform and Revolt

Imperial Reform in the Fifteenth Century

Contemporaries were exercised and perplexed by the deep social and economic transformations which they witnessed in the German lands at the close of the Middle Ages. From high-ranking prelates and chancery officials to urban councillors and syndics, from scholars and humanists to popular preachers and prophets, all were agreed that the Empire – as a salvific community and as a constitutional polity – must be set to rights. The watchword was reform, in both church and state. *Reformatio* (a recasting in Latin) bore different meanings for different audiences, but underlying them all was the conviction that reformation as renewal implied a return to first principles, to the good old order, be it the Empire in its heyday under the Hohenstaufen, or the Church in the age of apostolic Christianity: renovation, in other words, not innovation. It was in this tradition that the religious Reformers of the early sixteenth century stood. Their critique of the accretions and deformations of the Catholic Church was underscored by denunciations of the social and economic ills which confronted them in their own day; a return to the precepts of the Gospel – Christ's teaching on earth – was accompanied by a yearning for the simple life, a world without self-interest, greed, profit, or accumulation. In that, Martin Luther and his fellow-Reformers were reflecting and rehearsing the litany of grievances which made up the swelling corpus of reforming literature in the previous century, whose agenda came increasingly to dominate the sessions of the imperial diet. The times were out-of-joint: only an apocalyptic cleansing, many believed, could restore peace and public order. The corporate foundations of society, moreover, the pyramid of Estates, were being undermined by those who transgressed its carefully delineated gradations: 'let each remain in his Estate', said Luther, echoing the language of the reform tracts of the early fifteenth century.

The bulk of the reform literature and the prophecies of the fifteenth century, as well as the religious propaganda of the Reformation age, was only tangentially concerned with mundane economic and social discontents, but to those for whom the Empire had a salvific purpose (unlike mere national monarchies) or to those who held Christian doctrines to be the only template of a righteous life, justice, peace, and concord – the maxims of good order and the commonweal – must be upheld and practised by citizens both high and low in their daily lives. Where those maxims were ignored, or where a remedy for ills was not forthcoming, the lowly might rise up in rebellion and cast down the mighty from their seats. Whether the rebels' aims sought restitution and restoration of a fractured order, or encompassed the overthrow of the existing hierarchy and the creation of a new order, remains a hotly contested issue. Yet the context of both the secular application of Reforming doctrines and the aspirations of the rebellious commons was furnished in large measure by the swell of reform literature after 1400: the continuities between reform, Reformation, and revolt are fundamental to an understanding of popular protest in our period.

The principal forum for the reform proposals of the fifteenth century was the Councils of the Church held on German soil to end the schism of rival claimants to the papacy, and more broadly to determine the good governance of the Church. The first of these, convened at Konstanz from 1414 to 1418, had agreed that decisions of a General Council should be binding on all Christians, and provided for future assemblies to carry reform forward; the second, summoned to Basel in 1421 and which stuttered on at various venues until 1439, was called to address the unresolved issue of heresy in Bohemia under the radical Hussites, against whom a series of crusades had been launched, only to end in repeated *débâcles*. In the penumbra of its deliberations, however, there emerged a radical reform tract, penned by an unknown cleric, probably a native of one of the imperial cities of the south-west with good contacts to the circle of Emperor Sigismund, whose vision he claimed to enshrine.

This Reformation of Emperor Sigismund, although not printed until 1476, circulated in numerous manuscript versions; after its publication it went through eight editions up to 1522, and inspired (directly or obliquely) much of the reforming agenda of writers and publicists who came later. At the centre of the author's vision was the strengthening of the monarchy: a new emperor, hailed as a new Frederick of Hohenstaufen, the 'peace-rich', as the name Friedrich connotes in German, would arise to sweep away the arrogant, selfish princes and prelates, money-grabbers and war-mongers all, and so restore prosperity and peace to the German nation. The anonymous cleric drew upon imperial precedents, notably the so-called Mirror of the Swabians (*Schwabenspiegel*), a collection of laws compiled by a Franciscan friar in Augsburg around 1275, which in turn derived heavily from the more famous lawbook earlier in that century, the Mirror of the Saxons (*Sachsenspiegel*), composed in Latin by the legist Eike von Repgow, and translated by him into Low German. Both Mirrors expressly rejected the traditional justification of serfdom, above all by invoking Christ's sacrifice on the Cross, which had set all men free.

'It is an outrage', declared the Sigismund author, 'that one man should be so bereft before God that he can say to another "You are my own [property]". . . . It is the act of a heathen! For God has loosed us from all bonds, so that hereafter no one should claim such power over another. . . . Moreover', he went on, 'it has alas come to such a pass that members of the clergy, who should be God's own shield, take serfs unto themselves . . . I say plainly that no one who calls himself a Christian should behave thus. In the case of a nobleman, he should be stripped of his title and made to do penance if he will not desist; if a convent, it should be destroyed.'[*]

This was inflammatory language by any standard (not least from a priest), and it built upon passages in the *Schwabenspiegel* which then recur almost word-for-word in the Peasants' War of 1525, both in the local grievances of the peasants of Äpfingen near Biberach, and in the programme of the Twelve Articles of Upper Swabia. The excoriation of serfdom in the Reformation of Emperor Sigismund represents an exception in the reform literature of the fifteenth century, but other passages in this long tract addressed social and economic issues which remained running sores on the body politic well into

---

[*] *Reformation Kaiser Siegmunds*, ed. Heinrich Koller (*Monumenta Germaniae Historica 500–1500: Staatsschriften des späteren Mittelalters*, vol. 6) (Stuttgart, 1964), p. 278 f.

the sixteenth century. All, in various ways, reflected the commercialization of daily life, and the distortion in the exchange of goods and
in the exercise of trade which it had supposedly caused. The author
has relatively little to say about the practice of usury, which he
equates with greed and the lust for riches, rather than in its narrow
sense of taking excessive rates of interest, but he has plenty to say
about the chase for profit in general. He denounces those who buy
cheap and sell dear, particularly foodstuffs, evading or distorting the
market, a practice known as forestalling (*Fürkauf*), who 'deceive the
world with their sales and inordinate profits and oppress the poor'.[*]
And he extends his condemnation of speculators to the merchants
who trade in foreign markets, such as Venice, where they buy up
cloth and spices to sell at prices fixed by a cartel, and who dodge any
accusations of profiteering by bemoaning the great losses which they
have suffered on the high seas. Under the same heading he criticizes
those who step outside their learnt craft to deal on the side, a wine
merchant who trades in salt, or a tailor who also sells cloth, so that in
many cities four or five individuals, he declares, have cornered
enough trade for twenty men to make a living thereby. Although
such activity clearly contravened the corporate regulations of individual crafts, the author was no friend of guilds, either, whom he
accused of scratching each other's back. Councillors, for instance,
would come to underhand agreements to safeguard their mutual
interests, bakers overlooking the butchers' high meat prices,
butchers failing to point out the bakers' undersized loaves: the
victim of these underhand practices is always the commonweal.
Coinage, too, is counterfeit or debased; although the penalty for
counterfeiting is death, few culprits are ever caught and burnt. To
establish a sound coinage, all coin should be struck with the imperial
insignia on the obverse, and the mark of the minting lord or city on
the reverse. Commerce is also hindered by the many and excessive
tolls levied on goods passing by land or water; the majority should be
abolished, and toll-rates set every five years by honest inspectors. Not
only should waterways be free to all, the author extends the principle
to declare invalid any form of banal right – the control of forest,
pasture, or water – which burdens the peasantry.

We should not be surprised at the internal inconsistencies in the
agenda of the Reformation of Emperor Sigismund: removing tolls as
barriers to commerce while denouncing merchant companies;

---

[*] Ibid., p. 314.

demanding regulation of economic life while suspicious of those arch-corporatists and protectionists, the guilds. These were, after all, the proposals of a cleric, not of a professor of political economy. More seriously, the contradictions reflect the nature of German society and economy itself in the fifteenth century, an age in which the old order sat uneasily with the new: crafts and manufacturing amidst the agrarian economy; international trading companies located in cities with a guild regime; rulers consolidating and rationalizing their territories by recourse to the ancient instrument of serfdom.

By the closing decades of the century, many of the Sigismund tract's political aspirations had become the common coin of public discourse, manifest in the debates at the imperial diet of Worms in 1495, which outlawed feuding, proclaimed a general public peace, and instituted a universal poll-tax throughout the Empire, the so-called Common Penny. Social and economic ills were not yet on the agenda of the imperial diets, but they were addressed in the burgeoning pamphlet literature, sometimes with overtly apocalyptic overtones, and were subsequently taken up by the religious Reformers after 1517. This lineage can readily be observed in the draft of an imperial reformation, supposedly from the pen of an official of the archbishop of Mainz, Friedrich Weygandt, who intended to submit it to the 'parliament' of the peasant rebels set down to meet at Heilbronn in May 1525 at the height of the Peasants' War. The draft took up proposals adumbrated in a tract two years previously, the anonymous Needs of the German Nation (*Teutscher Nation notturfft*), also known – in a deliberate echo of its predecessor – as the Reformation of Emperor Frederick (that is, Frederick III), whose long reign from 1439 to 1493 had ended just before the great diet at Worms. What was new in Weygandt's draft was the explicit invocation of the Word of God as the template of all human conduct, but within this ideological framework the practical proposals were quite conventional. Apart from attacks on the upsurge of lawyers (a complaint not confined to Germany!) and the spread of Roman civil law, demands for the reduction or abolition of tolls and escort-fees, the establishment of a sound imperial coinage minted only from gold and silver, not base metals, and the institution of uniform weights and measures throughout the Empire all struck a familiar chord. Then Weygandt warmed to his theme: the existing trading companies (he mentions the Fuggers, Höchstetters, and Welsers of Augsburg by name) should be dissolved, and any further joint-stock enterprises should have their capital limited to 10000 florins – a figure that would have made a mockery of the Great Ravensburg Trading Company with ten times that share-capital, never mind the Fuggers who were on an altogether different plane. Weygandt did allow, however, that merchants might place money on deposit at 4 per cent in civic exchequers, though town councils were exhorted to lend such deposits to the poor at no more than 5 per cent: he was not an outright opponent of 'usury'.

Society and Economy in the Thought of the Religious Reformers

When Martin Luther issued his Address to the Christian Nobility of the German Nation on the Improvement of the Christian Estate in June 1520 – his most sweeping attack on the power of the papacy and the theology of the Roman Catholic Church – he concluded his philippic with a critique of German secular society, which linked the public ills of the Empire explicitly to the private failings of its citizens. There was an urgent need, he declared, to curb 'the excessive extravagance and expense of clothing which brings penury upon so many nobles and rich folk!' God had given the Germans enough wool, fur, and flax to clothe each Estate in its proper rank, so that 'we do not need to squander such huge sums on silks, velvets, articles of gold and other foreign imports'.* Even without the pope to fleece them, the Germans would still have had too many of these native robbers, the silk and velvet merchants. This Luther attributes to the desire to emulate others, upon which pride and envy thrive.

By the same token, Luther castigates the spice trade, the vessel which ships money out of the German lands, even though food and drink have by the grace of God always been plentiful enough, he asserts, as anywhere else. 'Perhaps I am putting forward foolish and impossible ideas', he asks rhetorically, as if intending to bring about the collapse of large-scale commerce, but for that reason 'God has caused the children of Israel to dwell far from the sea and forbad them to engage on any scale in commerce.' Luther then inveighs against the trading companies directly, whose activities lead to excessive and undeserved profits.

---

* *Luther's Works. American Edition*, ed. Jaroslav Pelikan and Helmut T. Lehmann, 55 vols (St Louis, MO/Philadelphia, 1955–86), vol. 44, p. 212 (translations amended by the present writer).

Verily we should bridle the Fuggers and other such companies. How can it come to pass in a godly and righteous manner that within a single lifetime wealth worthy of a king can be accumulated? I am no man for figures, but I do not understand how one hundred florins can yield twenty in return within a year or even how one florin generates another, since it does not come from tilling the soil or raising cattle, where wealth accrues not from human wits but from God's blessing.[*]

Alongside greed stand the sins of the flesh. Inordinate eating and drinking are held up by Luther as notorious German failings. The worst of it, he insists, is not the waste of money, but the vices of murder, adultery, robbery, blasphemy, and other evils to which they give rise. It is lamentable, moreover, that we should tolerate houses of ill-repute in our midst. It is better to have brothels, Luther concedes, than that the honour of wives and maidens be sullied, but 'if the children of Israel could exist without such an abomination, surely Christians should be able to do likewise!'[†]

Luther's stance, it is obvious, is that of a theologian and moralist, not of a secular reformer. In the few closing paragraphs of the Address to the Christian Nobility his concern is to highlight the harmful social consequences of the unChristian practices which he condemns, rather than to analyze the causes of those abuses. His strictures against monopolies and the larger trading companies are embedded in a general critique of luxury; his condemnation of usury as illegitimate profit is placed in the context of greed and licentiousness in general, the wanton behaviour known as 'grobianism' (from the German *grob*, coarse), which was particularly associated with the Germans and Dutch. In so doing he was transvaluing into religious categories the long-standing critique of Estates (*Ständekritik*), which found its principal expression in the welter of sumptuary laws issued by city councils and territorial princes. Such laws, designed originally to regulate expenditure, can be traced back to the thirteenth century, but they had their heyday – in itself a sign of turbulent times – between 1450 and 1550, when 260 were issued, more than half the number of all such edicts recorded since the year 1200. Sumptuary laws set down clearly what apparel was appropriate to each Estate, and the penalties for dressing beyond one's station.

---

[*] Ibid., pp. 212 f., 213 f.
[†] Ibid., p. 215.

Nuremberg, with its self-consciously exclusive patriciate, jealous of the finest gradations in status, yet dourly Franconian in its aversion to *grandezza*, offers a prime example. No one, mayor or councillor downwards to ordinary citizen or resident, even if originally from elsewhere, should wear shoes with excessive points, cloaks or jackets whose sleeves covered the hands (a precaution against trickery!), or velvet, pearls, and scarlet robes. Their womenfolk, especially the spouses of burgesses and notables, had always to be veiled in public; none, however mighty, should wear white headdresses with more than twelve pleats, skirts which trailed more than a hand's length along the ground, or with borders more than two fingers wide. They, too, were forbidden to wear pearls or scarlet, let alone high boots.[*] In the 1470s more than 1000 florins a year were accruing to the Nuremberg council from such fines!

Nuremberg was notorious for the surveillance of its citizenry, with secret denunciations of transgressions positively encouraged. Yet woe betide false accusations, as the wife of a sealmaker found to her cost in 1552. She was condemned to a day in the stocks for publicly berating the daughter of an organbuilder in the city for wearing a headband which was not fitting to her Estate. Nuremberg may well have been exceptional in the egalitarian rigour of its sumptuary laws. Other cities allowed their notables to wear finery: in Isny the burgesses had a special dining chamber where they foregathered in furs of marten and ermine, and fine silks. Nevertheless, the frequency of such legislation suggests that even stiff fines could not halt the march of fashion or the desire to ape one's betters. Moreover, sumptuary legislation made up only a fraction of the ordinances designed to regulate behaviour and prevent excess. There was a myriad of edicts setting out the correct conduct at marriages, baptisms, and funerals, or, more accurately, at the festivities thereafter, which were notorious for getting out of hand. Laws against gluttony, drunkenness, gambling, and blasphemy were legion – and heartily endorsed by the religious Reformers.

Since the Fall humanity had been beset by sin, and it was the duty of the clergy to call men and women to repent. But there is no doubt that the religious Reformers of the early sixteenth century, in common with the imperial reformers before them, believed that the spread of a commercial system with capitalist overtones lay at the

---

[*] *Die Freiburger Enquete von 1476. Quellen zur Wirtschafts- und Verwaltungsgeschichte der Stadt Freiburg im Breisgau im fünfzehnten Jahrhundert*, ed. Tom Scott (Freiburg im Breisgau, 1986), pp. 31–2.

root of all contemporary social and economic ills. Throughout the span of his career Luther attacked usury, beginning with his Small and Large Sermons Against Usury of 1518 and 1520, and concluding with his tract To The Parish Clergy, To Preach Against Usury of 1540. In 1524 he gathered together and elaborated upon his earlier writings in On Trade And Usury, which returned to the theme of the unnecessary import of luxury wares from India, and the resultant draining of wealth from Germany, particularly at the Frankfurt fair, described as the hole through which gold and silver disappeared. Nearer home it would be better, Luther observed, if the Germans left the king of England his woollens and the king of Portugal his spices. Yet when he turned to interest-payments, Luther was prepared to allow interest-taking in certain circumstances. Loans without risk were usury pure and simple. Hence he distinguished sharply between capital invested in a business, which by definition involved risk, and the buying of annuities with a guaranteed return, which was objectionable since it involved no risk at all. It was reasonable, Luther believed, for loans advanced as risk-capital to attract interest at between 4 and 6 per cent, though anything in excess of that rate was indeed usurious. However, Luther was also prepared to tolerate interest-payments as compensation for arrears or default on money lent, where the risk involved was both that of a real or actual loss, and a loss arising through foregone profit. This suggests that Luther had some appreciation – which is not the same thing as approval – of the intrinsic capacity of money to accumulate and that capital was a form of productive credit, a view which had in fact been adumbrated by Catholic scholastics in the fourteenth century, but which certainly went well beyond what many of his fellow-Reformers, such as Johann Agricola, or Johann Eberlin von Günzburg, would countenance. Agricola, for instance, like Luther a native of Eisleben in Saxony, in his commentaries on German proverbs in 1528 declared roundly, 'Striving for riches is avarice.' And the worst offenders were usurers, not simply those who bought annuities at no financial risk, but those who advanced capital to business enterprises. Agricola was particularly critical of the clergy as sellers of annuities, but he went on to contrast well-ordered government based on the honest toil of husbandmen, as in ancient Rome, where senators might be summoned from the plough, with the vast enterprise of Jakob Fugger in his own day, whom he blamed, *inter alia*, for striking a deal with the king of Portugal to drive up the price of spices, especially saffron and ginger. 'The laws of the Empire',

Agricola lamented, 'expressly forbad monopolies and forestalling . . . There is not one prince in Germany, it is said, who is not in debt to the Fuggers, which is why they ignore the imperial law.'*

The religious Reformers' hostility towards interest-taking and profit-making (both lumped together as 'usury') found little resonance, not least because interest-rates in Germany had fallen substantially from their medieval peak of 20 per cent or more to a standard level of 5 per cent after 1400. In any case, the prohibition on usury enshrined in canon law had already been circumvented by popes in the fifteenth century, who had declared the sale of annuities compatible with the law of the Church, while the Fifth Lateran Council in 1516 had approved the establishment of the so-called *montes pietatis*, the low-interest-charging public pawnshops championed by the Franciscan friars as a means of protecting the poor against truly usurious money-lenders. But the Reformers' suspicion of commerce and capital did indeed strike a strong chord in sixteenth-century Germany. Matters which had been beyond the purview of the great reform diet at Worms in 1495 (apart from sumptuary legislation) were brought on to the agenda of imperial diets in the second decade of the sixteenth century. In 1512 the assembly at Trier denounced monopolies, and the issue was taken up with renewed energy at Charles V's first diet, held at Worms in 1521 – the stage upon which Luther was called to account and condemned – not least because the emperor in his electoral capitulation had promised to take action against the trading companies. But countermeasures in the end were left to the princes and cities, the result of collusion between the emperor and his major financiers, the Fuggers, to block any decisive action at imperial level. This was an astute move, since the attitude of the leading cities to the large business firms in their midst was by no means uniform. In Augsburg, the headquarters of the Fuggers, Welsers, Höchstetters, and many other firms, religious unrest in the summer of 1524 at the proposed expulsion of the evangelical preacher Johannes Schilling spilled over into demands by the city's proletarians and poorer guildsfolk for the abolition of the trading companies and the overthrow of the council (as will be discussed later).

Hostility to the manifestations of early capitalism was also voiced

---

* Johann Agricola, *Die Sprichwörtersammlung*, vol. 1, ed. Sander L. Gilman (Berlin/New York, 1971), pp. 167, 172. Cf. the translation in *Manifestations of Discontent in Germany on the Eve of the Reformation*, ed. Gerald Strauss (Bloomington, IN/London, 1971), p. 120.

in Cologne and Ulm. In 1525 the craft guilds in Cologne submitted a list of 184 articles of grievance, in which they gave pride of place to the machinations of the great merchant houses, and demanded that these be investigated to see whether they were operating against the public interest. In particular, the guilds wanted new laws to regulate the import of luxuries from abroad, spices, gold, silver, silks, and the like, according to the commonweal. In Ulm twelve years earlier, the unrest had been domestic and more muted – complaints against the mayor, Hans Besserer, whose investment in a Stuttgart merchant company the guilds feared would hit their own trades. But in both Frankfurt am Main (where the 46 urban articles of grievance in 1525 were drawn up and then disseminated throughout northern Germany) and in Nuremberg, second only in rank to Augsburg as the home of merchant companies, there was no agitation against monopolies, putting-out, price-rigging, or forestalling. This should caution us against equating a political outcry at the highest level with widespread discontent at the grass-roots. Nevertheless, the debate in the imperial diet did not cease; the assault on trading companies was resumed in 1530, which prompted the Augsburg humanist and city secretary, Conrad Peutinger, at the instigation of the council, to compose a treatise in defence of monopolies, which broke the bounds of conventional economic thought, instinctively *dirigiste* and arcadian.

Peutinger's starting-point was a controversial one: he affirmed selfishness (in German *Eigennutz*, so often counterposed to *Gemeinnutz*, the commonweal) – or, as we should more soberly say, self-interest – as a fundamental component of human nature, and argued that expectation of profit was the only convincing motive for enterprise and risk-taking. Holding that supply was more important than demand in determining the level of prices, he propounded a law of price formation which emphasized market forces and discountenanced attempts by the authorities to set artificial tariffs. From there he reached a startling conclusion which stood the concept of monopoly on its head. What constituted a monopoly was any attempt to encroach upon the freedom of the individual to pursue his own interests according to his means and ability; by extension, any attempt to interfere in the level of prices was monopolistic. Far from being detrimental to the commonweal, the individual's pursuit of profit collectively conduced to the public good, since the latter implied the wealth and prosperity of as many citizens as possible. Adam Smith or Jeremy Bentham could not have put it better. With that, Peutinger undoubtedly let the Fuggers and their ilk off the hook, and he has often been condemned for that reason as a lackey of the merchant companies, in whose defence his treatise was written. But that facile judgement rather misses the point, namely, that for Peutinger it was economic *dirigisme* which was inimical to the general good. Yet at the same time Peutinger was too much the child of his age – and his urban environment – to accept that there should be a free market in the supply of essential foodstuffs: here councils should impose tariffs. Of course, Peutinger's attempt to argue that the large merchant houses were apostles of the free market was entirely specious. Their wealth and power were indeed based on political horse-trading: in return for the cession of regalian rights in the Tirolean mining industry, together with the granting of exclusive mining privileges, they were able to dictate prices, pay their workers in truck, and bring all stages of production and distribution under their control in a paradigm of vertical integration. They flourished, in other words, not through free-market competition but by achieving a virtual monopoly on the back of political guarantees (which Peutinger condoned, clearly reluctant to offend the Fuggers). However much the Fuggers – uniquely among the Upper German business houses – pioneered the independent firm, controlled by individuals from one family, rather than joint-stock ventures with outside participation, their business ethos was closer to the corporatist and protectionist spirit of the craft guilds than to unfettered free-market capitalism. The difference was that the city councils kept the latter under their thumb but were largely powerless against the former, who bought up rural estates as a security and threatened to withdraw from civic society – and the payment of civic taxes – if the urban authorities made life too difficult for them. The mercantile entrepreneurs and putters-out of early modern Germany, however eager for profit, were in general wedded to a patriarchal, not a capitalist, view of the world, whose norms were those of the landed aristocracy.

Hand-wringing over the monopolistic merchant companies may easily give the impression that the imperial diet reacted parlously to the economic problems of the day. In fact, as the sixteenth century wore on, it concerned itself more and more with measures designed actively to promote the economic well-being of the German lands, which foreshadow the mercantilist doctrines of the following century, that is to say, the policies of securing cheap domestic supplies of raw materials, of keeping reserves of bullion within Germany, and of

prohibiting the export of essential goods. In 1548 the first ordinances against the export of wool were proclaimed (though without
a corresponding ban on imports, which would have been truly
mercantilist), followed by a halt to leather exports in 1577. Imperial
prohibitions were in themselves largely useless unless echoed in territorial legislation, but there is little evidence that princes, particularly
in territories with extensive wool production such as Hessen and
Thuringia, were prepared to follow suit. In one respect, however, the
Empire was able to effect a startling change. After years of negotiations the imperial diet in 1559 at last agreed on an imperial coinage
ordinance, which established a fixed standard for a common cur-
rency throughout the German lands, thereby putting an end to two
centuries of monetary instability. The new coinage, the *Reichsthaler*,
was to be supervised not by the princes but by the imperial circles
(*Reichskreise*), which had been created by Maximilian at the beginning of the century as the regional judicial organs of the imperial
government. Although the ordinance made regional coinage associations (with competing currencies and fluctuating exchange rates)
redundant, it could not in itself guarantee the solidity of the new
coinage, as the terrible afflictions of rampant inflation and debasement at the onset of the Thirty Years War, the so-called *Kipper- und
Wipperzeit*, between 1618 and 1623 were to bring home.

The Empire as a plural polity was not the toothless lion of older
accounts; its judicial powers exercised by the imperial court of
chancery (*Reichskammergericht*) established in 1495, and its constitutional authority vested in the imperial aulic council (*Reichshofrat*)
after 1498 (though the boundaries of their respective competences
were never clearly drawn), were increasingly invoked in the course of
the sixteenth century. The imperial diets may have been inadequate
forums to deal with the secular ills of the age, as responsibility for
what became known as 'good police' (*gute Polizey*) devolved, largely
by default, upon the princely territories and urban magistracies, but
the Empire's supreme judicial organs took centre-stage, not only in
upholding law and order throughout the German lands at the level
of high politics (outlawing the feud, maintaining the public peace),
but also in resolving outbreaks of protest at local level, so that, in
Winfried Schulze's words, the sixteenth century in Germany witnessed the 'juridification' of social conflict after two centuries of
endemic popular protest,[*] as we will explore in Chapter 8.

---

[*] Winfried Schulze, 'Die veränderte Bedeutung sozialer Konflikte im 16. und 17. Jahrhundert', in
Hans-Ulrich Wehler (ed.), *Der deutsche Bauernkrieg 1524–1526* (Göttingen, 1975), pp. 277–302.

Urban Revolts in the Fourteenth Century

The historiography of urban revolts in the German-speaking lands has until recently been bedevilled by two largely unspoken assumptions: first, that the waves of urban unrest subsided in the mid-sixteenth century; second, that urban revolts were chiefly constitutional in character. It is sometimes forgotten that Erich Maschke, the historian who did so much to set these revolts in an analytic and comparative context, was at pains to stress that a cluster of revolts occurred in textile-manufacturing cities with early-capitalist division of labour, and that strikes in the booming mining centres were just as much a part of the fabric of urban protest as struggles over the division of political power.[*] He might have added the many protests by journeymen and apprentices against their conditions of employment, especially in the first half of the fifteenth century.

Nevertheless, it is now clear that the spasms of urban unrest continued up to and beyond the end of our period, with clusters in the 1580s and 1590s, again on the eve of the Thirty Years War, and continued unabated throughout the seventeenth and eighteenth centuries until the collapse of the *ancien régime*; indeed, the structural similarity between the latter and the guild revolts of the fourteenth century has been emphasized by Christopher Friedrichs,[†] which certainly weakens any attempt to identify the revolts as immediate responses to particular economic conjunctures. It is understandable, moreover, that historians have concentrated upon political struggles in the German towns and cities, because they display, through the involvement of the commons at large, the hallmarks of collective consciousness and action which are the necessary prerequisites of a social movement. Yet this approach threatens to marginalize sectional agitation – by an individual guild, or its apprentices, for instance – either by airbrushing it out of the picture altogether, or by relegating it to the level of reactive protest or mere rioting. For several decades it was left to East German Marxist historians to stress the economic and social undertow to urban protest, but their analysis was often vitiated by an insistence that revolts could simply be read off as a series of class struggles and by a naïve belief (which had been prevalent in the nineteenth century) that such movements were in some fashion democratic.

---

[*] Erich Maschke, 'Deutsche Städte am Ausgang des Mittelalters', in Wilhelm Rausch (ed.), *Die Stadt am Ausgang des Mittelalters* (Linz, 1974), pp. 1–44.
[†] See his essays listed in the Bibliography of Works in English.

Between 1301 and 1540 Maschke counted over 200 uprisings in more than 100 German towns; if we add revolts up to the Thirty Years War the number might well top 250. This figure far exceeds the total for any other European country in the same period – but what are its implications? Germany's nearest rivals in this regard are northern Italy and Flanders, and that is in itself suggestive: fragmented polities without central monarchical or princely authority, in which the cities were politically and economically dominant, so that, by extension, their regimes became the immediate target of discontent. Yet social and economic grievances were, it seems, much more prominent in Italian and Flemish communes than in German ones. To some degree this is a trick of the light: behind many of the 'political' revolts in the Hanseatic cities before and after 1400 lay grievances at the financial burdens incurred by the patriciate, either collectively as a city council, or as individual careerists, in extending the tentacles of power to the surrounding countryside, in a pale reflection of the Italian cities' domination of their *contadi* or the leading Flemish cities' influence over their 'quarters', whose motives were political only in the sense that 'political' was a cipher for economic exploitation. These wealthier and more powerful communes were never able to stifle or defuse overtly political opposition – unlike Italy, the towns of Germany were not full of 'tyrants', as Dante had described the solitary tribunes appointed from without to hold the ring amidst the competing urban factions and clienteles; nor were they prey to the vendettas of *mafioso* gangster dynasties such as the van Arteveldes in Ghent. But the German communes at the same time enjoyed considerably greater autonomy than their counterparts in England and France, where urban revolts (with a few notable exceptions in times of political or military emergency) were comparatively rare. In other words, the German cities stand at the mid-point of a spectrum, neither weak enough to be spared political factionalism on a scale which might tip over into revolt, nor strong enough to be forced into extreme solutions – importing foreign despots – to contain it. This point gains additional force when we realize that it was, almost without exception, the larger German communes, the free and imperial cities to the fore, which were susceptible to revolt, often repeatedly: the lesser towns, ruled by territorial princes, showed a much smaller incidence of popular protest, except in the two decades immediately preceding the Reformation.

Although struggles over the distribution of power were the undertow to urban unrest throughout our period, distinct phases, as well as a shifting geography, of protest can be identified. During the fourteenth and early fifteenth century there were clusters of revolts between 1330 and 1350, 1365 and 1385, and again between 1400 and 1430. Many of these uprisings were what used to be called 'guild revolts' (or even 'revolutions'!), that is to say, attempts by the craft guilds to wrest power (or a share of power) from the ruling patriciate. But this picture is too stark. Quite apart from the occasional instance of a patrician *fronde* (such as that of the von Auer family in Augsburg in the 1330s, mentioned in Chapter 2, and similar disturbances in Strasbourg in 1349), participation in these struggles was altogether more heterogeneous. Often sections of the urban elite – aspiring merchants, for example – might combine with the guild-masters to challenge the power of a council composed of ministerial or rentier families; at other times the craft guilds stood in direct opposition to the merchant guilds. In general, however, the participants were drawn from the ranks of the enfranchised burgesses, rather than from the lesser folk, those with mere rights of residence or the urban lower orders (*Unterschichten*), labourers and wage-workers. Moreover, the leading figures in the revolts came by-and-large from the wealthier guilds, for only the richer masters could afford the time and loss of earnings which council duty entailed (it was unpaid, expenses were usually modest, and it involved sitting on legal and administrative benches as well). In many south German communes these struggles were crowned with greater or lesser success, as in Ulm, Zürich, Strasbourg, and (temporarily) Basel. One revolt ended in spectacular failure: the attempt by the guilds to seize power in Nuremberg in 1348, which was crushed by the city's mercantile elite backed by imperial forces. Thereafter the city – as always the exception within Germany – continued to tolerate craft associations subject to civic regulation, but no guilds with a political voice.

In northern Germany, by contrast, it used to be thought that the guilds were much less successful in gaining a stake in the civic administration. It is certainly true that a guild constitution (*Zunftverfassung*) as the defining feature of the social polity was often missing in the north. But collective action revolved instead around other corporate institutions such as parishes, wards, lay brotherhoods, or even archery clubs. Moreover, the negative picture of political emancipation in the north has been too strongly coloured by the example of the mercantile coastal cities – Lübeck, Hamburg, Bremen, or the Wendish ports further east – or else by powerful inland communes such as Lüneburg (whose fortunes from its brine-pits had allowed it to oust the dukes of Braunschweig), which were indeed notoriously hostile towards the craft guilds. In Westphalia and Saxony the picture was quite different: the crafts wrested power in Braunschweig from the patriciate in 1374, quickly imitated by its neighbour Nordhausen the following year. Magdeburg had a guild constitution by 1330, after protracted internal unrest; in Münster the guilds had to wait until the mid-fifteenth century before they were granted a political voice. Sometimes, as in Münster and Osnabrück (though not in Braunschweig), opposition was expressed through the formation of a *Gesamtgilde* which embraced all the civic crafts in one political organ, an association quite unknown in the south. This unitary guild was to prove itself extremely powerful in the extraordinary events which attended the conversion of Münster between 1533 and 1535 from a city of Reformed Protestant inclination into the so-called Anabaptist Kingdom of Zion, a transformation accomplished by legitimate means, not force, thanks to the ease with which the city's peculiarly 'open' guild constitution allowed the council to be capsized.

The immediate context for the outbreak of revolt was often the annual elections to the council, which allowed charges of peculation and croneyism to be bandied about; frequently the commons demanded that the council open its books and account for its expenditure, particularly if new imposts had been levied in the preceding months. As resentment mounted, it was common for the citizens to form delegate committees to petition the council for redress. If their demands were met, a new slate of councillors could be hoisted into office at the elections, usually with much the same social background as those they replaced. If the council remained defiant, then open agitation – street protests, demonstrations, banner-waving processions, truculent assemblies before the town hall – might culminate in the banishment of the old council, confiscation of its estates, and the installation of a new regime. Physical violence was by no means unknown, but rarely spilled over into the kind of assassinations perpetrated, for instance, by the van Arteveldes and their henchmen in Ghent in the early 1380s.

A red thread running through protests in many Hanseatic cities at that time, and into the early fifteenth century, was opposition to extraordinary taxation or excessive expenditure which had been incurred as a result of the councils' foreign policies. Although few north German cities (as we have seen in Chapter 5) pursued an active territorial policy, preferring to acquire strategically situated

towns and lordships in mortgage, military expeditions against neighbouring lords and princes or the ambitions of individual councillors
might provoke internal dissent if they proved too costly. The
Braunschweig revolt of 1374, a beacon at the time, arose from the
imposition of an unprecedented excise to pay for territorial acquisitions; these turned out to be castles bought by councillors individually, though masked by the cloak of civic necessity, of which the new
council directed that its predecessors should forthwith be divested.
In Cologne in 1396 and Lübeck in 1408, the commune objected to
excessive expenditure on military expeditions against local lords,
adding, in the case of Lübeck, that no councillors should be allowed
to own landed estates beyond a certain distance from the city. A year
later in Rostock, a citizens' committee demanded that as a matter of
principle all landowners should be barred from office.

Interestingly, in southern Germany, where many imperial and free
cities pursued successful territorial policies, no revolts appear to
have been provoked by the acquisition of rural dependencies. The
reason was that, given the radial centrality of these cities, the creation of a protective zone with a market precinct, the suppression of
rival markets, and the securing of supplies through monopsony, lay
in the interests of all citizens, with many craftsmen actively alarmed
at the spread of rural competition, whereas in the mercantile cities
of the Hanseatic region, with their axial centrality, control of the
hinterland had much less economic rationale, so that their territorial policies were indeed often no more than the expression of
private ambitions. (The much more aggressive territorial expansion
of the leading Swiss cities, however, gave rise to rural resistance, as
will be discussed below.)

But not all Hanseatic revolts at the turn of the fourteenth century
can be pressed so readily into the framework of collective protest
against unaccountable patricians. Two revolts of the butchers
(*Knochenhauer*) at Lübeck in 1380 and 1384 stemmed from circumstances which reveal the other side of civic autonomy and what
Georg Schmidt has called a 'closed' or regulated economy (*gebun-
dene Wirtschaft*).* The butchers, a fractious trade in many cities
because their wealth sat uneasily with their precarious social
standing, as they rubbed shoulders with the knackers, were subject to

---

* Georg Schmidt, '"Frühkapitalismus" und Zunftwesen: Monopolbestrebungen und Selbstverwaltung in der frühneuzeitlichen Wirtschaft', in Bernhard Kirchgässner and Eberhard Naujoks
(eds), *Stadt und wirtschaftliche Selbstverwaltung* (Sigmaringen, 1987), pp. 77–114.

strict supervision, just as the lowlier bakers and tanners, both in terms of guaranteeing market supply and in order to maintain good quality and public hygiene. In Lübeck that meant not only the compulsion to deliver meat to the market rather than sell elsewhere (the principle of *Marktzwang*), but the requirement to hire their stalls from the council. The butchers twice sought to break this stranglehold, but without success, a sectional struggle whose outcome may well have been welcomed by the other guilds as consumers. Whether collective or sectional, however, there is little sign that the spate of rebellions in Hanseatic cities in the eight decades after 1350 stemmed from serious social and economic dislocations in the wake of plague and demographic collapse; there is no ready comparison between them and the clustering of rebellion in the 1370s and 1380s in other parts of Europe.

Urban Revolts on the Eve of the Reformation

The recrudescence of civic unrest in the closing decades of the fifteenth century equally finds little parallel beyond the German lands. Its underlying cause was the assertion by civic elites of their authority as magistrates ruling over subjects – *Obrigkeit* versus *Untertan* – as we have sketched in Chapter 2. In Tom Brady's words, 'sometime around 1450 came the watershed between an age of devolution of political voice to the guildsmen and an age of its re-concentration in the hands of the noble and mercantile elites'[*] – and even of wealthier craftsmen who differentiated themselves increasingly from those of inferior social status. This resurrection of oligarchy has never been adequately explained: it should, however, be set against the background of gradual population recovery, with renewed clamour for work side-by-side with the often contradictory desire to extend craft regulation, cap production, and embrace protectionism. In a bold stroke, Georg Schmidt has even suggested that the craft guilds were the authors of their own misfortunes, inasmuch as the pressure for legislation over wages, prices, and conditions of employment placed a heavy administrative burden on councillors who were neither salaried nor full-time officials, and who perhaps understandably retreated into closed decision-making, musing sourly that their

---

[*] Tom Brady, 'Economic and social institutions', in Bob Scribner (ed.), *Germany: A new economic and social history*, vol. 1 (London/New York/Sydney/Auckland, 1996), p. 276.

efforts earned little reward and less thanks. The fact that councillors, by rotation or co-option, often sat for years in office, circumventing the spirit if not the letter of urban constitutions, may have less to do with 'oligarchy' or 'corruption' than with the plain truth that qualified and financially independent councillors were hard to come by.

At a broader level, however, it is clear that urban magistracies were under the same pressures as princely chanceries. The press of business and the spread of written records demanded more efficient – which is not the same thing as accountable – administration: and to the bureaucratic mind the recipients of its decrees were not citizens but subjects. The charge on which municipal oligarchies should be arraigned is that, despite their high-falutin' airs, their administrations in many instances remained hopelessly amateurish, especially when it came to financial matters. One example may suffice. In the wake of its far-flung enquiry in 1476 into conditions in other south German cities, the council of Freiburg im Breisgau set about recasting the civic administration, chiefly with the aim of cutting costs. It decided that the number of officials on the Board of the Exchange, the town's financial watch-dog, should be reduced from six to four, but then changed its mind and put the number down to three. Although the savings were substantial, the measure backfired, since three men could not cope with the amount of paper-work. By June 1477 the Board of the Exchange was restored to five officials, but within a decade there were muttered criticisms of its conduct of business which culminated in a royal commission being despatched to Freiburg in 1490 by Maximilian to investigate the town's affairs. It recommended that the number of Exchange officials remain at five, but that three of them should not be councillors but ordinary guildsmen barred from holding any other office. Far from restoring stability, this concession merely opened the gates to further agitation, resulting in an attempted coup by a self-appointed popular tribune, Konrad Walzenmüller, in 1492. In its aftermath the council declared it intolerable that the commons' delegate committee, which had been appointed two years earlier, should continue to nominate three men to the Board of the Exchange, since the latter could transact no confidential business without its deliberations immediately being leaked to the citizenry at large. In 1495 the council proposed that the 1477 provisions be reinstated, but in the end had to agree that all five names be confirmed by itself and the commons' committee jointly, an arrangement which at last achieved a workable compromise, for it was still in place half a century later.

To couch the long-running unrest between council and commons in Freiburg after 1476 baldly in terms of a struggle between oligarchy and communality rather misses the point, for at its heart lay an intractable issue: where was the balance to be struck between accountability and confidentiality? There were perfectly good grounds for keeping some council business secret, but too often at the turn of the fifteenth century confidentiality became an alibi for political expediency, or a cloak for financial mismanagement.

The swell of urban revolts on the eve of the Reformation, although still concentrated in the larger cities, began to encompass smaller, less independent communities, where not surprisingly feelers were put out to the surrounding countryside. In Alsace, with its exceptional urban density, there were disturbances in Kaysersberg in 1521 and riots two years later in Cernay, but these were purely local events compared with the uprising in Rouffach in 1514, which in fact embraced the entire territory of the Upper Mundat, a lordship belonging to the bishop of Strasbourg surrounded by the Habsburg lands of Outer Austria. Here the grievances fell into two categories, without ever quite coalescing: the inhabitants of Rouffach itself complained at the town council's high-handed government, including excessive expenditure, arbitrary arrest, and restrictions on the usufruct of common – the usual catalogue of anti-oligarchical protest; these grievances were echoed in the Upper Mundat at large, but with the twist that the countryside also voiced outrage at discrimination in legal matters by the town council as their immediate superior. Parallel to these charges accusations of licentious conduct were levelled at the episcopal bailiff, who was alleged to have molested several female citizens and to have threatened their husbands with imprisonment if they dared complain, as well as jacking up the territorial tax and certain excises without reference to the bishop, Wilhelm von Honstein. Moreover, the grievances of the individual rural jurisdictions of the Upper Mundat (as opposed to the collective set of articles) almost without exception attacked the bailiff, not the Rouffach council. Faced with opposition from within and without, the latter closed ranks with the bishop's official – it was, in effect, acting as the long arm of the episcopal administration; in other words, unrest which at first sight seemed specific to the town in fact had a territorial dimension.

This emerges with even greater clarity in the same year in another revolt which engulfed much of the duchy of Württemberg, the so-called Poor Conrad uprising. Its proximate cause was the imposition of a new territorial excise, whose extra revenues were partly to be achieved by tampering with the duchy's weights and measures. More generally, the heavy-handed conduct of ducal officials at local level, in the administrative districts (*Ämter*) into which Württemberg was divided, caused resentment. Although the revolt brought the countryside up in arms (especially over damage to crops caused by game being allowed to roam the forest to provide good hunting for the lords), it seized the middling and poorer citizens of the smaller towns, as capitals of the *Ämter*, as well, whose civic dignitaries supplied the duchy with its local officials and represented the *Ämter* in the territorial diet. Duke Ulrich, for whom even revisionist historians cannot find a good word to say (except that he was not a drunkard), and who was shortly to be driven out of his principality by the forces of the Swabian League and exiled for 15 years, quashed the revolt by cutting a deal with the selfsame civic notables, with the result that nearly 1700 rebels were imprisoned and many executed.

Once the stormclouds of the Reformation burst upon the German urban communes, they not only washed away in many cases the uneasy consensus which had been reached between council and commons, but caused other wells of resentment to overflow. Martin Luther's 'freedom of a Christian' and invocation of the Gospel were interpreted by many urban Reforming preachers in an openly egalitarian sense: if Christ enjoined us to love our neighbours as ourselves, then the norms governing the civic community – often stylized as an Augustinian city of God in miniature – should be those of brotherliness, the commonweal, and equality of social and economic status. Hence urban revolts in the early 1520s sometimes took on the character of religiously legitimated class struggles, particularly in those cities which were in the throes of early capitalist development. This can be seen in the case of Augsburg, where the council's decision in August 1524 to expel the Reforming preacher, Johannes Schilling, a man with strong Zwinglian communal-congregational convictions, unleashed rioting in the Lower City amongst the poorer guildsfolk and lower classes, during which further demands were voiced for the abolition of the merchant companies and the overthrow of the council. These demands reflected the interests of the wage-labouring proletariat which had developed as the result of the putting-out system, particularly the weavers and tailors working on wage-contracts or piecework. But concerted action by an unholy alliance of patricians, merchants, and upper and middling guildsfolk soon put an end to the protest and ensured that there would be no recurrence throughout the century.

Elsewhere, plebeian groupings often provided a radical undertow to communal opposition movements, as in the Baltic Hanseatic ports of Wismar, Stralsund, and Rostock in the late 1520s. There it was not the activities of the large trading companies which fuelled discontent, but the nature of employment itself in seafaring communities, with a shifting and rootless class of casual labour in the docks: stevedores, boatmen, minor artisans, alongside paupers and beggars. Once the solid guildsfolk, under the slogan of the Gospel, used citizens' committees to force their way onto the merchant-dominated councils and to introduce Lutheran worship in the cities' churches they quickly severed their ties to the plebeians, who had threatened to develop into a permanent revolutionary force. But the very nature of their lives and occupations made organized and durable political agitation hard to sustain: in A. G. Dickens's words, 'they lacked leadership, cohesion and a clear sense of their own objectives.'* The radical citizens' committees which they formed – soviets, in all but name – petered out by the mid-1530s, as the Lutheran pastors exhorted the faithful to obedience and discipline. It comes as no surprise that radical religious doctrines, notably Anabaptism, found a ready audience amongst sections of the Baltic cities' populations.

In the early Reformation years the more astute city councils of Protestant persuasion were able to deflect much popular protest into well-established channels – attacks on the clergy. Violent forms of so-called 'parsons' storms' (*Pfaffenstürme*) had a venerable history in many German cities, stretching back in some cases to the thirteenth century, and erupting periodically thereafter. The Reformation merely concentrated and intensified these manifestations of popular disgust against those perceived as parasites upon the civic community. The varieties and causes of anticlericalism – a controversial issue in current scholarship – are too vast and complex to receive detailed investigation within the compass of this book. All that needs to be noted is that anticlericalism was not reserved for the upper echelons of the ecclesiastical hierarchy: it was directed against ordinary parish priests as well. Nor can it be said that hostility towards the regular clergy was necessarily greater than towards their secular counterparts, though the latter (as we have observed in Chapter 2) were not above stirring up popular feeling against the friars, whom they accused of usurping their parochial functions. If town councils

---

* A. G. Dickens, 'Some Hanseatic cities – and Erfurt', in idem, *The German Nation and Martin Luther* (London, 1974), p. 160.

were willing, either through conviction or expediency, to order clerical property to be inventoried, to confiscate church plate, to suspend clerical immunities, to require the clergy to swear an oath of citizenship, and to contribute to civic taxes – as happened during the Peasants' War in Alsace, when regional centres such as Wissembourg, Haguenau, Sélestat, or Colmar were under threat, with fifth columnists within their walls eager to ally with the peasant bands – then domestic unrest could be defused and the peasant rebels denied entry.

In northern Germany, Erfurt, with its vast territory, did not get off so lightly. In June 1521 the council had been the (complicit) beneficiary of a 'parsons' storm', in which students from the town's university, abetted by journeymen, apprentices, and local peasants, had sacked 43 houses belonging to canons of collegiate chapters, as well as the archbishop of Mainz's consistory court, as a means of demonstrating their impatience for the introduction of evangelical doctrines. But although the council, with Lutherans in its ranks, made cautious headway over the next three years, it was not acting fast enough for the surrounding peasants, as the great rebellion engulfed Thuringia in the spring of 1525. In April the council was obliged to admit a peasant army (said, implausibly, to have numbered 11 000) on condition that it left the citizenry unharmed – the unspoken invitation being to harm the clergy instead. That the rebels did with gusto, looting the houses of the clergy anew, and destroying the archbishop's prison and administrative headquarters, replete with records. But this time the council lost control of the situation. A newly elected council had to submit all its decisions for scrutiny by two committees drawn from the urban guild opposition and from the peasantry. In May 1525 they together presented a list of 28 articles which the council was sworn to adopt. Although known as the 'peasant articles', in reality the grievances reflected essentially urban discontents and, apart from their strictures against the clergy and its rapacity, were on the whole moderate in tone, calling for greater financial transparency, the maintenance of correct weights and measures, unrestricted trade, and an end to arbitrary taxation and illegal detention. None of this (as we have seen) was at all novel. Once the peasants had withdrawn from the city, and the rural rebellion in central Germany had gone down to sanguinary defeat, the council calmly proceeded to introduce Lutheran worship throughout the city, to reassert its authority over the city's territory, and to execute a handful of peasant ringleaders. There was never any real danger, despite appearances, that a 'popular front' of peasants and burghers would tumble Erfurt into revolutionary upheaval.

The explosive force of the new doctrines was none the less so manifest that preachers and magistrates lost no time in extolling the virtues of peace and dutiful obedience, and (more pertinently) in ensuring that proper channels of redress were open to citizens' discontents. That may account for the lull in urban unrest during the middle decades of the sixteenth century, though it certainly did not disappear entirely. In several cities where the Reformation had failed to make an impact in the 1520s, clamour for Reforming doctrines was often accompanied by civic unrest: muted in the case of Osnabrück, where after the Obergau revolt in 1525 the council edged towards the Reformation in the 1540s while trying to keep the lid on pressure from below; pandaemonic in the case of Münster, where apocalyptic Anabaptists in 1534 transformed the city into a 'kingdom of Zion', replacing the civil council with a theocratic monarchy and a board of elders.

Urban Revolts at the Turn of the Sixteenth Century

That urban revolts flared up again from the 1580s onwards has customarily been attributed to the spread of early absolutist policies and the deteriorating economic situation of many German cities. Both these arguments need to be treated with some reserve. The more closely one examines 'early absolutism', the more it appears a mirage, at least until the Thirty Years War, while the spectacular collapse of many Upper German business houses in the second half of the sixteenth century cannot, as we have argued in Chapter 5, be equated with any general urban economic downturn. What stands out is rather the extraordinary continuity of rebellion in certain cities throughout our entire period – Augsburg in the south, Cologne in the west, Lübeck and Braunschweig in the north, together with the Baltic ports of Wismar, Stralsund, and Greifswald. The immediate cause of many of the latter revolts was once again the arrogance and cliquishness of the ruling elites, though other motives, hitherto of peripheral significance, began also to emerge.

One of the most spectacular uprisings – on account of its violence, duration, and imperial ramifications – was the Fettmilch revolt in Frankfurt am Main between 1612 and 1614. What precipitated the first demonstrations was the occasion of the election in 1612 of King

Matthias as emperor, staged in Frankfurt, its traditional venue, at a time when confessional tensions within the Empire were running high, with the Protestant Union and the Catholic League having been formed shortly before. Under the terms of its constitution, the city was obliged to guarantee the safety of all those attending the coronation, from the emperor and the electoral princes downwards, on pain of suspension of its privileges. The citizens, already fed up with the haughty behaviour of the patriciate, its croneyism and legal chicanery, demanded that these privileges be publicly proclaimed. When, after some delay, the council rejected the citizens' demands as baseless, the enraged commons formed a committee to confront the council directly, and meanwhile took up arms. Other imperial cities hastened to offer their services as negotiators, while the emperor himself despatched the archbishop of Mainz and the land-grave of Hessen-Darmstadt as mediators. The provisional result in December 1612 was an accord which confirmed the political enfran-chisement of the guilds and the representation of the citizenry on the council. Instead of stabilizing the polity, however, this accord (as we have seen in other instances) merely served as a window for wider demands, which came to a head in 1614, when the old council was deposed and its members arrested and banished. In its place, a new citizens' council was installed. This chain of events had been stage-managed by a popular tribune, Vinzenz Fettmilch, from a family on the fringes of power, who had been repeatedly rebuffed from public office. Together with his henchmen, Fettmilch launched a thuggish assault on Frankfurt's Jewish quarter, plundering houses and finally driving the Jews out of the city. Two years earlier voices had been raised against the usurious rates of interest charged by the Jews, and the accord of December 1612 had set a ceiling of 8 per cent on all such loans, seemingly to no avail. Antisemitic violence – with peri-odic pogroms – had been a feature of many German cities in the later Middle Ages which housed Israelite communities. The upshot was frequently their expulsion, so that in the course of the sixteenth century Jewish groups were to be found predominantly in the coun-tryside (especially in the territories of the imperial knights), or in the smaller towns. By the time of the Fettmilch uprising, Jewish com-munities of any size, apart from Frankfurt itself, only existed in Friedberg in Hessen, in Worms and Speyer, and in Prague. Yet hos-tility towards the Jews in Frankfurt stretched back a century or more: the Frankfurt Articles of 1525, the most widely disseminated urban grievances of the Peasants' War, had attacked Jewish usury and pawnbroking. What had changed by 1612 was that antisemitic hatred had taken centre-stage, possibly as a result of growing impoverishment in the city (though the rebels' demand for cheap grain had also been heard in 1525).

Faced with imperial outlawry the solidarity of the Fettmilch rebels crumbled, so that by December 1614 the reinstated old council promptly abolished the guilds as political corporations (a fate which had earlier befallen several other imperial cities at the hands of Charles V in 1548), and readmitted the Jewish community. From the punishments meted out – executions, banishments, and fines – on well over 2000 inhabitants, it is clear that the revolt was much more than a political coup engineered by Fettmilch, but was indeed a broadly based communal opposition movement with antisemitism its driving force.

The protracted unrest in Aachen, which culminated at the same time as the Fettmilch uprising, although centring on control and accountability of the council, like so many earlier revolts, stemmed from circumstances which were entirely new: the co-existence of two religious confessions within one city, a Catholic party and a Protestant one with strong Calvinist leanings. Up to 1598 Aachen had been governed for the best part of twenty years by a Protestant council, but in that year it was deposed (through the intervention of the emperor) and replaced with a Catholic council, which thereupon resolved that only Catholics might hold public office. In so doing, it excluded from political power the bulk of the economic elite of the city, which began to turn itself into a self-conscious counter-elite, whose opposition to the council led to the formation of a citizens' committee in 1608 and further agitation in 1611. What made the situation in Aachen so complicated was that the success of the Catholic faction in re-Catholicizing the citizenry ensured the restoration of good relations with neighbouring Catholic lords, upon which much of Aachen's commercial prowess and the fortunes of the counter-elite in fact depended.*

Yet at the same time the council yielded to petitions from the craft guilds to curb the admission of new citizens and guildmasters, which the Calvinist mercantile counter-elite, committed to a free labour-market, demanded should be lifted. Along a quite different axis of interest, meanwhile, even Catholic citizens feared that Aachen's lib-

---

* Another *politique* faction of Catholics, however, was prepared to keep religious orthodoxy and political power separate.

erties as an imperial city might be jeopardized by too rigorous a Catholic policy, since it could lay the city open to Spanish Habsburg interference from the neighbouring duchy of Brabant. And that is exactly what happened: a hopelessly intractable situation was only brought to an end by Aachen's surrender to a Spanish army under General Ambrogio Spinola in 1614. The astonishing convolutions in the development of civic protest in Aachen were doubtless exceptional, but they serve to remind us how superficial it is to construe 'guild struggles' in our period as straightforward antagonisms between council and citizens, powerful and powerless. Sectional and class interests – potentiated in a confessional age – cut across or vitiated such facile distinctions.

Late Medieval Rural Rebellions

Rural unrest in the German-speaking lands between 1300 and 1600 shows one striking similarity to and one important difference from the incidence of urban rebellion. Rural revolts in late medieval Germany outstripped in frequency (though not so markedly as their urban counterparts) those in any other area of Europe. Moreover, the older view that rebellions subsided in the wake of the Peasants' War has also been revised. Though there were protests associated with the introduction of Reforming doctrines after 1525, as in the Bernese Oberland (though these expressed hostility towards their enforcement by city magistrates, not delayed enthusiasm), a certain lull did set in around the mid-sixteenth century, but by the 1570s rebellion was once again in full swing, leading up to and beyond the Thirty Years War. Where rural unrest diverged from the pattern in towns was in its geographical distribution, which also remained remarkably constant throughout the period, being concentrated overwhelmingly in Upper Germany, from the Alps in Switzerland and Austria northwards into the Upper Rhine and Swabia as far as the line of the river Main. Up to 1525 at least 60 rural rebellions have been identified by Peter Bierbrauer, but the label 'rebellion' requires comment.[*] He includes (rightly) the Appenzell Wars of 1401 to 1408, in which the rural communes of Appenzell allied with

---

[*] Peter Bierbrauer, 'Bäuerliche Revolten im Alten Reich: Ein Forschungsbericht', in Peter Blickle (ed.), *Aufruhr und Empörung? Studien zum bäuerlichen Widerstand im Alten Reich* (Munich, 1980), pp. 62–8.

the city of St Gallen to shake off the overlordship of the prince-abbot of St Gallen: but what began as a localized struggle developed into a territorial war of liberation, in which the rebels' League above the Lake (*Bund ob dem See*), concluded in 1405, quickly drew support from adjacent towns and communes in Vorarlberg, Graubünden, and Upper Swabia. The nobility, as allies of the abbot, responded by forming their own knightly association, the League of St George's Shield, two years later. The outcome of this territorial conflagration closely paralleled the struggle of the Inner Swiss cantons to establish political independence through leagues of mutual protection and assistance. The entire history of the Swiss Confederation after 1291 could with justice be written as a series of peasant wars of liberation, whose success was predicated upon alliances with powerful cities (Luzern, Bern, Zürich, St Gallen). But Bierbrauer also includes in his category of rebellion the mass demonstrations in 1476 associated with the visions of a simple shepherd boy in the village of Niklashausen, south of Würzburg, in Franconia. Peasants from across southern Germany flocked to the village to hear the visionary prophecies of the lad, Hans Böheim (known as the Drummer, or Piper, of Niklashausen), whose violent anticlerical tone spilled over into disavowal of temporal authority (the bishop of Würzburg was the ecclesiastical ruler of the district surrounding Niklashausen). Even if those who flocked to the village went as pilgrims, not as rebels, the boundaries between anticlerically heightened religious excitement and overt social defiance (as displayed by Böheim's followers when they marched to Würzburg to demand his release from captivity) are hard to draw. After all, the Hussite rebellion in Bohemia half a century earlier had been sustained by a unique blend of nationally coloured religious fervour and, on the part of the radical Taborites, at least, an explicit commitment to anti-feudal social egalitarianism and even primitive communism.

If it is right to apply the category of rebellion comprehensively rather than restrictively, it still remains the case that social unrest was almost exclusively an Upper German phenomenon. To this an explanation of beguiling simplicity has been given: the incidence of revolt coincided with the area of strong rural communes, in effect a swathe of territories embracing the Alpine lands, the Upper Rhine, Swabia, Franconia, and Hessen – but not Bavaria. This verdict, attractive though it is, raises more questions than it answers. At best it is a necessary, not a sufficient, explanation. Within the area under review, Franconia and Württemberg (until the Poor Conrad revolt of 1514) remained entirely free of uprisings. The revolts in Alsace hardly turned on the presence of strong communes (as we shall see), while the vast majority of revolts in Upper Swabia were directed (as we have noted in Chapter 6) against ecclesiastical, rather than secular, lords.

One tempting line of argument would be to suggest that unrest was concentrated in diminutive, unconsolidated, fragmented lordships, desperately trying to overcome their administrative 'backwardness'. The recourse to residential serfdom in Swabian monastic lordships offers some support for this idea. But the revolts were not confined to such jurisdictions, for even consolidated territories with unitary administrations could fall prey to rebellion, as did the archbishopric of Salzburg in 1462. Triggered by the levying of a consecration tax twice the rate imposed a decade previously, the jurisdictional districts (which comprised the peasant communes) and chartered markets withheld payment and submitted petitions complaining both about excessive feudal dues to landlords and the high-handed conduct of the archbishop's officials, especially their bending of justice and arbitrary increases in court fines. In the treaty which brought the revolt to an end the peasants were granted membership of the territorial Estates, though this political triumph proved cursory, and fresh disturbances seized Salzburg again in 1478 and 1504.

The distinction, therefore, was not between large and small, consolidated and fragmented, lordships, but between those which displayed a 'lack of integrational capacity' and those which had begun to establish an efficient and accountable public administration. That, it is held, explains the absence of rebellion in Bavaria. There rural communes (and market settlements) were well developed, but the consolidation of the duchy as a unitary territory had already reached a point where the wings of the local nobility had effectively been clipped, and where uniform territorial jurisdiction had bestowed upon the peasantry a measure of legal security and good property rights without encroaching upon the autonomy of local communities. Certainly the spread of hereditary tenures removed an immediate source of conflict, but the survival of serfdom (whether jurisdictional or residential, tenurial or personal) still provided material for ideological resistance. This has been confirmed by the various studies of Renate Blickle, whose findings suggest that Bavaria was by no means spared peasant unrest in our period, even if it remained quiet during the Peasants' War itself.[*]

---

[*] Renate Blickle, 'Agrarische Konflikte und Eigentumsordnung in Altbayern, 1400–1800', in Winfried Schulze (ed.), *Aufstände, Revolten, Prozesse* (Stuttgart, 1983), pp. 166–87.

'Integrational capacity' is, in any case, a two-edged sword, as the plethora of revolts in northern Switzerland during the fifteenth century demonstrates. If the hallmark of the Swiss Confederation was the singular alliance between rural communes and urban magistracies bent on carving out city-states, then the basis of that co-operation was always contested, never assured. The most remarkable feature of the formation of the Confederation was the emancipation of the rural population, as thousands of serfs bought citizen's rights as outburghers of the northern Swiss cities. In the Bernese Oberland, to take one example, half the serfs of Saanen had already bought their freedom by 1312; by the end of the fourteenth century, most of the peasants of the Lower Simmental had done likewise. This discharge of feudal bonds brought immediate advantage to Bern itself; indeed, it was the pursuit of a vigorous outburgher policy, which delivered around half the population of the Mittelland and Oberland into the subject status of rural citizens, obliged to pay taxes and render military service to the city, that allowed Bern to construct a vast rural territory: the physical acquisition of territory by conquest (such as the Vaud) came much later. Similar developments can be observed in Zürich and Luzern – the latter a spectacular case, since, as a city with a population of less than 4000 inhabitants, it is reckoned to have acquired 1000 outburghers in the 1380s alone. But what was the consequence? In most cases, the rural outburghers of the city-states were aghast to discover that they had merely exchanged their bonds of subordination to feudal nobles for subjection to urban patriciates, who used much the same array of feudal instruments (excepting serfdom as a legal category) to hold their peasants in check as had the jurisdictional and manorial lords they supplanted. Revolts in Zürich, Bern, Luzern, and even in the lowly Solothurn were endemic, because these cities were embarked upon a ruthless and predatory territorial policy. There was unrest in Zürich's rural territory in 1440–41, 1467–68, 1489, and 1515; and in Luzern's in 1434 and 1478. Bern became embroiled even more heavily in conflict, beginning with a revolt of the subjects of the abbey of Interlaken in 1445. From that protest sprang a general uprising of the Bernese Oberland, rallying to the so-called Evil League (*Böser Bund*), which later culminated in a revolutionary conspiracy of Interlaken's subjects between 1446 and 1451. Switzerland even experienced its own 'Peasants' War' among the subjects of Luzern, Bern, and Solothurn in 1513–14, though the disturbances never approached the scale of the events across the Rhine in 1525.

(The true Swiss Peasants' War of 1653 lies outside the scope of this study.)

The impact of state-building, whether by princes or by cities, upon local communities was a mixed blessing, and some have argued that there was functionally little difference between private feudal appropriation and public state taxation – that, in essence, is what Guy Bois has suggested in his analysis of the 'crisis of feudalism' in Normandy. Now that we have seen how the use of mortgages to tie the feudal nobility into princely service underlay territorial consolidation in Franconia, for example, the argument gains further point, and we will return to it. For the moment, it remains difficult to disentangle the causes behind rural revolts in the German lands up to 1525. With the exception of the monastic lordships examined in Chapter 6 – St Blasien and Schussenried – it is not easy to attribute the revolts to the repercussions of the late medieval agrarian crisis. There is certainly nothing in Germany to echo the English Peasants' Revolt of 1381. The intensification of lordship characteristic of the late Middle Ages, whether reflected in the spread of commercial pastoralism, in the tightening of jurisdictional controls, or in the expansion of local administration, may ultimately be traced to the dysfunction of lordship after the Black Death, but soon the process acquired a rationale of its own, which could in turn provoke resistance and revolt. At the same time – and this is only seemingly a paradox – the weakness of lordship, manifest in the failure of lords to offer their subjects protection, could unleash violent rebellion.

We have already referred in Chapter 6 to the exploitation which the mortgaging of lordships could entail. In time of war this sense of dereliction was even more acute. Three times within the space of five years subjects on the Upper Rhine rose up at the irruptions of French and Burgundian troops, including footloose mercenaries, in the wake of civil war in France. In 1439 in Strasbourg, in the Westrich bordering the Rhineland Palatinate in 1443, and the next year in Schwörstadt by Säckingen, burghers and peasants banded together to voice their anger at the craven failure of lords and magistracies to protect them against the marauding soldiery. This pattern was to be repeated on a much larger scale over a century later in eastern Austria, the frontline of resistance against the Turks, when calls for the abolition of all feudal lordship and its replacement by a peasant confederacy were heard. That goal had already struck a resonant chord on the Upper Rhine, for out of the leagues of resistance in the 1440s, known after the name of the peasant's laced boot as

Bundschuhe, a radical Bundschuh tradition is supposed to have developed by the end of the fifteenth century, which expressly invoked the struggle for peasant liberty in the Swiss Confederation, and strove to replace feudal lordship by republican communalism. Historians have been too eager to ascribe to these later Bundschuh revolts on the Upper Rhine – the rising in and around Sélestat in Alsace in 1493, and the three Bundschuh conspiracies under Joß Fritz, a serf of the bishop of Speyer, around Bruchsal in 1502, in Lehen by Freiburg im Breisgau in 1513, and a general rising planned for the whole of the Upper Rhine in 1517 – a coherence and revolutionary quality which they did not necessarily possess. It is perfectly true that these Bundschuh revolts broke the bounds of peasant society by actively seeking allies amongst townsfolk: their compass was territorial, not local, as we have already seen in the case of the contemporary Poor Conrad revolt in the duchy of Württemberg. But their distinctiveness is held principally to lie in the adoption of an overtly ideological slogan of freedom which transcended the particularity of local feudal custom, the principle of divine law, thereby foreshadowing the religiously inspired maxims of the Peasants' War.

Recent research has questioned this assumption both factually and conceptually. The evidence for the invocation of divine justice comes from the testimonies of two captured conspirators in 1517, who claimed that the Bundschuh flag, which Joß Fritz had already commissioned in 1502, but which had been left unfinished at the time of the Bundschuh's discovery, contained the legend 'Lord, stand by Thy divine justice', or that the flag displayed a white cross, images of the emperor, pope, Virgin Mary, St John the Baptist, Christ as the Man of Sorrows, and a kneeling peasant, as symbols of divine justice. Unfortunately, neither conspirator had actually seen the flag! Meanwhile, it has been suggested that the slogan of divine justice only penetrated rural society through the mediation of Reforming preachers after 1517, so that this ideological precept should properly be reserved for the Peasants' War itself. Quite apart from the recognition that the distinction between divine law and old (or customary) law is largely artificial (for in the spirit of reform as renovation, as we stressed at the outset of this chapter, the old law – embodying the original and uncorrupted social order – was itself godly), this historical revisionism overlooks the fact that the Bernese rebels in the Evil League of 1445 had invoked divine justice and claimed to be carrying out God's will. Rather than claiming the later

Bundschuh revolts as a self-fulfilling revolutionary tradition, fired by an overarching ideology, historians would be better advised to reflect that, as in any popular movement of liberation, whether the Bundschuh revolts were revolutionary depended neither upon the content nor upon the character of their demands in the abstract, but upon the particular and varying circumstances in which they were expressed. That of course applies, by the same token, to the Peasants' War itself.

Nevertheless, it is worth tracing briefly the three Bundschuh conspiracies under Joß Fritz, for they tellingly reveal the changes in tactics and objectives which Fritz was obliged to adopt to overcome the limits of peasant rebellion. His first conspiracy was directed against his overlord, the bishop of Speyer, and violent anticlericalism was its hallmark. The password 'God greet you, fellow. How fares the world?' earned the reply, 'We cannot rid ourselves of the plague of priests.' The demands of the conspirators envisaged abolition of the Church's privileges and power, expropriation of its property, and a return to apostolic poverty. Control of all ecclesiastical foundations was to be entrusted to the peasantry who would strictly limit the number of priests and determine communally their appointment and remuneration – exactly the powers which the rebels in 1525 also claimed. But the conspirators in the bishopric of Speyer on the right bank of the Rhine in 1502 went further, calling for all feudal dues to be swept away and serfdom to be abolished. With this programme Joß Fritz planned to bring the small towns of the bishopric onto his side, and carry the flame of rebellion onwards into the neighbouring territory of the margraviate of Baden-Durlach, but before these plans could come to fruition, the conspiracy was betrayed and Fritz fled for his life.

Eleven years later he resurfaced near Freiburg, and although his clandestine methods remained the same, his recruitment and objectives altered. He was determined to draw his ringleaders from the ranks of country craftsmen and village notables, rather than from the mass of agricultural smallholders, and these included the village priest of Lehen itself. Fritz also toned down the anticlerical invective – he was now operating in an area without major ecclesiastical landlords – and although the conspirators were required to recognize the authority of the pope and emperor, the religious litany of the password was replaced by the bland reply, 'In all the world the common man can find no comfort.' This time, moreover, the capture of towns became a principal strategic aim, not just the smaller towns on both banks of the Rhine, but the fortress of

Breisach and, above all, the capital of the Breisgau, Freiburg itself, to be achieved not by beleaguerment (he could not lay his hands on the necessary artillery), but by stealth, through arson during the town's bustling Martinmas fair. Fritz, it should be noted, made no effort to enlist the support of those urban groups most likely to be sympathetic to a rural uprising, the wine-growers and journeymen. How far he could have succeeded in winning over the population of a craft town caught in the throes of competition from rural crafts and village markets is a moot point, but, again, his cover was blown before the rebellion could be launched.

From the events of 1513 Joß Fritz had learnt an important lesson. To be successful, it was no use planning the conspiracy from one centre, or relying upon supporters with limited mobility. By 1517, in his last fling, Fritz was organizing simultaneously throughout Upper and Lower Alsace, the Breisgau, Baden, and the Black Forest. Subverting towns was as critical as raising the countryside, and cells of conspirators were discovered in many territorial towns in Alsace, as well as in some smaller imperial cities, such as Obernai and Rosheim. He chose his lieutenants not from those whose occupation tied them to a locality or to the rhythm of the seasons – the peasants – but from the legions of beggars, vagabonds, strolling-players, hawkers, quacks, and discharged mercenaries who thronged the highways of the Empire. He dispensed with all slogans except the cry of 'St George!' The trappings of religious ceremony and the evocative imagery of the flag were all but discarded. Similarly, all local and specific demands were dropped in favour of two general aims – the cancellation of debt- and interest-charges, and the abolition of feudal obligations – which would have struck at urban magistracies and rural lordships alike. The capture of towns, again by laying fire, was now to be the prelude to expelling or even killing the magistrates. Although the general conspiracy on the Upper Rhine was in its turn betrayed, Fritz's novel recruitment of the footloose and elusive ensured that the authorities found it very difficult to lay hands on the perpetrators, despite a leading henchman having coughed up the names of well over 100 conspirators.

What stands out in the Bundschuh conspiracies instigated by Joß Fritz is the discrepancy between tactical acuity and ideological vagueness. There is no question that Fritz's recognition of the importance of urban centres as strategic allies and as reservoirs of ordnance was correct, but he made little effort until 1517 to articulate demands which would find an immediate urban resonance; indeed, the ideological content of the conspiracies became increasingly peripheral, reduced to a few bald slogans. Fritz, a professional revolutionary to his fingertips, was an activist for whom agitation and subversion almost became ends in themselves, rather than the ideological champion of the peasantry, of whom he was ever more neglectful and dismissive. Or, to put it more charitably, the tactician overcame the ideologue. What ideological commitment there was resided in the vision of Swiss liberty, not Christian equality. Already in the Lehen Bundschuh Fritz had been determined to enlist the support of the Confederates before embarking on a major offensive. In 1517, too, Swiss reinforcements were to weld his contingents in the Breisgau and the Black Forest into a single formidable troop. The attraction was both practical and ideological. The Confederates' military superiority had been demonstrated by their defeat of Charles the Bold of Burgundy in 1477 and by their victory over Maximilian's army of the Swabian League at Dornach in 1499: the tactical implications of the rout of Swiss pikemen in the service of Milan by the French in 1515 at Marignano (today Melegnano) had not yet sunk in. But the example of Swiss republican liberty exerted, if anything, a more powerful fascination. The threat that south German communes might 'turn Swiss' and throw off feudal lordship was a constant preoccupation of the Habsburgs and their vassals around 1500. An incident in the Black Forest in 1518 makes the point. During a labour dispute in the silvermines around Todtnau one mineworker exclaimed that all they needed to press home their demands was to summon the Swiss over the mountains. This so alarmed the mining shareholders that they feared it would 'lead to great contempt and conspiracy (from which a Bundschuh might arise)'.[*] The example of the Swiss should make us chary of believing that only peasant rebellions with a religiously legitimated ideological programme were capable of developing revolutionary quality – as the prevailing historiography of the Peasants' War chooses to insist.

The Course and Causes of the Peasants' War

The series of uprisings which began at midsummer 1524 in the southern Black Forest and spread in waves throughout Upper and

---

[*] Albert Rosenkranz, *Der Bundschuh. Die Erhebungen des südwestdeutschen Bauernstandes in den Jahren 1493–1517*, 2 vols (Heidelberg, 1927), vol. 2, p. 309.

central Germany until the defeat of the last Salzburg rebels in July 1526, known collectively as the German Peasants' War or, in Peter Blickle's diction, the Revolution of the Common Man,[*] seized the same territories that had succumbed to social conflict throughout the later Middle Ages and articulated many of the same grievances that had been voiced in earlier revolts. In that sense, the Peasants' War stands in a continuum of rural protest, yet by geography and recruitment it far exceeded any other rebellion in pre-industrial Europe. For that reason alone it is otiose to search for single causes or exclusive aims. Two points of clarification, however, should be made at the outset. First, the chronological remoteness of the Peasants' War from the agrarian crisis of the late fourteenth century makes any direct causal link so feeble that it can be discounted. Hence it is incautious (to say the least) to see the War in the context of a supposed 'crisis of feudalism' (to pick up Peter Blickle's phrase), unless we can relate it to wider debates under that heading, spearheaded by the work of Robert Brenner and Guy Bois alluded to in Chapter 6, who have advanced a conceptual framework that permits European comparison. Second, the unquestioned impact of Reforming doctrines upon the rebels in terms of motivation, legitimation, and direction must not be allowed to foreclose an analysis of the War which gives due weight not only to programmes but also to processes: that is, to a reading of events which accepts that participants' perceptions might change over time, and that the many lists of articles of grievance may represent a stage in the unfolding of aspirations and mentalities, rather than demands which were normative and non-negotiable, and which had been implicit in the rebellion from the beginning.

The revolt began in an area which had already been destabilized by its proximity to the Swiss. The struggle against the Swiss, fought, in Tom Brady's words, almost as a civil war between the feudal nobility of south-west Germany and the republican cities and peasantries across the Rhine,[†] had already coloured the Bundschuh conspiracies under Joß Fritz (as we have seen); and it is perhaps significant that there is a final fleeting mention of him in the Hegau at the western end of Lake Constance in the winter of 1524, an old man with a grey beard who 'could not die until the Bundschuh had

---

[*] Peter Blickle, *The Revolution of 1525: The German Peasants' War from a new viewpoint* (Baltimore, MD/London, 1982).

[†] Thomas A. Brady, Jr, *Turning Swiss: Cities and empire, 1450–1550* (Cambridge, 1985).

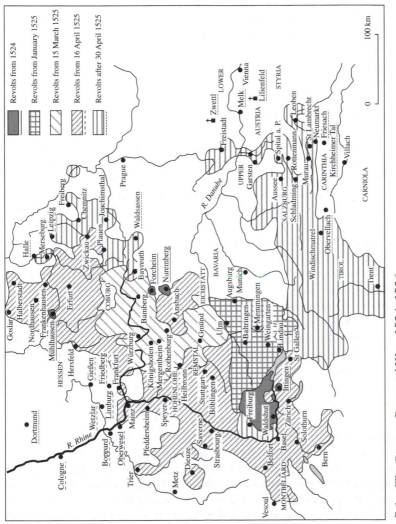

7.1   *The German Peasants' War, 1524–1526*

triumphed'. The southern Black Forest, moreover, was a district in which King Francis I of France was seeking to recruit mercenaries to fight the emperor in Italy, and the base from which Duke Ulrich of Württemberg set out to recapture the principality from which he had so deservedly been expelled. To the opportunities for making political mischief was added the spread of communal Reforming doctrines, radiating from Zürich under its Reformer Huldrych Zwingli into the countryside to the north, where local preachers gave his message a radical twist by refusing tithes and insisting that the church in the village be under the control of the parish, not the holder of the advowson, a demand which echoed the strength of the commune as a political institution.

Throughout the autumn and winter of 1524 the peasants of various lordships submitted petitions of grievance and demanded to negotiate, but none of their protests invoked biblical legitimation or put forward explicitly religious demands. The only exception was the villagers of Hallau, under the jurisdiction of Schaffhausen, the only member of the Swiss Confederation whose territory lay north of the Rhine, who clamoured in July for the communal election of pastors and an end to feudal obligations, declaring that they would have no lord but God alone. The fusion of secular and religious protest only became widespread after New Year 1525, and even then a clear ideological commitment was not always evident: the subjects of the landgraviate of Klettgau, next door to Schaffhausen, who stood under Zürich's protection, demanded that Scripture be the only judge of their grievances against their lord, Count Rudolf von Sulz, but the list of 44 articles which they presented early in 1525, despite the religious language of its preamble, was entirely concerned with specific infringements of their customary rights.

Nevertheless, although the peasants in the southern Black Forest still chose to act within the boundaries of their own lordships, the authorities were deeply alarmed that a 'great territorial war' might develop, as the town councillor of Villingen, Heinrich Hug, put it after witnessing the events in the Baar, the plain flanking the eastern slopes of the Black Forest. The reason for their fear was the agitation – and intimidation – of one of the most ruthless leaders of the Peasants' War, a serf of the abbey of St Blasien, Hans Müller from Bulgenbach. Müller led men from the county of Stühlingen (which had rebelled at midsummer) and other Foresters on a series of protest marches through the Black Forest northwards designed to carry the flame of rebellion northwards. In that he was successful, for aside from sporadic instances of violence (such as the sacking of the abbey of St Trudpert in December 1524) the peasants of Villingen and several Baar lordships, as well as from St Blasien, were in open defiance, during what has too readily been dismissed as a 'phoney war', already before the onset of mass rebellion in Upper Swabia in February and March 1525. Indeed, Müller had prepared the ground so well that he was able to raise a sizeable army in the spring which, styling itself the Christian Union of the Black Forest, embarked upon a campaign to force the leading towns of the south-west to capitulate, culminating in the surrender of Freiburg im Breisgau on 23 May.

By then the rebellion had engulfed all of southern Germany (except Bavaria) and much of central Germany – from Swabia to the Upper Rhine and Alsace, through Franconia, Hessen, and the arch-bishopric of Mainz to the Rhineland Palatinate, and northwards into Thuringia and Saxony. Common to all these areas were the Twelve Articles of Upper Swabia, drawn up at the beginning of March at the peasants' assembly in Memmingen, which provided the clarion and legitimation of rebellion, even though the social and legal condition of the peasantry in other parts of Germany did not always corre-spond to the Articles' provisions, notably in their demand for the abolition of serfdom as repugnant to Christian freedom, for serfdom had largely disappeared (as we have seen in Chapter 6) in the secular lordships of Franconia and throughout Thuringia.

The Twelve Articles embodied, in summary, four heads of demands: (1) communal control of pastors (who should preach the Gospel as the Reformers understood it) and tithing; (2) the aboli-tion of serfdom and servile dues; (3) the restoration of communal usufructs; (4) the easement of legal and financial burdens upon individual tenants or peasant families. The Articles insisted in con-clusion that, should any be found to be incompatible with the Word of God, they would be disclaimed. Because the Articles represent a redaction of many local Swabian grievance lists, it is not always apparent what gave rise to certain complaints. The tenth Article, for instance, complains that some have appropriated meadows or arable that once belonged to the community, which should be restored to common ownership. But whether the enclosure or alienation of land had been undertaken to promote pastoralism or to settle landless men on new smallholdings is not mentioned. The general tenor of the Twelve Articles is far from revolutionary – not surprisingly, since they were composed by the lay enthusiast, Sebastian Lotzer, a journeyman furrier, with commentary and biblical glosses by the Reforming preacher of Memmingen, Christoph Schappeler. The latter's preamble disavows any intention of disobedience, invokes Christian love, peace, and, concord, and accuses the enemies of the Gospel of stirring up unrest by their failure to accept the truth of the new teachings. But it has been pointed out that, if the Articles had been implemented, they would have undermined the foundations of feudal lordship to the point of collapse: their moderate language, in other words, concealed a revolutionary purpose.

Moreover, while the Christian Union of Upper Swabia, embracing the three armies who had assembled at Memmingen – the Baltringen, Allgäu, and Lake Constance bands – broadly speaking eschewed violent retribution upon their lords, ecclesiastical and secular, the same cannot be said for the Odenwald-Neckar valley band in Franconia, which destroyed over 200 castles in the bishopric of Bamberg alone within the space of ten days; or the Mühlhausen-Thuringian army, which in a week-long campaign through the Eichsfeld at the beginning of May plundered scores of castles and convents, as well as coercing half a dozen nobles to join their army as common members; or of the numerous bands in Alsace which stormed the convents and ecclesiastical foundations which littered the left bank of the Rhine – the 'parsons' lane' (*Pfaffengasse*) of the Empire – with such gusto. Revolutionary violence against persons was, by contrast, relatively uncommon. The massacre of Count Ludwig von Helfenstein and other nobles at Weinsberg near Heilbronn in mid-April sent shock-waves throughout Germany precisely because it was so exceptional. Likewise, Thomas Müntzer's execution of three of Count Ernst von Mansfeld's servants in the name of God's law, as the combined Thuringian armies were encamped at Frankenhausen, was an act of people's justice which went well beyond most rebels' understanding of divine legitimation.

Although the Twelve Articles were adopted in certain areas regardless of regional variations in the structure and exercise of lordship, in others they were modified to take account of local circumstances. That was true in Württemberg, where hostility was vented at the Austrian government of occupation, rather than at local feudal lords (which allowed Duke Ulrich to pose, implausibly, as the champion of his subjects), and in Alsace, where the hatred of clerical lords, the attack on the use of ecclesiastical courts to hear temporal cases, and opposition to a host of tolls, excises, and taxes had already been voiced in the Bundschuh revolts. Yet in the archbishopric of

Salzburg, where rural grievances closely paralleled those in Swabia, the Twelve Articles were not adopted at all. This raises the possibility that their invocation was sometimes contingent and tactical, rather than principled and ideological.

What the Twelve Articles reflect, in broad terms, is a reaction to the increasing burdens of lordship (whether one wants to call that feudalism or seigneurialism). For that reason the debate whether the Peasants' War was a political or a socio-economic movement rather misses the point, since lordship itself relied, inextricably, upon both instruments of exploitation. By the same token, the rebels were the victims both of long-term social and economic changes (the aftermath of the late medieval agrarian crisis) and of more recent political and jurisdictional developments (the consolidation and concentration of lordship as state-building in miniature, often through recourse to serfdom): self-evidently, the former conditioned the latter. Indeed, the way in which lords chose to shore up their power was pre-eminently by mobilizing judicial rights to augment their revenues: by jacking up court fines; by interfering in rights of inheritance (the seizure of chattels); by shortening leases; or by using lordship over serfs to increase labour-services. All this was only possible, it is usually held, because the population was recovering, with consequent pressure upon land and its use (succession to tenancies, access to the common), which gave lords – for the first time in 150 years, in many cases – some leverage over their peasants. Against this background, the silence of the Twelve Articles on the transformation of rural economy and society in Swabia (as described in Chapters 4 and 6) is all the more puzzling. They evidently reflect the interests of the tenant farmers, the enfranchised members of the village commune alone: they ignore altogether the spread of rural craftsmen and the rise of a cottar class, and the tensions to which they gave rise, except perhaps obliquely in Article 10 (though then only from the perspective of the possessing peasantry). Only in the Federal Ordinance, the Twelve Articles' sister manifesto which regulated military discipline within the Christian Union and the conduct of negotiations with outsiders, is there a fleeting reference to craftsmen who might wish to emigrate in pursuit of a livelihood, namely that they should inform the Union of any looming danger from abroad and return home to fight if required. The status of the Twelve Articles as a programme which embraced the interests of the rural population at large, therefore, is somewhat problematic.

A possible solution to this dilemma has recently been proposed in the light of events in the abbey of Ottobeuren. There the revolt began as a traditional piece of bargaining between landlord and tenants, that is, the rural oligarchy of possessing peasants. Only after the elite had lost control of the situation did the rebels turn to radical political activism – but they were the cottars and landless, the rural poor whose voice had been drowned out in the Twelve Articles themselves. At the point where the tenant farmers were still willing to negotiate with the abbot (who had fled) – in mid-April 1525 – other Ottobeuren subjects joined in the storming of castles in the surrounding district. This argument (which, in passing, is sceptical of the view that tenant farmers in general were under threat from pressure on land caused by a population recovery) still needs to be tested for other lordships. Be that as it may, some initial moderates were not precluded from subsequently adopting more radical aims, so that we are still left with the problem of why radicalization should have occurred: whether it was driven by the impact of a religious ideology, or by a response to unfolding opportunities and broadening perceptions of what could be achieved – or by both.

Political Programmes in the Peasants' War

Similar difficulties attend any assessment of the political vision which underlay the Twelve Articles. As a general principle, those who subscribed to the Articles committed themselves to brotherly love and the advancement of the Christian commonweal, but what that meant in practice was another matter. Leaving aside the radical religious programme of Thomas Müntzer in Thuringia, who claimed that all things should be held in common (though this maxim, extracted under torture, is open to several interpretations), there is little trace of any enthusiasm for Christian socialist egalitarianism, in which private property would disappear; rather, the peasants were desperate to repel the encroachment upon their property rights and individual family livelihoods. More broadly, few rebels sought to renounce secular politics in favour of a community of saints (as the radical Hussites in Bohemia had done, and as Müntzer may have envisaged), but rather to recast the political order in their own interests, to replace vertical by horizontal channels of authority. That desire was shaped by the existing pattern of lordship. Where territorial fragmentation was the norm (in Upper Swabia, on the Upper Rhine, and in Franconia), the peasants proposed to establish a corporative-confederate constitution, within which autonomous village and urban communes would voluntarily ally in Christian Unions without abandoning their sovereign rights (there were obvious parallels with the Swiss Confederation). Where unitary territories with a hierarchy of Estates existed (as in Württemberg, Salzburg, Tirol, and the southern margraviate of Baden), the peasants were prepared to recognize the territorial courts, diet, and administration (and even the prince), but were determined to replace a constitution of Estates (*landständische Verfassung*) by a commons' constitution (*landschaftliche Verfassung*), in which the local communes would elect representatives to the diet, who in turn should nominate a commons' council to administer the government alongside the territorial ruler. In several of these territories, indeed, the peasantry was already represented (Baden, Tirol, and obliquely through the district administration in Württemberg). It is also the case, as Horst Buszello has noted, that in the territorially defined revolts the peasants had a natural focus for their aims, but in areas of territorial fragmentation negotiations with local lords by the regional armies quickly became pointless, so that the rebels came to demand a 'reformation' of the political order on the basis of divine law.[*]

These observations suggest that it is not always easy to make a direct connection between the invocation of Scripture and a particular political vision, and that the commitment to divine law varied in relevance and intensity. How central, indeed, was religion to the Peasants' War? Was its role functional – not so much the cause of rebellion as the means of its rapid diffusion – or ideological – supplying both legitimation and programme to the peasant rebels? In the case of the Christian utopias which were propounded in the course of the War, Thomas Müntzer's religious covenant in Thuringia or Michael Gaismair's blueprint for a Territorial Constitution in Tirol, the issue appears straightforward, but that is not altogether the case.

Müntzer certainly believed that he was leading the elect into battle against the godless, whose extirpation was assured, but after the *débâcle* at Frankenhausen he turned in chagrin upon his followers, accusing them of pursuing creaturely ends rather than God's purpose. If there was truth in that charge, then the blame lay with Müntzer himself. In the varying leagues which he had formed, first defensive, then offensive, as conscious reconfigurations of the Old

---

[*] Horst Buszello, *Der deutsche Bauernkrieg von 1525 als politische Bewegung* (Berlin, 1969).

Testament covenant between God and his chosen people Israel, he had created a disciplined and effective framework for supraregional action, yet he steadfastly refused to offer any detailed programme for those leagues to adopt, for the sovereignty of the elect was but the necessary interim before Christ's parousia, and the order of Christ's kingdom was not for man to determine. Although Müntzer may have sketched the outlines of a new polity in the so-called Constitutional Draft (a document whose source problems are worthy of the Hydra), the demands his followers expressed turned out to be reworkings of the Twelve Articles of Upper Swabia.

By contrast, Gaismair's plan for a peasant republic in Tirol was so full of detailed proposals that it has received a barrage of contradictory interpretations. There is no disagreement that its guiding principle was that of a Christian commonwealth, directly indebted to the theocratic doctrines which Gaismair had encountered through his contacts with Zwingli in Zürich in the winter of 1525. The Word of God was to form the legal framework of the republic; and a university was to be set up whose sole purpose was to teach and interpret Scripture. Ecclesiastical foundations were to be dissolved and their buildings handed over to hospitals and orphanages, and their assets distributed to the poor and needy. All social distinctions and privileges (including the liberties of towns) were to be abolished, so that Christian equality should prevail. But Gaismair went on to address the economic and commercial needs of Tirol, including the future of its extensive mining industry, by adumbrating measures which went well beyond the simple rural arcadia beloved of most Reformers (as discussed earlier in this chapter). Gaismair described how the agricultural output of Tirol might be increased along the lines of the Italian system of mixed commercial agriculture, with olives, vines, and grain grown side-by-side (*coltura promiscua*). Manufacturing, on the other hand, was to be strictly regulated, with two markets under state control, while artisan and manufacturing production was to be centrally located and controlled by a superintendent appointed and salaried by the state. In the case of the mining industry, all foreign mining companies (he instances those villains we have encountered elsewhere, the Augsburg companies of the Fugger, Höchstetter, Paumgartner, and others) were to be expropriated, and the smelting of silver and lead was to be run by a state collective, with the price of ore to be determined by a state tariff, not market forces.

Gaismair's debt to Zwingli has encouraged some commentators to regard these proposals as a blueprint for a Christian socialist society, in which individual ownership of the means of production and free-market enterprise were to be outlawed. This interpretation ignores the formidable textual problems surrounding the Tirolean Constitution (which cannot be pursued here), but also the silences and omissions: this is a document *par excellence* which demands to be read against the grain. Gaismair was not opposed to the individual holding of land by peasant proprietors; he did not discount the continuance of wage-labour in the mines; and he said nothing about the native Tirolean mining companies (with which his own family had been involved). The thrust of the mining articles was to shore up the position of the labour-employing petty-capitalist mining share-holders against the onslaught of oligopolists from the south German cities. In general terms, Gaismair's plan can be seen as an early example of mercantilist theory within a state which must safeguard and promote its own resources (including manufactures), and accumulate reserves of bullion. Yet on account of Tirol's location along a vital artery of commerce between the Mediterranean and the German lands the plan at the same time encouraged imports and restricted exports (which was quite contrary to conventional mercantilist thought). The Territorial Constitution is significant because it shows not only how far the Peasants' War could unleash creative energies in the pragmatic description of a new Christian society, but also how much that vision echoed and elaborated the imperial reform tradition of the fifteenth century, as did Friedrich Weygandt's blueprint for the peasant assembly at Heilbronn already discussed.

Even so, it is beyond doubt that the Peasants' War represented a quantum leap in the evolution of rural rebellion in the German speaking-lands – or indeed in Europe. Does this justify its description as a 'revolution of the common man'? Peter Blickle is convinced that the new religious doctrines of the Reformers provided the ideological legitimation and motor of rebellion which had been lacking in late medieval peasant revolts; moreover, that ideological force was so powerful that it could effortlessly override any tensions or differences of interest which existed within the rural communes, or between the countryside and the towns. Against that view both practical and theoretical objections may be entered. The willingness of townsfolk to ally with the peasants was not as great as Blickle suggests. Certainly the peasants were able to win over hundreds of small towns which lived in symbiosis with their surrounding countryside, the so-called 'peasant burgher towns' whose inhabitants were in large part farmers. But the attitude of the larger craft towns was altogether lukewarm. Almost all who joined the peasant bands were coerced, or were pre-empting the threat of looting and destruction. Far from being alliances of principled solidarity under the sign of the Gospel, that is to say, communities of interest, most alliances were communities of action, that is, of mutual convenience or defensive necessity with no active solidarity or ultimate common purpose. In many towns where rich ecclesiastical institutions prompted a groundswell of anticlericalism the peasants demanded admittance ostensibly to revenge themselves upon the clergy, claiming that they would leave the citizens unharmed. But magistrates were understandably reluctant to take the rebels' assurances at face value, and hastened to shore up support among their commons by taking firm action against the clergy and convents themselves, as we have already noted in the case of the Alsatian cities.

The theoretical objection is more fundamental. Blickle believes that *only* ideology – maxims of divine justice and the Word of God – was capable of transforming a series of local uprisings circumscribed by feudal lordship into a general war of liberation throughout Upper Germany, in short, a revolution. But there are two drawbacks to this argument. The distinction between revolts under the old (or customary) law and under divine law cannot truly be sustained, as we have already argued in the case of the Bundschuh revolts. Moreover, it is not always clear what the peasants understood by divine law. Some historians have suggested that the rebels in 1525 conceived of divine justice in legal rather than theological terms – that its foundations lay in natural godly justice (the order of Creation), rather than the Bible, and that what they understood by the slogan differed widely over time and space, amounting in the end to little more than the law which abetted the peasants and assailed their lords, a strangely voluntaristic attitude. Yet even if this criticism is overstated, it does raise the question whether religious ideology was indeed indispensable in transforming rebellion into war. The emancipation of the Swiss communes – as we have seen in the case of Appenzell – involved a general territorial war without recourse to religious slogans. Subsequently, the driving force behind the Bundschuh conspiracies (and, as we might well conjecture, Hans Müller's agitation in the Black Forest in 1524) was a vision of Swiss freedom – in other words, republican, not religious, liberty. Furthermore, in early 1525 supraregional alliances transcending local feudal jurisdictions in two instances in Swabia – the Kempteners' solidarity with the subjects of the bishop of Augsburg and the abbey of Rothenfels; and the formation of the Lake Constance band – preceded the adoption of divine justice as an overarching legitimating principle: the latter did not enable or engender the former. The peasants' recourse to religious principles, in other words, might be as much instrumental as ideological. It was left to Reformers such as Schappeler, heavily influenced by Zwingli, to fuse Swiss republican freedom with religious liberty, as can be seen in the hitherto anonymous tract of mid-1525, now plausibly ascribed to him, To the Assembly of the Common Peasantry.

Peasant Revolts in the Sixteenth Century

Although the Peasants' War ended in sanguinary defeat, the spirit of sedition lingered on – either in rumours of fresh unrest in southwest Germany, or in the transvaluation of secular rebellion into radical religious fervour on the part of some of Müntzer's supporters who embraced militant Anabaptism – Hans Hut in Franconia, or Hans Römer in Thuringia, where the latter sought to instigate a chiliastic rebellion in Erfurt at the end of 1527. Politically, however, the peasants did wrest some concessions from their lords. In new territorial constitutions genuine attempts were made to safeguard the legal rights of subjects and to ease their economic burdens. The abbey of Kempten, for instance, which had incurred the peasants' hatred before and during the War, continued to be prey to conflict, but experienced no further revolt because the peasants' territorial corporation (Landschaft) had wrested legal means of redress from the abbot in 1525. Sometimes, though, the lords ratted. In 1532 Archduke Ferdinand of Austria (by then king of the Romans) rescinded the territorial ordinance for Tirol which he had promulgated six years earlier, containing substantial concessions to his subjects. But in many parts of southern Germany territorial assemblies in which the commons were represented continued to function right up to the Napoleonic Wars.

Nevertheless, rural revolt did not cease, though its character and causation changed. In the aftermath of the Peasants' War peasants increasingly resorted to strategies of protest which did not imply a recourse to violence, but sought legal channels of redress. When that failed, resistance could manifest itself in novel forms, as in the Owingen revolt in Hohenzollern in 1584, when 73 men quit the village in late August and only returned in November after an imperial edict promised them immunity until their case was settled – an act of some sacrifice since it took place at harvest-time! Although further revolts did occur in the south-west – the landgraviate of Klettgau rose in 1595, there was unrest in Upper Swabia in the lordships of Rothenfels and Staufen the following year, and troubles on the Upper Rhine broke out before and after 1600 – the incidence of rebellion began geographically to disperse. Much of central and northern Germany, which had been on the periphery of revolt in 1525, now succumbed to a wave of unrest stretching from the Palatinate and the Lower Rhine in the west, through northern Hessen to Lower Saxony, mostly confined to smaller territories, such as the multitude of independent counties in the Wetterau. Although the burdens of seigneurialism continued to provoke resistance, revolts in the latter part of the sixteenth century were frequently caused by the weight of imperial or territorial taxation, a fiscal appetite fed both by the expense of war and by the administrative costs of principalities reliant upon new bureaucracies. Significantly, however, religion all but vanished as a legitimating principle (and only half as many revolts were directed against ecclesiastical lords as a century earlier).

For the first time, moreover, the Austrian crown lands in the east (as opposed to Tirol and Vorarlberg) became the theatre of persistent and embittered rebellion, culminating in the Lower Austrian Peasants' War of 1596–97, and its Upper Austrian namesake of 1626. Subjects who had to bear the brunt of Ottoman military advances were particularly prone to revolt, especially if abandoned by their lords: the Wendish peasants in Croatia in 1573 were so disenchanted with their noble overlords that they declared all feudal lordship null and void and planned to replace it with a republic on confederal lines. But resistance to the Habsburg archduke-emperors themselves had more complex and protracted causes. Just as the mortgaging of lordships before 1500 had aroused a sense of legal and economic exploitation on the part of the peasantry, a century later the Habsburgs had begun to resort to what Hermann Rebel has termed 'lien administration', deliberately augmenting the mortgageable value of their estates in Lower Austria by forcing emphyteutic (that is, improving) leases upon their tenants and by stepping up *corvées*, particularly in cash (the so-called *Robotgeld*).* The mortgagees them-

---

* Hermann Rebel, *Peasant Classes: The bureaucratization of property and family relations under early Habsburg absolutism, 1511–1636* (Princeton, NJ, 1983).

selves behaved as 'bureaucratic capitalists', both intervening directly in commercialized agricultural production and by seeking to control the market through enforcing rights of pre-emption or monopsony, backed by the coercive legal and military power of the state. Here the argument for a continuity between private feudal appropriation and public state taxation (the Guy Bois thesis) seems particularly pertinent.

But the Austrian peasants at the beginning of the seventeenth century faced yet another threat. Many had embraced Lutheranism and now found themselves the victims of a Habsburg policy of re-Catholicization, in which they stood to be stripped of their tenancies if they resisted. Rebel sees the 1626 war in Upper Austria, therefore, as a struggle by individualized peasant landholders, often plunged into debt, to preserve the meagre advantages of their status over against the lodgers and landless in the face of an unrelenting state bureaucracy which was squeezing them financially and confessionally. There are distinct echoes here of the east European social systems discussed in Chapter 6, not least the domanial economy (*Gutswirtschaft*). Indeed, the term 'economic lordship' (*Wirtschaftsherrschaft*), as an interval type of feudal regime between western rental landlordship and eastern *Gutsherrschaft*, which we have already encountered on the borderlands of the Elbe, was originally coined by Alfred Hoffmann to describe the system prevailing in the central Austrian lands. The susceptibility of the Austrian crown lands to rebellion after 1550 should make us pause before relegating peasant unrest in east Elbia to 'a lower level of class struggle' (in Marxist parlance) without actual revolt. It remains true, none the less, that the incidence of peasant rebellion across the span of northern Germany from east Frisia to the Baltic was much less than in Upper Germany. As long as historians believed that the peasant commune in northern and eastern Germany was weak and underdeveloped, the explanation seemed self-evident. But since we now know that peasant communes were vigorous in territories such as Brandenburg and east Prussia, the explanation crumbles – and revolts did indeed occur. In 1440 subjects of the bishopric of Ermland (or Warmia, as it is sometimes known in English), an enclave surrounded by the Teutonic Order's Prussian territory, offered manifest resistance to the cathedral chapter, which was bent upon introducing new forms of economic exploitation. Although the protest did not spill over into violence, the peasants proved remarkably intractable, spurning several offers of mediation by the territorial diet, precisely because they insisted that their village charters be observed to the letter. Only after two years did the protest cease, but not before the bishop had arrested the leading agitators. During the Peasants' War there was a very brief rising in the Samland, just north of Ermland, in which the various socio-ethnic groupings – German peasants, Prussian freemen, and Prussian peasants – made common cause to resist the administrative changes which had come about as a result of the secularization of the Teutonic Order's territory. A generation later, there was renewed unrest in what was by then the duchy of Prussia, centred on the administrative district of Insterburg (Černja-hovsk), where the ethnic Lithuanian peasants complained at labour-services, particularly ploughing in distant fields, imposed by German officials. Among the Lithuanian peasantry, who were pastoralists rather than husbandmen, living in hamlets, not nucleated villages, the commune as a socio-legal institution was indeed rudimentary, but that did not stop them rebelling. Elsewhere east of the Elbe the advance of *Gutsherrschaft* gave rise to constant legal suits between peasants and lords: between 400 and 600 judgements were handed down in such cases by the Brandenburg court of chancery between 1560 and 1620. The absence of active revolt should not be equated with passive acquiescence. The exercise of feudal lordship in its various manifestations remained contested throughout the German-speaking lands until the nineteenth century.

8 Deviancy and Conformity

Standards of Living

Across the sixteenth-century German landscape blew the chill winds of social dislocation and confessional division. The struggle for daily subsistence in an age of gathering inflation pushed many to the margins of existence; the pressures of religious conformity and social discipline drew sharper lines between those who were honourable and those seen as marginals. The critique of the nobility prompted it to insist on ever more tightly drawn tests of ancestry and honoura-bility, defined by 'purity of the blood'; the threat to their economic livelihood prompted craftsmen and journeymen to restrict opportu-nities for working women; the competition for resources within vil-lages drove growing numbers of peasants down into the ranks of cottars and landless. The fear of a loss of social cohesion and the hardening of the boundaries of cultural identity led to a search for scapegoats, those who were perceived as outsiders and blamed for contemporary misfortunes – heretics, witches, Jews. Once it was thought that the political authorities themselves – princely chanceries or city magistrates – were responsible for the new emphasis on discipline and obedience, and hence for the willingness to identify and criminalize as deviants those who did not conform to social and religious norms, but it is now appreciated that the desire to marginalize and to persecute was as deeply rooted in the mentali-ties and anxieties of the common people themselves. However, although there are parallels to be drawn between material adversity and cultural attitudes, historians are rightly reluctant to posit simple causal links: social behaviour may respond in complex and oblique ways to external pressures, while wider institutional constraints may colour and shape cultural predispositions.

What can be said with confidence is that the livelihood of those Germans who depended upon wage-labour was being visibly undermined as the sixteenth century progressed: the increase in prices began to outstrip that of wages in a ratio of perhaps 3:2. But this bald statement is far from self-explanatory. Wilhelm Abel once classically described the fifteenth century as the 'golden age of the artisan', or of the wage-worker, and although this view has been severely qualified in recent years it remains true that the debasements of the period did not lead to an erosion of the purchasing power of money in real terms, and hence to price inflation. Knut Schulz has suggested, based on his researches on the Upper Rhine, that the debasement of the coinage remained without negative consequences because it merely represented a realignment of the available money in circulation to the volume of goods for sale. How that hypothesis might be tested in practice remains unclear. What is not in doubt is the diametrically opposed trend after 1500, when the fineness of struck coin remained largely intact while the purchasing power of money declined rapidly – after 1530, at least. The famous price-scissors – the most frequently used and least understood economic metaphor applied to our period – began to open once again, this time to the disadvantage of wages. That supply and demand – a recovering population, and the onset of harvest failures and famine in successive years (especially from 1527 onwards) – in part account for the rise in cereal prices is well known. But the failure of wages to keep pace cannot be explained by purely economic factors. For all their efforts, earnestly pursued if feebly rewarded, to stem the rise in price of essential foodstuffs (for which 'forestalling' and 'regrating' were invariably blamed, even though they were often as much the consequence of the authorities' interference in the workings of the market as its cause), magistrates succeeded in setting a cap on wage-rates, not least because they could count on the (tacit) approval of those guildmasters who employed wage-labour.

Although the purchasing power of wages was declining in real terms before 1550 (as evidence from Saxony suggests), the rapid deterioration set in only after mid-century, as Tables 8.1 and 8.2 illustrate. Though they present statistics from one city alone (with an exceptionally good archival survival), the figures for Basel are

Table 8.1 Index of food prices in Basel, 1450–1600

Period	Grain (spelt)	Wine	Butter	Eggs	Beef	Herrings
1450–1474	66	82	93	88	88	93
1475–1499	100	100	100	100	100	100
1500–1524	106	110	107	–	117	100
1525–1549	165	164	140	–	142	145
1550–1574	293	221	220	200	199	230
1575–1599	408	290	293	400	262	350

Source: Adapted from Knut Schultz, *Handwerksgesellen und Lohnarbeiter. Untersuchungen zur oberrheinischen und oberdeutschen Stadtgeschichte des 14. bis 17. Jahrhunderts* (Sigmaringen, 1985), p. 437, tables I and II.

Table 8.2 Relation of food prices to wine-growers' wages in Basel, 1450–1600

Period	Food price index*	Index of daily wages	Index of purchasing power of wages
1450–1474	77	–	–
1475–1499	100	100	100
1500–1524	108	100	93
1525–1549	157	100	64
1550–1574	253	118	47
1575–1599	355	168	47

* Calculated on a basket of 50% grain, 10% wine, 20% fats, 20% protein (eggs, beef, herrings).

Source: Adapted from Schultz, *Handwerksgesellen und Lohnarbeiter*, p. 437, table III.

broadly echoed for other German cities about which we have reliable evidence, such as Cologne. What stands out in Table 8.1 is not so much the palpable upward pressure on the price of foodstuffs, but how far the price of grain, in this instance spelt, the constituent of everyday rough bread, had outstripped other foodstuffs by the end of the century. But even then the figures need to be interpreted with caution: in second place came eggs, which doubled in price between 1550 and 1600 for no very obvious reason (perhaps a switch from carbohydrates to proteins in the face of bread shortages?), while in third place came herrings, scarcely a staple of the daily diet, but which (as we have mentioned in Chapter 5) may have been over-fished in the Baltic, or else may have migrated to other spawning-grounds.

There can be endless argument, too, whether the basket of comestibles used to establish the food price index in Table 8.2 is correctly weighted. Eggs and herrings became very expensive, but beef much less so, and historians are often surprised at the quantity of meat in early modern diets, even amongst ordinary folk. As contemporary price tariffs show, the range of meat on offer was not confined to beef; pork was much more common and, in the sheep-rearing areas of Germany, mutton. Moreover, there was scarcely a part of the beast that was not consumed – lights, brains, heart, tongue, tail, hoof, or trotter – all cheap and nourishing fare alongside the more expensive ribs and haunches. Nevertheless, the figures speak an unambiguous language: between 1500 and 1600 the purchasing power of wages in Basel had halved, a collapse also observable in Augsburg. Whether that spelt widespread immiseration is less clear, given what is known about the proportion of wages paid in kind. Nevertheless, the number of those whom the municipal records describe as *Habenichts* (either propertyless, or, sometimes more pointedly, destitute) was on the up, though whether it reached 50 to 60 per cent of the urban population in the later sixteenth century, as is frequently asserted, needs to be treated with some scepticism.

Climate Change, Subsistence Crises, and Economic Downturn

By the second half of the sixteenth century it is proper to speak of a price revolution, whose European causes have long been a commonplace of the historical literature (the inflow of bullion from the Americas or, more precisely, its squandering on expenditure – armies, courts, buildings – which brought no return on capital). But longer-term secular changes within European society in general must be accorded at least equal importance in explaining renewed pressure on resources and therewith prices. The recovery of population from the 1470s onwards, as noted in Chapter 3 and discussed in Chapter 7 in the context of the Peasants' War, placed severe strains on grain supplies within an inelastic agricultural regime. More recently, however, the focus has switched to changes which were specific to much of northern and central Europe, above all the onset, around 1560, of what has been termed the 'little ice age', which is supposed to have lasted until around 1630 or beyond. This period of worsening climate was characterized by a general fall in annual temperatures, a shortened growing season, with more protracted winters, cold polar airstreams, and a lowering of the snowline. The pioneering research on climate change in the German-speaking lands has been undertaken by the Swiss historian, Christian Pfister, particularly his observations on fluctuations in the Grindelwald glacier between 1570 and 1680.* It is no criticism of Pfister's work to point out that alpine Switzerland is hardly typical of the German uplands and plains! What subsequent investigation has been undertaken still largely concentrates on Upper Germany rather than the north. But even if the evidence for climatological change is accepted wholesale (and it has already been deployed, as we shall see, in the aetiology of witchcrazes), it provides no easy answer to the shifting balance of land-use and crop-yields. To take the Upper Rhine, in close proximity to Switzerland, as an example: on its left bank it was, then as now, the driest and warmest region of Germany. There, in the later sixteenth century, it appears that vines disappeared from the valley floors and rolling uplands. If that was a consequence of climate deterioration, then the outcome may on two counts have been positive, rather than negative: the land available for grain cultivation increased, and vines became confined to the slopes on the foothills of the Vosges when greater exposure to sunlight, together with mineral-rich and better-draining soils, created a meso-climate much more favourable to the production of quality – and hence high-value – wines than the marshy plain. The most that can be said by way of generalization is that any 'little ice age' was on the whole a central European phenomenon, rather than a coastal one, and that both bread-grains and vines, as Mediterranean crops, were at greater risk of harvest failure when grown north of the Alps than in the south.

---

* Christian Pfister, *Bevölkerungsgeschichte und historische Demographie* (*Enzyklopädie Deutscher Geschichte,* vol. 28) (Munich, 1994).

Yet the evidence for severe and protracted subsistence crises after 1500 is incontrovertible, with the early 1570s, mid-1580s, and late 1590s witnessing grievous famines and death in many German lands, and a consequent leap in grain prices (but, significantly, perhaps, not at first in western Pomerania on the Baltic seaboard). The 1570s, for instance, marked the onset of widespread pauperism amongst the peasantry of the county of Hohenlohe in northern Württemberg, much later than in areas of rural industries and by-employment.

While the 'little ice age' obviously affected the rural economy in the first instance – though with self-evident implications for the subsistence of artisans and traders who bought their bread at market – it is arguable whether the urban economy suffered a general downturn in the German lands towards the end of the sixteenth century. Here the argument is bedevilled by the obvious regional variations within Germany (to which we have earlier alluded), not least the distinction between the Hanseatic League and the Upper German centres of manufacturing and finance, as well as the need to set the fortunes of individual companies against the collective economic performance of towns and cities. We have already noted that in northern Germany certain cities of the Hansa, particularly the leading ports of the North Sea and the Baltic, continued to prosper up to and beyond 1500, even if the Hansa as a whole was in commercial retreat. For southern Germany, we have also stressed that the difficulties of several international trading companies were seized upon as opportunities by their middle-ranking counterparts, eager to step into their rivals' shoes. Nevertheless, there is a widely held view that the Upper German economy was definitely in recession in the later sixteenth century. Recent dissenting voices such as Franz Mathis do not help their case by attempting to rebut a notion of 'crisis',* whereas the argument is simply about the scale of a downturn that would occur in any business cycle. Those who know the economy of the Upper German cities best have in fact argued along rather different lines. Against the view that the shift in commercial activity to the Atlantic and overseas – manifest in the rise of Antwerp and Seville – damaged the Upper German economy, Wolfgang von Stromer has suggested that, initially at least, merchants and manufacturers from metropolises such as Nuremberg or Augsburg benefited, since there was increased demand in these distant markets for the goods produced

---

* Franz Mathis, *Die deutsche Wirtschaft im 16. Jahrhundert* (*Enzyklopädie Deutscher Geschichte*, vol. 11) (Munich, 1992), p. 81.

in Upper Germany – metalware, weapons, precision instruments, light textiles.[*] At first, too, the Upper German trading and banking houses were heavily involved in overseas investment, sometimes in partnership with the monarchs of the colonial powers (the Portuguese crown, for instance, shared its pepper monopoly in Europe with the Nuremberg family firm of Imhoff). Such investment was both risky and costly, but it could bring fabulous rewards. It cannot be denied that royal bankruptcies and the dislocations of war dealt a severe blow to these overseas trading houses, but at the level of the regional economy it is less clear that the decades after 1550 signalled a severe downturn. Augsburg's fustian production was still on the increase at the end of the century, with an annual output of 410 000 pieces in 1595 rising to 430 636 in 1612, even though it was detectably slower to react to changing fashions in textiles than Nuremberg, which had already begun to invest in other mixed fabrics and in new areas of linen manufacture in eastern Europe. The seventeenth century, moreover, witnessed the full flowering of Augsburg as a centre of the decorative and applied arts, with the city's workshops bustling with gold- and silversmiths, engravers, printers, cabinet-makers, and ivory-carvers. These, of course, were luxury trades which do not necessarily tell us much about the performance of the quotidian economy. What remains true, however, as we emphasized at the end of Chapter 5, is that Augsburg's regional economic pre-eminence was achieved at the expense of middle-ranking cities on the periphery of its economic unit. A tidy balance-sheet, therefore, is hard to draw up; all that can confidently be said is that many of the economic indicators were pointing downwards, not upwards, as the century drew to a close: in the encircling gloom, beacons such as Augsburg and Nuremberg shone out all the more strongly – but perhaps they were will-o'-the-wisps.

Honour and Social Cohesion

Under the threat of social and economic dislocation the desire to uphold one's status – individually in noble lineages, collectively in urban corporations and village communities – grew apace. To that end, concepts of honour were applied more vigorously to affirm

---

[*] Wolfgang von Stromer, 'Verflechtungen oberdeutscher Wirtschaftszentren am Beginn der Neuzeit', in Wilhelm Rausch (ed.), *Die Stadt an der Schwelle zur Neuzeit* (Linz, 1980), p. 33.

exclusivity and conformity, while maxims of discipline and solidarity were deployed against those perceived as a threat to social cohesion and good order. Three snapshots from recent research illustrate how these precepts were deployed throughout the society of Estates.

After mid-century there are clear signs of a crisis of legitimacy among the German lesser nobility. A critique of the self-perception and behaviour of the nobility was nothing new: we have already referred to Sebastian Franck's highly moralistic condemnation in Chapter 6; his strictures were taken up in yet more violent language by the Tübingen poet Nikolaus Frischlin in 1580. How rattled were the objects of his scorn can be seen from the storm of outrage on the part of the knighthood of Swabia, Franconia, on the Upper Rhine, and in the Wetterau; Frischlin himself narrowly escaped assassination. Erik Midelfort has with some justice described the response to Frischlin's tirade as paranoia, but even those who sought to defend nobility both as a moral virtue and as a social Estate found the going tough, as Cyriacus Spangenberg discovered in his *Mirror of the Nobility* in 1591/94. What began as an apologia ended as a hand-wringing lament at the degeneration of the nobility in his own day:

> Now nothing bars lords from heaven but their damnable, stinking, fleshly pride, so that they think too well of themselves to have to learn anything godly, and their shameful contempt for the Word . . . refusing . . . to be instructed and punished by it.*

This, as the diction shows, was written from a Lutheran perspective, all the more remarkable since among the first 'nobles' academies' to be founded as finishing-schools for scions of the aristocracy, with a strict, almost monastic, regime, was the Lutheran Collegium Illustre in Tübingen.

By the end of the century further academies for the schooling of noblemen had been founded in Hessen, Nassau, the Rhineland Palatinate, and later Saxony. The concomitant of a newly fostered sense of *noblesse oblige*, however, was the application of much stricter criteria of nobility – the proof of noble ancestry through three or four generations, and the invocation of the principle of 'purity of

---

* Cyriacus Spangenberg, *Adels Spiegel*, 2 vols (Schmalkalden, 1591/94), vol. 2, fo. 385v. Cited in H.C. Erik Midelfort, 'Curious Georgics: The German nobility and their crisis of legitimacy in the late sixteenth century', in Andrew C. Fix and Susan C. Karant-Nunn, *Germania Illustrata. Essays on early modern Germany presented to Gerald Strauss* (Kirksville, MO, 1992), p. 236.

the blood'. In Westphalia, for instance, a patent of privilege was proclaimed in 1570, which listed those families who had met the test of noble ancestry and who had possessed a landed estate which qualified them for membership of the territorial diet. This drawing-in of horns was by no means peculiar to the German lands, of course, but the attack on the very principle of nobility and noble virtue seems to have been particularly virulent there, and was only gradually blunted by the chivalric education which young nobles received in the *Ritterakademien*.

A similar concern to define and protect one's identity and interests can be observed amongst urban artisans – not simply craftmasters, but journeymen as well. At a practical level this was expressed both in measures designed to restrict access to the guilds – stiffening entry qualifications by demanding a more elaborate masterpiece or insisting on testimony of a certain level of wealth – and by persistent (and largely fruitless) attempts to curb unregulated competition from hawkers, or informal artisan activity beyond the town walls (as noted in Chapter 5). But hand-in-hand with legislation went an increasing preoccupation with definitions of honour, above all legitimate birth, for in German the two terms *ehrlich* (honourable) and *ehelich* (legitimate) echoed each other. Illegitimacy, however, was only one among several stigmas: any contact with the so-called 'dishonourable' professions – knacker, hangman, grave-digger, sowgelder (known in German sardonically as *Nonnenmacher*, 'nun-maker'), street cleaner, bailiff – brought pollution in its train, even to the point where to mention such persons without a salvatory formula (*salvo honore, salva venia*) ran the risk of dishonour. It needs to be stressed, though, that the categories of dishonourable occupations were anything but watertight. Throughout all of Germany they included shepherds, and in much of northern Germany linen-weavers, too, though not in the south where, initially, in both town and countryside the greatest numbers were concentrated. That suggests that the boundaries of honour and dishonour were socially constructed, rather than a reflection of any intrinsic uncleanliness of occupation, but why linen-weavers fell victim to such odium is indeed puzzling: the fact that linen-weaving involved a high proportion of female labour may certainly hold one clue.

Indeed, within the urban economy, women more generally became the objects of marginalization and degradation during the sixteenth century. Though the impact of the Reformation undoubtedly played a role, the origins of their exclusion lay much further back: in the triumph of the craft guilds and their corporatist ethos in the later Middle Ages. For these guilds were not only ruled by males, their rituals and ceremonies (such as the initiation of journeymen into mastership) were exclusively male, too, which bound their members more closely together in psychological and cultural ways, as well as in terms of material interest. Once the Reformers had redefined gender roles in a way which allowed men to be both father and bread-winner, but relegated women to the sole function of motherhood, the path to occupational exclusion was open: the workshop became a male preserve. Shrinking economic opportunities could only reinforce this trend. Skilled trades which were transformed by the introduction of new machinery were either redesignated as unskilled and handed over to women on lower rates of pay; or else the new technology was deemed so advanced, as with the introduction of the knitting-frame, that only men were capable of operating it, so that women were consigned to 'unskilled' hand-knitting: not so much Catch-22 as Stitch-22!

There were perceptible knock-on effects among journeymen, who saw their chances of becoming masters, and of marrying and establishing their own households, ever more squeezed. For them honour was more than an abstract ideal: it constituted 'symbolic capital', for a loss of honour deprived the journeyman of the right to work. Hence in the course of the century journeymen showed themselves increasingly hostile to women in the workplace. 'Honour' was invoked as a device to set them apart from female competition; in 1597 the journeymen cordmakers of Frankfurt am Main petitioned to have unmarried women ('maids') excluded from employment altogether, and around the same time Nuremberg's ringmakers came under pressure from their journeymen to restrict the scope of women's work. Journeymen's notions of 'honour', however, were not necessarily those of the (male) magistrates and guildmasters: the latter emphasizing paternal authority, thrift, and diligence; the former comradeship, bravery, and prodigality – the virtues of bachelordom, not the settled household.

Within rural society conflicts over resources and livelihood were rarely expressed in the language of honour, but they did revolve around the privileges conferred by membership of the commune, together with the maintenance of discipline and stability within the commune, both of which by implication rested upon notions of eligibility and honourable conduct. After 1500, and especially after mid-century, growing competition over usufructs placed a premium on

communal inclusion and set those with lesser or no communal rights
at a perceptible disadvantage. That was particularly manifest in conflicts over forest and woodland pasture, for the danger of deforesta-
tion through overuse prompted the feudal authorities – often in the
teeth of village resistance – to issue ordinances restricting access to
the forest. In Württemberg after 1550, for instance, the ducal administration had to intervene in repeated village disputes between
peasant proprietors and farm labourers, or between large- and small-
holding peasants, the former eager to reserve felling, pannage, and
estovers to themselves, the latter clamouring for access to woodland,
both for timber and to graze their beasts on acorns and beechmast.
But the real struggle was less over communal resources than over
property and inheritance within the peasant families themselves. In
the county of Hohenlohe in northern Württemberg attempts to
control land-use and the marketing of agricultural produce at a time
of population pressure in mid-century were matched, and indeed
underpinned, by efforts to discipline all those who might present a
threat to the status of the possessing tenants, that is to say, women,
youths, and the village poor. In that, the male heads-of-household
were abetted by the pastors of what had become a Lutheran territory, who regarded social disorder as the result of the decay of the
family and its integrity, rather than of structural tensions within rural
society. As Thomas Robisheaux has put it:

> The reform of marriage and the family [as the pastors exhorted
> their flock] can . . . only be understood in the context of the
> social conditions in the village at this time. The rise in popula-
> tion, scarcity of land, the rapid spread of rural poverty, and,
> after 1570, the ever present threat of famine: All these condi-
> tions meant that families survived only through carefully
> protecting their land and resources. The access to land and
> wealth . . . was inseparably bound up with courtship and mar-
> riage.[*]

Here we can see the appeal of stronger patriarchal authority and
marital discipline; and it is no accident that Hohenlohe's first marriage
law of 1572 decreed that all property arrangements at marriage had to
be regulated publicly in the presence of the parents and of the count's

---

[*] Thomas Robisheaux, *Rural Society and the Search for Order in Early Modern Germany* (Cambridge,
1989), p. 106.

local officials. These pressures led, in the longer term, to an erosion of communal solidarity, in the sense that communal control of land, forest, and water became of less importance than the peasants' access to credit – to commercial, rather than fixed, wealth, as Robisheaux puts it; with the counts acting as the peasants' main creditors.

German Jewry in the Confessional Age

The fate of the Jews in the German-speaking lands also confirms the general pattern of a search for social conformity which consigned those who stood outside the cultural and religious norms to marginality. Up to the time of the Black Death, the number of Jewish communities had grown in tandem with the proliferation of urban foundations, perhaps totalling 1000 settlements in the mid-fourteenth century. Most of these were to be found – almost by definition – in the profusion of lesser towns, but there were sizeable communities in many of the cathedral cities (where the bishops protected them in order to tax them), and in a string of imperial cities. In response to persecution and expulsion, as we have noted in Chapter 3, the Jews had largely dispersed throughout the countryside, settling in very small communities in Hessen, Franconia, and the Palatinate, where they remained largely undisturbed for the next few centuries. But this was by no means the whole story, for the rise of confessional politics complicated the picture.

Many of the leading Reformers, in a mixture of visceral antipathy and theological rigorism, advocated strongly anti-Jewish measures to the authorities (who, for reasons of fiscal advantage, were sometimes reluctant to comply). Luther's antisemitism, which became more strident as he grew older, is well known, but theologians in southern Germany who embraced the communal ethos of Reformed Protestantism could show themselves just as unbending. Martin Bucer, the leading south German Reformer after Zwingli's death, tried to persuade Landgrave Philip of Hessen, the leader of the Protestant Schmalkaldic League, to expel the Jews from his territory (though without success). In the end, Jews were driven out of many north German Lutheran lands – Saxony, Braunschweig, Hannover, and subsequently Brandenburg and Silesia. Yet the attitude of the Reformers had not always been initially hostile. Both Wolfgang Capito, Martin Bucer's fellow-Reformer in Strasbourg, and Andreas Osiander, the Lutheran pastor of Nuremberg, were known to be sympathetic to Judaism. What changed in the course of the century was the confessional environment, with both Protestant camps very much on the defensive in the face of a Catholic counter-offensive, until the Religious Peace of Augsburg in 1555 brought relief for the Lutheran signatories of the Confession of Augsburg a generation earlier, though not to the Reformed Protestants who remained outlaws under the imperial constitution until the Westphalian peace settlement in the aftermath of the Thirty Years War. The Protestant sense of beleaguerment – laced with forebodings of apocalypse – stiffened their self-perception as 'watchmen in Zion', the guardians of the New Israel, which by definition set them squarely against the children of the Old Israel, the Jews.

In the few cities where Jewish communities survived, the rise of confessional antagonisms could easily turn against the Jews as a convenient scapegoat. That, as we have seen in Chapter 7, was the case in Frankfurt am Main, where antisemitism provided the undertow to the resentments which burst forth in the Fettmilch rising. It also accounts for the unusual chain of events in Dortmund in the closing decades of the sixteenth century. The city had finally adopted the Reformation in Lutheran guise in the 1570s, after protracted struggles between an evangelically minded party and the firmly Catholic magistrates. But the Catholic elite did not take the defeat lying down, and intrigued with Emperor Rudolf II to restore the old faith, and even to bring in the Jesuits. For the majority of the citizens, their Lutheranism became a badge of communal identity and solidarity in the face of looming imperial intervention, with the upshot that in reprisal they turned against the Jewish community in Dortmund – which had survived because it enjoyed imperial protection – and expelled it in 1595. While it is true, therefore, that the very fact of dispersion reduced the likelihood of concerted persecution, and that issues of toleration and protection were increasingly determined by the perception of economic advantage rather than religious and cultural antipathy, it is hard to follow Jonathan Israel all the way when he concludes benignly that, compared with the later Middle Ages, by the last third of the sixteenth century 'Jewish life was more secure and relatively free from active persecution', or that 'religion ceased to dictate the terms and form of Jewish settlement'.[*]

---

[*] Jonathan I. Israel, 'Germany and its Jews: A changing relationship (1300–1800)', in R. Po-Chia Hsia and Hartmut Lehmann (eds), *In and Out of the Ghetto: Jewish–Gentile relations in late medieval and early modern Germany* (Washington, DC/Cambridge, 1995), p. 299.

The Beginnings of Witch-Hunting

By the later sixteenth century the fears and psychoses that once had attached themselves to Jews – the accusations of ritual murder, the poisoning of wells, the defiling of the Host – had been displaced onto those suspected of witchcraft. The belief in magic and its power to inflict both harm and good is as old as mankind itself, but the growing conviction that all magic derived from a pact with the devil, and the readiness to bring persons to trial on suspicion of sorcery, even if they had perpetrated no actual crime, contributed after 1500 to a deep insecurity or even panic in many parts of central Europe, which discharged itself in bouts of mass persecution which have rightly been termed a witchcraze. Over the last twenty years a veritable avalanche of research has swept over the European witchcraze, and the beginnings of a consensus about its origins and dispersion have now emerged, though much is bound to remain speculative, since there will always be scope for debate about the psychological mainsprings of witch persecution, that is, the collective and unconscious mentalities which disposed social groups to identify some in their midst as alien and malign. Three principal constituents in the transvaluation of witchcraft can be identified. What once was seen as sorcery became redefined as heresy, for any pact with the devil was an affront to the God of Christianity, which is why Jews were spared such accusations; witchcraft was no longer the property of 'wise' or 'cunning' men and women as individuals, but was the manifestation of a collective will, hence it depended upon secret compacts – conspiracies – not only with the devil but between persons; and the practice of sorcery became overwhelmingly (though never exclusively) associated with women. These three elements conduced in turn to three consequences. What once had been punished by banishment now led to execution, often after confessions extracted under torture; the prosecution of individuals gave way to mass trials, horribly prefiguring the 'show trials' of Stalinist Russia; and the emphasis on women encouraged sorcery to be identified with sexual perversion. The belief not merely in a pact with the devil, but in sexual intercourse with Satan and the existence of succubi or incubi, heightened the neurotic fear of witches. In this light, the witchcraze becomes all too predictable.

And that should counsel us to caution. For the persecution of witches in the German-speaking lands was not steady, but sporadic, not comprehensive but localized, and even at the height of the witchcraze there were always voices, both theological and judicial, raised against persecution (or at least against the forensic procedures employed). They did so less in a precocious spirit of Enlightenment rationalism (for most men and women in the sixteenth and seventeenth century continued to believe in the reality of witchcraft), than from scepticism either that the accused had been correctly identified or that the evidence of harmful magic (black magic) was anything other than flimsy or unprovable.

Moreover, the initial signs of a harsher attitude towards witchcraft were detectable beyond the German-speaking lands, specifically in the area around Lake Geneva in the duchy of Savoy in the decades after 1400. Here the first explicit links were made between sorcery and heresy, accompanied by strongly antisemitic overtones (the notion of the witches' sabbath or synagogue, and accusations of ritual murder). Throughout the fifteenth century witch trials, conducted either by the Inquisition or before the civil courts, took place in France, Italy, and Burgundy, as well as England, rather than in the German lands, though Alsace and Lorraine within the boundaries of the Empire also witnessed prosecutions (with Lorraine a century later in the forefront of witch-hunting in Catholic Europe). Yet it was Alsace which produced the most assiduous persecutor of witches towards the end of the fifteenth century, the Dominican friar Heinrich Kramer from Sélestat, known by his latinized surname as Institoris (merchant or trader), who composed the first comprehensive manual of witchcraft, the *Malleus Maleficarum*, literally the 'hammer of sorcery', but known in its personalized form as the Hammer of Witches.

Theologically, Kramer said nothing new: rather, he played fast and loose with what the Church fathers had said about witchcraft, twisting their utterances to suit his own purpose. The novelty of the *Malleus* lay in its insistence that witches actually performed harm (as opposed to the theological tradition which affirmed that magic had no direct effect), and that it ascribed black magic above all to women. Those features would doubtless have remained without resonance, were it not for two circumstances. Kramer's writing coincided with a period of poor climate, harvest failure, and famine from the 1470s into the 1490s in much of Upper Germany, in other words a context which encouraged the afflicted to seek scapegoats for the damage to beasts and crops – a prefiguration of the consonance between the onset of the 'little ice age' from the 1560s and the rise in witch-hunting. More importantly, Kramer's was the first tract

against witchcraft to be disseminated in print; between its publication in 1486 and its last reprint in 1669 it went through thirty editions. That in itself proves little (apart from the lurid fascination of
Kramer's outpourings), for the *Malleus* was in fact initially outsold by
a counter-tract composed by the Konstanz jurist Ulrich Molitor, in its
German version *Von Unholden und Hexen* (On Demons and Witches),
which appeared in ten editions around 1500 alone. The true significance of the *Malleus* lay in the fact that, being accessible in print, it
was cited almost straight away by theologians on the western fringes
of the Empire in the archbishopric of Trier as a manual against
witches, though Kramer's own preaching in the region (he had been
appointed papal inquisitor for Upper Germany in 1478) certainly
helped to popularize the tract. Kramer's barnstorming, nevertheless,
did not unleash a sustained period of witch-hunting, for the incidence of persecution died back in the 1520s. But his misogyny certainly chimed with a new view of women as sexual predators,
observable from the 1450s onwards, and subsequently the stock-in-
trade of many religious Reformers in the following century. The
depictions of women riding on devils, beasts, or tools (such as
broomsticks) with overtly lascivious intent became markedly more
frequent, as can be illustrated by considering Albrecht Dürer's
engraving *A Witch Riding Backwards on a Goat*, from around 1505.
The naked woman clutches one of the goat's horns in her left hand,
while the right holds a distaff. Her features firmly set, her mouth
ajar, her tresses streaming backwards as she flies: these suggest a
virago, a woman powerful and unbiddable. The image reeks of
sexual reversal and disorder – the goat as the symbol of lust, the
backward ride on an animal as the sign of humiliation for those who
had transgressed the codes of sexual honour. These were medieval
commonplaces, but for the first time they are explicitly linked to
sorcery, though Wolfgang Behringer warns against seeing too close a
connection between the image depicted and the beliefs of the artist:
it may merely be that the witch had become a popular motif in the
portrayal of women.[*]

All the same, as the sixteenth century wore on, there were understandable reasons why communities should come to identify women
in their midst as sexually dangerous and prey to devilish influence.
For accusations of witchcraft were levelled above all at unmarried
women: maids (those not yet married), widows (not yet re-married),

---

[*] Wolfgang Behringer, *Hexen: Glaube, Verfolgung, Vermarktung*, 2nd edn (Munich, 2000).

and spinsters (those who had never married). With population increase came later marriage, while the proportion of women who never married rose from 5 to 15 or even 20 per cent: as a result, the number of 'masterless' women grew apace. Quite apart from the issue of sexuality, moreover, accusations of witchcraft commonly arose within the female domain, surrounding birth, the raising of children, the care of the sick, or the tending of animals. But this cannot explain the remarkable fact that latterly women were prepared to accuse themselves of having made pacts with the devil, or why denunciations of sorcery so frequently came from other women. Here Heide Wunder has suggested that village gossip among women revolved less around objects and events than around relations between women, the affirmation of solidarity or exclusion.[*]

The Witchcraze of the Late Sixteenth Century

The era of active persecution, culminating in a genuine witchcraze, began in the 1560s and lasted, in its first fling, until the late 1620s (though there were further bouts thereafter). The regional variation in witch-hunting is at first glance bewildering, but several observations can usefully be made at the outset. The legal basis for the trial and punishment of witches changed. The criminal lawcode of the Empire drawn up under Charles V, the so-called *Carolina* of 1532, had only listed black magic under its provisions (and left imprecise the issue of confiscation of property of those condemned), but after mid-century several territories, among them Württemberg in 1567 and Saxony in 1572, promulgated new criminal codes which declared all magic to be the work of the devil, so that many more persons fell into the judicial net. Investigation and prosecution were entrusted throughout the German lands to the civil, not the church, courts (that was true even in the ecclesiastical principalities); in the *Malleus* Kramer had already insisted that sorcery was so abominable and such a threat to public order that the civil magistrates must not hesitate to intervene. In the longer term, that meant that Protestant territories were not held back – if they so chose – from hunting witches as vigorously as Catholic ones, for clearly they could not have admitted the Inquisition across their borders. Yet it remains the case

---

[*] Heide Wunder, *"Er ist die Sonn', sie ist der Mond." Frauen in der frühen Neuzeit* (Munich, 1992), p. 199.

that Catholic authorities were more likely to execute witches than Protestant ones, by a ratio of around two to one, even though all three confessions – Catholic, Lutheran, and Reformed (Calvinist) – were deeply split within their own ranks over the issue of witchcraft. It might be tempting to argue that, since witchcraft was equated with heresy, Catholics had the added advantage (from their own point of view) of branding adherents of the Reformation as heretics, and were perhaps less scrupulous, therefore, in distinguishing religious from social deviancy. But, if truth be told, Erik Midelfort's despairing comment of thirty years ago still holds good: 'The reasons for such a striking difference [between Catholics and Protestants] are not obvious and have never been made clear.'[*]

What can be said is that the accusations of witchcraft across the confessional divide often served as a veil for latent secular tensions, and some alleged sorcerers were also indicted on other criminal charges. Many of the larger territories and the more powerful imperial cities never allowed the fear of harmful magic to get out of hand: Lutheran Württemberg, Catholic Bavaria, and the Rhineland Palatinate (Calvinist after 1561) refused to countenance mass witch trials, as did Frankfurt am Main, Nuremberg, and Augsburg. Of Protestant territories, those of middling rank witnessed the greatest number of witch trials, particularly the lands of the imperial counts such as Nassau, Büdingen, Schaumburg, or Lippe. Among Catholics, the greatest persecutors were undoubtedly the prince-bishops and prince-abbots, rather than secular rulers, particularly after 1600: Archbishop Ferdinand of Bavaria in Cologne presided over 2000 executions between 1612 and 1637; Bishop Philipp Adolf von Ehrenberg sanctioned 900 executions in Würzburg within the space of a mere eight years, from 1623 to 1631. Inspired by confessional zealotry these Counter-Reformation prelates may have been, but it needs to be stressed that the decision actively to persecute witches might depend on the individual incumbent: a change of bishop could bring a rapid halt to the witchcraze. Recent research has qualified this argument even further. Before 1600 in the archbishopric of Trier 350 witches were executed during the rule of Johann VII von Schönenberg (1581–99). This witch-hunt was once ascribed to the archbishop's own persecution complex, but it is now clear that the impulse came largely from below, within the local communities,

---

[*] H. C. Erik Midelfort, *Witch Hunting in Southwestern Germany 1562–1684: The social and intellectual foundations* (Stanford, CA, 1972), p. 33.

whose committees of investigation (secular Inquisitions in minia-ture!) wrested judicial authority from the territorial administration, leaving it almost paralyzed. Such initiatives by villagers have also been identified in the counties of Nassau-Saarbrücken and Pfalz-Zweibrücken (the area of the modern Saarland), in the lands of the Teutonic Order, and in the duchy of Lorraine.

And this gives us an important clue to the causes of the witchcraze after 1560. As a Trier chronicler put it: 'Because everyone generally believed that crop failures over many years had been brought on by witches and malefactors out of devilish hatred, the whole land rose up to exterminate them.'* The correlation between climate deterio-ration and subsistence crises – the 'little ice age' – on the one hand and spasms of intense witch-hunting on the other cannot be doubted. After 1600 renewed bouts of plague and the devastation of the Thirty Years War only added to the sense of insecurity and panic, though in the 1620s and 1630s there was no neat coincidence between witch-hunting and military emergencies. We should not, in short, fall victim to a mechanical determinism, for state policy (as we have seen) could influence the extent of persecution, and it was the administratively weaker territories on the whole that were most sus-ceptible to the witchcraze.

But cutting across confessions and types and size of territories went a further shift in state policy. The sixteenth century saw a hard-ening of the arteries in terms of cultural and behavioural attitudes – this was the age of what has been termed social disciplining. That was manifest in the proliferation of new law codes, harsher punish-ments for crimes, or closer supervision and regulation of everyday life by the authorities. Yet the emphasis on disciplining was not simply a hegemonic device, designed to tighten the control of rulers over the ruled: it applied as much to the rulers themselves. Self-disci-pline, a new asceticism and religious intensity, combined with hos-tility towards popular culture and its often unruly expression, was its hallmark: Protestant puritanism was matched by Catholic zealotry. In their sermons both Catholic and Protestant preachers denounced witches and sorcery as the source of climate catastrophes, famine, and disease. The elites were led into sanctioning witch-hunting, not because they had been struck by some kind of collective madness, but because their increasingly dour view of the world encouraged

---

* Cited in Wolfgang Behringer 'Weather, hunger and fear: Origins of the European witch-hunts in climate, society and mentality', *German History*, 13 (1995), p. 7.

them to seek rational theological grounds for combating evil and the work of the devil. The authorities' willingness to engage in witch-hunting on a large scale must be set in the context of a struggle to re-establish order – or, as Wolfgang Behringer has put it, of a search to impose order and discipline on a society whose values had been open, vivacious, pleasure-seeking, and this-worldly.[*]

'Good Police' and Social Disciplining

The search for order in the German lands can be observed before the hardening of confessional divisions, and even before the Reformation itself. As part of the long process of state-building, princes and magistracies concerned themselves increasingly with what is known as 'good police' (in German *Polizey*), that is, not only the disciplining of their subjects but an active engagement in chari-table provision, and economic improvement. That may be seen as part of a wider recognition that political consolidation and stability depended upon reaching an accommodation with those now cast as citizens under public jurisdiction. In 1555 the imperial court of chancery declared itself willing for the first time to hear suits by sub-jects against their lords, with the sanction that lords were liable to be stripped of their fiefs if condemned. This right of appeal became the stock-in-trade of legal textbooks, and was frequently invoked by local communities, often incurring considerable expense. Whether this 'juridification of conflict' amounted, in Winfried Schulze's diction, to a more rational form of conflict resolution may nevertheless be doubted, since it underestimates the extent to which subjects before the sixteenth century had been able to negotiate 'treaties of lord-ship' with their feudal superiors.

By 1500, none the less, 13 principalities in Germany had issued police ordinances; more broadly, the sixteenth century witnessed a spate of territorial constitutions (which contained police provisions): Württemberg's first statute in 1495, when the territory was raised to a duchy, was followed by another five up to 1567; similarly, in Austria seven statutes were issued in the fifty years from 1527 to 1577. But there is no doubt that a practical concern for public welfare was ini-tially promoted where Reforming doctrines were eagerly embraced. The first ordinances for civil poor relief (as opposed to the Church's

---

[*] Ibid. p. 20.

charity) were issued by Nuremberg in 1522, and by Augsburg and Strasbourg a year later. Luther was approached by the council of the small Saxon town of Leisnig in 1523 to give advice on public welfare provision; his Ordinance for a Common Chest at Leisnig was the Reformer's first attempt to put his religious beliefs into social-ethical practice, though he subsequently backed away from the communal-egalitarian implications of the ordinance, and in any case regarded the Leisnig experiment as something of a failure. Protestant communities – both Lutheran and Zwinglian – were likewise the first to address the reform of morals on a broad front, issuing marriage statutes, and establishing consistory courts to supervise marriage and morals (taking the place of the Catholic church courts), as wedlock became the social and ethical ideal instead of celibacy, in what Lyndal Roper has termed the 'holy household'.[*]

By mid-century, however, the concern for discipline and welfare was shared by Catholic and Protestant alike. Tridentine Catholicism was no less keen on personal self-discipline or hostile towards the bawdiness of popular culture than the Reformers. While the period after 1550 in the Empire is often described as the confessional age, in social, cultural, and ethical attitudes there was not a great deal to separate the three confessions. What did change was the legal framework, for the Religious Peace of Augsburg of 1555 created a new imperial church law alongside Catholic and Protestant ecclesiastical law, with the result that confessional allegiance became not merely a matter of conscience or belief, but a legal and political distinguishing-mark which added yet another facet to the plural polity of the Holy Roman Empire.

Confession, therefore, constituted a tangible criterion of inclusion or exclusion, conformity or deviancy. The expression of confessional identity combined with the spread of moral rigorism and an ascetic view of the world to create a society which was not only obsessed with order but all too eager to define and defend itself by identifying and persecuting those perceived as a threat to that order.

In Augsburg there hangs a painting, from the brush of an unknown master around 1600, of the annual ball staged by the city's patrician families. The artist had an ulterior purpose: to depict the changes in fashionable dress that had taken place throughout the sixteenth century. As the column of patrician lords and ladies snakes its way across the canvas, we see in the foreground the brightly

---

[*] Lyndal Roper, *The Holy Household: Women and morals in Reformation Augsburg* (Oxford, 1989).

coloured, slashed and pleated gowns and cloaks, broad-brimmed hats or elaborate headdresses common around 1500. But then the garments become plainer, the decoration less extravagant, the colour more sombre, until by the end of the century all are dressed in black, bare-headed, with men and women uniformly in lace ruffs. A Catholic or a Protestant image? Either, or both, for Augsburg was confessionally mixed, and so was its elite. The sobriety of dress mirrored the sobriety of the age: the search for order was also the search for conformity, regardless of confessional divisions. Yet those confessional divisions were ultimately to become the occasion for the utter collapse of order, when German society was thrown into turmoil, as the struggle for European hegemony plunged the Empire into the chaos of the Thirty Years War.

It is often argued that the particularity of the German lands led ultimately to the paralysis of the Empire as a body politic: the competing interests of princes and of cities, compounded in a confessional age, cancelled each other out. And this verdict has sometimes been extended to its economy and society: the efflorescence of the German economy in the merchant leagues and cities gave way to sclerosis and introspection; the social order, locked into the rigid hierarchy of Estates, was barely disrupted in the west, and underwent a feudal reaction in the east. But such a judgement is too coloured by narratives of the rise of the early modern state and strong centralized monarchies. At the edges of the German-speaking lands the Swiss Confederation and the Dutch Republic survived and prospered as polycentric territories; indeed, economic rivalry between cities and the integration of town and country were the hallmark of Dutch mercantile greatness. But they were republican polities, both in their legal constitution and in their social values. The German lands of the Empire, by contrast, remained wedded to a feudal-aristocratic order. And that even the Thirty Years War was unable to destroy.

Bibliography of Works in English

Apart from studies of the Reformation, German history between 1300 and 1600 is poorly served by works in English. And much of what there is deals in any case with political and constitutional matters, rather than with social and economic. A general outline up to 1500 is provided by F. R. H. Du Boulay, *Germany in the Later Middle Ages* (London, 1983), with bibliography. The author's self-deprecating tone and quaint style should not be allowed to obscure the book's genuine merits. We are now fortunate, however, in having the twin-volumed *Germany: A new social and economic history*, vol. 1 ed. Bob Scribner; vol. 2 ed. Sheilagh Ogilivie (London/New York/Sydney/Auckland, 1996). The first volume covers the period 1450 to 1630; the second, 1630 to 1800. Volume 1, in particular, should be the first port-of-call for those seeking detailed information (including references to the German literature). It is cited below as Scribner, *Germany*.

Chapter 1: The Political Geography of Germany, 1300–1600

A basic orientation is to be found in Tom Scott, 'Germany and the Empire in the fifteenth century', in C. T. Allmand (ed.), *The New Cambridge Medieval History*, vol. 7: *c.1415–c.1500* (Cambridge, 1998), pp. 337–66 (with bibliography). There are two studies of individual principalities: Henry J. Cohn, *The Government of the Rhine Palatinate in the Fifteenth Century* (Oxford, 1965; repr. Aldershot/Brookfield, VT, 1992); and Lawrence G. Duggan, *The Governance of the Bishopric of Speyer to 1552* (New Brunswick, NJ, 1978). Although political studies, both works contain much useful information on social and economic affairs. The same applies – though with a greater emphasis on social history – to a string of works on individual cities, though none spans the entire period, and most take the Reformation as their backdrop: Gerald Strauss, *Nuremberg in the Sixteenth Century: City politics and life between Middle Ages and modern times*, revised edn (Bloomington, IN, 1976); Miriam Usher Chrisman, *Strasbourg and the Reform: A study in the process of change* (New Haven, CT/London, 1967); Susan C. Karant-Nunn, *Zwickau in Transition,*

1500–1547: The Reformation as an agent of change (Columbus, OH, 1987). Short but stimulating is Hans R. Guggisberg, *Basel in the Sixteenth Century: Aspects of the city republic before, during and after the Reformation* (St Louis, MO, 1982).

On political representation and the growth of territories Francis L. Carsten, *Princes and Parliaments in Germany from the Fifteenth to the Eighteenth Century* (Oxford, 1959) is still fundamental. On the lure of Swiss confederal republicanism to south German cities, see the path-breaking study by Thomas A. Brady, Jr, *Turning Swiss: Cities and empire, 1450–1550* (Cambridge, 1985). On the rulers of the period there is in English only Gerhard Benecke, *Maximilian I: An analytical biography* (London/Boston, MA/Melbourne/Henley-on-Thames, 1982), which is barely biographical or analytic. The condition of the Empire on the eve of the Reformation is described in the essays of A. G. Dickens, *The German Nation and Martin Luther* (London, 1974), a splendid book which ranges much more widely than its title suggests. On the way in which imperial politics was shaped by local and regional structures, the essays in Thomas A. Brady, Jr, *Communities, Politics, and Reformation in Early Modern Europe* (Leiden/Boston/Cologne, 1998) offer fundamental insights. On rural communes and communalism, some of Peter Blickle's many essays have now been collected in *From the Communal Reformation to the Revolution of the Common Man*, transl. Beat Kümin (Leiden/Boston/Cologne, 1998). Blickle's views on communalism as the guiding principle of early modern German history are contained in his essay *Obedient Germans? A Rebuttal: A new view of German history*, transl. Thomas A. Brady, Jr (Charlottesville, VA/London, 1997). For a critique of this interpretation see two essays by Bob Scribner: 'Communities and the nature of power', in Scribner, *Germany*, pp. 291–325; and 'Communalism: Universal category or ideological construct? A debate in the historiography of early modern Germany and Switzerland', *Historical Journal*, 37 (1994), pp. 199–207.

The topography of sixteenth-century Germany, as presented by pioneers such as Sebastian Münster and Sebastian Brant, is discussed in Gerald Strauss, *Sixteenth-Century Germany: Its topography and topographers* (Madison, WI, 1959).

Chapter 2: Society and Hierarchy

The best survey of social structure is offered by Christopher Friedrichs, 'German social structure, 1300–1600', in Scribner, *Germany*, pp. 233–58. Apart from his remarks there is very little in English on the situation of the nobility in the Holy Roman Empire before the seventeenth century. There is nothing, for instance, to set alongside Hamish Scott (ed.), *The European Nobilities in the Seventeenth and Eighteenth Centuries*, 2 vols (London/New York, 1995). Useful comparative insights (but with little on Germany itself) can be gained from Jonathan Dewald, *The European Nobility, 1400–1800* (Cambridge, 1996), and the penetrating study by Hillay Zmora, *Monarchy, Aristocracy and the State in Europe, 1300–1800* (London/New York, 2001). For the junkers of east Elbia see under Chapter 6. A few older works have examined the fate of the imperial knights: H. H. Kehrer, *The von Sickingen and the*

German Princes, 1262–1523 (Ann Arbor, MI, 1981); Hajo Holborn, *Ulrich von Hutten and the German Reformation,* transl. Roland H. Bainton (New Haven, CT, 1937; repr. Westport, CT, 1978); W. R. Hitchcock, *The Background to the Knights' Revolt, 1522–23* (Berkeley/Los Angeles, 1958), as well as the broader survey by M. J. LeGates, 'The Knights and the problem of political organizing in sixteenth-century Germany', *Central European History,* 7 (1974), pp. 99–136. A lively insight into one notorious robber-knight is provided by Henry J. Cohn, 'Götz von Berlichingen and the art of military autobiography', in J. R. Mulryne and Margaret Shewring (eds), *War, Literature and the Arts in Sixteenth-Century Europe* (Basingstoke/London, 1989), pp. 22–40.

Apart from Friedrichs cited above there is little in English on the self-perception of urban elites and their relation to the rural nobility, but on urban mentalities more generally, and the guilds in particular, see Antony Black, *Guilds and Civil Society in European Political Thought from the Twelfth Century to the Present* (London, 1984), ch. 9, and Hans-Christoph Rublack, 'Political and social norms in urban communities in the Holy Roman Empire', in Kaspar von Greyerz (ed.), *Religion, Politics and Social Protest: Three studies on early modern Germany* (London, 1984), pp. 24–60. From a north German perspective see also Heinz Schilling, *Religion, Political Culture and the Emergence of Early Modern Society: Essays in German and Dutch history* (Leiden, 1992). On humanists and the urban milieu, see Maria Grossmann, *Humanism in Wittenberg, 1485–1517* (Nieuwkoop, 1975); E. H. Zeydel, *Sebastian Brant* (New York, 1967); and Lewis W. Spitz, *Conrad Celtis: The German arch-humanist* (Cambridge, MA, 1957). The fine social gradations within urban communities are explored in Miriam Usher Chrisman, *Conflicting Visions of Reform: German lay propaganda pamphlets, 1519–1530* (Atlantic Highlands, NJ, 1996), and the differences of interest between guilds (within the Reformation context) by Philip Broadhead, 'Guildsmen, religious reform and the search for the common good: The role of the guilds in early modern Augsburg', *Historical Journal,* 39 (1996), pp. 577–97. Outburghers are discussed in Tom Scott, *Freiburg and the Breisgau: Town–country relations in the age of reformation and Peasants' War* (Oxford, 1986), and for Switzerland by Tom Scott, 'Liberty and community in medieval Switzerland', *German History,* 13 (1995), pp. 98–113. The fate of the urban poor is dealt with in comparative perspective by Robert Jütte, *Poverty and Deviance in Early Modern Europe* (Cambridge, 1994), and in a fine case-study by Lee Palmer Wandel, *Always Among Us: Images of the poor in Zwingli's Zurich* (Cambridge, 1990).

On rural society (apart from the works listed under Chapters 6 and 7), see the outstanding local study by Thomas Robisheaux, *Rural Society and the Search for Order in Early Modern Germany* (Cambridge, 1989), which examines the county of Hohenlohe in northern Württemberg, and for the duchy of Württemberg as a whole the anthropological approach of David Sabean, *Power in the Blood: Popular culture and village discourse in early modern Germany* (Cambridge, 1984), which is suitably dismissive of the harmony purportedly enshrined in communal values.

For women, see under Chapter 3; for Jews, see under Chapter 8.

Chapter 3: Population and Household

There is disagreement on almost every aspect of Germany's population in this period (though not on the long-term trends): the appropriate geographical basis of calculation, the multipliers to be used in arriving at household size, and the density of settlement before and after the waves of epidemic in the fourteenth and fifteenth centuries. Almost the only guide in English (which also contains comments on climate change) is Christian Pfister, 'The population of late medieval and early modern Germany', in Scribner, *Germany*, pp. 33–62. But his findings are at some variance, in the case of towns, with the compilation by Paul Bairoch, Jean Baton, and Pierre Chèvre, *La population des villes européennes/The Population of European Cities* (Geneva, 1988), *s.v.* Allemagne/Germany; Autriche/Austria; Suisse/Switzerland; and France (for Alsace and Lorraine). For urban populations even more revisionist are Tom Scott and Bob Scribner, 'Urban networks', in Scribner, *Germany*, pp. 113–43, who argue that the urban quotient of the German population was appreciably lower than usually thought.

On family and household, as well as on patterns of reproduction, Germany echoes the rest of western Europe. See, therefore, Michael Mitterauer and Reinhard Sieder, *The European Family: Patriarchy to partnership from the Middle Ages to the present*, transl. Karla Oosterveen and Manfred Hörzinger (Oxford, 1982); and Arthur E. Imhof, *Lost Worlds: How our European ancestors coped with everyday life, and why life is so hard today*, transl. Thomas Robisheaux (Charlottesville, VA/London, 1996). For the rural population see also Thomas Robisheaux, 'The peasantries of western Germany, 1300–1750', in Tom Scott (ed.), *The Peasantries of Europe from the Fourteenth to the Eighteenth Centuries* (London/New York, 1998), pp. 111–42.

On women and gender there is a general European survey by Merry E. Wiesner, *Women and Gender in Early Modern Europe*, 2nd edn (Cambridge, 2000), and for Germany itself two outstanding works: Heide Wunder, *He is the Sun, she is the Moon: Women in early modern Germany*, transl. Thomas Dunlap (Cambridge, MA, 1998); and Merry E. Wiesner, *Working Women in Renaissance Germany* (New Brunswick, NJ, 1986). See also the latter's usefully compact survey, 'Gender and the world of work', in Scribner, *Germany*, pp. 209–32, and the special issue of *German History*, 17/1 (1999) on 'Gender in early modern German history', ed. Ulinka Rublack.

Chapter 4: Economic Landscapes

On the concept of economic landscapes see fundamentally Tom Scott, 'Economic landscapes', in Scribner, *Germany*, pp. 1–31. A general account of the European economy in this period from the pen of a German historian naturally contains much material on central Europe, but Hermann Kellenbenz, *The Rise of the European Economy: An economic history of continental Europe 1500–1750*, transl. Gerhard Benecke (London, 1976) is longer on description than explanation. A more conceptual approach (but one which is too inclined to see the evil hand of capitalism at every turn) is offered by

Peter Kriedte, *Peasants, Landlords and Merchant Capitalists: Europe and the world economy, 1500–1800*, transl. Volker Berghahn (Leamington Spa, 1986).

The cycles of agricultural depression and recovery are still dominated by Wilhelm Abel, *Agricultural Fluctuations in Europe: From the thirteenth to the twentieth centuries*, transl. from the 3rd edn (1978) by Olive Ordish (London, 1980), even though the first edition appeared in 1935! A useful modern survey is given by Heide Wunder, 'Agriculture', in G. R. Elton (ed.), *The New Cambridge Modern History*, vol. 2: *The Reformation*, 2nd edn (Cambridge, 1990), pp. 23–47. Very much stuck in the Abel mould is Werner Rösener, 'The agrarian economy, 1300–1600', in Scribner, *Germany*, pp. 33–62. In addition to his 'Peasantries of western Germany' cited above, see also Thomas Robisheaux, 'The world of the village', in Thomas A. Brady, Jr, Heiko A. Oberman, and James D. Tracy (eds), *Handbook of European History 1400–1600: Late Middle Ages, Renaissance and Reformation*, vol. 1: *Structures and Assertions* (Leiden/New York/Cologne, 1994), pp. 79–112.

The development of a central European cattle-trade is examined by Ian Blanchard, 'The continental European cattle trades 1400–1600', *Economic History Review*, 2nd series 39 (1986), pp. 427–60. Rural manufacturing is the subject of two essays by Hermann Kellenbenz, 'The fustian industry of the Ulm region in the fifteenth and early sixteenth centuries', in N. B. Harte and K. G. Ponting (eds), *Cloth and Clothing in Medieval Europe: Essays in memory of Professor E. M. Carus-Wilson* (London, 1983), pp. 259–76; and 'Rural industries in the west from the end of the Middle Ages to the eighteenth century', in Peter Earle (ed.), *Essays in European Economic History* (Oxford, 1974), pp. 45–88. Although not directly concerned with Germany, the essay on the new draperies by Robert S. DuPlessis, 'One theory, two draperies, three provinces, and a multitude of fabrics: The new drapery of French Flanders, Hainaut, and the Tournaisis, *c*.1500–*c*.1800', in N. B. Harte (ed.), *The New Draperies in the Low Countries and England, 1300–1800* (Oxford, 1997), pp. 129–72 is of fundamental importance. Salt-mining is explored by Rudolf Palme, 'Alpine salt-mining in the Middle Ages', *Journal of European Economic History*, 19 (1990), pp. 117–36; and ore-mining by Philippe Braunstein, 'Innovations in mining and metal production in Europe in the late Middle Ages', *Journal of European Economic History*, 12 (1983), pp. 573–91.

There is depressingly little in English on the nature of early capitalism and the putting-out system. William J. Wright's survey, 'The nature of early capitalism', in Scribner, *Germany*, pp. 181–208 is at least a starting-point, and it is better than his monograph, *Capitalism, the State and the Lutheran Reformation: Sixteenth-century Hesse* (Athens, OH, 1988), though the latter does shift the focus away from urban capitalists to princely entrepreneurs. It is nevertheless extraordinary that the only work on the Fuggers was published in the nineteenth century: Richard Ehrenberg, *Capital and Finance in the Age of the Renaissance: A study of the Fuggers and their connections*, transl. H. M. Lucas (New York, 1896; latest repr. New York, 1963). There is, however, a monograph on another merchant house: Fritz-Wolfgang Ringling, *Sixteenth Century Merchant Capitalism: The Haug-Langnauer-Linck and relatives of Augsburg as a case study* (Rochester, NY, 1979).

Chapter 5: Commercial Networks and Urban Systems

The principal theoretical issues (including central-place theory) are discussed in Tom Scott and Bob Scribner, 'Urban networks', in Scribner, *Germany*, pp. 113–43. For the Hanseatic League the best study remains Philippe Dollinger, *The German Hansa*, transl. D. S. Ault and S. H. Steinberg (London, 1970), which has been reissued with a new introduction by Mark Casson (London/New York, 1999). There is also an east German account by Johannes Schildhauer, *The Hansa: History and culture*, transl. Katherine Vanovitch (Leipzig, 1985), whose rich illustrations help to redress the view that the Hanseatic cities lagged behind their south German and Swiss counterparts culturally and intellectually. On the Hansa's overseas trade see T. H. Lloyd, *England and the German Hansa, 1157–1611* (Cambridge, 1992). On the capital of the Hansa in the west, Cologne, see Franz Irsigler, 'Industrial production, international trade and public finances in Cologne (XVIth [*recte*: XIVth] and XVth century)', *Journal of European Economic History*, 6 (1977), pp. 269–306. There is a brief survey of Nuremberg by Wolfgang von Stromer, 'Commercial policy and economic conjuncture in Nuremberg at the close of the Middle Ages: A model of economic policy', *Journal of European Economic History*, 10 (1980), pp. 119–29, and a wide-ranging monograph on Augsburg: Martha White Paas, *Population Change, Labor Supply, and Agriculture in Augsburg, 1480–1618: A study of early demographic–economic interactions* (New York, 1981). Note also the comparative study by Herbert Eiden and Franz Irsigler, 'Environment and hinterland: Cologne and Nuremberg in the later Middle Ages', in James A. Galloway (ed.), *Trade, Urban Hinterlands and Market Integration c.1300–1600* (London, 2000), pp. 43–57.

That leads on directly to issues of market competition and town–country relations. From the undisputed master of Upper German conditions, see Rolf Kießling, 'Markets and marketing, town and country', in Scribner, *Germany*, pp. 145–79. Decidedly inferior is Etienne François, 'The German urban network between the sixteenth and the eighteenth centuries: Cultural and demographic indicators', in Ad van der Woude, Akira Hayami, and Jan de Vries (eds), *Urbanization in History: A process of dynamic interactions* (Oxford, 1990), pp. 84–100. For south-west Germany see Scott, *Freiburg and the Breisgau* cited above; Tom Scott, 'Economic conflict and co-operation on the Upper Rhine, 1450–1600', in E. I. Kouri and Tom Scott (eds), *Politics and society in Reformation Europe* (Basingstoke/London, 1987), pp. 210–31; Tom Scott, *Regional Identity and Economic Change: The Upper Rhine, 1450–1600* (Oxford, 1987); and most recently Tom Scott, 'Town and country in Germany, 1350–1600', in S. R. Epstein (ed.), *Town and Country in Europe, 1300–1800* (Cambridge, 2001), pp. 202–28, which also discusses the formation of rural territories and city-states. These are also examined by Christopher R. Friedrichs, 'The Swiss and German city-states', in Robert Griffeth and Carol G. Thomas (eds), *The City-State in Five Cultures* (Santa Barbara, CA/London, 1981), pp. 109–42; and most recently by Peter Johanek, 'Imperial and free towns of the Holy Roman Empire – city states in pre-modern Germany?', in Mogens Herman Hansen (ed.), *A Comparative Study of Thirty City-State Cultures* (Copenhagen, 2000), pp. 295–319. For Switzerland see Scott, 'Liberty and community' cited above.

A comparison with the Low Countries is particularly illuminating. Alongside the older works of David M. Nicholas, 'Town and countryside: Social and economic tensions in fourteenth-century Flanders', *Comparative Studies in Society and History*, 10 (1968), pp. 458–85, and his book-length study, *Town and Countryside: Economic and political tensions in fourteenth-century Flanders* (Bruges, 1971), should now be set Peter Stabel, *Dwarfs Among Giants: The Flemish urban network in the late Middle Ages* (Leuven/Apeldoorn, 1997).

Chapter 6: Lordship and Dependence

The conceptual issues surrounding the 'crisis of feudalism' can be pursued in T. H. Aston and C. H. E. Philpin (eds), *The Brenner Debate: Agrarian class structure and economic development in pre-industrial Europe* (Cambridge, 1985), and in Guy Bois, *The Crisis of Feudalism: Economy and society in eastern Normandy, c.1300–1550* (Cambridge/Paris, 1984). The feud and the mortgage are brilliantly analyzed for one region of Germany by Hillay Zmora, *State and Nobility in Early Modern Germany: The knightly feud in Franconia, 1440–1567* (Cambridge, 1997), and in his article, 'Princely state-making and the "crisis of the aristocracy" in late medieval Germany', *Past and Present*, 153 (1996), pp. 37–63. The views of Otto Brunner are now accessible in English: *Land and Lordship: Structures of governance in medieval Austria*, transl. from 4th edn and ed. Howard Kaminsky and James Van Horn Melton (Philadelphia, 1992). The editors' 70-page introduction says all that is needed about the remarkable intellectual influence of Brunner's thesis, which now deserves to be consigned to the curiosity cabinet of history.

There are few studies in English of individual lordships, but for the Teutonic Order see Michael Burleigh, *Prussian Society and the German Order: An aristocratic corporation in crisis, c.1410–1466* (Cambridge, 1984). For southwest Germany in a later period, but with implications for preceding centuries, see David M. Luebke, *His Majesty's Rebels: Communities, factions, and rural revolt in the Black Forest, 1725–1745* (Ithaca, NY/London, 1997). On the thorny question of serfdom, readers have little to guide them in English except for Heide Wunder, 'Serfdom in later medieval and early modern Germany', in T. H. Aston, P. R. Coss, Christopher Dyer, and Joan Thirsk (eds), *Social Relations and Ideas: Essays in honour of R. H. Hilton* (Cambridge, 1983), pp. 249–72. But see also Luebke above.

On structures of east Elbian lordship and dominion we are much better served. See the general critique by Edgar Melton, '*Gutsherrschaft* in east Elbian Germany and Livonia, 1500–1800: A critique of the model', *Central European History*, 21 (1988), pp. 315–49; and the numerous studies by William W. Hagen: 'Village life in east-Elbian Germany and Poland, 1400–1800: Subjection, self-defence, survival', in Tom Scott (ed.), *The Peasantries of Europe from the Fourteenth to the Eighteenth Centuries* (London/New York, 1998), pp. 145–89; 'Capitalism and the countryside in early modern Europe: Interpretations, models, debates', *Agricultural History Review*, 62 (1988), pp. 13–47; 'How mighty the junkers? Peasant rents and seigneurial profits in sixteenth-century Brandenburg', *Past and Present*, 108 (1985), pp. 80–116; 'Working for the junker: The standard of living of manorial laborers in Brandenburg, 1584–1810', *Journal of Modern History*, 58 (1986), pp. 143–58; and 'Seventeenth-century crisis in Brandenburg: The Thirty Years' War, the destabilization of serfdom, and the rise of absolutism', *American Historical Review*, 94 (1989), pp. 302–35. His views are now summarized in *Ordinary Prussians: The Brandenburg junkers and their contentious villagers, 1500–1840* (Cambridge, forthcoming). There are also useful essays in Daniel Chirot (ed.), *The Origins of Backwardness in Eastern Europe: Economics and politics from the Middle Ages until the early twentieth century* (Berkeley, CA, 1989). On the situation of the Polish gentry and magnates, see Antoni Mączak, 'The conclusive years: The end of the sixteenth century as the turning-point of Polish history', in E. I. Kouri and Tom Scott (eds), *Politics and Society in Reformation Europe* (Basingstoke/London, 1987), pp. 516–32. On the rather different situation in Silesia, where *Gutsherrschaft* and *Gutswirtschaft* by no means coincided, see Richard C. Hoffmann, *Land, Liberties, and Lordship in a Late Medieval Countryside: Agrarian structures and change in the duchy of Wrocław* (Philadelphia, 1989). On northern Bohemia see Sheilagh Ogilvie, 'The economic world of the Bohemian serf: Economic concepts, preferences and constraints on the estate of Friedland, 1583–1692', *Economic History Review*, 2nd series 54 (2001), pp. 430–53.

Chapter 7: Reform and Revolt

There is an excellent collection of sources in translation on reform plans and social grievances in Germany up to the Reformation in Gerald Strauss (ed.), *Manifestations of Discontent in Germany on the eve of the Reformation* (Bloomington, IN/London, 1971), but very little by way of secondary literature. See, however, Dickens, *German Nation and Martin Luther* cited above. On sumptuary laws, there are some remarks in Robert Jütte, 'Daily life in Germany', in Scribner, *Germany*, pp. 327–53. For Luther's social and economic thought – and a discussion of Michael Gaismair's Christian republic in the Peasants' War – see Tom Scott, 'The Reformation and modern political economy: Luther and Gaismair compared', in Thomas A. Brady, Jr, and Elisabeth Müller-Luckner (eds), *The Reformation between the Late Middle Ages and Early Modern Times* (Munich, 2001), pp. 273–302.

Urban revolts before the sixteenth century are the exclusive preserve of Rhiman A. Rotz: '"Social struggles" or the price of power? German urban uprisings in the late Middle Ages', *Archiv für Reformationsgeschichte*, 76 (1985), pp. 64–95; 'Investigating urban uprisings (with examples from Hanseatic towns, 1374–1416)', in W. C. Jordan (ed.), *Order and Innovation in the Middle Ages: Essays in honor of Joseph R. Strayer* (Princeton, NJ, 1976), pp. 215–33, 483–94; 'Urban uprisings in Germany: Revolutionary or reformist? The case of Brunswick, 1374', *Viator*, 4 (1973), pp. 207–23; 'The uprising of 1374: Source of Brunswick's institutions', *Braunschweigisches Jahrbuch*, 54 (1973), pp. 61–73; 'The Lubeck rising of 1408 and the decline of the Hanseatic League', *Proceedings of the American Philosophical Society*, 121 (1977), pp. 1–45. It is time this imbalance was redressed. On the development of *Obrigkeit* see Thomas A. Brady, Jr, 'Economic and social institutions', in Scribner, *Germany*, pp. 259–90. On urban unrest during the Reformation see, apart from Dickens, *German Nation and Martin Luther*, Philip Broadhead, 'Popular pressure for reform in Augsburg, 1524–1534', in Wolfgang J. Mommsen (ed.), *Stadtbürgertum und Adel in der Reformation/The Urban Classes, the Nobility and the Reformation* (Stuttgart, 1979), pp. 80–7; and for Erfurt, R. W. Scribner, 'Civic unity and the Reformation in Erfurt', *Past and Present*, 66 (1975), pp. 29–60. Both these articles broach the topic of anticlericalism, on which (since it lies outside the scope of this book) see merely Peter A. Dykema and Heiko A. Oberman (eds), *Anticlericalism in Late Medieval and Early Modern Europe* (Leiden/New York/Cologne, 1994). (On anticlericalism in the Peasants' War see below.) On the Anabaptists in Münster, see R. Po-chia Hsia, 'Münster and the Anabaptists', in R. Po-chia Hsia (ed.), *The German People and the Reformation* (Ithaca, NY/London, 1988), pp. 51–69.

Revolts in German communes at the turn of the sixteenth century and beyond have been extensively explored by Christopher R. Friedrichs: 'Citizens or subjects: Urban conflict in early modern Germany', in Miriam Usher Chrisman and Otto Gründler (eds), *Social Groups and Religious Ideas in the Sixteenth Century* (Kalamazoo, MI, 1978), pp. 46–58, 164–9; 'Urban politics and urban social structure in seventeenth-century Germany', *European History Quarterly*, 22 (1992), pp. 187–216; 'Urban conflicts and the imperial constitution in seventeenth-century Germany', *Journal of Modern History*, 58 supplement (1986), pp. 98–123; 'German town revolts and the seventeenth-century crisis', *Renaissance and Modern Studies*, 26 (1982), pp. 27–51; 'The Fettmilch uprising in German and Jewish history', *Central European History*, 19 (1986), pp. 186–228.

Rural revolts before the Peasants' War are poorly treated in the English literature. Apart from Peter Blickle's essay, 'Peasant revolts in the German empire in the late Middle Ages', *Social History*, 4 (1979), pp. 223–39, there is a reconstruction of the events at Niklashausen in 1476 by Richard Wunderli, *Peasant Fires: The drummer of Niklashausen* (Bloomington/Indianapolis, IN, 1992), whose style is even more bizarre than the events it purports to 'reimagine'. The author stresses that he 'wrote this book for people who are not professional historians', which is just as well. On the Bundschuh revolts see Scott, *Freiburg and the Breisgau* cited above.

On the Peasants' War, by contrast, the literature is plentiful, including an edition of sources in translation: Tom Scott and Bob Scribner (eds), *The German Peasants' War: A history in documents* (Atlantic Highlands, NJ/London, 1991). The dominant interpretation of the War is that of Peter Blickle, *The Revolution of 1525: The German Peasants' War from a new perspective*, transl. from the 2nd edn (1981) by Thomas A. Brady, Jr, and H. C. Erik Midelfort (Baltimore, MD/London, 1982). Blickle's views have not found universal acceptance. For a critique see Tom Scott, 'The Peasants' War: A historiographical review', *Historical Journal*, 22 (1979), pp. 693–720, 953–74 (which also surveys the spate of literature on the 450th anniversary of the War in 1975), and Bob Scribner, '1525 – revolutionary crisis?', in Monika Hagenmaier and Sabine Holtz (eds), *Krisenbewußtsein und Krisenbewältigung in der Frühen Neuzeit – Crisis in Early Modern Europe: Festschrift für Hans-Christoph Rublack* (Frankfurt am Main/Berlin/Bern/New York/Paris/Vienna, 1992), pp. 25–45. Two sets of essays have been published: the first, Janos Bak (ed.), *The German Peasant War of 1525* (London, 1976) is a scrappy collection; the second, Bob Scribner and Gerhard Benecke (eds), *The German Peasant War – New Viewpoints* (London, 1979) is altogether more useful. From a range of articles on various aspects of the War, six may be selected: on the beginnings of the War in the Black Forest and the role of religious radicalism, Tom Scott, 'Reformation and Peasants' War in Waldshut and environs: A structural analysis', *Archiv für Reformationsgeschichte*, 69 (1978), pp. 82–102; 70 (1979), pp. 140–69; on anticlericalism, Henry J. Cohn, 'Anticlericalism in the German Peasants' War', *Past and Present*, 83 (1979), pp. 3–31; on the role of the imperial cities, Thomas F. Sea, 'Imperial cities and the Peasants' War in Germany', *Central European History*, 12 (1979), pp. 3–37; on tensions within the village community, Govind Sreenivasan, 'The social origins of the Peasants' War of 1525 in Upper Swabia', *Past and Present*, 171 (2001), pp. 30–65; on wine-growing regions in the War, Roy L. Vice, 'Vineyards, vinedressers and the Peasants' War in Franconia', *Archiv für Reformationsgeschichte*, 79 (1988), pp. 138–57; and on the aftermath of the War, Thomas F. Sea, 'The economic impact of the German Peasants' War: The question of reparations', *Sixteenth Century Journal*, 8 (1977), pp. 74–97. For the links between the Peasants' War and Anabaptism see the fine study by James M. Stayer, *The German Peasants' War and Anabaptist Community of Goods* (Montreal/Kingston, Ont./Buffalo, NY, 1991). An important comparative study is that of Paul Freedman, 'The German and Catalan peasant revolts', *American Historical Review*, 98 (1993), pp. 39–54. The extensive literature on peasant revolts after the Peasants' War is surveyed by Tom Scott, 'Peasant revolts in early modern Germany', *Historical Journal*, 28 (1985), pp. 455–68, and by Thomas Barnett-Robisheaux, 'Peasant revolts in Germany and central Europe after the Peasants' War: Comments on the literature', *Central European History*, 17 (1984), pp. 384–403. The 'juridification' of social conflict is expounded by Winfried Schulze, 'Peasant resistance in sixteenth- and seventeenth-century Germany in a European context', in Kaspar von Greyerz (ed.), *Religion, Politics and Social Protest: Three studies in early modern Germany* (London, 1984), pp. 61–98. On the Austrian lands up to the Peasants' War of 1626 see the important study by Hermann Rebel, *Peasant Classes: The bureaucratization of property and family relations under early Habsburg absolutism, 1511–1636* (Princeton, NJ, 1983), whose methodology, strongly anthropological in approach, has still to be taken up by other scholars of revolts in the German-speaking lands. See also Hermann Rebel, 'Peasantries under the Austrian Empire, 1300–1800', in Tom Scott (ed.), *The Peasantries of Europe from the Fourteenth to the Eighteenth Centuries* (London/New York, 1998), pp. 191–225.

Chapter 8: Deviancy and Conformity

For recent reflections on the flimsy evidence for an economic downturn in Augsburg, see Thomas Max Safley, 'Bankruptcy: Family and finance in early modern Augsburg', *Journal of European Economic History*, 29 (2000), pp. 53–75. This is a topic which urgently invites comparative investigation for Germany as a whole – especially from those with no axe to grind.

The question of honour and dishonour has come to the fore in recent research on Germany. For the nobility, see H. C. Erik Midelfort, 'Curious Georgics: The German nobility and their crisis of legitimacy in the late sixteenth century', in Andrew C. Fix and Susan C. Karant-Nunn (eds), *Germania Illustrata: Essays on early modern Germany presented to Gerald Strauss* (Kirksville, MO, 1992), pp. 217–42. For towns, see Kathy Stuart, *Defiled Trades and Social Outcasts: Honor and ritual pollution in early modern Germany* (Cambridge, 1999). For the countryside, see, alongside his monograph *Rural Society and the Search for Order* cited above, Thomas Robisheaux, 'Peasants and pastors: Rural youth control and the Reformation in Hohenlohe, 1540–1680', *Social History*, 6 (1981), pp. 281–300. On the moral supervision exercised over women see Lyndal Roper, *The Holy Household: Women and morals in Reformation Augsburg* (Oxford, 1989). Recently the focus of enquiry has widened to embrace patterns of criminality, suicide, and infanticide. Three such studies are: Ulinka Rublack, *The Crimes of Women in Early Modern Germany* (Oxford, 1999); David Lederer, 'The dishonorable dead: Perceptions of suicide in early modern Germany', in Sibylle Backmann, Hans-Jörg Künast, Sabine Ullmann, and B. Ann Tlusty (eds), *Ehrkonzepte in der Frühen Neuzeit* (Berlin, 1998), pp. 349–65; Alison Rowlands, '"In great secrecy": The crime of infanticide in Rothenburg ob der Tauber, 1501–1615', *German History*, 15 (1997), pp. 179–99.

The literature on the Jews in Germany is now likewise extensive. See the two studies by R. Po-chia Hsia, *The Myth of Ritual Murder: Jews and magic in Reformation Germany* (New Haven, CT/London, 1988); and *Trent 1475: Stories of a ritual murder trial* (New Haven, CT/London, 1992); and the collection of essays in R. Po-chia Hsia and Hartmut Lehmann (eds), *In and Out of the Ghetto: Jewish–gentile relations in late medieval and early modern Germany* (Washington, DC/Cambridge, 1995), as well as Miri Rubin, *Gentile Tales: The narrative assault on late medieval Jews* (New Haven, CT/London, 1999).

The number of works on witchcraft is positively hypertrophic: this is a craze which must surely pass. The essential works in English for the German-speaking lands are: H. C. Erik Midelfort, *Witch Hunting in Southwestern Germany 1562–1684: The social and intellectual foundations* (Stanford, CA, 1972), which has stood the test of time extremely well; for the south-east its counterpart is Wolfgang Behringer, *Witchcraft Persecutions in Bavaria: Popular magic, religious zealotry and reason of state in early modern Europe*, transl. J. C. Grayson and David Lederer (Cambridge, 1997) – excellent, but prolix. Behringer's article, by contrast, 'Weather, hunger and fear: Origins of the European witch-hunt in climate, society and mentality', *German History*, 13 (1995), pp. 1–27, covers a vast range of issues succinctly. On women and witchcraft see the essays by Lyndal Roper, *Oedipus and the Devil: Witchcraft, sexuality and religion in early modern Europe* (London/New York, 1994). On Dürer's *Witch* see Charles Zika, 'Dürer's witch, riding women and moral order', in Dagmar Eichberger and Charles Zika (eds), *Dürer and his Culture* (Cambridge, 1998), pp. 118–40, 225–8.

The impact of the Reformation has ensured that issues of public welfare, charity, and 'police' have received extensive attention. For present purposes see merely R. W. Scribner, 'Police and the territorial state in sixteenth-century Württemberg', in E. I. Kouri and Tom Scott (eds), *Politics and Society in Reformation Europe* (Basingstoke/London, 1987), pp. 103–20; and, for reference, Marc Raeff, *The Well-Ordered Police State: Social and institutional change through law in the Germanies and Russia 1600–1800* (New Haven, CT/London, 1983). On charity, see Thomas Max Safley, *Charity and Economy in the Orphanages of Early Modern Augsburg* (Atlantic Highlands, NJ, 1997), and the more general study by Carter Lindberg, *Beyond Charity: Reformation initiatives for the poor* (Minneapolis, MN, 1993). The same self-denying ordinance applies to the literature on confessionalization. See R. Po-chia Hsia, 'The structure of belief: Confessionalism and society, 1500–1600', in Scribner, *Germany*, pp. 355–77, and his *Social Discipline in the Reformation: Central Europe, 1550–1750* (London/New York, 1989). The best modern introduction to the Thirty Years War is Ronald G. Asch, *The Thirty Years War: The Holy Roman Empire and Europe 1618–1648* (New York, 1997).

Select List of Works in German

Much of the subject matter of this book is only covered by works in German. Rather than compile an exhaustive list of authorities, I have confined myself to a short selection of those books and articles which I have found particularly suggestive. Omission of titles should not be taken to imply that the works in question have not been consulted. A project such as the present one would have been made immeasurably harder, however, had I not been able to consult the *Enzyklopädie Deutscher Geschichte*, currently in progress, published by R. Oldenbourg Verlag in Munich. This enterprise seeks to provide in convenient volumes of around 100 pages a conspectus of current research on a huge range of topics from the Middle Ages to modern times, each volume divided into three sections – overview, problems and directions of research, and bibliography. The volumes I have found most useful are:

Vol. 1. Peter Blickle, *Unruhen in der ständischen Gesellschaft 1300–1800* (1988).

Vol. 3. Winfried Reininghaus, *Gewerbe in der frühen Neuzeit* (1990).

Vol. 10. Walter Achilles, *Landwirtschaft in der frühen Neuzeit* (1991).

Vol. 11. Franz Mathis, *Die deutsche Wirtschaft im 16. Jahrhundert* (1992).

Vol. 13. Werner Rösener, *Agrarwirtschaft, Agrarverfassung und ländliche Gesellschaft im Mittelalter* (1992).

Vol. 14. Karl-Friedrich Krieger, *König, Reich und Reichsreform im Spätmittelalter* (1992).

Vol. 18. Rudolf Endres, *Adel in der frühen Neuzeit* (1993).

Vol. 24. Heinz Schilling, *Die Stadt in der frühen Neuzeit* (1993).

Vol. 28. Christian Pfister, *Bevölkerungsgeschichte und historische Demographie* (1994).

Vol. 32. Werner Paravicini, *Die ritterlich-höfische Kultur des Mittelalters* (1994).

Vol. 34. Wolfgang von Hippel, *Armut, Unterschichten, Randgruppen in der frühen Neuzeit* (1995).

Vol. 35. Ernst Schubert, *Fürstliche Herrschaft und Territorium im späten Mittelalter* (1996).

Vol. 38. André Holenstein, *Bauern zwischen Bauernkrieg und Dreißigjährigem Krieg* (1996).
Vol. 40. Dieter Berg, *Deutschland und seine Nachbarn 1200–1500* (1997).
Vol. 42. Helmut Neuhaus, *Das Reich in der frühen Neuzeit* (1997).
Vol. 44. Michael Toch, *Die Juden im mittelalterlichen Reich* (1998).
Vol. 46. Rainer Gömmel, *Die Entwicklung der Wirtschaft im Zeitalter des Merkantilismus 1620–1800* (1998).

Two general works also deserve particular mention: Peter Moraw, *Von offener Verfassung zu gestalteter Verdichtung: Das Reich im späten Mittelalter* (*Propyläen Geschichte Deutschlands*, vol. 3) (Berlin, 1985), and Ernst Schubert, *Einführung in die Grundprobleme der deutschen Geschichte im Spätmittelalter* (Darmstadt, 1992). Works used in several chapters are only cited once.

Chapter 1: The Political Geography of Germany, 1300–1600

Ehlers, Joachim, (ed.), *Ansätze und Diskontinuität deutscher Nationsbildung im Mittelalter* (Sigmaringen, 1989).
Isenmann, Eberhard, 'Reichsstadt und Reich an der Wende vom späten Mittelalter zur frühen Neuzeit', in Josef Engel (ed.), *Mittel und Wege früher Verfassungspolitik* (Stuttgart, 1979), pp. 9–223.
Schmidt, Georg, *Der Städtetag in der Reichsverfassung* (Stuttgart, 1984).
Schubert, Ernst, *König und Reich: Studien zur spätmittelalterlichen deutschen Verfassungsgeschichte* (Göttingen, 1979).
Seibt, Ferdinand, and Winfried Eberhard (eds), *Europa 1500. Integrationsprozesse im Widerstreit: Staaten, Regionen, Personenverbände* (Stuttgart, 1987).

Chapter 2: Society and Hierarchy

Andermann, Kurt, *Studien zur Geschichte des pfälzischen Niederadels im späten Mittelalter* (Speyer, 1982).
Blickle, Peter, *Landschaften im Alten Reich: Die staatliche Funktion des gemeinen Mannes in Oberdeutschland* (Munich, 1973).
Blickle, Renate, 'Nahrung und Eigentum als Kategorien in der ständischen Gesellschaft', in Winfried Schulze (ed.), *Ständische Gesellschaft und soziale Mobilität* (Munich, 1988), pp. 73–93.
Diefenbacher, Michael, 'Stadt und Adel – Das Beispiel Nürnberg', *Zeitschrift für die Geschichte des Oberrheins*, 141 (1993), pp. 51–69.
Domsta, Hans J., *Die Kölner Außenbürger: Untersuchungen zur Politik und Verfassung der Stadt Köln von der Mitte des 13. bis zur Mitte des 16. Jahrhunderts* (Bonn, 1973).
Groebner, Valentin, *Ökonomie ohne Haus: Zum Wirtschaften armer Leute in Nürnberg am Ende des 15. Jahrhunderts* (Göttingen, 1993).
Hofmann, Hans Hubert, '*Nobiles Norimbergenses*: Beobachtungen zur Struktur der reichsstädtischen Oberschicht', *Zeitschrift für bayerische Landesgeschichte*, 28 (1965), pp. 114–50; reprinted in Theodor Mayer (ed.), *Untersuchungen*

zur gesellschaftlichen Struktur der mittelalterlichen Städte in Europa (Konstanz/ Stuttgart, 1968), pp. 53–92.

Press, Volker, *Adel im Alten Reich: Gesammelte Vorträge und Aufsätze*, ed. Franz Brendle and Anton Schindling (Tübingen, 1998).

Scott, Tom, (ed.), *Die Freiburger Enquete von 1476: Quellen zur Wirtschafts- und Verwaltungsgeschichte der Stadt Freiburg im Breisgau im fünfzehnten Jahrhundert* (Freiburg im Breisgau, 1986).

Scott, Tom, 'Der "Walzenmüller-Aufstand" 1492: Bürgeropposition und städtische Finanzen im spätmittelalterlichen Freiburg im Breisgau', *Zeitschrift des Breisgau-Geschichtsvereins ('Schau-ins-Land')*, 106 (1987), pp. 69–93.

Wunder, Heide, *Die bäuerliche Gemeinde in Deutschland* (Göttingen, 1986).

Zotz, Thomas, 'Adel in der Stadt des deutschen Spätmittelalters: Erscheinungsformen und Verhaltensweisen', *Zeitschrift für die Geschichte des Oberrheins*, 141 (1993), pp. 22–50.

Chapter 3: Population and Household

Abel, Wilhelm, *Geschichte der deutschen Landwirtschaft vom frühen Mittelalter bis zum 19. Jahrhundert*, 2nd edn (Stuttgart, 1967).

Blaschke, Karlheinz, 'Entwicklungstendenzen im Städtewesen Sachsens', in Wilhelm Rausch (ed.), *Die Stadt an der Schwelle zur Neuzeit* (Linz, 1980), pp. 245–58.

Dietrich, Richard, 'Das Städtewesen Sachsens an der Wende vom Mittelalter zur Neuzeit', in Wilhelm Rausch (ed.), *Die Stadt an der Schwelle zur Neuzeit* (Linz, 1980), pp. 193–226.

Henning, Friedrich-Wilhelm, *Das vorindustrielle Deutschland 800 bis 1800*, 4th edn (Paderborn/Munich/Vienna/Zürich, 1985).

Schirmer, Uwe, *Das Amt Grimma 1485–1548: Demographische, wirtschaftliche und soziale Verhältnisse in einem kursächsischen Amt am Ende des Mittelalters und zu Beginn der Neuzeit* (Beucha, 1996).

Wunder, Heide, *'Er ist die Sonn', sie ist der Mond': Frauen in der Frühen Neuzeit* (Munich, 1992).

Wunder, Heide, and Christina Vanja (eds), *Weiber, Menscher, Frauenzimmer: Frauen in der ländlichen Gesellschaft* (Göttingen, 1996).

Chapter 4: Economic Landscapes

Ammann, Hektor, 'Die Anfänge der Leinenindustrie des Bodenseegebiets', *Alemannisches Jahrbuch*, 1953, pp. 251–313.

Ammann, Hektor, *Die wirtschaftliche Stellung der Reichsstadt Nürnberg im Spätmittelalter* (Nuremberg, 1970).

Held, Wieland, *Zwischen Marktplatz und Anger: Stadt-Land-Beziehungen im 16. Jahrhundert in Thüringen* (Weimar, 1988).

Henning, Friedrich-Wilhelm, *Landwirtschaft und ländliche Gesellschaft in Deutschland 800–1750*, 2nd edn (Paderborn/Munich/Vienna/Zürich, 1985).

Holbach, Rudolf, *Frühformen von Verlag und Großbetrieb in der gewerblichen Produktion (13.–16. Jahrhundert)* (Stuttgart, 1994).

Huppertz, Barthel, *Räume und Schichten bäuerlicher Kulturformen in Deutschland* (Bonn, 1939).

Irsigler, Franz, 'Intensivwirtschaft, Sonderkulturen und Gartenbau als Elemente der Kulturlandschaftsgestaltung in den Rheinlanden (13.–16. Jahrhundert)', in Annalisa Guarducci (ed.), *Agriculture as a Factor in the Modifying of the Environment: A five-century survey (1200–1700)/Agricoltura e trasformazione dell'ambiente secoli XIII–XVIII* (Florence, 1984), pp. 719–47.

Kießling, Rolf, *Die Stadt und ihr Land: Umlandpolitik, Bürgerbesitz und Wirtschaftsgefüge in Ostschwaben vom 14. bis ins 16. Jahrhundert* (Cologne/Vienna, 1989).

Stromer, Wolfgang von, 'Gewerbereviere und Protoindustrien in Spätmittelalter und Frühneuzeit', in Hans Pohl (ed.), *Gewerbe- und Industrielandschaften vom Spätmittelalter bis ins 20. Jahrhundert* (Stuttgart, 1986), pp. 39–111.

Chapter 5: Commercial Networks and Urban Systems

Ammann, Hektor, 'Die Diesbach-Watt-Gesellschaft: Ein Beitrag zur Handelsgeschichte des 15. Jahrhunderts', *Mitteilungen zur vaterländischen Geschichte*, 37 (1928), pp. 1–133, appendix pp. 1–81.

Behr, Hans-Joachim, 'Die Landgebietspolitik nordwestdeutscher Hansestädte', *Hansische Geschichtsblätter*, 94 (1976), pp. 17–37.

Blickle, Peter, 'Zur Territorialpolitik der oberschwäbischen Reichsstädte', in Erich Maschke and Jürgen Sydow (eds), *Stadt und Umland* (Stuttgart, 1974), pp. 54–71.

Dirlmeier, Ulf, 'Mittelalterliche Zoll- und Stapelrechte als Handelshemmnisse', in Hans Pohl (ed.), *Die Auswirkungen von Zöllen und anderen Handelshemmnissen auf Wirtschaft und Gesellschaft vom Mittelalter bis zur Gegenwart* (Stuttgart, 1987), pp. 19–39.

Dubler, Anne-Marie, *Handwerk, Gewerbe und Zunft in Stadt und Landschaft Luzern* (Luzern/Stuttgart, 1982).

Fritze, Konrad, *Am Wendepunkt der Hanse: Untersuchungen zur Wirtschafts- und Sozialgeschichte wendischer Hansestädte in der ersten Hälfte des 15. Jahrhunderts* (Berlin, 1967).

Gasser, Adolf, *Entstehung und Ausbildung der Landeshoheit im Gebiet der Schweizerischen Eidgenossenschaft* (Aarau/Leipzig, 1930).

Irsigler, Franz, 'Frühe Verlagsbeziehungen in der gewerblichen Produktion des westlichen Hanseraumes', in Konrad Fritze, Eckhart Müller-Mertens, and Johannes Schildhauer (eds), *Zins – Profit – ursprüngliche Akkumulation* (Weimar, 1981), pp. 175–83.

Kirchgässner, Bernhard, 'Organisationsprobleme des südwestdeutschen Handels zwischen Schwarzem Tod und 30jährigem Krieg (1350 bis 1650)', in *Bausteine zur geschichtlichen Landeskunde von Baden-Württemberg* (Stuttgart, 1979), pp. 221–37.

Leiser, Wolfgang, 'Das Landgebiet der Reichsstadt Nürnberg', in Rudolf

Endres (ed.), *Nürnberg und Bern: Zwei Reichsstädte und ihre Landgebiete* (Erlangen, 1990), pp. 227–60.

Marchal, Guy P., *Sempach 1386: Von den Anfängen des Territorialstaates Luzern* (Basel, 1986).

Meynen, Emil, (ed.), *Zentralität als Problem der mittelalterlichen Stadtgeschichtsforschung* (Cologne/Vienna, 1979).

Mörke, Olaf, 'Die Fugger im 16. Jahrhundert: Städtische Elite oder Sonderkultur? Ein Diskussionsbeitrag', *Archiv für Reformationsgeschichte*, 74 (1983), pp. 141–62.

Peyer, Hans Conrad, 'Wollgewerbe, Viehzucht, Solddienst und Bevölkerungsentwicklung in Stadt und Landschaft Freiburg i. Ue. vom 14. bis 16. Jahrhundert', in Hermann Kellenbenz (ed.), *Agrarisches Nebengewerbe und Formen der Reagrarisierung im Spätmittelalter und 19./20. Jahrhundert* (Stuttgart, 1975), pp. 79–95.

Raiser, Elisabeth, *Städtische Territorialpolitik im Mittelalter: Eine vergleichende Untersuchung über verschiedene Formen am Beispiel Lübecks und Zürichs* (Lübeck/Hamburg, 1969).

Stromer, Wolfgang von, 'Verflechtungen oberdeutscher Wirtschaftszentren am Beginn der Neuzeit', in Wilhelm Rausch (ed.), *Die Stadt an der Schwelle zur Neuzeit* (Linz, 1980), pp. 21–40.

Wunder, Gerhard, *Das Straßburger Landgebiet: Territorialgeschichte der einzelnen Teile des städtischen Herrschaftsbereichs vom 13. bis zum 16. Jahrhundert* (Berlin, 1967).

Chapter 6: Lordship and Dependence

Andermann, Kurt, 'Leibeigenschaft im pfälzischen Oberrheingebiet während des späten Mittelalters und der frühen Neuzeit', *Zeitschrift für historische Forschung*, 17 (1990), pp. 281–303.

Andermann, Kurt, 'Raubritter – Raubfürsten – Raubbürger? Zur Kritik eines untauglichen Begriffs', in Kurt Andermann (ed.), *'Raubritter' oder 'Rechtschaffene vom Adel'? Aspekte von Politik, Friede und Recht im späten Mittelalter* (Sigmaringen, 1997), pp. 9–29.

Bittmann, Markus, *Kreditwirtschaft und Finanzierungsmethoden: Studien zu den wirtschaftlichen Verhältnissen des Adels im westlichen Bodenseeraum 1300–1500* (Stuttgart, 1991).

Blickle, Peter, *Studien zur geschichtlichen Bedeutung des deutschen Bauernstandes* (Stuttgart/New York, 1989).

Blickle, Renate, 'Leibeigenschaft: Versuch über Zeitgenossenschaft und Wirklichkeit, durchgeführt am Beispiel Altbayerns', in Jan Peters (ed.), *Gutsherrschaft als soziales Modell: Vergleichende Betrachtungen zur Funktionsweise frühneuzeitlicher Agrargesellschaften* (Munich, 1995), pp. 53–79.

Enders, Lieselott, 'Entwicklungsetappen der Gutsherrschaft vom Ende des 15. bis zum Beginn des 17. Jahrhunderts, untersucht am Beispiel der Uckermark', *Jahrbuch für Geschichte des Feudalismus*, 12 (1988), pp. 119–66.

Enders, Lieselott, 'Die Landgemeinde in Brandenburg: Grundzüge ihrer Funktion und Wirkungsweise vom 13. bis zum 18. Jahrhundert', *Blätter für deutsche Landesgeschichte*, 129 (1993), pp. 195–256.

Endres, Rudolf, *Adelige Lebensformen in Franken zur Zeit des Bauernkrieges* (Würzburg, 1974).

Görner, Regina, *Raubritter: Untersuchungen zur Lage des spätmittelalterlichen Niederadels, besonders im südlichen Westfalen* (Münster, 1987).

Grees, Hermann, *Ländliche Unterschichten und ländliche Siedlung in Ostschwaben* (Tübingen, 1975).

Harnisch, Hartmut, *Bauern – Feudaladel – Städtebürgertum: Untersuchungen über die Zusammenhänge zwischen Feudalrente, bäuerlicher und gutsherrlicher Warenproduktion und den Ware-Geld-Beziehungen in der Magdeburger Börde und dem nordöstlichen Harzvorland von der frühbürgerlichen Revolution bis zum Dreißigjährigen Krieg* (Weimar, 1980).

Harnisch, Hartmut, *Die Herrschaft Boitzenburg: Untersuchungen zur Entwicklung der sozialökonomischen Struktur ländlicher Gebiete in der Mark Brandenburg vom 14. bis zum 19. Jahrhundert* (Weimar, 1988).

Hoffmann, Alfred, 'Die Grundherrschaft als Unternehmen', *Zeitschrift für Agrargeschichte und Agrarsoziologie*, 6 (1958), pp. 123–31.

Hüllinghorst, Bernd, '"Daß keine ärmere geplagte leute in der Graffschaft Lippe wohneten!" Die lippische Leibherrschaft im 17. Jahrhundert', in *Der Weserraum zwischen 1500 und 1650: Gesellschaft, Wirtschaft und Kultur in der Frühen Neuzeit* (Marburg, 1993), pp. 93–113.

Kaak, Heinrich, *Die Gutsherrschaft: Theoriegeschichtliche Untersuchungen zum Agrarwesen im ostelbischen Raum* (Berlin/New York, 1991).

Köhn, Rolf, 'Der Hegauer Bundschuh (Oktober 1460) – ein Aufstandsversuch in der Herrschaft Hewen gegen die Grafen von Lupfen', *Zeitschrift für die Geschichte des Oberrheins*, 138 (1990), pp. 99–141.

Kriedte, Peter, 'Spätmittelalterliche Agrarkrise oder Krise des Feudalismus?', *Geschichte und Gesellschaft*, 7 (1981), pp. 42–68.

Lütge, Friedrich, *Geschichte der deutschen Agrarverfassung vom frühen Mittelalter bis zum 19. Jahrhundert*, 2nd edn (Stuttgart, 1967).

Militzer, Klaus, 'Auswirkungen der spätmittelalterlichen Agrardepression auf die Deutschordensballeien', in Udo Arnold (ed.), *Von Akkon bis Wien: Studien zur Deutschordensgeschichte vom 13. bis zum 20. Jahrhundert* (Marburg, 1978), pp. 62–75.

Ribbe, Wolfgang, and Johannes Schulze (eds), *Das Landbuch des Klosters Zinna* (Berlin, 1976).

Rösener, Werner, 'Zur Problematik des spätmittelalterlichen Raubrittertums', in Helmut Maurer and Hans Patze (eds), *Festschrift für Berent Schwineköper zu seinem siebzigsten Geburtstag* (Sigmaringen, 1982), pp. 469–88.

Sabean, David W., *Landbesitz und Gesellschaft am Vorabend des Bauernkriegs* (Stuttgart, 1972).

Sablonier, Roger, *Adel im Wandel: Eine Untersuchung zur sozialen Situation des ostschweizerischen Adels um 1300* (Göttingen, 1979).

Schenk, Winfried, *Mainfränkische Kulturlandschaft unter klösterlicher Herrschaft: Die Zisterzienserabtei Ebrach als raumwirksame Institution vom 16. Jahrhundert bis 1803* (Würzburg, 1988).

Schmidt, Christoph, *Leibeigenschaft im Ostseeraum: Versuch einer Typologie* (Cologne/Weimar/Vienna, 1997).

Scott, Tom, 'Wandel und Beharrung der Untertänigkeit: Die südwestdeutsche Leibherrschaft/Leibeigenschaft in komparativer Sicht', in Markus Cerman and Robert Luft (eds), *Untertanen, Herrschaft und Staat in Böhmen und im 'Alten Reich'* (Munich, forthcoming).

Troßbach, Werner, '"Südwestdeutsche Leibeigenschaft" in der Frühen Neuzeit – eine Bagatelle?', *Geschichte und Gesellschaft*, 7 (1981), pp. 69–90.

Ulbrich, Claudia, *Leibherrschaft am Oberrhein im Mittelalter* (Göttingen, 1979).

Chapter 7: Reform and Revolt

Bauer, Clemens, 'Conrad Peutinger und der Durchbruch des neuen ökonomischen Denkens in der Wende zur Neuzeit', in Clemens Bauer *et al.* (eds), *Augusta 955–1955* (Augsburg, 1955), pp. 219–28.

Bierbrauer, Peter, 'Bäuerliche Revolten im Alten Reich: Ein Forschungsbericht', in Peter Blickle (ed.), *Aufruhr und Empörung? Studien zum bäuerlichen Widerstand im Alten Reich* (Munich, 1980), pp. 1–68.

Blaich, Fritz, *Die Reichsmonopolgesetzgebung im Zeitalter Karls V.* (Stuttgart, 1967).

Blaich, Fritz, *Die Wirtschaftspolitik des Reichstags im Heiligen Römischen Reich* (Stuttgart, 1970).

Blickle, Peter, (ed.), *Revolte und Revolution in Europa* (Munich, 1975).

Blickle, Peter, '*Es sol der Schwanberg noch mitten in Schweitz ligen.* Schweizer Einflüsse auf den deutschen Bauernkrieg', *Jahrbuch für fränkische Landesforschung*, 60 (2000), pp. 113–25.

Blickle, Renate, 'Agrarische Konflikte und Eigentumsordnung in Altbayern, 1400–1800', in Winfried Schulze (ed.), *Aufstände, Revolten, Prozesse: Beiträge zu bäuerlichen Widerstandsbewegungen im frühneuzeitlichen Europa* (Stuttgart, 1983), pp. 166–87.

Bulst, Neithard, 'Kleidung als sozialer Konfliktstoff: Probleme kleidergesetzlicher Normierung im sozialen Gefüge', in Neithard Bulst and Robert Jütte (eds), *Zwischen Sein und Schein: Kleidung und Identität in der ständischen Gesellschaft, Saeculum*, 44/1 (1993), pp. 32–46.

Buszello, Horst, *Der Deutsche Bauernkrieg von 1525 als politische Bewegung* (Berlin, 1969).

Koller, Heinrich, (ed.), *Reformation Kaiser Siegmunds* (Stuttgart, 1964).

Maschke, Erich, 'Deutsche Städte am Ausgang des Mittelalters', in Wilhelm Rausch (ed.), *Die Stadt am Ausgang des Mittelalters* (Linz, 1974), pp. 1–44.

Remling, Ludwig, 'Formen und Ausmaß gewerblicher Autonomie in nordwestdeutschen Städten (14.–16. Jahrhundert)', in Bernhard Kirchgässner and Eberhard Naujoks (eds), *Stadt und wirtschaftliche Selbstverwaltung* (Sigmaringen, 1987), pp. 60–76.

Schilling, Heinz, 'Bürgerkämpfe in Aachen zu Beginn des 17. Jahrhunderts: Konflikte im Rahmen der alteuropäischen Ständegesellschaft oder im Umkreis der frühbürgerlichen Revolution?', *Zeitschrift für historische Forschung*, 1 (1974), pp. 175–231.

Schmidt, Georg, '"Frühkapitalismus" und Zunftwesen: Monopolbestrebungen und Selbstverwaltung in der frühneuzeitlichen Wirtschaft', in Bernhard Kirchgässner and Eberhard Naujoks (eds), *Stadt und wirtschaftliche Selbstverwaltung* (Sigmaringen, 1987), pp. 77–114.

Schulze, Winfried, *Bäuerlicher Widerstand und feudale Herrschaft in der frühen Neuzeit* (Stuttgart/Bad Cannstatt, 1980).

Schulze, Winfried, 'Die veränderte Bedeutung sozialer Konflikte im 16. und 17. Jahrhundert', in Hans-Ulrich Wehler (ed.), *Der Deutsche Bauernkrieg 1524–1526* (Göttingen, 1975), pp. 277–302.

Scott, Tom, 'Freiburg und der Bundschuh', in Hans Schadek (ed.), *Der Kaiser in seiner Stadt: Maximilian und der Reichstag zu Freiburg 1498* (Freiburg im Breisgau, 1998), pp. 333–53.

Scott, Tom, 'Der "Butzenkrieg": Der Aufstand zu Rufach 1514', in Heinrich Richard Schmidt, André Holenstein, and Andreas Würgler (eds), *Gemeinde, Reformation und Widerstand: Festschrift für Peter Blickle zum 60. Geburtstag* (Tübingen, 1998), pp. 355–69.

Scott, Tom, 'Südwestdeutsche Städte im Bauernkrieg: Bündnisse zwischen Opportunismus und Solidarität', in Bernhard Kirchgässner and Hans-Peter Becht (eds), *Stadt und Revolution* (Stuttgart, 2001), pp. 10–36.

Wunder, Heide, 'Der samländische Bauernaufstand von 1525: Entwurf für eine sozialgeschichtliche Forschungsstrategie', in Rainer Wohlfeil (ed.), *Der Bauernkrieg 1524–26: Bauernkrieg und Reformation* (Munich, 1975), pp. 143–76.

Chapter 8: Deviancy and Conformity

Behringer, Wolfgang, *Hexen: Glaube, Verfolgung, Vermarktung*, 2nd edn (Munich, 2000).

Heinrich Kramer (Institoris), *Malleus Maleficarum*, ed. Günter Jerouschek and Wolfgang Behringer (Munich, 2000).

Schilling, Heinz, (ed.), *Die reformierte Konfessionalisierung in Deutschland – Das Problem der 'Zweiten Reformation'* (Gütersloh, 1986).

Schulz, Knut, *Handwerksgesellen und Lohnarbeiter: Untersuchungen zur ober-rheinischen und oberdeutschen Stadtgeschichte des 14. bis 17. Jahrhunderts* (Sigmaringen, 1985).

Glossary

Ackerbürger   literally, 'citizens of the field', that is, towndwellers whose livelihood derived from agriculture, including wine-growing and market-gardening.

Banalities   the rights vested in a feudal lord by virtue of his judicial right to command or prohibit (the 'ban'), for instance over milling or brewing.

Bannmeile   the zone around a chartered market within which no other market might be held. This market precinct originally often extended to a radius of one (German) mile.

Bauernlegen   the expropriation of peasant farms, as practised in parts of east Elbia.

Bloomery   the first forge in an iron-works through which the metal passes after melting.

Bucking   the bleaching of linen in a lye, that is, an alkaline solution (commonly milk).

Cabinet government   government in which the ruler relies on a circle of personal advisers, rather than on an established staff of salaried officials.

Cameral lordship   a lordship under the direct rule of the territorial prince, rather than in the hands of feudal lords as his vassals.

Cameralism   the German variant of the doctrine of mercantilism (*q.v.*), which, aside from its commitment to bullionism and autarky, stressed the representation and splendour of the prince and his court, and a general concern for the welfare of the prince's territory and subjects, including an active policy of repopulation after the Thirty Years War.

Canton   the modern term canton is anachronistically applied to the members of the Swiss Confederation, who in the sixteenth century were known as *Orte* (places). In contemporary usage it was applied to the regional associations of imperial knights (*Ritterkantone*).

Catch-crop   A secondary crop grown on the same land as the main crop, before or after the latter's planting, intended to reinvigorate the soil.

Cattle-gate   a pasture for cattle.

Church-ale   a festival usually celebrating the saint's day of the church's patron saint.

Coltura promiscua   the Italian system of mixed commercial agriculture, whereby crops are grown intermingled, for instance, corn, vines, and olives.

Consistory   (Catholic) the diocesan court; (Protestant) the clerical board supervising morals.

Coppicing   the cutting-over of young trees before they become timber-trees, in order to provide staves for spokes, hoops, baskets, and the like.

Corvée   the French term for unpaid labour required to be performed by serfs for their lords.

Crofting   the laying-out on grass of linen in order to bleach it.

Cupellation   the ancient process of extracting silver from argentiferous lead by means of heating in a small cup or hearth, superseded by liquation (*q.v.*).

Custumal   the customs of a village, set down in writing, which formed the legal basis of relations between lord and peasant.

Eigenbehörigkeit   the legal status of those tenants in many parts of north-west Germany which, while not binding them to the lord's jurisdiction, did not entitle them to hereditary possession, and which sometimes entailed substantial payments. Although not deriving from the age of classical manorialism, this status may be loosely compared with villeinage (*q.v.*).

Erbuntertänigkeit   hereditary subjection of the tenant to the landlord, obliged to accept existing restrictions, but with the right to buy himself free.

Estovers   the right to take wood from the forest for domestic use.

Forestalling   the buying-up of goods before they reach market, in order to corner the market or to drive prices up.

Formariage   marriage to a subject outwith the lord's jurisdiction, or beyond the village community.

Fürkauf   the practice of forestalling (*q.v.*), but often used more broadly to imply any distortion of the direct relationship between producer and consumer.

Gesindezwangdienst   the compulsion of peasants' children to work for fixed terms as servants on the lord's estates, as practised in parts of east Elbia.

Gutsherrschaft   the intensification of seigneurialism by eliding landlordly and jurisdictional authority, observable in parts of east Elbia from the fourteenth century onwards.

Gutswirtschaft   the intensification of commercial agriculture on large domains (latifundia, *q.v.*), practised in parts of east Elbia from the sixteenth century onwards.

Hackling   dressing flax by splitting and combing the fibres with a hackle.

Heriot   the payment to the lord on the death of a peasant (not necessarily of servile status), usually the best head of cattle (for men) or best dress (for women).

Hintersasse   a towndweller with rights of residence rather than full citizenship.

Hofmark   the compact commercial estate, farmed by direct wage-labour, rather than by the *corvées* (*q.v.*) of serfs, found in parts of Bavaria, as opposed to the large commercial estates (latifundia, *q.v.*) of east Elbia.

Hurdling   the temporary enclosure of land by fencing with portable frames to create pastures for sheep or cattle.

Landschaft   in general terms, a landscape; more specifically, the commons of a territory as a political entity, sometimes represented as a corporation or Estate in the territorial diet (assembly).

Landwehr   the rampart-and-ditch constructed by some German cities to mark off and defend the boundary of their rural territory.

Latifundium (plural: **latifundia**)   large commercial estates reliant upon dependent labour, characteristic of parts of east Elbia, and reminiscent of the plantation estates of the colonial New World economies with their use of indentured labour.

Leibeigenschaft   serfdom attaching to the person (in German *Leib*, body); in parts of south-west Germany where this form of serfdom was revived in the late Middle Ages the unfreedom attached to the serf by virtue of residence under the lord's jurisdiction, rather than as a form of hereditary personal bondage.

Liquation   the smelting of argentiferous rock in a series of furnaces at high temperature, allowing the silver to run off and leaving the lead burnt up as white lead (lead oxide), which could be returned to its metallic state by reduction through charcoal.

Lohheckenwirtschaft   an alternate system of husbandry, in which coppicing (*q.v.*) succeeded tillage in rotation.

Marktzwang   the compulsion to deliver goods or produce to one specified market (cf. monopsony).

Mediatization   the surrender of a prince's direct (immediate) loyalty as a vassal of the emperor by succumbing to the rule of another prince.

Meierei   a dairy-farm.

Meierrecht   a form of tenancy, prevalent in north-west Germany, loosely analogous to the English copyhold, whereby the farmer had secure (though not necessarily hereditary) written title to his holding.

Mercantilism   a loose body of doctrines designed to augment the state's economic power and resources, principally by a reliance on bullionism (the accumulation of a treasury of wealth) and self-sufficiency (autarky). Cf. *cameralism.*

Merchet   the fine paid by a serf to his lord for permission to marry.

Monopsony   the compulsion to sell goods to one purchaser, or the situation where a purchaser is powerful enough to exert undue influence over the price of goods.

Neifty   bodily, or corporeal, serfdom, attaching to the person, as opposed to villeinage (*q.v.*), that is, tenurial bondage.

Pannage   the right to pasture swine in the forest.

Putting-out system   the practice whereby a merchant advances to a dependent wage-worker either working-capital, or the tools of trade, or (most commonly) the raw materials, in return for delivery of a finished, or semi-finished, product at an agreed price.

Realleibeigenschaft   a form of serfdom prevalent in parts of Westphalia and Bavaria, whereby bodily or personal serfdom was attached really, that is, tenurially, to the tenancy held from the lord.

Regrating   the buying-up of goods at market, especially foodstuffs, with the intention of reselling at a later date at a higher price in the same market. Cf. *forestalling.*

Retting   softening the fibres of flax by steeping or moistening.

Schäferei   a sheep-farm.

Schollengebundenheit   literally, 'tying to the sod' (i.e. the soil), the tenurial subjugation of the peasantry in east Elbia.

Serfdom   the unfreedom of the peasant under a feudal lord, either attaching to the person as a hereditary stigma, or to the land held from the lord. Cf. *neifty* and *villeinage.*

Stallage   the tax paid for the right to erect a stall at market.

Usufruct   the use of and benefit from a resource (such as the common land), without ownership of it.

Usury   the taking of excessive rates of interest; often used more broadly to describe profit-taking of any kind.

Villeinage   serfdom attaching to the unfree tenure of land held from a feudal lord, usually in return for *corvées* (*q.v.*).

Vorwerke   the commercially run farms of feudal lords east of the Elbe (as opposed to the vast latifundia, *q.v.*), sometimes confusingly translated as 'manors'.

Wirtschaftsherrschaft   an interval type of lordship, encountered in parts of central Austria and the borderlands of the river Elbe, which combined commercial leases on the larger peasant farms with a direct labour-force of landless workers on single domains.

Acknowledgements

I am grateful to Cambridge University Press for permission to include material first published in contributions to *The New Cambridge Medieval History*, vol. 7: *c.1415–c.1500*, ed. C. T. Allmand (1998), and to *Town and Country in Europe, 1300–1800*, ed. S. R. Epstein (2001). I am also indebted to Edward Arnold Publishers for permission to reproduce extracts in revised form from two essays in *Germany: A new social and economic history*, vol. 1, ed. Bob Scribner (London/New York/Sydney/Auckland, © Arnold, 1996).

Dr H. J. Cohn kindly subjected the text to critical scrutiny; his careful and constructive comments have much improved it. I would also like to acknowledge the advice and support of the Series Adviser, Professor Joseph Bergin, who first proposed the volume, and who awaited its protracted completion with forbearance. The faults which remain fall to the author. In preparing the text and the maps I am most grateful for the help of Maggie Farrington and Sandra Mather.

Tom Scott
Langholm, 2001

Index of Names and Places

Germany and the German-speaking lands are not separately indexed, but the Holy Roman Empire is. Merchant houses are listed under the cities in which they had their headquarters, but the Fuggers are accorded a separate entry. Reform tracts, as well as urban and rural leagues, are indexed below; wars and popular revolts are listed in the Index of Subjects.

Index of Subjects

There are no agreed terms in English for the intensified seigneurialism and the intensified commercial agriculture of East Elbia. These have therefore been entered under their respective German terms, Gutsherrschaft and Gutswirtschaft.